About the author

DAVID LOWES has been active in labour movement politics for over twenty years. Between 1984 and 2003 he was an activist in the Liverpool City Branch of NALGO/UNISON, and held various positions. Involvement in campaigns against rate-capping, poll tax and privatization led to a doctoral thesis from John Moores University on labour movement campaigns to defend local democracy, jobs and services in the 1980s. A member of the Conference of Socialist Economists and London Socialist Historians Group, he has become involved in the latest phase of anti-capitalist struggle.

The Anti-Capitalist Dictionary

movements, histories & motivations

DAVID E. LOWES

FERNWOOD PUBLISHING
Nova Scotia

SIRD
Kuala Lumpur

ZED BOOKS
London & New York

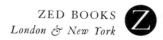

To my father
John Francis Lowes,
a lifelong advocate for the interests of working people,
29 June 1924–16 July 2002

The *Anti-Capitalist Dictionary* was published in 2006 by

Published in Canada by Fernwood Publishing Ltd, 8422 St Margaret's Bay Road (Hwy 3) Site 2A, Box 5, Black Point, Nova Scotia, BOJ IBO

Published in Malaysia by Strategic Information Research Development (SIRD), No. 11/4E, Petaling Jaya, 46200 Selangor

Published in the rest of the world by Zed Books Ltd, 7 Cynthia Street, London N1 9JF, UK, and Room 400, 175 Fifth Avenue, New York, NY 10010, USA
www.zedbooks.co.uk

Copyright © David E. Lowes 2006

The right of David E. Lowes to be identified as the author of this work has been asserted by him in accordance with the Copyright, Designs and Patents Act, 1988

Designed and typeset in Monotype Van Dijck
by illuminati, Grosmont, www.illuminatibooks.co.uk
Cover designed by Andrew Corbett
Printed in Malta by Gutenberg Press Ltd

Distributed in the USA exclusively by Palgrave Macmillan, a division of St Martin's Press, LLC, 175 Fifth Avenue, New York, NY 10010

A catalogue record for this book is available from the British Library
Library of Congress Cataloging-in-Publication Data available

Library and Archives Canada Cataloguing in Publication
    Lowes, David E.
        The anticapitalist dictionary: movements, histories and motivations / David E. Lowes.
    Includes bibliographical references and index.
    ISBN 1-55266-199-7
        1. Anti-globalization movement—Dictionaries.   I. Title.
    HC15.L69 2006   330.12'2   C2006-900910-4

ISBN 983 2535 808 Pb (SIRD)

ISBN 1 84277 682 7 Hb (Zed)
ISBN 1 84277 683 5 Pb
ISBN 978 1 84277 682 7 Hb
ISBN 978 1 84277 683 4 Pb

Contents

Preface

On one of the many occasions when I have been asked to explain the thinking behind this book, a friend remarked that it appeared to lack balance. What he meant, of course, was that it did not include, among other things, entries that address ideas and movements from a purely capitalist perspective. I could not offer a direct refutation of his assessment, because to all intents and purposes he was right. This work is not intended to be a 'dictionary of politics'. There are plenty of publications that use that title, in one form or another, but their authors also recognize that subject matter is selected according to an overall schema. The *Oxford Concise Dictionary of Politics* (1991), for example, focuses on 'concepts, people and institutions … referred to in academic and *scholarly* writing about politics' (my emphasis). Though entitled 'dictionary' to accommodate bookshelf categories, this book represents a counterbalance to orthodox counterparts by way of a praxis that aims to invigorate today's progressive anti-capitalism through an explication of the historical interrelationship between activity, concepts, issues and organizations. In fact, there are entries that refer to or describe ideas, institutions and movements that favour capitalism, but these are included due to their relevance to anti-capitalism and to explain why they generate disapproval.

To state that anti-capitalism is as old as capitalism itself might appear to some as a statement of the obvious and to others as a tautology. Naomi Klein, for example, writes in Mike Prokosch and Laura Raymond, *The Global Activist's Manual* (2002), that it is something that 'ebbs and flows, lies dormant for years, then rushes back onto the scene in a brand new outfit and under an assumed name'. For a variety of reasons, the genealogy of this oppositional force – permanent or recurring, depending on your point of view – has been ignored, obfuscated or trivialized by many in the media, the universities and established political parties. Before the disintegration of the Soviet bloc, in the atmosphere of the Cold War and at the hand of sectarian dogmatists, for example, the heredity of anti-capitalist thought and action was all too often the victim of selective analysis and presentation – whether sympathetic or hostile.

Even today, in the so-called developed world, there are consistent campaigns to marginalize the traditions and values of those who campaign for a fairer and more open society – not least by self-proclaimed advocates of progress, like the 'New Labour' project in Britain. Curiously, however, this modern-day tendency is afflicted by a central contradiction, whereby progressive values that look forward to a new, better society are characterized as backward-looking by those enchanted by neoliberal nostrums that hark back to an imaginary idyll. The trend is not new, however, as there have been many attempts to demonize anti-capitalist resistance and tradition over the generations. The pejorative use of the term 'Luddite' to portray working people as reactionary is but one such example that belies a reality described by Eric Hobsbawm in *Primitive Rebels* (1972) as collective bargaining by riot. Other examples include the circumstances surrounding the trial and execution of the Haymarket Martyrs and the use of the term 'anarchy' as a synonym for chaos and lawlessness to demonize movements like the Diggers, Enragés and Levellers and to discredit alternative socio-economic theories.

All this might have a ring of truth about it, but any critically minded reader will still ask why this book is being written. The short answer to this question lies with the enduring sequence of protests that began in Seattle in November 1999, grabbed the attention of the corporate media and sent shock waves through the self-congratulating institutions of the new world order. To the surprise of many commentators, this latest manifestation of anti-capitalist discontent did not lose its impetus in the wake of atrocities committed in the United States of America in September 2001 and the repression of dissent that followed. On the contrary, the movement continues to flourish and acquire fresh momentum from successive international crises. Following protests at the Fifth Ministerial meeting of the World Trade Organization held in September 2003 at Cancún in Mexico, organizers have even started choosing increasingly remote or inaccessible venues for meetings.

Nevertheless, it is always imperative to provide a counterbalance to misrepresentation – from whatever quarter it originates. In this respect, the book is intended to complement the endeavours of anti-capitalist activists, authors and organizations in combating unfavourable coverage, making the activities and ideas of the movement available to the widest possible audience and thereby contributing to the growth, understanding and development of the movement. As a quick reference resource, for example, it provides self-contained entries that introduce and explain concepts and issues that are important to today's movement. In so doing, it also demonstrates how the meaning and relevance of some of these have changed over time and illustrates a linkage between past and present activity that might be unfamiliar to people who are involved or interested in the movement's current manifestation. After all, progressive anti-capitalism has many roots and inspirations and all are part of an evolving historical struggle for the enlightenment and liberation of all humanity, to realize unfettered personal and collective development, expression and fulfilment.

USING THIS DICTIONARY

An alphabetical format has been adopted to make information readily accessible and entries have been chosen on a thematic basis. In other words, they focus on ideas, issues and concepts, but include references to movements, organizations, people and publications that form part of, or have informed or inspired, anti-capitalist ferment. Entries for individual people have been omitted, though individuals are referred to where their influence or input is considered to be relevant. This reflects the fact that today's movement is bigger than one person or group and that activists reject the established media and political practice of reducing ideas and movements to personalities.

For those who require additional detail, relevant publications are included in the text and, where appropriate, online sources of further information are also provided, as is a bibliography. The inclusion of Internet addresses recognizes the global accessibility of the medium, as well as the fact that it is a favoured tool of many anti-capitalist activists, movements and organizations. Web addresses are also included in the hope of making available, through searches and links pages, some of the additional sites that contain public interest content.

Adopting an alphabetical format means that it is not possible to provide a chronological account of the development of anti-capitalist ideas. Some form of sequential perspective can be achieved by cross-referencing entries, however, and for anyone interested in the evolution of progressive anti-capitalist thought there is a 'timeline' at the end of the book. When taken as a whole, therefore, the book does provide a historical context, albeit a less than perfect one.

Due to the internationalist principles and perspective that pervade progressive politics, the subject matter is not limited to Britain or to the English-speaking world. To reflect and accommodate this diversity, books have their English title first followed by the original in brackets; journals have their original title first, followed by a translation in brackets; and organizations start with whatever is common usage followed by the translation – all using roman script. Where possible, cited works are English-language editions available from the British Library. If no such translation can be found, details of the edition identified are provided instead.

Now to the potentially thorny question of cross-referencing. Small capitals are used to indicate each cross-reference, and, where a candidate for cross-referencing appears more than once in an entry, it is indicated as such on the first occasion that it is mentioned and is not repeated. As a general rule, cross-referencing serves one of two purposes. First of all, it indicates the existence of a more complete description, where previous knowledge of a concept, organization or technical term will afford a greater understanding of a particular entry and of the debate, problem or interpretation pertaining to it. The second purpose is to demonstrate linkage between ideas, concepts, movements, organizations and so on, especially where such connections have been obscured by time or through deliberate intent.

Ultimately, the book is not designed to be read cover to cover, but it is for the reader to decide what is the best way for her/him to use it. S/he can follow the alphabetical format and cross-references, use the general index or browse casually. The most important thing is that each reader finds the book useful and hopefully illuminating, interesting and stimulating. As Stéphane Mallarmé (1842–1898) is reputed to have said, *La vraie bombe c'est le livre.*

ACKNOWLEDGEMENTS

There are many people to whom I owe a debt of gratitude for their advice and encouragement in the research, preparation and writing of this book. These include, but are not restricted to, Ian Cook, Andrew Ford, Helen King, Rasigan Maharajh, Steve Wright, and Anna Hardman and her colleagues at Zed. Most thanks go to Sarah, however, for her forbearance, support and understanding. That said, I take full responsibility for any errors or weaknesses in the text.

A

ACCOUNTABILITY is often used to denote an element or quality of DEMOCRACY that is equated with good governance, but the term generally means that those who hold and exercise a degree of POWER have a responsibility to explain and justify their conduct. Elected representatives, appointed officials and other public office holders are therefore required to demonstrate that they have discharged their duties appropriately. Issues raised by anti-capitalists, for example, include the granting of EXPORT CREDITS to firms that supply military equipment to oppressive regimes or when aid is given to environmentally destructive projects like dam construction in which national companies have a financial interest. Accountability is often considered to be less effective than TRANSPARENCY, though, because it can only occur after a decision or action has taken place. The process of holding individuals, parties or governments answerable for their actions can be conducted in a variety of ways, including through media investigation or legal challenges in the courts, but it is considered to be the ultimate function of elections. In reality, however, the extent to which officials explain themselves to voters is extremely limited, while falling numbers of people bothering to vote in elections suggests that fewer see a vote cast once every few years as an adequate method of making a government and elected representatives keep their promises.

Those disenchanted by an electoral process that fails to deliver accountability either become apathetic or cynical, or in the case of the anti-capitalist movement they turn to extra-parliamentary opposition. The latter groups and individuals do so in order to make public their concerns and thereby put pressure on people and institutions that would otherwise be beyond reproach. In particular, attention is focused on the policies and practices of non-elected international institutions like the INTERNATIONAL MONETARY FUND, the WORLD BANK and on CORPORATIONS and the impact that they have on working people, society and the environment. Faith in the responsibility of national governments is seriously undermined, for example, when domestic policy options are circumscribed by international institutions or by the threat of an international corporation to withdraw investment.

Similarly, large corporate donations to political parties appear to have an influence on policy decisions that ordinary members can only dream of. In Britain, for example, a change in the New Labour government's policy of banning tobacco advertising occurred after a £1 million donation to the Labour Party from an interested person, although the money was returned after a public outcry. Similarly, in the USA, the collapsed and discredited energy corporation Enron had been a major donor to the presidential election campaign of George W. Bush and its officials were subsequently involved in deciding the administration's energy policy. The principle of accountability is therefore equally relevant to membership organizations like political parties and trade unions – where there are demands for appointed officials and leaders to be directly responsible to rank-and-file members. Likewise, there are also demands for NON-GOVERNMENTAL ORGANIZATIONS to be accountable to donors, supporters and the people whom they aim to help. See also TAXATION.

FURTHER INFORMATION

Corporate accountability: www.corpwatch.org; www.corporatewatch.co.uk
Governmental accountability in Canada: www.probeinternational.org
Accountability for Africa's problems: www.data.org

ACQUIRED IMMUNE DEFICIENCY SYNDROME (AIDS) is believed by the majority of medical opinion to develop as a consequence of contracting the Human Immunodeficiency Virus (HIV). First observed in the 1980s, the disease was given its current name in 1982, while HIV was identified by Robert Gallo and Jean Luc Montagnier in 1984 and named two years later. Due in part to the unpleasant, debilitating nature of the disease – if untreated, death results from a chronic attack on the immune system that renders it unable to combat even the most common infections – related issues raise particularly strong feelings.

The fact that the disease can be transmitted sexually is reason enough for conservative groups and individuals to stigmatize those infected according to their lifestyles; see Dennis Altman, *AIDS and the New Puritanism* (1987). Infection is therefore portrayed, in stereotypical fashion, as the result of heterosexual and homosexual promiscuity. Similarly, transmission between drug users who share unsterilized needles and syringes is considered to be the consequence of inappropriate behaviour. Sections of the MEDIA, for example, used to refer to AIDS as a 'gay plague', while religious fundamentalists consider it to be a punishment from their god.

Such simplistic and prejudicial views ignore the fact that the disease can also be transmitted from mother to child during birth, breastfeeding or while the baby is in the womb. Hospital patients and haemophiliacs have also been infected during blood transfusions and the use of infected blood products, although this is now rare due to the introduction of screening procedures. On the other hand, misconceptions and irrational views like the belief that HIV can be transmitted by breathing, touching, holding or shaking hands, hugging and kissing or by sharing cooking and eating utensils only serve to fuel discrimination.

The disease and its consequences are now a global problem, with over 42 million people estimated to be living with HIV in 2004 and 20 million deaths having resulted from AIDS-related illnesses. Today, children and heterosexual adults constitute the majority of people living with AIDS or HIV and live predominantly in developing countries, particularly sub-Saharan Africa, where access to treatment is limited. In Botswana, for example, more than 1.6 million people are infected and in Lesotho the figure is 330,000 out of a population of just under 1 million. Elsewhere, South Africa was estimated to have 4.7 million infected people in 2002, while in 2003 the numbers of infected people in Nigeria and Ethiopia were judged to be 3.7 million and 2.4 million, respectively. The same year 4.6 million people were estimated to be living with the disease in India and a further 1.5 million in China. Due to social and economic collapse in Eastern Europe and Central Asia, an estimated 1.7 million people had become infected by 2004, while the World Health Organization estimated the number of cases in Russia to have exceeded 257,000, Ukraine 500,000 and Estonia 3,700 in the same year.

The debates that rage around the prevention and treatment of AIDS/HIV are recorded by Shereen Usdin, *The No Nonsense Guide to HIV/AIDS* (2003), and these reflect themes that motivate sections of the anti-capitalist movement. Although a cure or vaccine is not available at present, treatments exist that can delay the onset of AIDS. HIV, for example, can be treated with antiretroviral therapy to help repair the immune system, assuage associated symptoms and thereby increase the life expectancy and the quality of life of someone affected – even if their condition has already progressed to AIDS. Such therapy can also reduce the chances of the virus being transmitted from mother to newly born child. All this depends on a government's willingness or ability to afford the levels of investment in health care necessary to fund such treatment. As Christine-Anne d'Adesky, *Moving Mountains* (2004), attests, lack of funding is still the main reason why most AIDS-related deaths occur in developing countries, where there is a particular need for health-care, sex education, employment and treatment funding. For some of these countries, spending is restricted by loan conditions imposed by the INTERNATIONAL MONETARY FUND and the WORLD BANK, while for others international debt repayments either exceed spending on health care or seriously restrict funds available for all welfare spending (see INTERNATIONAL DEBT).

Pharmaceuticals corporations from developed countries, like Eli Lilly in the USA, stand accused of profiteering at the expense of people living with HIV/AIDS. Campaigners allege that such CORPORATIONS set prices at levels poorer nations cannot afford and refuse to waive intellectual property rights to allow the production of cheaper generic drugs. International agencies like Médicins sans Frontières and Oxfam, for example, have campaigned for developing countries to be allowed to manufacture generic medicines. Their calls have met with limited success, but still face resistance from corporations that argue that generic products are less effective than their patented versions. Even when a government can afford to fund antiretroviral therapy, research and prevention measures, pressure has to be maintained to ensure those adequate standards of care and prevention are actually provided. Dissemination of information about safer sex, the dangers of sharing needles or the distribution of clean needles and syringes takes place in many developed countries and in Uganda, Zambia and Senegal. Such initiatives are undermined, however, by pronouncements like those of the president of the Vatican's Pontifical Council for the Family, Cardinal Alfonso Lopez Trujillo, who claims that condoms do not prevent HIV infection.

Where governments fail to provide adequate levels of health care or are guilty of mismanagement, affected individuals, families and communities organize and participate in activist campaigns to make sure that their views are heard and their knowledge and experiences used to inform necessary change. In South Africa, for example, activists and organizations like the Treatment Action Campaign seek to ensure that affordable treatments are made available. Such groups also campaign to protect the RIGHTS of people who are living with HIV/AIDS, especially in relation to employment opportunities, health care and life insurance. Ultimately, the failure or refusal to listen to the concerns of those affected raises questions about the ACCOUNTABILITY of representatives of government – politicians, health officials, researchers, medical bureaucrats and doctors – and of pharmaceuticals corporation executives as well.

FURTHER INFORMATION

Activist oriented campaigns: www.actupny.org/indexfolder/links.html
Statistics: www.avert.org/statindx
World development and global health crisis: www.worldbank.org/aids
United Nations HIV/AIDS Program: www.unaids.org

ACTIVISM/ACTIVIST are terms used to describe a person or group of people who take action in furtherance of a cause – writing letters or emails, attending protests, making speeches, joining boycotts or taking part in DIRECT ACTION and CIVIL DISOBEDIENCE – to bring about environmental, political or social change. An activist can be a member of a campaigning organization – a NON-GOVERNMENTAL ORGANIZATION, political party or TRADE UNION, for example – but not a paid official. There is therefore a strict distinction between people who join an organization or become active in support of a particular cause so that they can create or pursue a career for themselves and those who are prepared to use their own time and resources unselfishly. Nevertheless, you do not have to belong to an organization to be an activist – many anti-capitalists are happy to be part of a movement that does not set standards or conditions for membership.

Numerous forms of activism and causes inspire people to become active. Historical examples include anarchists, communists, DIGGERS, ENRAGÉS, LUDDITES, socialists and those like the Chartists and suffragists who campaigned for an extension of the vote. Some of these causes, ideas and issues still motivate groups of people like students and workers to take action. Other themes are to be found on the pages of this tome, while still more are covered by Mike Prokosch and Laura Raymond in *The Global Activist's Manual* (2002), and Randy Shaw, *The Activist's Handbook* (1996), who adopt a specifically American context. In the spirit of anti-capitalism, the editorial collective Notes from Nowhere also provide further evidence of the activities and motivations of anti-capitalists in *We Are Everywhere* (2003). The Internet is also used as a resource and a tool for the development of networks, the distribution of information via email lists and the practice of HACKTIVISM.

At its most fundamental, activism can involve the practice of everyday life, as in the case of 'conscious living' outlined by Duane Elgin, *Voluntary Simplicity* (1981). Elgin advocates reducing the level of consumption and

5

therefore the need to sell one's time for money — ideas often advocated by those concerned with ecological and environmental concerns and a possible antidote to ALIENATION. The downshifting of lifestyle and a respect for nature are also values to be found among anti-corporate activists, who advocate greater respect for the RIGHTS of consumers, as well as the employees of CORPORATIONS. In cultural terms, some activists work to create their own MEDIA, while the use of existing media to combat ADVERTISING and its domination of popular culture is termed Culture Jamming or sniggling — advocated by people like Kalle Lasn, *Culture Jam* (1999).

Examples of the practice include setting up pirate radio stations to transmit alternative ideas or the use of pop music by bands like Chumbawamba for the same purpose. In the latter case, the term 'guerrilla communication' is used to describe the use of a spectacle — a festival or gig — to PROTEST and change the opinions of observers — such as the dousing of Britain's deputy prime minister at the Brit Awards. This type of activity bears comparison to the ideas of the SITUATIONIST INTERNATIONAL, which, during the revolts in France in May 1968, advocated the disruption of conventional media to create confusion.

FURTHER INFORMATION

Activists magazine: www.activistmagazine.com
Culture Jammer Encyclopaedia: www.sniggle.net
Global action database: www.agp.org
List of environmental organizations: www.envirolink.org

ADVERTISING is the paid promotion of a BRAND in order to stimulate demand and is usually part of an overall promotional strategy that can include publicity, public relations, personal selling and sales promotion. Set up in 1843, Volney Palmer in Philadelphia, USA, is credited with being the first advertising agency. The emergence of such organizations was symptomatic of growing competition between companies during the nineteenth century, which, in turn, necessitated the development of new ways of obtaining and increasing market share. Then, with the proliferation of monopolies, CORPORATIONS faced the possibility that market prices would become fixed or change beyond their control. They therefore used advertising to promote a differentiation between products that would enable demand to be manufactured as a way of varying price and therefore maximizing profits.

According to economists there are two main types of advertising that can be used to achieve short- or long-term increases in sales, an increase in market share, improved awareness of brand or an improvement of image. These include ads that provide information about a commodity's availability, uses, advantages, price, quality and terms of sale; and those that seek to persuade people that they want or need a particular brand. In practice, such differentiation is often difficult to define, especially where imagery is used to present a persuasive message, such as the presentation of cigarette smoking as a symbol of chic behaviour, freedom and independence. In this way, commodities are associated with things that are considered to be appealing, in order to make the product seem equally desirable, such as in the use of airbrushed female and male images, picturesque landscapes or the inclusion of buzzwords with a favourable association.

Advertising now intrudes into every realm of life on billboards, buses, bus stops, park benches and taxis on the street, as well as neon signs. At home, printed flyers are shoved through the door and telephone marketing invades privacy. Adverts also interrupt Internet use, radio listening, television and video viewing and appear in magazines and newspapers. At work, corporate logos appear on office stationery and on payslips, and even schools are used to advertise the corporations that sponsor them or provide 'free' curriculum materials. The same organizations seek to reinforce their message by broadcasting radio and television commercials that contain slogans, jingles and catchphrases designed to lodge in the memory and encourage people to buy a particular brand. Ironically, the 'soap opera' was specifically produced to facilitate a break in commercials, not the other way round, and now provides a vehicle for a form of covert advertising. This involves the placement of branded products so that they are visible in television programmes, films and other entertainment media and become associated with an actor, cast, movie or programme.

Other techniques include making sure that a brand is widely recognized and its name remembered through repetition in the hope that it will eventually be used as a noun or a generic term – the brand name Hoover, for example, is used subconsciously as a synonym for a vacuum cleaner. The testimony of ordinary users can also be employed as a way of endorsing a brand or COMMODITY – 'eight out of ten people asked...', for example – as can an appeal to authority through the approval of 'experts', such as in the promotion of something as 'scientifically tested' or 'clinically proven'. The testimony of ordinary citizens also has the added advantage of implying that the brand is widely used, while other techniques, associated with the promotion of designer wear, encourage people to believe that they are unique and therefore need things that are supposed to embody or express their manufactured individuality. Even the imagery and symbolism of capitalist antitheses ANARCHISM, COMMUNISM and SOCIALISM have been appropriated and used as selling points.

The roles of advertising and public relations become contentious when they overlap in the service of corporations, government agencies, governments or politicians. The Committee for Public Information, or Creel Committee, which organized publicity on behalf of the US government during World War I, is credited with being the first example of this kind of activity. Towards the end of the twentieth century, marketing culture took over politics in Britain and the USA as New Labour under Tony Blair and the Democrats led by Bill Clinton used a variety of techniques including opinion polling and focus groups to evaluate public opinion. This two-way approach is intended to help clients listen as well as communicate messages, although it also involves high-tech techniques for distributing information to those being consulted. This can include satellite feeds, the Internet, broadcast faxes and database-driven phone banks to recruit supporters for a particular cause or issue and can just as easily be used as means of one-way propagandizing.

In fact, Edward Bernays (1891–1995), one of the pioneers of public relations, argued in *Propaganda* (1928) that the scientific manipulation of public opinion was necessary to overcome chaos and conflict in society. Critics like John Stauber and Sheldon Rampton, *Toxic Sludge is Good for You* (1995), doubt that such practices really serve the interests of DEMOCRACY and freedom of speech, especially when they deliberately marginalize or deny the feasibility of alternative economic and social ideas. This can be achieved through the creation of front groups – organizations that purport to serve a public cause while actually serving the interests of a sponsor – and is called a third party technique. No wonder public relations is disparaged as the 'black art', 'spin' and the work of 'spin doctors' or 'flacks', as in Stuart Ewen, *PR! A Social History of Spin* (1996), and Nicholas Jones, *Sultans of Spin* (1999).

Alternative forms of practice are available from organizations such as Adbusters, which cater for non-governmental organizations like Friends of the Earth, Greenpeace, trade unions and non-profit organizations. In contrast to normal advertising and public relations bodies they will only help create a campaign if they agree with the cause. They also aim to inspire people to become activists, so that they will present a challenge to existing power structures and the domination of commercial forces through social marketing campaigns like Buy Nothing Day and TV Turnoff Week. Although Naomi Klein points out in *No Logo* (2000) the irony of merchandising to promote a 'buy nothing day', via the Cable News Network, the use of existing means and methods is a central aspect of the attempt to subvert them.

Others prefer to parody corporate and political advertisements in order to subvert the original message – hence the term 'subvertising'. This can be an image that is subtly different to a recognizable corporate logo or an alteration to an existing advert that draws attention to an alternative or critical point of view, thereby sabotaging the original message of politicians, corporations and others. 'Just do it... or else!', for example, has been used to comment on Nike's alleged use of sweatshops. Subverts appear as graffiti, a sticker left in a prominent position, the rewording of billboards or as spoof T-shirts. Advocates consider subvertising to be a form of creative resistance to corporate disinformation that pollutes physical or mental commons, and a call to action.

FURTHER INFORMATION

Adbusters: www.adbusters.co.uk; www.adbusters.org
Billboard Liberation Front: www.billboardliberation.com
Exposing deceptive and manipulative PR campaigns: www.prwatch.org
Pictorial subverts: www.subvertise.org

ALIENATION is a concept the understanding and interpretation of which has varied over time and according to its application to a particular field. In sociological terms, for example, it refers to an individual divorced or isolated from society as a whole and from other people, due to societal constraints on the ability to express and appreciate individuality. While Jean-Jacques Rousseau (1712–1778) is credited as first describing human beings as alienated from their natural state by the constraints of society, he did not use the actual term in his discourse. Georg W.F. Hegel (1770–1831), on the other hand, understood alienation in idealistic terms, as the gap between particular and universal consciousness – between self-understanding and ignorance. Alternatively, Ludwig Feuerbach (1804–1872) adopted a materialist approach that depicted man as alienated from himself by the creation and worship of an imagined superior being – the estrangement of man from his true nature by the process of deification. The concept's revolutionary, anti-capitalist

9

usage originated with Karl Marx (1818–1883), who developed Hegel's and Feuerbach's approaches when first outlining his ideas in *Excerpts from James Mill's Elements of Political Economy* (1844) and *Economic and Philosophical Manuscripts* (1844) – especially the section on 'Estranged Labour'.

Marx identified capitalist SOCIAL RELATIONS as the source of modern-day alienation, which is basically an estrangement (*Entfremdung*) of an individual from their potential. This process could be a consequence of individual action or the condition in which an individual, group, institution or society exist. Viewed in this way, RELIGION, philosophy, common sense, art and morals each represents a form of alienation (*Entausserung*), whereby people defer to an ideal standard and give up the power to change things or control their own destiny. Similarly, Marx saw the institutions of the STATE – law courts, parliament and social institutions – as removed from the practice of everyday life and therefore another example of how people have lost their potential to govern their own lives through social interaction.

More specifically, it is through the day-to-day operation of capitalist society that human beings are alienated from their true potential. First and foremost, people are forced to work in return for money that allows them to acquire the means to sustain their own lives and those of their family. They do not live in order to work freely, creatively, productively or self-consciously as a free expression and enjoyment of life. Time spent at work is literally an alien life. The division of labour and the production line mean that individuals are not involved in the design and creation of the complete product. They are not allowed to use and extend their range of skills as activity is divided into repetitive tasks that do not require creative thought or social interaction. In this way, workers are not allowed to cooperate in creative activity and therefore become alienated from each other and from the productive process.

Alienation from potential through the reality of working life – the fact that objects produced do not contain any expression of personal creativity – is but one part of the process. Having sold their labour-power to earn a living, the worker has no control over the work they are told to do or over what they produce. As they expend their labour-power for the benefit of their employer, the product of their endeavours belongs to someone else. In this way, they are alienated from the products of their working lives. The commodities produced are appropriated by the employer and therefore appear to have no relation to the people who created them – leaving the producer without power over their product and dependent on wages paid by their employer. Once they are offered for sale, commodities only relate to each other and to the people who created them through the medium of exchange-value. At this point, relations between producers are also mediated by the way commodities relate to each other and the process of alienation is therefore one of REIFICATION, by which relations between people are understood as relations between things.

As well as being alienated from the product of their work, from themselves and from other people, humans are also alienated from their 'species being' (*Gattungswesen*) – their essence, their nature, their very humanity. Essentially, this means that the person is unaware of and therefore unable to realize their full potential as a sentient being. Marx argues that the solution to all these forms of alienation requires a complete inversion of the productive process to permit free, creative work that allows individuals to express their own essence and personality through the act of producing and in the objects produced. The individuality and personality of the producer could then be recognized in their product – by themselves and by others. Furthermore, knowledge of another person's enjoyment of the product would provide additional fulfilment, because the creation of an object has fulfilled another person's human needs. In this manner, work represents a genuine human relation through the affirmation of the self and the satisfaction of others' needs.

While investing elements of oneself – individuality, personality and so on – in an object can still be seen as a form of alienation or fetishism, its social aspects remain positive and distinct from capitalist, private property relations. Because the private ownership of the means of production is viewed as the source of alienation and therefore an obstacle to the realization of human potential, the abolition of human self-alienation necessitates the abolition of PRIVATE PROPERTY and associated relations of production. In turn, such a seismic change requires a collective, revolutionary effort to effect a transformation of the material conditions of productive social existence. Thus the revolutionary potential of the concept remains separate and distinct from the subsequent adaptations and reinterpretations of psychologists, philosophers and sociologists and survives the attempt by Louis Althusser (1918–1990) in *For Marx* (1969) and *Reading Capital* (1970) to dismiss alienation as an idealistic aberration in Marx's early writings.

Today, disaffected youth tend to use the term 'anomy' or 'anomie' to express feelings of alienation and purposelessness. Used by Émile Durkheim (1858–1917) in *Le Suicide* (1897) to denote a condition or malaise in individuals, characterized by an absence or diminution of standards or values, a more general meaning implies a disorder due to the absence of law, order, organization, rules or structure. In anti-capitalist terms, the individualism promoted by NEOLIBERALISM is consistent with an increasing feeling and reality of isolation among people, with the promotion of self-interest above all else favouring predation over cooperation. Fears about the process and effects of GLOBALIZATION are fed by societal changes in economic fortunes and the significant discrepancy between the ideological theories and values espoused by politicians and corporate representatives and the experiences of everyday life. The reality of mass, capitalist society that is characterized by large, mobile, urban populations is that people are constantly confronted by unfamiliarity whether at work, on their way to it or during leisure time.

FURTHER INFORMATION

István Mészáros: www.marxists.org/archive/meszaros/works/alien/meszaro1.htm

ANARCHISM refers to sets of theory, doctrine and movements that reject the need for any differentiation between STATE and society. More specifically, anarchists and anarchism deny the need for the existence of political and legal institutions, governments, laws, political parties and coercive organizations like the police and military; all of which are organized as separate entities and considered to hold POWER over people, property or territory. In contrast, the free association of all citizens is a prerequisite of anarchism and, as a result, government is only considered to be legitimate if it has the detailed consent of all those governed. This demand is deemed to be incompatible with the functioning and organization of the modern state as a set of institutions that form an integral part of society and yet make decisions for and about its members without direct consultation. The rejection of government and state has been advocated by pro-capitalist individualists who promote a free-market combination of anarchism and liberalism, but more often by the anti-capitalist versions of anarchism.

The oldest reference to 'anarkhian' is attributed to the playwright Aeschylus (525–456 BCE), who used the word in *Seven against Thebes* around 467 BCE. As part of the historical struggle against capitalism, the development of anarchist ideas can be traced back to the DIGGERS and LEVELLERS of the English Revolution. There is a shared antipathy to PRIVATE PROPERTY as the source of inequality and stress on the importance of social equality as a condition necessary for the maximum liberty of all. In fact, opponents of the Levellers used 'anarchism' as a pejorative term, indicating chaos and disorder, in an attempt to discredit their demands. The practice was repeated against the ENRAGÉS during the French Revolution and appears to have originated with Plato (428/7–348/7 BCE), *The Republic*, Book Eight, and Aristotle (384–22 BCE), *Politics*, Book Six. Although he did not use the term, William Godwin (1756–1836) is credited with providing the first description of a decentralized society based on autonomous communities in his *Enquiry Concerning Political Justice* (1793) and as anticipating many of the theoretical propositions and ideas that would later become associated with anarchism.

George Woodcock (1912–1995), *Anarchism* (1986), records that the socialist thinker Pierre-Joseph Proudhon (1809–1865) adopted the term as a positive appellation in *What is Property? (Qu'est-ce que la propriété)* (1840). His subsequent contributions to the theoretical exposition of a self-regulated society composed of individuals and voluntary associations dedicated to cooperative working, mutuality and federalism provided the bases from which Mikhail Bakunin (1814–1876), Piotr Kropotkin (1842–1921) and others proceeded. Although Anselme Bellegarrigue (1820–?) produced *L'Anarchie, Journal de l'ordre* (*Anarchism, Journal of Order*) in 1850, most of Proudhon's followers referred to themselves as 'mutualists'. These included Ramon de la Sarga (dates unknown), who in 1845 established the anarchist journal *El Porvenir* (*The Future*) in La Coruña, Spain, and Francisco Pi y Margall (1824–1901), who attempted to put his federalist ideas into practice during the Spanish Revolution of 1873.

Mikhail Bakunin reformulated anarchist doctrine by advocating collective ownership of the means of production, and in *The Paris Commune and the Idea of the State* (1871) advocated REVOLUTION by spontaneous uprising as a means of abolishing the state. This new approach received support in France, Italy and Spain, partly as a consequence of the endeavours of Giuseppe Fanelli (1829–1877), who established branches of the International Workingmen's Association (IWMA) in Madrid and Barcelona. In similar fashion to the mutualists before them, however, Bakunin's followers preferred to be known as 'collectivists' and only called themselves anarchists after expulsion from the IWMA in 1872 and following the creation of the Anarchist International at Saint-Imier, Switzerland – which existed between the years 1873 and 1877. Piotr Kropotkin broadened Bakunin's collectivist approach into anarchist communism by advocating the collective ownership and organization of the means of production and distribution, together with a vision of society as a federation of free communist groups and decentralized industry. In *Mutual*

13

Aid (1897), Kropotkin justified his theories in evolutionary terms, arguing that cooperation equalled or surpassed competition.

An individualist strategy that advocated the 'propaganda of the deed' originated in Italy towards the end of the nineteenth century, having first been articulated by Errico Malatesta (1853–1932) as a tactic of employing insurrectionary acts to inspire mass revolt. Several high-profile figures fell victim to assassination, including French president Sadi Carnot in 1894; the Austrian empress in 1898 and the king of Italy in 1900. Leon Czolgosz (1873–1901) killed the president of the United States of America, William Mckinley, in 1901. Regardless of a strong tradition of anarcho-pacifism and associated nonviolent views like the Christian anarchism of Leo Nikolayevitch Tolstoy (1828–1910), the authorities were quick to misrepresent the nature, theory and history of anarchism in order to cultivate public revulsion. In a development that has clear similarities to events in the early twenty-first century, governments of the day equated anarchism with acts of TERROR that required eradication.

In *Reflections on Violence* (1906) and other works, Georges Sorel (1847–1922) contributed to the development of syndicalist theory, partly as a consequence of disillusionment with Bakuninian strategy. The ideas of Sorel and others were developed into anarcho-syndicalism in recognition of the need to develop a mass movement, the effective suppression of anarchism in general and public disgust at the tactic of assassination. Anarcho-syndicalism advocated the creation of revolutionary mass trade unions as a template for the structure of a new society – practising industrial democracy – and as the organization through which the overthrow of existing structures could be executed in the form of the general strike. In the USA, the International Workers of the World (IWW) espoused similar ideas in their proposal for an Industrial Commonwealth, although they never described themselves as anarcho-syndicalists or syndicalists.

In Spain, anarchists were influential in the trade-union movement, where the Anarchist Federation of Iberia (Federación Anarquista Ibérica), an activist-led organization, was founded in 1927 by Buenaventura Durutti (1896–1936), Juan García Oliver (1901–1980) and others. During the revolutionary period of 1936–39, the National Labour Federation (Confederación Nacional del Trabajo) and associated militia took control of the regions of Aragon and Catalunya, placing factories and railways under the control of workers' committees. Land was confiscated and organized into libertarian communes, along lines advocated by Kropotkin. The actions of the Communist Party of Spain (Partido Comunista de España) towards the end of the period contributed to the destruction of anarchist organizations and, ultimately, the victory of Franco. The victory of fascism in Spain therefore heralded the end of anarchism as a mass movement – as it had in Italy a decade or so earlier and did in Germany during the 1930s.

In Japan, during the first half of the twentieth century, Shusui Kotoku (1871–1911) and other anarchists were executed for an alleged plot to assassinate the emperor and, following World War I, the anarchist Black Federation was founded, as was a Syndicalist Federation. Japanese anarchism was effectively extinguished in 1935, however, under the auspices of measures taken against the Anarchist Communist Party for allegedly plotting armed insurrection. In tsarist Russia, the influence of anarchism and Bakunin was evident in the organization and tactics of Narodnaya Volia (the People's Will) and the Social Revolutionaries (Partiya Socialistov-Revolucionerov), though the latter adopted the organizational form of a conventional political party under Viktor Chernov (1876–1952). Following the revolution of 1917, Nestor Makhno (1889–1934) and his followers established an anarchist community in part of the Ukraine until they were forced into exile in 1921. Anarchist activism in the USA was largely associated with European immigrants, most notably the **HAYMARKET MARTYRS** and those, including Alexander Berkman (1870–1936) and Emma Goldman (1869–1940), who were imprisoned and exiled under the 1903 congressional order banning foreign anarchists from entry to or residence in the USA. Nevertheless, a minority of anarchists remained active in the IWW, until its suppression after World War I.

In the second half of the twentieth century anarchist federations, groups and ideas existed mainly on the margins of progressive politics – largely because of a **HEGEMONY** that emphasized **CAPITALISM** and **COMMUNISM** as the only viable alternatives. Appealing to those who rejected the strictures of this cold war dichotomy, anarchist elements and influences were discernible in the **STUDENT** and **NEW LEFT** movements of the 1960s and 1970s. The commune and squatting movements that established the 'Free City of Christiania' in Copenhagen, Denmark, and similar areas in Barcelona, Spain, and Berlin in the erstwhile Federal Republic of Germany were also influenced by anarchist thinkers like Robert Paul Wolff, *In Defense of Anarchsim* (1970). Meanwhile, popular interest was engendered by anarcho-punk in the 1970s, epitomized by the band Crass in Britain, while individuals like Bob Black, *The Abolition of Work and Other Essays* (1985), and Noam Chomsky, *Profit over People* (1999), continue to promote progressive libertarian ideas.

In the aftermath of the cold war, a myriad of anarchist federations and groups maintain a prolific presence among contemporary anti-capitalist, anti-globalization and anti-war movements. They are perhaps most noticeable as the BLACK BLOC tactic employed at demonstrations against the G8, WORLD BANK, World Economic Forum and WORLD TRADE ORGANIZATION meetings. MAY DAY has also been rejuvenated in London as a day of protest and festivity. Analogies have also been drawn between anarchist ideas and the decentralized, non-authoritaian practices of ZAPATISTA autonomous municipalities, Indymedia, Peoples' Global Action and the SOCIAL FORUM.

FURTHER INFORMATION
Anarchist FAQ: www.infoshop.org/faq/index.html
Anarchist Encyclopedia: www.recollectionbooks.com/bleed/gallery
On-line News Service: www.ainfos.ca/en
Organizations: www.broadleft.org/anarchis.htm; flag.blackened.net/af/links.html

ARMS TRADE involves the sale and purchase of military hardware – ammunition, guns, missiles, bombs, vehicles, helicopters, planes, ships – tear gas and riot-control equipment, as well as the technology and know-how to make and use them. Much has been made by G8 countries of attempts to halt the proliferation of nuclear, chemical and biological weapons, especially preventing them falling into the hands of non-state forces. Meanwhile, however, controls on the sale of conventional weapons, especially to allies, have been relaxed and sales increased; thus in *Undermining Global Security* (2004) Amnesty International pinpoints the expansion of the European Union as a contributory factor. Furthermore, although the United Nations Commission on Human Rights categorizes depleted uranium weapons and cluster bombs alongside nuclear, chemical and biological weapons as having 'indiscriminate effect', they have been used in Afghanistan, Iraq and Serbia.

The top five arms-exporting countries are: the USA, Britain, France, Russia and China, while Britain, France, Germany and Sweden are involved in one-third of all arms deals. The fact that the USA, Britain and France all make more from arms sales than each gives in aid is not the only relationship between arms and aid. Many arms sales are made to the recipients of overseas aid and are guaranteed by government subsidies and support for arms exports in the form of EXPORT CREDITS. Such TRADE often involves countries about which human rights organizations have expressed concern and where there is civil unrest or tensions between neighbouring countries.

A non-exhaustive list of countries that are affected by one or more of the above factors includes: Algeria, Angola, Chile, Colombia, Egypt, India, Indonesia, Israel, Jamaica, Kenya, Nepal, Pakistan, Philippines, Saudi Arabia, Syria, Turkey and Uzbekistan. Even poor and indebted nations are courted over arms sales, as in the case of Britain attempting to sell military air traffic control systems to Tanzania. Speaking to a conference held in Australia during February 2004, James Wolfensohn, president of the WORLD BANK, claimed that developing countries spend twenty times as much on military spending as they do on development.

Opposition to the manufacture and sale of arms comes from various sources including charities, peace organizations, trade unions, religious and political groups and therefore encompasses a variety of opinions and reasons for opposition. These include arguments that exporting arms to oppressive regimes impacts on the human rights of local people and that supplying arms to those involved in conflict or tension with neighbours undermines security. Exporting arms is also seen as encouraging military spending over and above economic development, education, health and other welfare provision and as reinforcing the militaristic approach to problem solving. Hence, Paul Hawken, *The Ecology of Commerce* (1993), has advocated an international tax on arms manufacturers.

Goals vary from regulating and reducing arms trade to ridding the world of nuclear and other weapons of mass destruction and abolishing the trade altogether through the reorganization of military industry for civil purposes. With a United Nations conference on small arms scheduled for 2006, Amnesty International, the International Action Network on Small Arms (IANSA) and Oxfam are campaigning for an international treaty – similar to the 1997 treaty banning landmines – to outlaw the sale of weapons used to violate human rights or humanitarian law. ACTIVISTS also participate in DIRECT ACTION and CIVIL DISOBEDIENCE at events like Europe's biggest arms exhibition– the Defence Systems and Equipment International held in London – to publicize the need for alternatives to the production and sale of arms and the use of military force to resolve conflict. They also argue that the UNITED NATIONS and CIVIL SOCIETY should be the primary route for the resolution of international disputes by peaceful means in line with the principles of peace, JUSTICE and democratic values.

FURTHER INFORMATION

Campaign Against the Arms Trade: www.caat.org.uk

European Network Against the Arms Trade: www.antenna.nl/enaat
Global network for the elimination of nuclear weapons: www.abolition2000.org
Joint Amnesty International, IANSA and Oxfam Campaign: www.controlarms.org

ASYLUM is the practice of granting nationality or leave to stay in a country to people who fear persecution in their place of origin or their adopted home. See also REFUGEE.

AUTONOMIA refers to the autonomous network movement of social self-organization that was prevalent in the North of Italy in the 1970s and similarly important in Rome. Its roots can be traced back to the early 1960s and the ideas of working-class autonomy expressed in the journals *Contrapiano* (*Counter Planning*), *Quaderni Rossi* (*Red Notebooks*), *Potere Operaio* (*Workers' Power*) and *Classe Operaia* (*Working Class*), by people like Sergio Bologna, Antonio Negri, Alberto Asor Rosa and Mario Tronti. Antecedents of the Autonomia also included groups to the left of the Partito Comunista Italiano (Communist Party of Italy, PCI) such as Lotta Continua (Struggle Continues, LC), Avanguardia Operaia (Workers' Vanguard, AO) and Potere Operaio (Workers' Power, PO) – named after the journal. These groups were born out of the social unrest of the 1960s that spawned the NEW LEFT, reflected the regional political traditions in Italy and were similarly influenced by the effects of population migration from South to North.

Despite losing members to Autonomia, the Marxist–Leninist AO remained a competitor during the 1970s, as did LC, whereas other groups chose to dissolve in the wake of the PCI's 'historic compromise' with the Christian Democrat government in 1973. PO, for example, disbanded after many of its members left to help form the 'Autonomous Committees' (Autonomia) inside factories that featured younger, militant workers who were hostile to political orthodoxy, parties and trade unions. This move, together with the ideas that informed it, also found a receptive audience among cultural figures, ecologists, environmentalists, radical youth, students, women's groups and autonomous collectives. For these people, the refusal of organizational forms and the freeing of everyday life from labour-time had more appeal than the centralism advocated by Franco Piperno and Oreste Scalzone; although they too joined the Autonomia after a year or so.

Between 1974 and 1977, Autonomia appeared in northern and central Italy, including Padua in the north-east – where Antonio Negri worked and had brief links with activists – and at the Porto Marghara Petro-Chemical Centre on the outskirts of Venice. Underground radio stations such as Radio Alice in Bolgna, Radio Sherwood in Padua and Radio Onda Rossa in Rome promoted the street protests of 1977 that personified protesters as *passamontagna* (ski mask over the face). In response, the government made a disputed link between the Autonomia and the Brigate Rosse (Red Brigades) and instigated a period of repression that culminated in the arrest, on 7 April 1979, of professors, writers, journalists and others linked to the movement.

Autonomia appealed to the counterculture through its rejection of capitalist relations in and beyond the factory. While the refusal to work (*il rifiuto del lavoro*) appeared in the workplace as struggles against increased productivity, opposition to the social factory – unpaid housework, schooling and other activities linked to the maintenance of the workforce – gave many a theoretical basis for their rejection of society. Repudiation of the work ethic and of alienated labour in favour of personal and community development and fulfilment appealed to those disenchanted with Keynesian planning, socialist productivism and the PCI's failure to address questions of self-fulfilment and assertion (*autovalorizzazione*).

In contrast to the PCI, Autonomia argued that the fulfilment of human needs is not only relevant to those in paid employment but is an equally valid goal for alienated social labourers – the subject of unpaid surplus work and part of the state's extension of the wage–work nexus over society. It therefore remains a distinctive feature of the movement that it advocated abolition of the STATE in the name of social labourers whom it recognized as a potential revolutionary force with a desire to enjoy life rather than have to earn it. Even so, some sections, notably in Rome, continued to assert the primacy of workers in paid employment. Steve Wright, *Storming Heaven* (2002), provides an extensive account of the movement.

FURTHER INFORMATION

Current thinking – aut-op-sy: lists.village.virginia.edu/~spoons/aut_html
Archives of Autonomist Marxism can be found at:
www.eco.utexas.edu/Homepages/Faculty/Cleaver/txarchintro.html;
www.emery.archive.mcmail.com/public_html/rednotes/index.html

B

BIOCENTRIC thinking is an aspect of deep ecology that affords intrinsic worth to all 'natural' things. In this fashion, biocentrism, or ecocentrism, as it is also known, places nature at the centre of its value system, whereas anthropocentrism grants that privilege to humanity and is equated with civilization, industrial society and hence CAPITALISM. Although mainstream environmental groups and Green parties also aim to reduce human impact on the earth, deep ecologists consider them to be reformist. See also ECOLOGY and ENVIRONMENTALISM.

FURTHER INFORMATION

Earth First: www.earthfirst.org/
Left biocentrism: www.ic.org/pnp/biocentrism.html; www.greens.org/s-r/32/32–
    12.html

BIODIVERSITY or biological diversity is defined by Article 2 of the United Nations Convention on Biological Diversity (1992) as: 'The variability among living organisms from all sources, including, *inter alia*, terrestrial, marine and other aquatic ecosystems and the ecological complexes of which they are part: this includes diversity within species, between species and of ecosystems.' The introduction of the term 'biological diversity' is credited to Thomas E. Lovejoy in his Foreword to Michael Soulé and Bruce Wilcox's *Conservation Biology* (1980). The first use of 'biodiversity' has, on the other hand, been attributed to the contribution of Edward O. Wilson to the National Forum on Biodiversity held in 1986 in Washington DC, USA, and the published findings of the conference, edited by Wilson and Frances M. Peter: *Biodiversity* (1988). See also ECOLOGY, ENVIRONMENTALISM and GENETIC ENGINEERING.

FURTHER INFORMATION

Convention on Biological Diversity: www.wcmc.org.uk/igcmc/convent/cbd/cn_cbd.
    html
Biodiversity: books.nap.edu/catalog/989.html

BIOPIRACY refers to the use of life in the form of animals and humans, microorganisms and plants, including their cells, genes and organs, without the knowledge or consent of their originators or owners. As such, the concept assumes a right to own and use biological resources through the patenting process. Vandana Shiva, *Biopiracy* (1997), for example, argues that the multilateral agreements like the World Trade Organization's TRADE-RELATED INTELLECTUAL PROPERTY RIGHTS (TRIPS) and the NORTH AMERICAN FREE TRADE AGREEMENT (NAFTA) make all living organisms and their components liable to be patented. More importantly, these agreements impose a legal obligation on signatories to recognize patents registered in any member country, although many developing countries do not have procedures by which intellectual property can be registered. Furthermore, Article 102 of the 1952 Patent Act in the USA allows existing methods and technologies to be patented in the USA, so long as the knowledge is new to that country. This means that even ancient knowledge and traditions from other cultures and countries can be registered in the USA and by virtue of TRIPS and NAFTA they have to be recognized by all signatories as the PRIVATE PROPERTY of the individual or corporation that acquired a patent for them. Examples include patents granted on the properties of the 'brinjal', 'Jamun' and 'Karela' plants that have been used as traditional remedies for diabetes in India, while agrochemical, biotech and pharmaceuticals CORPORATIONS are also acquiring patents on gene sequences, human stem cells and protein.

Although the specific concept of biopiracy is linked to the provisions of TRIPS and NAFTA, prior to the 1992 Convention on Biological Diversity (CBD) corporations were able to use and take biological resources without any need to offer recompense. The CBD was designed to give countries sovereignty over biological resources and traditional knowledge, so that corporations seeking to acquire and use such resources, through bioprospecting, would need prior consent and therefore to offer a share of the proceeds to the source nation. Bilateral contracts have been signed between the Merck pharmaceuticals corporation and the Costa Rican National Institute of Biodiversity, which also has contracts with another nineteen firms. Similarly, the Diversa and Nature Limited corporations have agreements with the Mexican government that allows them to explore the utility of biological resources in Chiapas and traditional Mayan knowledge.

Such bilateral arrangements are intended to lay the foundation for benefit sharing, but critics like GRAIN and Third World Network argue that it is impossible to estimate the potential value of discoveries and therefore agree

21

a level of remuneration that is either fair or realistic. Other complications include the fact that a species might not be unique to just one country. Similarly, if genetic modification is recognized as constituting a new product that warrants its own patent, any payment of royalties to the original source becomes null and void. In contrast, the concepts of collective and communal knowledge and nature – natural resources – are synonymous for the indigenous peoples of biodiversity-rich countries like Brazil, India and Malaysia and inimical to intellectual property rights. Patents, however, confer monopolies to corporations on medicinal and other inventions that result from their research, which means, in turn, that local production can be prevented and prices charged that make food, health and medicinal products inaccessible.

Alternatively, Richard Stallman, *Biopiracy or Bioprivateering?* (2001), argues that rather than offering a solution to monopolization, the biopiracy thesis contributes to the PRIVATIZATION of public knowledge and property by advocating a fairer distribution of corporate profits. The concept is also considered to be flawed because it is based on the fundamental premiss that animal and plant varieties are available to be owned – whether by corporations, countries or indigenous peoples. As a solution, collective, cumulative innovation and knowledge, it is suggested, should be recognized as a public resource and a GLOBAL COMMONS.

FURTHER INFORMATION

Charter of Farmers Rights: www.agobservatory.org/library.cfm?refID=29551
Biopiracy and the Americas: www.alternet.org/story/16057

BIOSPHERE was proposed by Eduard Suess (1831–1914) in 1875 as the name for the conditions that support life, and the concept redefined by Vladimir I. Vernadsky (1863–1945) in *The Biosphere* (1926) to mean the sum of all ecosystems. The term can therefore be used to refer to all places where life is possible, the ecological interactions of the planet as a whole and those parts of the earth – the atmosphere, land and water – which support or are capable of supporting the existence of plants and animals. The global biosphere plays a crucial role in the carbon cycle, regulating the storage or release of carbon into the atmosphere, and has passed into more common usage along with BIODIVERSITY as the possible impact of GLOBAL WARMING has been recognized. See also ECOLOGY, ECOSYSTEM and ENVIRONMENTALISM.

BIOTECHNOLOGY is defined by Article 2 of the United Nations Convention on Biological Diversity (1992) as 'any technological application that uses biological systems, living organisms, or derivatives thereof, to make or modify products or processes for specific use.' Fari, Bud and Kralovánszky, *History of the Term Biotechnology* (2001), note that Károly Ereky (dates unknown) coined the term 'biotechnology' in 1917 and outlined his theory of technology based upon biochemistry in 1919. In general terms, however, industrial practices like brewing, wine-making, leather processing and the production of starch, yeast, alcohol, meat, milk and vegetable products fit the UN definition.

While there are applications that do not use living organisms, today's biotech corporations like Amgen, Biocon, Genetech, Monsanto, Shantha Biotech and ZymoGenetics are associated with research and production of modified animals and plants for agricultural, industrial, medicinal and, more rarely, marine and aquatic purposes using GENETIC ENGINEERING. The vast majority of these CORPORATIONS are based in industrialized countries of North America and Europe.

BLACK BLOC refers to a tactic adopted during demonstrations whereby a group of protesters don black attire and masks in order to raise the profile of their presence, carry out acts of CIVIL DISOBEDIENCE and counter police attacks on demonstrators, while evading the identification of individual activists. Media commentators first used the term *der schwarze Block* to describe participants in the squatter movement, Autonomen and Rote Armee Fraktion (Red Army Fraction) protests in the erstwhile Federal Republic of Germany during the 1980s. The tactic also bears comparison with the *passamontagna* who took part in street protests by the AUTONOMIA in 1970s' Italy, but first appeared in the USA during protests against the Gulf War of 1991 and is now synonymous with an anarchist presence at anti-capitalist protests. Similar activities and motivations also apply to the other non-hierarchical movements like the Tute Bianche (White Overalls) and the White Overalls Movement Building Libertarian Effective Struggles (WOMBLES)

The Tute Bianche were founded in the Leoncavallo social centre of Milan, Italy, as a movement against GLOBALIZATION, CAPITALISM and for international debt relief. Wearing padded overalls or chemical suits and helmets as protection against the police, they adopt a similar approach to the black bloc, having no predefined strategy other than not alienating other demonstrators; they take decisions on the spur of the moment. Their white attire provides a collective identity at demonstrations, affords a degree of anonymity to individuals and is intended to symbolize the invisibility of people without RIGHTS and POWER, as well as those rendered ghosts by neoliberal policies. The WOMBLES also don white overalls and protective clothing at protests to resist police aggression and facilitate freedom of movement and communication. Evident at Prague, Hallowe'en and May Day protests, they encourage equal participation in organizing action and hold open meetings to discuss ideas, tactics and decision-making.

FURTHER INFORMATION

Tute Bianche in Italian: www.tutebianche.org; in English: www.nadir.org/nadir/
    initiativ/agp/free/tute/
WOMBLES: www.wombles.org.uk

BOURGEOISIE is the term used by Marx and Engels to describe the class of people who own the means of production and run the polity. The word was taken from the French where it originally meant city dweller, but was used in the seventeenth and eighteenth centuries to distinguish between urban upper and lower classes and those from a rural background. The French aristocracy also used the term pejoratively to imply that merchants who traded for PROFIT and employed others to work for them were money-grubbing exploiters whose values of hard work, legal process, morality, PRIVATE PROPERTY, sanctity of the family and thrift made for dull conformity.

Those who aspire to bourgeois status – the self-employed who own their own means of production, work for themselves and therefore control their own labour-time as artisans or run family farms or small shops – were labelled petit bourgeois. This group also included people who subsisted on stipends or private wealth, like academics, doctors and lawyers, though such roles are now more often than not salaried; a process mirrored by the takeover of small farms and businesses by industrial-scale competitors. For a discussion of the process of 'proletarianization', see Harry Braverman (1920–1976), *Labour and Monopoly Capital* (1974). The appearance of publicly traded CORPORATIONS, run by managers and owned by shareholders, has led some to question the relevance of these categories, while others contend that this form of bureaucratic and technocratic domination is merely a modern-day expression of the nineteenth-century experience. See also CLASS.

BOYCOTT is a form of nonviolent DIRECT ACTION that originated in 1880 when members and supporters of the Irish National Land League ostracized the eponymous Captain Charles Cunningham Boycott (1832–1897). As land agent for the Lough Mask tenantry of Lord Erne, County Mayo, Ireland, Boycott implemented rent rises that exacerbated already harsh living conditions. The tactic has since developed into one of not buying, selling or trading the products of certain individuals, companies or countries in an attempt to exert pressure and thereby secure a change in policy and practice.

Examples of campaigns that have employed the tactic in more recent times include the campaign for India's independence from Britain, the civil rights movement in the USA, the anti-apartheid movement's ostracizing of South Africa, and the refusal to participate in elections that are considered to be discriminatory. The tactic remains popular today, with calls for boycotts of, among other things, Burma, Esso, Israel and World Bank Bonds, and even extends to 29 November, designated 'International Buy Nothing Day'.

FURTHER INFORMATION

Burma: www.freeburmacoalition.org
Esso: www.stopesso.com
Israel: www.ism-london.org
World Bank Bonds: www.econjustice.net/wbbb

BRAND is a type of INTELLECTUAL PROPERTY that allows advertisers to make distinctions between different traders and their otherwise identical products. Strictly speaking, a brand is registered as a trade mark to associate commodities with particular producers, in the hope that consumers identify with a product and thereby generate demand. In practice, a brand can be represented by a label, logo, name or symbol and is a COMMODITY in itself, often available for sale to the highest bidder with a price equivalent to or greater than the physical means of production such as factories or machinery.

Ironically, some of the most familiar brand names have found that with success comes scrutiny and notoriety – witness, for example, Coca-Cola's attempt to brand tap water as 'Dasani' in Britain. Revelations about exploitative practices that result in environmental degradation or include the use of sweatshops, CHILD LABOUR and subsistence wage rates, made possible by repressive regimes, have, for example, combined to sully brand images that are often promoted by multimillionaire celebrities. Making connections between the plight of those who produce a commodity and those who promote

25

or consume it helps to demystify the allure of the brand and exposes the process of REIFICATION upon which the success of branding relies.

FURTHER INFORMATION

A critical look at McDonald's: www.mcspotlight.org
List of top brands of 2003: bwnt.businessweek.com/brand/2003/index.asp

BRETTON WOODS SYSTEM refers to an agreement, reached in 1944, to establish an international monetary and payments regime in which fixed exchange rates were a prerequisite for the operation of the GENERAL AGREEMENT ON TARIFFS AND TRADE. Each country therefore undertook to maintain the EXCHANGE RATE of its currency within a value of plus or minus 1 per cent. The agreement provided for international cooperation in the control of short-term CAPITAL FLOWS to avoid sudden currency depreciation or fluctuations in exchange rates. Other features included the creation of the International Bank for Reconstruction and Development – also known as the WORLD BANK – and the INTERNATIONAL MONETARY FUND (IMF). While both institutions were intended to support the international exchange rate and payments system, the latter would do so through short-term loans to member states experiencing problems and the former via long-term assistance for economic reconstruction and development.

Due to the devastation of European economies during World War II and the withdrawal of Soviet-bloc countries, the system was plagued by a lack of resources and shelved in 1947. As a means of supporting European economic recovery, the USA developed the Marshall Plan to provide unilateral aid in the form of grants instead of loans and developed the Truman Doctrine whereby aid was granted to nations in return for a pro-US stance. In addition to these factors, the dollar was the only currency whose VALUE was linked to gold. This set of circumstances contributed to the dollar's standing as the principal currency in the international system underwriting TRADE and payments. The USA therefore dominated the international system until 1971 when it unilaterally suspended dollar–gold convertibility. Since 1976, when the articles of the IMF were amended to allow floating exchange rates, its policies and practices and those of the World Bank have been criticized for enforcing a neoliberal agenda, while helping to preserve the HEGEMONY of the the US Treasury and Federal Reserve over the international system.

FURTHER INFORMATION

A view of Bretton Woods today: www.brettonwoodsproject.org/index.shtml

C

CAPITAL FLOWS can be short, medium or long term, private or public and can move in or out of a country. All have some effect on the **EXCHANGE RATE** because money entering or leaving a country has to be converted from one form of currency to another. Medium- or long-term flows are considered to be less disruptive, because they have a less dramatic effect on exchange rates and are often associated with investment in plant, machinery and factories, transference of technology and the creation of jobs and commodities. In contrast, short-term capital flows – also known as 'hot money' – are connected to profits generated by interest-rate levels, but they can also be speculative whereby investors gamble on the expected appreciation or depreciation of stock and bond markets and of a given currency.

In the last quarter of the twentieth century, a rapid growth of short-term flows led to increased instability in international financial markets – following the dismantling of the **BRETTON WOODS SYSTEM** in the 1970s and the consequent removal of capital controls and **DEREGULATION** of financial markets. Before the East Asian Crisis of 1997, for example, private capital flows to developing countries were seven times their 1990 level and five times greater than aid flows. Short-term, volatile investment in East Asia had the effect of inflating property and share prices, while in South America countries experienced inflows of capital in the early 1990s that fuelled a consumption boom and hyperinflation, as Miles Kahler, *Capital Flows and Financial Crises* (1998), notes. The values of national currencies also increased and trade deficits developed, as exports became more expensive and imports comparatively cheap. As the situation became unsustainable, fears of devaluation led foreign investors to withdraw their capital, thereby fuelling a collapse in the value of national currency – nearly 50 per cent in some cases – and exchange rate crises.

Replacing the original Bretton Woods principles with those of **NEOLIBERALISM** means that exchange rates are floating, unregulated, and that governments that wish to discourage capital flight can either raise interest rates or use reserves to protect the value of their national currency. Higher interest rates exacerbate the consequences of capital flight, however, fuelling economic recession, bankruptcy for banks and businesses, and redundancy, lower wages and high rates of unemployment for people in general. They also make it more expensive for governments to borrow, at a time when tax revenue is falling due to economic recession, and spending on social and welfare provision is therefore reduced as governments introduce austerity measures to balance budgets and reduce consumer demand. All in all, the consequences of short-term capital flows have a disproportionate effect on national populations in general and on the poor in particular. Whereas mobile international investors can withdraw capital before losses are incurred and escape any reduction in living standards, the populations affected enjoy no such luxury. See also REGULATION and TOBIN TAX.

FURTHER INFORMATION

Capital Flows and Exchange Rate Policy: www.fpif.org/briefs/vol4/v4n17cap_body.
   html
A Case for Capital Controls: attac.org.uk/attac/document/bond-capital-controls.
   pdf?documentID=72

CAPITALISM defined in general terms is a social, political and economic system characterized by the private ownership of property and the production and sale of commodities for PROFIT as opposed to use by the producer(s). In other words, the means of producing, distributing and exchanging commodities are owned privately and operated for the financial gain of their owners. The term is also used to refer to a phase in the development of human history that corresponds to the said social, political and economic features and was, according to the *Oxford English Dictionary* (1993), first used in 1854. Debates rage over when 'capitalism' actually came into being and over characteristics which appear to constitute different stages of its development, but writers as different as Max Weber (1864–1920), *General Economic History* (1923) and Karl Marx (1818–1883), *Capital* (Volumes I–III), identify certain features as common to capitalism. There is, however, less of an accord over the merits of these features and the benefits they provide to people in general.

The private ownership and use of money or credit – capital – for the purchase of labour-power, materials, finished or unfinished commodities and other forms of capital, such as machinery, is generally accepted as developing in Western Europe between the fifteenth and nineteenth centuries and forms a central feature of capitalism. In addition to production for sale, referred to above, five other features are considered to define capitalism as a mode of production; none of which should be considered to be more or less important. In the *Communist Manifesto* (1848), for example, Marx and Engels argue that people are forced to find employment because, 'having no means of production of their own, [they] are reduced to selling their labour-power in order to live'. The fact that a person's potential for work becomes a COMMODITY that is sold for money – a wage – as part of a contractual relationship with an employer is considered to be symptomatic of the capitalist mode of production, which tends to reduce all SOCIAL RELATIONS to an interaction between commodities.

Even money, the predominant medium of exchange in capitalism, is treated as a commodity to be bought and sold under the control of banks, financial institutions and other intermediaries. As part of this trait, interest is charged for credit or debt facilities – such as mortgaging a factory – that are used to finance the purchase or sale of commodities. Production or enterprise can also be financed by issuing bonds and shares, which allows the resources of others to be used and controlled by the capitalist, without consultation with those employed. Whereas bonds make it possible to turn the debt portions of interest rates into commodities, share trading has the effect of commoditizing the ownership of CORPORATIONS. Advances in communications technologies have also made it possible to trade equity, fluctuations in markets, future prices and much more.

To all intents and purposes, owners of corporations – be they shareholders, individuals, partnerships or families – control the productive process. In other words, they decide the hiring and firing of employees, their working conditions and workplace environment, how much is produced, the techniques employed in production, and how and to whom products are sold. There are certain legal or regulatory constraints, but as long as they have the financial means, owners are free to do as they please; even where they delegate day-to-day decision-making through a managerial hierarchy. The one other mediating factor is that of competition between different types of capital, corporations and producers for market share, especially where the same or similar commodities are produced (see ADVERTISING and BRAND). Under such circumstances, capitalist endeavours face pressure to cut costs through the introduction of labour-saving practices and technology designed to increase productivity while maintaining or reducing costs.

While the characteristics described above have been more or less evident since the first appearance of capitalist societies, analysts have identified

29

stages that are associated with the way the defining features operate. The earliest form of capitalism is therefore labelled merchant or mercantile and corresponds to a period that runs from the fifteenth to the eighteenth century when Western European nations like England, France, the Netherlands, Portugal and Spain embarked on a process of overseas colonization and trade. The following epoch is defined by rapid growth and industrialization facilitated by technological progress, such as the use of steam engines in small individually owned firms. This industrial phase is a particular feature of nineteenth-century capitalist practice, epitomized by minimal state intervention and whose exponents sought justification in the theories of Adam Smith (1723–1790), David Ricardo (1772–1823) and LAISSEZ-FAIRE.

The early years of the twentieth century witnessed the development of large-scale industrial processes such as steel production, shipbuilding and the concentration of activity into large firms. These events involved the introduction of economies of scale and the formation of cartels and monopolies in an attempt to neutralize the disadvantageous effects of competition. People like John Hobson (1858–1940), in *Imperialism* (1902), argued that the rise of monopoly capitalism concentrated wealth, reduced purchasing power and forced the STATE to seek markets overseas. Vladimir (Ulyanov) Lenin (1870–1924) adopted a similar thesis in *Imperialism, the Highest Stage of Capitalism* (1916), as has Immanuel Wallerstein *World-systems Analysis* (2004). The second half of the last century witnessed the emergence of multi- or trans-national corporations and renewed attempts to reduce costs by moving production overseas to take advantage of cheaper labour and mitigate the problems of competition from developing countries – a process that has come to be known as GLOBALIZATION.

Other characteristics and techniques, such as forms of PRIVATE PROPERTY, markets and trade, existed before capitalism, so too criticisms of these and other features such as an uneven distribution of wealth and POWER. One of the things that makes capitalism different, however, is that it espouses values and sets standards that are considered to be universal, but that it fails to live up to. Prime examples of this disparity between principles and practice include the notions of EQUALITY and FREEDOM. While everyone is held to be equal before the law or as electors, vast inequalities exist in the economic realm. Similarly, the free market is supposed to allow corporations as employers and individual employees to meet as equals, who then enter into contractual arrangements on this basis. In reality, however, those who need employment in order to survive are in an inferior bargaining position and therefore have to accept an unequal distribution of returns for their work and are often restricted in their attempts to organize collectively in a TRADE UNION. Such arrangements form the basis of EXPLOITATION and are particularly evident where corporations from industrialized countries employ workers and even children in the developing world to take advantage of comparatively lower wage rates. Neoliberal economists, entrepreneurs and politicians even advocate maintaining a 'natural rate of unemployment' to bolster the superior position of employers and to keep wage demands in check.

These social relations involve a truncated form of freedom, evident in the process of ALIENATION, whereby people seeking employment have little or no control over the work they do, although they have a theoretical freedom to enter into any type of arrangement they wish. In fact, the mere existence of property impinges on the freedom of those who are excluded from the advantages ownership entails. Freedom to challenge the existing state of affairs is also limited due to legal arrangements such as intellectual and private property rights that protect current owners and the advantages enjoyed by them. Such circumstances are reinforced through networks in which the privileged and wealthy attend the same educational institutions – schools and universities – and develop into the judicial and administrative echelons of the STATE, the boardrooms of corporations, banks and structures through which corporations and other organizations conduct business and execute their plans. A combination of networks, property rights and the profit motive are also considered to contribute to a reckless exploitation of natural resources regardless of the detrimental impact on society and environment.

Further contradictions exist in the advocacy of state intervention in the economy in order to minimize REGULATION, because it limits the profitability of corporations, while objecting to state intervention elsewhere. Free markets are also considered to be synonymous with DEMOCRACY, although there are plenty of non-democratic examples where there is also interdependence between private property, free markets and liberal economics. These include, but are by no means restricted to, modern-day examples like Burma, Hong Kong and Indonesia in Asia. During the second half of the last century, military regimes also prevailed in Argentina, Brazil and Chile in Latin America, and in Greece, Portugal and Spain in Europe, where capitalist interests were protected and even promoted. These and other criticisms are levelled at capitalism from a variety of quarters that include ANARCHISM, COMMUNISM, SOCIALISM and many of today's anti-capitalist and anti-globalization groups and organizations.

FURTHER INFORMATION

Arguments in favour of capitalism: www.capitalism.org
How capitalism works in the United States of America: www.theyrule.net

CHILD LABOUR refers to children who are in some form of paid employment. This can be in factories producing goods for export as high-profile Western brand names, or selling commodities, working as tourist guides, as domestic helpers in the home, on family-run farms and in small family businesses – shops, restaurants and so on. While child labour is concentrated in the developing world – essentially as a consequence of POVERTY – the practice also exists in the so-called developed world, usually within limitations laid down by law, most notably as child actors and child singers, but sometimes not, as in cases of child prostitution. Child labour was commonplace in Britain until legislation in the nineteenth century regulated the hours and the conditions in which children could work; a process that also took place during the early years of the twentieth century in the USA. Nevertheless, restrictions still vary between nations and child exploitation is often linked to HUMAN TRAFFICKING.

Western individuals, corporations, nations and other entities are also complicitous – whether knowingly or not – through the sale and purchase of products assembled or otherwise manufactured by children. Child labour not only represents a form of EXPLOITATION, it also contradicts the liberal notion of freely negotiated contracts between employers and employees and contravenes the UNIVERSAL DECLARATION OF HUMAN RIGHTS and the United Nations Convention on the Rights of the Child (1989). Child workers suffer abuse in a number of ways, including: denial of educational opportunities, exposure to workplace injury, risk of physical and sexual abuse from adult employers and colleagues, stunted physical development and poor health due to working conditions without adequate lighting or ventilation. Some children are also involved in armed conflict, either in guerrilla forces, militias or even state-organized groups as in the case of the war between Iran and Iraq. The fact that the Convention on the Rights of the Child defines a child as any person under the age of 18 years or age of majority recognized by a particular nation has led some to question Britain's inclusion of 16- and 17-year-olds in its armed forces.

FURTHER INFORMATION

About the Convention on the Rights of the Child: www.unicef.org/crc/crc.htm

CIVIL DISOBEDIENCE is a strategy or act that involves the refusal to obey or the deliberate breaking of specific laws, thereby defying state authority on the grounds of moral objection. Such activities are calculated to capture MEDIA interest, usually through a dramatic demonstration of intense feeling and commitment, and thereby draw attention to a particular cause. The tactic is also designed to stretch the resources of and provoke an extreme reaction from those enforcing the law. Popular revulsion at any overreaction is expected to increase sympathy for the protesters, engender support for their cause and exert pressure on government to change legislation or policy. In order to maintain the moral high ground, civil disobedience is strictly nonviolent and, with the exception of the targeted law or policy, law-abiding. Civil resisters therefore acquiesce peacefully to arrest and imprisonment, and do not retaliate when attacked or beaten by opponents or those policing their action so that there is not even an implied attempt to usurp the STATE.

Henry David Thoreau (1817–1862) is credited with introducing the term in his 1849 essay *On the Duty of Civil Disobedience* in which he justified his refusal to pay taxes in PROTEST at slavery and war with Mexico. The tactic was used and developed by Mohandas Gandhi (1869–1948) in campaigns against British colonial South Africa during the first decade of the twentieth century and the use of Passbook laws to control the movement of people, and, later, against British rule in India. His campaign in India was termed satyagraha – an insistence of truth – and involved civil resisters – satyagrahi – refusing to salute the Union Jack. There were also a series of protests, such as those of 1930–31 involving the Dandi March to make salt from the sea. From 1942 the campaign was also referred to as the 'quit India' movement.

In the USA, Martin Luther King (1929–1968) and the civil rights movement adopted civil disobedience techniques, such as black people refusing to give up bus seats to whites, picketing whites-only restaurants and white people riding in 'negro only' rail cars. The mass democratic movement in South Africa adopted similar tactics, during the 1940s and 1950s, to expose the inequities of apartheid through non-compliance, ungovernability and the creation of alternative forms of organization.

Civil disobedience was also practised by those who opposed the war in Vietnam and refused the draft in protest at the introduction of conscription. In Britain, the Campaign for Nuclear Disarmament and others opposed to nuclear weapons have employed civil disobedience tactics, such as forming a peaceful blockade or occupying a facility, thereby breaking the law of

33

trespass. Likewise those who refused to register for or pay the 'poll tax' between 1989 and 1991 were civil resisters.

Environmental campaigners also adopt the practice, like Greenpeace activists using boats to blockade radioactive waste shipments and Earth First tree-sitters shutting down the logging of ancient forests. More recently, techniques have been applied to the Internet as HACKTIVISM and electronic civil disobedience as virtual blockades and sit-ins were staged against the Mexican and US governments to draw attention to the war being waged against Zapatista resistance and the indigenous peoples of the Chiapas region in Mexico. Other examples include the staging of protests against the 2003 war on and subsequent occupation of Iraq. Likewise, anti-capitalist activists have employed blockades and demonstrations in attempts to shut down meetings, such as those of the WORLD TRADE ORGANIZATION (WTO) in Seattle, USA, November 1999, the G8 Summit in Genoa, Italy, July 2001 and the WTO in Cancún, Mexico, September 2003.

FURTHER INFORMATION

Civil Disobedience index: www.actupny.org/documents/CDdocuments/CDindex. html

Thoreau's essay: www.cs.indiana.edu/statecraft/civ.dis.html

CIVIL LIBERTIES are constitutional or other legal regulations that are intended to limit the coercive power of the state. Examples include freedom from arbitrary arrest; freedom of assembly, association and movement; freedom of speech; the right not incriminate oneself; and trial by jury. See also RIGHTS.

CIVIL SOCIETY is a concept that can be traced to Thomas Hobbes (1588–1679), John Locke (1632–1704) and Jean-Jacques Rousseau (1712–1778), and was used by Georg W.F. Hegel (1770–1831) and Karl Marx (1818–1883) to distinguish between society in general and the STATE. Along similar lines, the Centre for Civil Society, based at the London School of Economics, includes in its definition institutions, organizations and behaviour situated between the state, the business world and the family. Such a broad sweep encompasses charitable, not-for-profit, cooperative and voluntary organizations; economic, political and social movements like alternative media; consumer bodies, professional associations, trade unions, sexual orientation and environmental groups. Also included are non-governmental organizations, policy think-tanks, religious groups that are not part of the established church, and cultural, social, sports and other civic clubs – basically all forms of social participation and engagement.

Even though the state is part of society in its day-to-day functioning – as law courts and the institutions of government, for example – it is presented and presents itself as something that is separate and distinct from the competition and fragmentation of normal SOCIAL RELATIONS. The state is therefore deemed to rule over individuals and organizations that influence the way people and society function, in the public – as opposed to private – interest. In contrast, some anti-capitalist and anti-globalization activists use the term when referring to groups involved in resistance or agitation for social development and public interest in the domain of social life; a view that is at odds with attempts to include businesses and CORPORATIONS in a United Nations definition. The term is also favoured by representatives of the G8, the INTERNATIONAL MONETARY FUND, the ORGANIZATION FOR ECONOMIC COOPERATION AND DEVELOPMENT and the WORLD BANK when referring to non-governmental organizations and citizen groups that lobby them in an attempt to influence policy and practice.

FURTHER INFORMATION
United Nations: www.un.org/partners/civil_society/home.htm

CLASS is a socio-economic category, the conception of which varies according to the manner of its application, be it academic, market research based or anti-capitalist, but which generally indicates a division or order of society. In everyday use, the understanding of class is subject to further confusion because the English language conflates grade, rank and status as factors that determine membership of a particular class. Political scientists, sociologists and market researchers, on the other hand, base their definitions on forms of economic stratification, according to which classes are separated by gaps between wealth controlled or income received. In his essay *Class, Status and Party* (1924), Max Weber (1864–1920) used the German-language distinction between class and status to define the former in terms of economic categories such as employee, entrepreneur, wealth and so on, and the latter as involving social customs such as honour and prestige. He took the distinction further, by suggesting that status can, in part, be determined

35

by class but not vice versa and that class has an impact on long-term 'life chances', such as educational performance, health prospects and earnings potential.

Social scientists who study voting behaviour, like the National Centre for Social Research, which conducts and publishes the British General Election Study, attempt to correlate class, in the form of distinctions between employment categories, with political and social behaviour. Such models can be bipolar, referring to a division between a ruling, upper class of rich and powerful, as opposed to a lower, subordinate class of average or below average earners. They also differentiate further by introducing a middle-class category comprising managers and highly paid professionals, usually engaged in non-manual employment labelled 'white collar', in contrast to manual or 'blue collar' workers who form the lower or working class. The concept of a 'middle class' depends on personal perception of status, however, because indicators include education, consumption patterns and the conditions or environment in which people work and live. As with all models of social structure, classifications face difficulties when they attempt to accommodate real-world variability. Examples of such problems include deciding where agricultural workers fit with a scheme of middle- and working-class voters or to which class a family belongs if the job of each partner falls into different employment categories.

As noted by Lizabeth Cohen, *A Consumer's Republic* (2003), the advertising industry uses market research to correlate consumption patterns with class in order to decide how and where to promote particular commodities. In contrast to the British General Election Study, for example, which distinguishes between owners and managers, the surveys used for the purposes of **ADVERTISING** divide class into six categories. At the top of this ladder are higher and intermediate managerial, administrative and professional workers, followed by those who undertake clerical, junior managerial or supervisory roles. Then come skilled manual workers, who are followed by the semi-skilled and unskilled, while pensioners and casual workers come at the bottom of the heap. Perhaps inevitably, the construction and application of such classifications only serve to confuse further the concept of class.

In anti-capitalist terms, issues of class have formed a central aspect of **ANARCHISM**, **SOCIALISM**, syndicalism and other tendencies, but it is with the ideas of Karl Marx (1818–1883), Friedrich Engels (1820–1895) and subsequent Marxists that class as a force for human liberation is usually associated. Similarly, the celebrated phrase from the *Communist Manifesto*

(1848) that 'the history of all hitherto existing society is the history of class struggle' is linked indelibly to both men, even though revolutionaries like Louis Auguste Blanqui (1805–1881) recognized class antagonism as a motor of social change. Viewed in this way, the concept is far removed from its market research and social science interpretations, especially as it is offered as the key to human liberation.

Paradoxically, academia and capitalist society in general use their own subdivisions of economics, politics, philosophy and sociology to interpret Marx. They therefore portray his definition of class membership – as relating to ownership and control of the means of production or not – as economic reductionism: that is, explaining societal factors in reference to the realm of the economy.

This interpretation is wrong on two counts. First of all, in *Capital* (Volume I) Marx distinguished between a research method, which recognizes that fixed and stable notions are actually components in flux, and the presentation of reality as theory. What this means in terms of his overall approach is that his conception of class should not be understood as one factor or another, because it represents a totality – economic, political and sociological all at the same time. Classes are not regarded as static entities, for example, but as the product of human social relations that change over time and involve, but are not reduced to, a shared experience of the productive processes. The material conditions of not owning or controlling means of production reduces people to selling their labour-power in order to survive and makes those who work for a wage a 'class in itself'. On the other hand, recognition of a common interest, of divisions in society and one's position in it and the organization of class members into trade unions or political parties to further their interests as a whole, means that the class in itself has become a 'class for itself'.

The unequal relation between those who own and control the means of production as factories, mines, farms and so on – the **BOURGEOISIE** – and the wage worker or **PROLETARIAT** results in constant conflict because without human labour-power production is impossible; even though the worker receives less than an equal share of the proceeds. Struggle occurs in the factory over health and safety, wages, working conditions, productivity and working hours, and in society as a whole over the social wage – education, health and welfare provision. In Marxist terms, the proletariat not only represents a challenge to the profits of the bourgeoisie, it is also the agent of human liberation from the consequences of **PRIVATE PROPERTY** – ALIENATION,

37

EXPLOITATION and POVERTY. Such forms of antagonism are variously referred to as class conflict, class struggle and class war.

While a simplistic dichotomy of bourgeoisie and proletariat is not appropriate to the categorization of each individual in society, it nevertheless represents an understanding of society, through which a strategy for human emancipation can be developed. Some, like Jan Pakulski and Malcolm Waters, *The Death of Class* (1996), argue against the relevance of class, while others deliberately seek to conflate the revolutionary strategy with pejorative motivations based on resentment and desire for privilege. Paradoxically, critics of class analyses spend an inordinate amount of time and energy propounding class-based myths such as individuals avoiding work in order to live off societal wealth created by others, and overnight success or wealth portrayed as a result of dishonesty. Similar examples of IDEOLOGY include neoliberal emphasis on individualism, competition and the realization of identity through the purchase of commodities as a short-term advancement in economic and social status and therefore an antidote to the recognition of common interests. All of which are reinforced by the notion that everyone has an interest in present-day society because it is the only one that can guarantee increased standards of living; an appearance supported, inadvertently, by class struggles to improve welfare provision and ameliorate poverty.

Whereas some radical movements are not organized along class lines, like those motivated by issues of ethnicity, feminism, national liberation or sexual orientation, the two often coincide, as in the emergence and growth of the NEW LEFT in the second half of the twentieth century. Likewise, many anti-capitalist and anti-globalization activists reject the vanguard party ideas associated with Karl Kautsky (1854–1938), Vladimir (Ulyanov) Lenin (1870–1924), Georg Lukács (1885–1971), Leon Trotsky (1879–1940) and others and are disenchanted with western party politics in general. Nevertheless, the movement involves alliances between subordinated and directed social groups who, although they might not accept class analyses, are opposed to people and organizations – like politicians, corporate executives and CORPORATIONS, the INTERNATIONAL MONETARY FUND, the WORLD BANK and the WORLD TRADE ORGANIZATION – that dominate and direct economic and social life. In fact, the development of an anti-capitalist consciousness that favours mass activity over professional party organization is comparable to the analyses of Rosa Luxemburg (1871–1919) and those of autonomist, class-struggle or open Marxism taking place around the ideas of self-organization in Britain, Germany, Italy and North America.

FURTHER INFORMATION
British Election Study: www.essex.ac.uk/bes/index.html
A World Bank view: poverty.worldbank.org/library/view/6242/
Sources on autonomist, class-struggle and open Marxism: www.libcom.org/library

CLIMATE CHANGE see GLOBAL WARMING

COLLECTIVISM refers to theory and practice – goals and procedures – that relate to the organization and decision-making of a freely formed and self-governing association or group of cooperating individuals. So defined, its origins can be traced to the form of anarchism outlined in *Statism and Anarchy* (1872) by Mikhail Bakunin (1814–1876) and espoused by his followers who advocated the collective ownership of the means of production and were known as 'collectivists'. They and subsequent proponents argue that PRIVATE PROPERTY should be abolished in favour of communal, collective and public forms of organization/ownership whereby everyone has equal decision-making powers, equal responsibility for decisions, and works for the equal benefit of all. Such relations therefore form a prerequisite of real equality – based on the absence of hierarchical structure – that precludes notional ideals of EQUALITY. Examples of this latter idealism include 'equality before the law', where legal representation is bought according to wealth, and the ideals of 'one person, one vote', which do not explain the disproportionate influence corporate executives appear to exert on government officials.

Collectivist principles are based on the view that the interests of individuals are best served when they act as part of a coordinated group and that collective welfare is constituted by the well-being of every member. Cooperation is therefore considered to be more efficient than competition and rivalry. Furthermore, the voluntary association of consenting individuals who agree to the collective production and ownership of goods is considered to obviate the use of coercive force and therefore the need for a STATE or political system. Then, as now, collectivism constitutes the opposite to primacy of the individual (the theory of rational individualism), private property and the operation of the state machine as in Marxist–Leninist socialism.

Perhaps the most enduring example of collective organization and practice is that of the TRADE UNION, which involves the benefits of collective bargaining to secure wage rises and other forms of support based on membership. Attempts have also been made, not least by the NEW LEFT in the USA, to establish collectives by people who reject bourgeois roles and values such as work, school and family organization, to allow experimentation in new ways

39

of living by merging daily life and **POLITICS**. The experience afforded by such projects offers a valuable insight into problems faced by those who attempt to establish alternative organizational forms alongside existing society. The idea that society can be changed through withdrawal and the creation of better and more appealing alternatives has, for example, led to situations where mere survival becomes the goal and measure of success. Furthermore, success depends on attracting like-minded people who are committed to certain ideals, while principles of tolerance, passivity and relaxed membership criteria have often left collectives open to abuse from people who try to dominate or freeload.

Defined very broadly, collectivism can include **CORPORATIONS** and communes and be understood as any doctrine that argues for the priority of public over private/individual interests. Many anti-capitalist activists, like those involved with A-Infos, the European Counter Network, Indymedia and Notes from Nowhere, operate as collectives. It is therefore no coincidence that the features of political, economic and social organization they advocate – like replacing market mechanisms with public responsibility, the public ownership of utilities, and state regulation to protect the environment and workers – are the same ones attacked by **NEOLIBERALISM**. According to the latter, any society that is not **LAISSEZ-FAIRE** – that has a mixed economy or public welfare provision – is termed collectivist because certain features are owned, run or provided collectively for all and not restricted to one group or individual. Paradoxically, however, those who argue for giving free rein to corporations are advocating a form of collectivism whereby the interests of individual employees and consumers are presented as being tied to the interests and characteristics of a particular corporation. The anti-collectivist argument that collectives risk suppressing individual rights and sacrificing them for the alleged good of the group therefore appears to be self-defeating.

FURTHER INFORMATION

A-Infos: www.ainfos.ca/en
European Counter Network: www.ecn.org
Indymedia: www.indymedia.org
Notes from Nowhere: artactivism.members.gn.apc.org

COMMODITY is a product, according to capitalist economists, the price of which varies in response to fluctuations in its availability (supply) and the extent to which people think they need or want that particular product (demand). In the critique of political economy, outlined by Karl Marx (1818–1883) in the first chapter of *Capital* (Volume I), a commodity is any product, good or service, the primary purpose of which is availability to be bought and sold for money – in other words, to be exchanged. As CAPITALISM is based on the commodity system of production, almost everything is available for exchange, including: art, computers, national currencies, factories, food, homes, labour-power, machines, medicine, money, radio and television airwaves, raw materials and shares. More and more things have been commoditized over time to allow their owners to make a PROFIT by selling them for a price greater than that which they cost to buy.

A further aspect of the Marxist critique involves the argument that the worth of people to society is dependent on the price they can achieve for their labour-power as their saleable commodity, and that relations between them are reduced to impersonal and uncontrollable forces of the labour market. Moreover, the production of commodities requires the expenditure of human effort, labour-power, but the SOCIAL RELATIONS that take place between producers are obscured by the end product. The tendency to turn everything into a commodity means that people exist and relate to each other not as human beings, but as things – see REIFICATION. This process is important, because it results in a differentiation between appearance and reality, thereby concealing EXPLOITATION, the class interests of people and the political significance of employment and other social relations. As human relations appear as relations between commodities, the process is described as 'commodity fetishism' because inanimate objects are imbued with human qualities. People therefore appear to exist in a world of things and this is also a factor in their ALIENATION.

COMMUNISM refers to an ideal form of society, the political movement that advocates and agitates in favour of the creation of such a society and the self-described states that existed in the twentieth century as the Union of Soviet Socialist Republics (USSR), in Eastern Europe and in Asia. As a consequence of cold war propaganda and concomitant Soviet hegemony, communism became synonymous with the social, political and economic organization of these states, but this belies the various versions of communism that are indicated by adjectives like: anarchist, crude, libertarian, primitive, scientific and utopian, or the prefix 'Euro'. Furthermore, the distinction between communism, SOCIALISM and social democracy is

41

largely a twentieth-century convention, brought about by the creation of the Third International by the USSR in 1919 to encourage the formation of communist parties on the Bolshevik vanguard model and thereby distinguish between revolutionary and gradualist organizations. For most of the nineteenth century, communism, socialism and social democracy had been fairly interchangeable.

Certain characteristics can, however, be identified as fundamental to any conception of communism. In the first instance, the absence or abolition of the private ownership of property – excluding personal effects – accompanies the social ownership of the means of production and exchange. Production is therefore organized for use – to realize the potential for abundance – rather than for the sale and consumption of commodities for PROFIT. The other essential principle is EQUALITY, defined as the absence of hierarchy including the absence or abolition of classes, social divisions including the division of labour and non-exploitative SOCIAL RELATIONS. These criteria originated with Claude-Henri de Rouvroy, Comte de Saint Simon (1760–1825). Although not an avowed communist, his basic theory of a rationally planned and collectively controlled mode of production based on modern industry was outlined in *Letters from an Inhabitant of Geneva to his Contemporaries* (*Lettres d'un habitant de Genève à ses contemporains*) (1803). In fact, the term is attributed to the secret revolutionary societies of Paris in the 1830s, like the German émigré Ligue des Juste (League of the Just) and the Société des Saisons (Society of the Seasons) led by Louis-Auguste Blanqui (1805–1881). Subsequently introduced to Germany by Moses Hess (1812–1875), the term first appeared in England in 1843.

Communism has therefore been applied retrospectively to describe the ideas of Gerrard Winstanley (1609–60) and other DIGGERS in seventeenth-century England and those espoused by François Noel (Gracchus) Babeuf (1760–1797) during the Executive Directory period of the French Revolution. Babeuf's *Conspiracy of Equals* (*Conspiracion des Égaux*), for example, advocated a regime of literal equality based on the collective ownership of property, fixed wages, expropriation of the rich, the allocation of work according to capacity, a centralized distribution system of all produce and the collectivization of the industrial sector. These ideas were to form the basis of the state ownership schemes advocated by Louis Blanc (1811–1882), *The Organization of Labour* (*L'Organisation du Travail*) (1840), while the programme of the Société des Égaux (Society of Equals) informed the plot, *coup d'état* and post-revolutionary dictatorship strategy of Louis-Auguste Blanqui.

The development of communist theory led to the introduction and application of various subcategories like agrarian, crude, primitive, scientific and utopian. Such differentiation was used by Friedrich Engels (1820–1895) and Karl Marx (1818–1883) in the *Communist Manifesto* (1848) to distinguish their own brand of communism and to demonstrate the synchronized development of ideas and societal organization. According to this approach, primitive communism refers to a tribal organization of human society – described by Lewis H. Morgan (1818–1881), *Ancient Society* (1877) – where productive relations are based on collective ownership of the means of production and an absence of classes, STATE, hereditary status, exploitation or economic stratification. Such societies are typically non-authoritarian, broadly egalitarian in terms of social and economic relations, operate a collective right to basic resources, and PRIVATE PROPERTY exists in the form of personal possessions – weapons, household articles, clothing and so forth.

In reference to the development of human history, crude communism is defined as predating the capitalist mode of production and therefore the development of machine industry that offers the potential for abundance. First expressed in sixteenth-century England, it is typified in *Utopia* (1516) by Thomas More (1478–1535) as a primitive idyll believed to be superior to the feudal system. Communism of production based on machine industry was popularized by Étienne Cabet (1788–1856) in *Travels in Icaria* (*Voyages en Icarie*) (1839), a name he later gave to the colony he founded in the USA. By variously advocating class reconciliation as opposed to class struggle, amelioration of social conditions, reorganization of the labour process, communal ownership and free distribution of essential goods and services according to need, Cabet was categorized as utopian. So too was Robert Owen (1771–1858), *A New View of Society* (1816), who set up communities named New Lanark in Scotland and New Harmony in the USA; as did Wilhelm Weitling (1809–1864), *Guarantees of Harmony and Freedom* (*Garantien der Harmonie und Freiheit*) (1842), under the name of Communia. Similarly, Charles Fourier (1772–1837), *Theory of the Four Movements* (*La Théorie de Quatres Mouvements*) (1808), advocated the founding of experimental communities and was also labelled utopian.

Marx and Engels considered their form of communism to be scientific, because it was based on a materialist analysis and study of society and socio-economic development, as opposed to an emotional or ethical yearning for reconciliation of rich and poor. In similar fashion to Blanqui, they saw class struggle as the revolutionary driving force behind the history of human

43

development, but came to this conclusion through materialist study and dialectical analysis. They also rejected his conspiratorial approach, advocating instead a political movement of the working class to achieve not just political revolution but human emancipation. Their ideas on the matter were outlined in the *Manifesto* which was written at the request of the second congress of the Communist League (Bund du Kommunisten) – the name adopted by the League of the Just from June 1847.

Marx and Engels worked briefly with Blanquists and Chartists, during 1850, as part of the World Society of Revolutionary Communists and with non-communists in the International Working Men's Association from 1864 to 1876. In 1889, the Second International was established as a loose federation of trade unions and political parties that involved communists and non-communists in debating tactics and policy. Participants included August Bebel (1840–1913), Eduard Bernstein (1850–1932), Jean Jaurès (1859–1914), Karl Kautsky (1854–1938), Vladimir (Ulyanov) Lenin (1870–1924), Rosa Luxemburg (1871–1919), Yulii Martov (1873–1923) and Georgii Plekhanov (1856–1918). The idea of communism was also influenced by anarchist thinkers, before and after their exclusion from the International in 1896. Objecting to what he considered to be an innate authoritarianism in the approach of Marxian communism, for example, Piotr Kropotkin (1842–1921) advocated a form of anarchist communism. In *The Conquest of Bread* (1892), *Fields, Factories and Workshops* (1899) and *Mutual Aid* (1902), he advanced his proposals for a society in which the means of production and distribution would be both owned and organized collectively in a federal society of free communist groups and decentralized industry.

In the second decade of the twentieth century a radical communism, strongly influenced by a distrust of those social-democratic parties that had supported and taken national sides in World War I, developed in around the Communist, or Third, International. A defining feature of the movement was its rejection of agreements or alliances with reformist parties and a mistrust of electoral involvement. The movement was also associated with Council Communism in Germany, the Communist Workers Party of Germany (Kommunistische Arbeiter Partei Deutschlands) and revolutionary unions like the General Workers Union of Germany (Allgemeine Arbeiter Union Deutschlands). In Saxony, Otto Rühle (1874–1943) and the factory-based General Workers Union (Allgemeine Arbeiter Union Einheitsorganisation) advocated a workers' democracy based on a federation of workers' councils, elected at workplaces, as an antidote to Bolshevism, parties and parliament. Other leading figures included Anton Pannekoek (1873–1960), Herman Gorter (1864–1927) and Paul Mattick (1904–1981).

Elsewhere left communists in Russia under Nikolai Bukharin (1888–1938) opposed the Brest–Litovsk peace treaty, argued for a revolutionary war, opposed national self-determination and supported a voluntarist approach to REVOLUTION. In the Netherlands, the movement is associated with the Communist Workers Party (Kommunistische Arbeiders Partij Nederland), the International Communist Group (Bond van Internationale Kommunisten) and the Revolutionary Socialist Workers Party (Revolutionair Socialistische Arbeiders Partij), later known as the Marx–Lenin–Luxemburg Front, led by Henk Sneevliet (1883–1942). Amadeo Bordiga (1889–1970) and his supporters in the Italian Socialist Party (Partito Socialista Italiano) had a tenuous link to left communism until Bordiga was imprisoned in 1926, after which Italian left Communism developed in exile under Ottorino Perrone (1897–1957). The movement was also identified with Sylvia Pankhurst and the Communist Workers Party of Britain. These and other groups, including followers of Daniel De Leon (1852–1914), the Industrial Workers of the World and the numerous parties in the USA that used 'Socialist Labor' in their title, were polemicized by Lenin in *Left-Wing Communism, an Infantile Disorder* (1920).

Left communists had supported the Bolshevik Revolution of October 1917 and the Communist International, but retained a critical view of its development and Bolshevik methods. Following the formation of the International Left Opposition by Leon Trotsky (1879–1940) and his supporters, there was a brief association between the two tendencies, although this foundered over tactical alliances with reformist groups and entrism. Nevertheless, individuals and groups often moved from one to the other, examples of which include the Workers Group (Grupo de Trabajadores) in Mexico, the International Communist League (Ligue des Communitistes Internationalistes) in Belgium and the Revolutionary Communists of Germany (Revolutionäre Kommunisten Deutschlands), formed in exile.

Although the partisans of the cold war sought to equate communism with the organization, practices and theorization of self-proclaimed communist states, a number of factors conspired to challenge this perception. These included the creation of the Fourth International by Trotsky and his supporters in 1938, the disbanding of the Communist International in 1943, the Chinese Revolution of 1949 under Mao Zedong (1893–1976) and the subsequent Sino–Soviet split. Similarly, denunciation of Josef (Dzhugashvili) Stalin (1879–1953) three years after his death was compounded by the repression of Czechoslovak, Hungarian and Polish attempts to pursue independent policies and practices. Alternative approaches to communism developed in response to such events, most prominently in the form of the NEW LEFT that generally eschewed established Communist parties and Eurocommunism. Advocates of the latter sought to adapt their programmes according to national circumstances, adopt gradual as opposed to revolutionary tactics, cooperate with other progressive parties and groups and work on the basis of a mixed economy to expose the shortcomings of capitalist society. Although such ideas were influential in France and Spain, they were most prominent in Italy where the Communist Party (Partito Communista Italiano) sought to reinterpret the ideas of Antonio Gramsci (1891–1937).

Self-professed Communist parties remain in power in the People's Republic of China, Vietnam, Laos, North Korea and Cuba, although only Cuba still has its original leader, Fidel Castro. Whereas the Soviet bloc disintegrated in the 1990s, China, Vietnam and Laos still describe themselves as communist even though they have introduced market reforms, private enterprise and, in China, private property. The collapse of the Soviet Union led to a splintering or disappearance of many Marxist–Leninist parties that had been recognized and supported by Moscow. Many groups and political parties continue to call themselves communist and agitate for revolution, including Maoists, Marxist–Leninists and Trotskyists. Council and left communism also have supporters, as do anarchist communism and the autonomist movement, which has its roots in the AUTONOMIA that developed in Northern Italy.

FURTHER INFORMATION

Communist documents: www.marxists.org
Organizations: www.broadleft.org
Left communism: www.internationalism.org

CONSUMERISM is a pejorative term used to indicate a level of consumption that exceeds the satisfaction of basic needs and wants. All human beings maintain and reproduce themselves – mentally and physically – through the consumption of air, food, water and, depending on the climate, clothing and shelter from extremes of weather. Intellectually, people also make use of various educational opportunities, enjoy art, literature and other forms of CULTURE. The idea that there is a level and direction of consumption that is excessive was introduced by Thorstein Veblen (1857–1929) in his *The Theory of the Leisure Class* (1899). Veblen used the term 'conspicuous consumption' to denote unusual purchasing patterns through which people attempt to enhance their social status according to the amount or expense of the commodities they accumulate or consume. Such action subordinates human individuality and personal development to the purchase of brand names, designer labels and the statements made by the ownership and display of expensive cars, houses, jewellery and other luxury items; possibly in an attempt to remedy feelings of ALIENATION. Personal relationships also become restricted to an interaction between people with similar interests in the pursuit of wealth, luxury and the consumption of similar products – see REIFICATION.

All forms of society involve consumption, and, as the process destroys what has been produced, replacement requires a cycle of production and consumption. In capitalist society, this process takes on unique and extreme characteristics due to the fact that commodity production for PROFIT displays an increasing dependency on the generation of higher and higher levels of consumption over and beyond basic needs. The drive to maintain and increase profits results in the constant differentiation of consumer goods and the manipulation of consumers through ADVERTISING to convince them that they need to purchase a newly available product or replace an existing one. This creation of demand takes place on a number of levels and even includes children as a target for marketing strategies, where certain products and foods are particularly aimed at the young consumer.

As a result, more and more waste is generated for disposal in landfill sites; a process that is accompanied by a paradox whereby profit margins are diminished by workers' demands for the higher incomes that are necessary to finance further consumption. In an attempt to maintain profitability emphasis is placed on the maximization of production at minimum cost, and this results in a form of 'productivism' that concentrates on achieving higher levels of output without consideration of the consequences for people, society or the environment. Moreover, the creation of commodities for sale to the public means that more items and resources are also produced, consumed and disposed of as part of the production process itself. These trends are not simply economic. Lizabeth Cohen's *Consumer's Republic* (2003), for example, records how governments in the USA equated consumption with patriotism and encouraged shopping as an antidote to trauma in the aftermath of World War II and the September 2001 atrocities.

The implications of consumer society are not only evident in the industrialized world. The STRUCTURAL ADJUSTMENT PROGRAMMES advocated by the INTERNATIONAL MONETARY FUND and the WORLD BANK for economic expansion or recovery in developing countries tend to promote an increase in exports. This emphasis on overseas demand means that domestic production is geared to the consumption patterns of other nations, which leaves farmers and manufacturers overly reliant on the health of other economies and their decision whether or not to subsidize their own producers. In fact, the overwhelming export potential for developing countries lies in agricultural products like bananas, beef, coffee and sugar; although agricultural sectors are heavily subsidized by the European Union and by North American governments. Furthermore, the land and resources that go into growing crops and livestock for export – including animal feed – are lost to local consumption needs and often involve deforestation; a process exacerbated by the consumption of wood and paper in parts of Europe, Japan and North America – the so-called developed world.

Consumption beyond minimal and basic needs is accepted and advocated by those who oppose capitalist excess; an example of which includes the 'potential for abundance' tenet of COMMUNISM. Similar ideas are advocated by J.W. Smith, *World's Wasted Wealth* II (1994), and by TRADE UNIONS that campaign for a reduction in the working week without a loss of pay, based on improved productive capacity. These alternatives argue for production that is geared to a redistribution or more equitable distribution of wealth – social and private – and promote the organization of production to facilitate SUSTAINABLE DEVELOPMENT, education and welfare as opposed to conspicuous display, the accumulation of capital and profit. The goal of environmental protection forms an integral aspect of such thinking, with investment and growth strategies targeted at reducing pollution in the production and consumption processes, including the development of new, cleaner technology and the repair of existing damage. Others like Duane Elgin, *Voluntary Simplicity* (1993), seek a more direct approach involving a change in lifestyle, while organizations like Adbusters mount 'buy nothing' campaigns to get their message across.

FURTHER INFORMATION

Anti-consumerism: www.enough.org.uk/
Discussion of issues: www.globalissues.org/TradeRelated/Consumption.asp
United Nations facts and figures: stone.undp.org/hdr/reports/global/1998/en/

COPYLEFT represents the antithesis of INTELLECTUAL PROPERTY because it uses existing COPYRIGHT regulations to place a document, idea or programme in the public domain as a universally available product that remains freely available. This involves a requirement whereby conditions of use and amendment permit anybody to copy, use, modify and redistribute a particular item – together with anything derived from it – so long as the distribution terms are retained and others are thereby authorized to use, copy, change and distribute any new version accordingly. Copyleft therefore prevents people and CORPORATIONS from making changes to a document, idea or programme in order to restrict access and therefore allows knowledge to grow beyond the resources or imagination of any individual entity. All such criteria are covered by the Free Software Foundation versions of the GNU Free Documentation License.

FURTHER INFORMATION

General outline: www.gnu.org/copyleft/copyleft.html
Application to documents: www.gnu.org/copyleft/fdl.html

COPYRIGHT is a form of INTELLECTUAL PROPERTY protection that applies to creative work such as art, films, literature, music, sound recording and software and prevents others from making copies, issuing copies, performing in public, broadcasting, using online, distorting or mutilating the copyrighted work. Criteria differ from country to country, but a work can only be copyrighted if it includes some element of originality and skill. Copyright protection then applies for a set period of time, but only to the form of arrangement, expression or selection as opposed to facts, ideas, information or function. While other forms of intellectual property, like patents, require ideas to be registered, a copyright applies as soon as there is a record of what has been created, but it does not constitute a monopoly on the right of use. Copyrights are often assigned or licensed to CORPORATIONS for royalties and such practices are common in the book publishing and music industries.

The origin of the modern form of copyright is attributed to eighteenth-century England, during the Industrial Revolution, when the Statute of Anne came into force in 1710 and recognized authors, rather than publishers, as the primary beneficiaries. Several international treaties have since been agreed with the intention of normalizing standards. These include the Berne Convention of 1886, the Universal Copyright Convention 1954, the Trade-Related Aspects of Intellectual Property Rights agreement 1994, the WORLD INTELLECTUAL PROPERTY ORGANIZATION Copyright and Performance and

Phonograms treaties of 1996 and the European Union Copyright Directive 2001.

Justification for the existence of copyright relies on the argument that it encourages and rewards creative work and that it allows corporations to benefit and thereby invest in and encourage the development of new talent. Where an employee creates something suitable for a copyright as part of their paid employment, however, the copyright is automatically assigned to the employer. In contrast, critics like Lawrence Lessig, *Free Culture* (2004), contend that such regulations are restrictive. Other objections include the view that copyright extends the practice of EXPLOITATION into the intellectual realm and serves to restrict creativity by reinforcing the perception that the only rewards for creativity are monetary – as opposed to personal development and expression. Thus, as an item of property to be sold, creativity is subjugated to the logic of commodity production whereby output becomes formulaic in response to market demand or development is constrained by the need for rapid turnover so that 'creative' products can be bought and sold for PROFIT. Ultimately, the practical efficacy of copyright is constantly being undermined by advances in technology, like photocopying, sound and image recording and the advent of the Internet. Alternative formulas are also being developed to challenge restrictions and include the creative commons project, COPYLEFT and open source software.

FURTHER INFORMATION
Creative Commons: creativecommons.org/
Free Software: www.fsfeurope.org/

CORPORATE LOBBY GROUP is an organization that attempts to exert an influence on the policy and decision-making processes of governing bodies at local, regional, national and international levels in furtherance of the interests of one or more CORPORATIONS. Although national governments are ostensibly in control of their economic, political and social jurisdictions, they are subjected to lobbying from a variety of groups and bodies including corporations, non-governmental organizations, think-tanks and trade unions. Lobbying takes a variety of forms and often employs public relations and ADVERTISING techniques, but is most contentious when accompanied by party funding or the creation of ostensibly independent organizations to influence public opinion in the interests of a sponsor. Such practices are open to allegations of corruption, more so than attempts to exert influence through the publication of research and regular reports, for example, although a combination of methods might be practised at one time or another.

Cooperation also takes place between corporations through trade associations, lobby groups and think-tanks and these can be organized along industry lines, across sectors or national boundaries. On a national level, for example, the Business Roundtable, founded in the USA in 1972, attempts to influence environment, consumer, health-care, international trade and social security policy on behalf of over 200 banks and corporations in America. The European Roundtable of Industrialists plays a similar role on behalf of Europe's largest corporations, has nearly 50 affiliates and seeks to persuade governing institutions at the national and European Union levels to pursue the neoliberal agenda of DEREGULATION and PRIVATIZATION. As a bridge between organizations on both continents, the Transatlantic Business Dialogue (founded in 1995) represents the interests of around 150 American and European corporations and specializes in alerting the European Commission and the US government to the dangers of 'barriers' to transatlantic trade.

At the transnational level, the International Chamber of Commerce (ICC) has existed since 1919, is based in Paris and, as the largest corporate lobby group, represents corporations from more than 130 countries. Extremely influential with institutions of international governance, including the G8 and UNITED NATIONS, the ICC was responsible for writing parts of the abortive MULTILATERAL AGREEMENT ON INVESTMENT and has permanent representation at the WORLD TRADE ORGANIZATION. Activities include advocating open trade, market economy systems and business self-regulation, which translates into attempts to weaken the KYOTO PROTOCOL, the United Nations Convention on Biodiversity (1992) and the Basel Convention on the Control of Transboundary Movements of Hazardous Wastes and Their Disposal (1989).

Although it is not strictly a lobby group, corporate delegates to the World Economic Forum (WEF), founded in 1971, are given the opportunity to influence the institutions of international governance and many national governments at annual meetings that facilitate fraternization between representatives from those institutions. At its most visible, the WEF invites 2,000 or so academics, corporate executives, journalists and politicians to the elite Swiss ski resort of Davos, to enable the exchange of information and the formulation of policy among and on behalf of the world's leading corporations. WEF membership is dominated by Asia, Europe and the USA and by corporations with an annual turnover of US$1 billion or more. Corporate membership is dependent on payment of an annual fee; attendance at the annual meeting is also fee-based, as is the right to contribute to regional and annual agendas as an Institutional, Knowledge or Annual Meeting Partner.

The WEF was instrumental in devising and creating the World Trade Organization and since January 2000 its meetings have become a focus for protests by those who reject the consequences of unregulated capitalism. Criticism of private, informal meetings between corporate executives, international financial institutions and political leaders prompted the WEF to invite organizations like Friends of the Earth, Greenpeace and Focus on the Global South, but it has since refused to extend that invitation to those it considers to be negative in outlook. Opponents of corporate lobbying consider such activity to be anti-democratic because of the influence it exerts over the policy and practice of institutions of national and international government, which stands in direct contradiction of the fundamental democratic principle of one person, one vote. The economic strength of individual corporations that provides the basis for their influence is also enhanced by the adoption of a collective approach, a tactic of which they, paradoxically, disapprove when it is adopted by employees. The determination of policy without the knowledge or consent of voters is also considered to undermine any claim of ACCOUNTABILITY.

FURTHER INFORMATION
Official sites: www.iccwbo.org; www.weforum.org
A critical view of the WEF: www.citizen.org/documents/WEFreport.pdf
Centre for Responsive Politics: www.opensecrets.org/
Corporate Europe Observatory: www.corporateeurope.org/

CORPORATIONS are non-governmental bodies that have been registered with and authorized by the STATE – originally as a group of investors – to gather private funds and conduct business in a designated area of commercial activity. More specifically, it is a collective organization with a constitution or charter that details its duties, purpose and responsibilities; in return for which it is accorded privileges not available to ordinary businesses or groups of individuals. The laws of the state where corporations are registered or operate regulate their activities, and undertakings outside their legal or constitutional remit are *ultra vires*. Depending on the local convention, such organizations are also known as companies or firms, while those registered on a non-profitmaking basis are often referred to as 'non-stock' or 'membership' corporations.

In fact, corporations originated in Europe as non-profit projects that provided services, utilities and other forms of infrastructure of a public nature: banking and insurance; hospitals and universities; as well as diplomatic functions and defending trade routes. The practice continued in the USA following independence and well into the twentieth century in the form of postal, broadcasting and other communication services like the British Broadcasting Corporation, which was incorporated in 1926. Until recently, the term was also synonymous with the agencies of local government in the cities and towns of Britain. Then as now, the ultimate state sanction is revocation of charter, but from the seventeenth century on corporations grew in power and independence as they served the imperial purposes of controlling trade, resources and territory in Asia, Africa and the Americas.

The first such entity was the British East India Company, which operated under the title of 'The Governor and Company of Merchants of London Trading into the East Indies'. Set up in 1600, its charter included the shipment of raw material to Britain for manufacture and the export of finished goods. Others followed, like the Dutch United East Indies Company (Vereenigde Oostindische Compagnie) formed in 1602 and a West Indies version founded in 1621. Similarly, a French East India Company (Compagnie des Indes Orientales) was established in 1664 and followed by a Swedish Company (Svenska Ostindiska Companiet) in 1731. Although these corporations existed for different lengths of time, the origin of today's corporate form can be traced back to mid-nineteenth-century Britain and dissolution of the territorial power of the East India Company in 1858. This move followed the Joint Stock Companies Acts of 1844 and 1856 that allowed companies to define their own purpose and granted them legal status equivalent to that of a person, while the Limited Liability Act 1855 protected the personal assets of shareholders from the consequences of their corporate behaviour.

In 1886 the US Supreme Court decided in *Santa Clara County* v. *Southern Pacific Railroad* that a corporation should be recognized as a 'natural person' under law and therefore be entitled to the rights specified under the 14th Amendment to the Constitution, which was adopted to protect emancipated slaves. Similar protections are afforded to the Anonymous societies, known as *Société Anonyme* in the French-speaking world and as *Sociedad(e) Anónima* in Spanish and Portuguese. Meanwhile share- or stock-based corporations are known as *Aktiengesellschaft* in Germany and *Società per Azioni* in Italy, while limited liability is indicated by the terms *Gesellschaft mit beschränkter Haftung* and *Società in Accomandita per Azioni*. Depending on the national requirements corporate status is indicated in its title as Incorporated (Inc.), Limited (Ltd), Limited Liability Company (LLC), Public Limited Company (PLC), Publicly Listed Company (Plc), Proprietary (Pty) or Unlimited.

Although corporate personhood is distinguished, in law, from that of a natural person, a group of people registered as a corporation has the right to employ people, own PRIVATE PROPERTY, sign contracts and sue or be sued in the courts. In legal terms, a corporation might be an 'artificial' or 'moral' person(s), but this abstract category forms the basis for the idea that corporations and individual employees enter into fair and free contracts as equals; even though corporations exercise POWER over the lives and professional activities of their members. Corporations also enjoy privileges not available to ordinary individuals or groups of individuals. As indicated earlier, the shareholders of a limited corporation – be they people, pension funds, trusts or other corporations – are not liable for the organization's debts and obligations, or such liability is limited to the cost of the shares they hold. Without such a caveat there would be little incentive to buy and sell shares as commodities.

Corporate governance involves the distribution of rights and responsibilities among those who manage the activities and interests of a corporation. This normally involves a board of directors, officers that include a chief executive, president and treasurer, and shareholders who approve corporate performance at general meetings. In reality, individual shareholders have little say, as the major holdings belong to other corporate interests and investment funds that are mainly interested in the payment of dividends. Directors and officers can also be major shareholders due to their privileged positions within corporations that allow them to award themselves preferential and new stock options. They also pay themselves allowances for attending board meetings, and award themselves large salaries, free medical insurance and generous pension provision, together with expense-account allowances and the use of company cars and homes – even when corporate profits and stocks fall.

Such behaviour leads to calls for ACCOUNTABILITY and union campaigns like Executive PayWatch mounted by the American Federation of Labor and Congress of Industrial Organizations (AFL–CIO) and those against 'fat-cat' bosses organized by Amicus and Unison in Britain. Others like the Alliance for Sustainable Jobs and the Environment raise concerns about the negative impact corporations have on communities, the environment, society and workers and the extent to which they operate beyond the effective control of the nation-state. Sportswear firms like the Italian Kappa and British JJB Sports, for example, have been accused of trading with Burma despite its human rights record, and in 2004 British American Tobacco agreed to shift production to China to take advantage of low production costs and secure access to the domestic market. Such trends were first noted by R.H. Coase in *The Nature of the Firm* (1937).

There is also a pattern of corporations breaking or circumventing laws and the (re)introduction of regulations to remedy or prevent repetition. The Bank of Credit and Commerce International collapsed in 1991, for example, amid allegations of money laundering, tax evasion and illegal acquisition of banks and real estate. Likewise, in the USA Enron imploded in 2001 and ex-directors and officers now face charges of banking and securities fraud, insider dealing, exaggerated financial statements and off-books partnerships and transactions. According to neoliberal economic theory, however, corporations are granted legal privileges in return for accountability and REGULATION. In practice, few questions are asked about international activities so long as the host nation benefits. Many American corporations, for example, register in the State of Delaware, because it does not tax activities that take place outside its boundaries and grants greater powers to boards of directors, while the State of Nevada allows corporations to be set up without a record of who owns them.

As Ted Nace notes, in *Gangs of America* (2003), this process began with the East India Companies that acquired raw materials from pre-capitalist societies and exported finished products back to them. Joint-stock corporations have also operated in more than one country since the nineteenth century and their growth through international mergers can be traced to the 1930s when Lever Brothers and Margarine Unie formed Unilever. There are also examples of corporations being involved in determining national economic policy through the staging of a *coup d'état*, as in the case of United Fruit in Guatemala 1953 and copper-mining companies in Chile 1973. Even today, corporations like Shell and British Petroleum are accused of controlling land, military forces, ports and railroads in Africa and Latin America.

Since the 1970s national boundaries have become less important to industrial and financial corporations, which use centralized head offices to coordinate global management and control of legally distinct entities. These MULTINATIONAL CORPORATIONS (MNCs) benefit from free-trade areas and the deregulatory agenda of the INTERNATIONAL MONETARY FUND, WORLD

BANK and WORLD TRADE ORGANIZATION. To a certain extent, MNCs have been able to invert the practices of the East India Companies by moving production to developing countries and importing cheaply produced commodities to the industrialized world at inflated prices and therefore profits. In the absence of capital controls, MNCs are also able to invest profits abroad or move capital, commodities and production through subsidiary firms and subcontractors. Such power gives them added leverage when bargaining with governments – particularly in the developing world – to secure favourable taxation policy, reductions in consumer and environmental protection and lower standards of labour, human and animal rights. To this extent they appear to be beyond government control, and their ability to destabilize weak economies by withdrawing or threatening to withdraw investment, unless governments acquiesce to their demands, raises questions concerning the nature and efficacy of DEMOCRACY.

Of the 100 largest economies, 51 are MNCs and the rest nation-states. In 2001, for example, the respective turnover of the USA-based corporation Wal-Mart was similar to that of Sweden, while ExxonMobil exceeded that of Turkey, General Motors that of Saudi Arabia and General Electric that of Poland. The wealth and power of corporations is increasingly equated with the control of domestic political agendas through the ownership of media institutions that influence the outcome of public discourse. Corporate ownership in the form of Berlusconi and Murdoch not only dominates the popular media, but sponsorship and funding also determine university curricula, research funding and therefore the career prospects of academics and graduates. Likewise political parties, such as Forza Italia, act as fronts for corporate interests and depend on the financial largesse of corporations, leaving those without resources marginalized. Last but not least, the apparently ubiquitous presence of the products that corporations promote through aggressive ADVERTISING also contributes to accusations of an agenda for international domination that involves the destruction of indigenous, local and other forms of custom and CULTURE.

FURTHER INFORMATION

About multinationals: www.multinationalmonitor.org; www.transnationale.org
Corporate accountability: www.asje.org

CULTURE, in general terms, refers to any human activity that involves cultivation and development. This applies in the sphere of aesthetic production – art, literature and music – as well as in anthropological study of the way people live in a particular society. In the German idealist tradition of Gottfried Leibniz (1646–1716), Immanuel Kant (1724–1804), Johann Fichte (1762–1814), Friedrich Schelling (1775–1854) and Georg W.F. Hegel (1770–1831), 'culture' is equated with objective mind or spirit and its embodiment in human activity. Alternatively, it is considered to be a prerequisite for civilization or the higher ideals of FREEDOM and happiness. As a mental and spiritual realm perceived to be superior to and therefore different from the experience of everyday existence, the concept becomes an ideal to be accepted or affirmed and a standard against which humanity is evaluated. This translates into the measurement of behaviour or norms, concrete artefacts, and beliefs or values against absolute ideas about human beauty and quality.

In capitalist society, such preconceived criteria have become synonymous with certain social activities such as the appreciation and consumption of particular commodities. Examples include works of art – drawing, installation, painting, performance, photography, sculpture, video and so on – items of fashion, cuisine, literature as defined by a 'canon', and music represented as harmony, lyricism and resonance in ballet, opera and other forms of orchestral composition. The processes through which these products and practices are afforded meaning and therefore classified as worthy of appreciation are subtle and involve a number of mediators. These include people who are presented as uniquely qualified to be 'critics' and therefore able to appreciate, interpret, judge and comment on worth. Educational institutions and the MEDIA communicate similar messages and undertake analogous roles, while the mere inclusion of a painting in an art gallery, the publication of a book or staging of a play implies that a certain standard has been achieved.

Such mores are embedded in social relationships that revolve around the enjoyment of a product or activity, which, in turn, is dependent on income or wealth that facilitates the purchase of artefacts, tickets for performances at prestigious venues and the leisure time necessary for participation in such pastimes. The distinction between 'high' and 'low' culture, with the former being equated with 'fine', expensive goods and a level of education necessary to appreciate them, represents a form of CONSUMERISM in which elite consumption symbolizes status and becomes a means through which people relate to each other. Aesthetic value defined as universal truth thus becomes a way of codifying and mystifying social hierarchy and involves the myriad interactions explored by Pierre Bourdieu (1930–2002) and Jean-Claude Passeron, *Reproduction in Education, Society and Culture* (1977). Paradoxically, given the original idealistic justification, the dictates of fashion, be it in the form of art, clothing or music, conflate aesthetics and innovation in order to generate consumption through a constant changing of criteria that suggest or signal an individual's position in status groups. Cultural styles and movements drift in and out of vogue among high-status consumers and involve media celebrities who hire 'consultants' to advise them on their purchases and who join with producers to determine the rate and direction of changes to that which is considered to be de rigueur.

At the other end of the spectrum low, mass, pop or popular culture is prevalent in modern capitalist society. Perhaps ironically, the same mediators of high culture are involved in determining the content of its counterpart, especially industries that disseminate information in the form of film, printed publications, television and as news. As Jean Baudrillard observes in *Simulations* (1984), these are the very media through which the public see pictures of the world presented as reality, via a selection, interpretation and presentation of incomplete 'facts' as whole and immutable. The defining features of popular culture include its broad appeal and the mass production and consumption of commodities of a superficial and transitory quality in various formats, such as comics, computer games, pulp fiction novels and video/DVD.

Low and high culture are therefore juxtaposed as literature versus genre novels, opera against music hall, or popular music and symphony; while the choices involved in eating out, listening to music, visiting cinema or watching television serve to define and reinforce societal divisions of CLASS, ethnicity, gender, race and region. In an attempt to counteract such influences, underground, sub- or counter-cultures have developed to establish an independent identity, but achieve little more than an illustration of the manner in which the forces of domination prevail. In other words, groups whose behaviour, preferred artefacts and values are meant to challenge or resist established practices usually express their difference through the same consumption patterns – that is, in terms of alternative forms of art, fashion, literature and music.

Members of the Frankfurt School or Institute for Social Research (Institut für Sozialforschung), for example, argued that such phenomena had devastating implications for human emancipation and radical social change. Although Max Horkheimer (1895–1973) and Herbert Marcuse (1898–1979) contributed to analyses, the approach is epitomized in the work of Theodor Adorno (1903–1969), including *Prisms* (1981) and *The Culture Industry* (1991). Influenced by Walter Benjamin (1892–1940) and Friedrich Pollock (1894–1970), Adorno concluded that the commercialization, commodification and standardization of the 'Culture Industry' amounted to REIFICATION and IDEOLOGY. Through the market place, for example, VALUE is equated with price and creativity is degraded and neutralized by mechanical reproduction for sale. Commercial culture therefore serves to integrate, pacify and thereby reinforce the status quo by encouraging unquestioning consumption that has a fetishistic character of diffusing human identity through its equation with commodities.

Adorno therefore advocated an aesthetic approach that promotes the struggle to understand art, music, literature, philosophy and so on as the way of establishing real value. For Adorno avant-garde and innovative art and music, especially the atonal music of Arnold Schoenberg (1874–1951), resisted appropriation by the market system due to the critical effort required for appreciation. Even here, however, there are perpetual attempts to reduce that which is different to the status of COMMODITY and thereby neutralize the very substance of its value – the detachment from prevailing social norms. Such a fate befalls conceptual art when it is deemed to be 'collectable', for example, in spite of the original approach that considered the ideas of the artist to be more important than the creation of commercially marketable works. Similarly, the idea that the abilities, experience, skills and training involved in the production of artefacts constitutes worth obscures the fact that even creative workers are exploited if they work for an employer or on commission for CORPORATIONS and wealthy people who purchase their artefacts for decorative or investment purposes.

Uncritical affirmation of existing social conditions is also reinforced by certain academic approaches to appreciation that emphasize a strict interpretation of text – be it clothing, film, photographs or written language. Such formal methods seek to prevent any discussion of creative intention, psychology, biography or reader response. Alternative viewpoints focus on the framing of objects, the ways in which artefacts are consumed – read, received and interpreted – and consider audience reaction or discourse to be at least as important as an individual piece of work. In postmodernist style, for example, aesthetic values are attributed to individual perception and group construction, so that meaning is believed to vary according to the social and political context in which a particular form of culture occurs or is viewed. In this way, universal aesthetic truth or value is replaced by decentred, provisional or tacit interpretation and reinterpretation based on the method of deconstruction advocated by Jacques Derrida (1930–2004), *Letter to a Japanese Friend* (1983), among others.

This brings us back to the questions of universal or fundamental principles as conceived by the modernist approach to aesthetics and the extent to which the abstraction of beauty, freedom and happiness to the cultural realm serves the repressive function of escapism through distraction from everyday drudgery. While culture offers temporary relief from real-life experience and therefore acts to perpetuate existing conditions, it also embodies the dynamic confrontation between ordinary experience and symbolic representation and expression of human potential. William Morris (1834–1896), *News from Nowhere* (1890), for example, sought to equate all creative work with art and thereby demystify the division of labour, whereby cultural artefacts and their production are presented as separate, specialist and distinct. By challenging the distinctions between the two, the aim is to realize human creativity as a liberating force and source of enjoyment. In *The Soul of Man under Socialism* (1891), Oscar Wilde (1854–1900) located the value of creativity in the experience of the creator, for which the enjoyment of the observer is incidental. More recently, anti-capitalist groups like the Movement of the Imagination and the Art and Revolution Collective see the combination of creativity with ACTIVISM and political and social relevance as crucial to meaningful artistic expression. This is based on the creation of new forms of resistance that involve dance, music, theatre and puppetry to inspire participants and observers into radical, progressive social change.

FURTHER INFORMATION

Anti-capitalist groups: www.artandrevolution.org; www.movementoftheimagination.org

Frankfurt School: www.marxists.org/subject/frankfurt-school

D

DEEP ECOLOGY is a bio- or eco-centric way of analysing issues that affords intrinsic value to all 'natural' things, so that nature as opposed to humanity forms the basis of its value system and therefore constitutes the opposite of anthropocentrism. See also ECOLOGY.

FURTHER INFORMATION
Foundation for Deep Ecology: www.deepecology.org

DEMOCRACY is a nebulous concept employed as a value judgement in current-day capitalist parlance to imply approval or accreditation of a given system of government. Rooted in the Greek *demos*, meaning 'people', and *kratein*, 'to rule', the term implies that, in some undefined sense, ultimate decision-making power rests with the population. Although now equated with universal adult suffrage, for long periods slaves, women, the illiterate, the propertyless, felons and emancipated blacks in the South of the USA were excluded from voting and standing for election. The issue of candidature, suffrage and hence democracy became associated with progressive values through campaigns to universalize such rights by groups like the Chartists and suffragettes in Britain, social-democratic parties in Europe and women's suffrage groups, the Southern Christian Leadership Conference and Student Non-violent Co-ordinating Committee in the USA. As with many progressive causes, however, the term was originally used negatively, by Aristotle (384–322 BCE) and Plato (427–347 BCE) and, similarly, had pejorative implications when it was reintroduced in the eighteenth century.

Despite the fact that 'democracy' is often prefixed by 'delegated', 'direct', 'directed', 'industrial', 'liberal', 'participatory', 'representative' and 'social', when the MEDIA and politicians use the term they invariably mean a combination of its liberal and representative versions. In practice, this involves one or more of the following: competition between parties, elections, political liberties – freedom of association and free speech, the rule of law – including a judiciary ostensibly independent of the legislature, separate executive and legislative functions and universal suffrage. Such systems also employ a small number of people – compared to the size of the population – to represent, indirectly, the 'will of the people'. Although the most basic democratic principle implies rule by the majority – in this case indirectly through representatives – liberal democracy conspires to negate this principle according to certain eighteenth- and nineteenth-century conventions.

The first of these is attributed to Edmund Burke (1729–1797), particularly his acceptance speech following election to parliament in Bristol, England, in November 1774. Stated briefly, this doctrine depicts representatives as free agents who, having been chosen on the basis of their qualities and general principles, are not directed by those who elected them. On the contrary, they act according to their conscience and reason to represent what they consider to be the interests of all their constituents and therefore the best interests of the nation as a whole, even if it means activity outside of their borders to protect that interest. Not surprisingly, a version of this paternalistic view was employed by bishops and lords, who opposed an extension of the franchise under the first Reform Act 1832, on the basis that the disenfranchised were already represented, albeit virtually. Although the principle is still espoused by governments to defend unpopular decisions, the fact that representatives vote largely according to party instruction makes such reasoning untenable.

That representatives are not bound to vote in accordance with the wishes of the electorate is indicative of a second defining feature of liberal democracy: that the majority should not be allowed to challenge and reform certain values or impinge on the liberty of minorities. This doctrine is associated with Aristotle; James Madison (1751–1836), *The Federalist* (1788); John Stuart Mill (1806–1873), *On Liberty* (1859); and Alexis de Tocqueville (1805–1859), *Democracy in America* (1835–40); who variously feared that the poor majority would expropriate the rich minority – thereby infringing private property rights. Ironically, this 'tyranny of the majority' thesis has been enshrined in constitutional law and used to justify a diffusion of electoral will through the creation of second chambers and professional bureaucracy, even while the disenfranchisement of and discrimination against people on the basis of property, race and sex was tolerated. Such inconsistencies led to accusations that democracy meant little more than elite rule justified in terms of elections and maintained by a manufactured electorate. After all, early proponents of equal, political rights for all – such as Thomas Hobbes (1588–1679), *Leviathan* (1651: ch. 16), and John Locke (1632–1704), *Two Treatises of Government* (1690) – were not democrats.

Whether modern-day representation is compatible with precepts developed during the English Revolution, whereby the LEVELLERS, among others, understood the term to mean a deputed right, is open to question. As indicated earlier, party representatives are more akin to delegates to the extent that they represent a body or group and therefore refrain from independent activity. Taken at face value, this implies greater levels of ACCOUNTABILITY and responsibility to electors, but only if delegates act according to prior commitments, implement decisions approved by voters and are subject to recall if they transgress in any way. The delegation of powers to unelected civil servants, like central banks, for example, would appear to stretch principles of accountability and obviate the direct transmission of public preferences or rights to an equal say in decision-making. Wherever representatives rule indirectly, therefore, questions remain about what percentage of votes need to be cast in order to make a government legitimate – do governments need to obtain more votes than any single competitor or a majority over all other contestants?

In contrast, direct democracy means that all citizens are able to participate in debate and decision-making, rather than electing somebody to act on their behalf; as advocated by anarchists and considered to be an ultimate goal of COMMMUNISM. According to such views, all adult members of a society are free to participate directly in decision- and law-making, which means the absence of representatives and therefore the disappearance of distinctions between the STATE and CIVIL SOCIETY. Athenian democracy (*c.* 500–330 BCE) is often cited as an example, albeit that it was based on an electorate that excluded foreigners, slaves and women and therefore equated to less than a quarter of the adult population. The principle of direct democracy was advocated by Jean-Jacques Rousseau (1712–1778), *The Social Contract* (1762), on the basis of principles that are consistent with ANARCHISM. Put simply, the will of the individual cannot be delegated and people are only free if they are required to abide by laws they have willed into existence.

Karl Marx (1818–1883), *The Civil War in France* (1871), cited the Paris Commune of the same year as an example of direct democracy, where POWER was decentralized and the division between executive and legislative functions abolished through popular control over civil society. He described such arrangements as 'the dictatorship of the proletariat' to signify a return to the principle of majority rule conceived on the basis of LIBERATION rather than repression. The term was later associated with the Soviet Union, where the dictatorship was guided by the Communist Party of the Soviet Union (CPSU,

Kommunistischeskaya Partiya Sovetskogo Soyuza). With some prescience, this practice was predicted to become a dictatorship of the party within the proletariat by Karl Kautsky (1854–1938), *Dictatorship of the Proletariat* (1918). Nevertheless, direct democracy is considered to be compatible with the goals of accountability and TRANSPARENCY, not least because the opportunity for people to determine their own future is expected to encourage participation, and to engender debate and familiarity with the issues and needs of others.

Unlike the abstract nature of representation, direct democracy affords the possibility of a practical application of the principle of EQUALITY. Some, like Joseph Schumpeter (1883–1950), *Capitalism, Socialism and Democracy* (1948), however, consider the proposition to be impractical, because capitalist economies require people to be available for work rather than making decisions about how they live their lives. As a form of compromise between the two, participatory democracy has been developed to include an increased use of direct involvement through consultative bodies, public inquiries and referenda, while ultimate decision-making is left with representatives so as to ensure that liberal rights and values remain protected. Other forms of direct involvement are mostly considered to be feasible at the local level where knowledge of issues is more likely and the consequences of decision-making tangible, as takes place in Hungary and, according to Joseph Zimmerman, *The Initiative* (1999), in thirty-four states of the USA.

Advocates of electronic democracy and government, like access2democracy, see advances in communications and information technology making participation in decision-making processes more accessible, expansive and direct. The Internet, for example, is advocated as the means through which information can be accessed and shared, and deliberation and participation take place. This can involve forums, discussion and message boards, networks and weblogs and therefore undermines the objection that everyone has to be at the same place and same time for direct democracy to work. Open Source Government is also proposed and practised by groups like GNU project and Indymedia as an alternative to hierarchical, centralized and corporate dominance, because it allows grassroots involvement in the creation and approval of policy regardless of location. Where practised, such cooperation to resolve problems and issues does away with the need for representatives.

In the absence of such alternatives, Vilfredo Pareto (1848–1943), *The Mind and Society* (1935), and Schumpeter came to the pessimistic conclusion that democratic government tended towards rule by an elite – the very opposite of the tyranny of the majority! Anti-capitalists like the Student Alliance to Reform Corporations see the funding of political campaigns, candidates and parties by wealthy individuals and companies in return for favourable policy decisions as a modern-day manifestation of this tendency. There is therefore scepticism about the ritual of elections, which, regardless of turn-out, are portrayed as giving mass approval to the status quo. Perhaps a more honest concept is that of 'directed democracy', advocated by Muhammad Ayub Khan (1907–1974), whereby participation takes place within an official party and an elite makes decisions in the public interest. This proposition bears analogy with the theory, if not the practice, of democratic centralism by the CPSU in the USSR, its Warsaw Pact allies, the Communist International and its affiliated parties.

Robert Michels (1875–1936), *Political Parties* (1911), also drew the conclusion that the internal decision-making and organization of political parties tended towards elite control – a view supported by the findings of Eric Shaw, *Discipline and Discord in the Labour Party* (1988). Michels's criticisms are shared by anarcho-syndicalists and syndicalists, who distrust political parties in particular and liberal democracy in general; this stance gained widespread support in Britain, France, Germany, Italy, Spain and the USA during the first half of the twentieth century. As a solution they advocated associations of workers (*syndicats*) formed on the basis of trade or industry and the organization of society practising industrial democracy through the TRADE UNION. G.D.H. Cole (1889–1959) proposed similar ideas in *Self-Government in Industry* (1917), as did Beatrice and Sydney Webb, *Industrial Democracy* (1898). The diversity of such schemes can be illustrated in reference to Germany where post-World War II factory councils (*Betriebsrate*) include share ownership and worker representation on boards of directors, and pre-war workers' councils (*Arbeiterrate*). The latter represented outright ownership and the practice of direct democracy whereby workers in the community of the factory or firm are expected to make all decisions.

The idea of democratic control in the workplace stands in contradistinction and as complete anathema to the reality of modern-day corporate control and influence, as described by Greg Palast, *The Best Democracy Money Can Buy* (2002). Organizations like Jubilee Research campaign to democratize international bodies like the INTERNATIONAL MONETARY FUND, WORLD BANK and WORLD TRADE ORGANIZATION. Meanwhile, at the national level, Public Citizen and others work to obtain an equal voice and equal access to resources, opportunities and information for consumers, producers and workers to enhance their involvement in decision-making processes. Groups like the **ZAPATISTAS** and the **SOCIAL FORUM** initiative also put ideas about alternative approaches to democracy into practice. This involves a combination of consensus decision-making associated with indigenous cultures and direct democracy in order to gather the views of people and guard against elite rule. Such approaches are also the complete opposite of constitutional government that limits democratic involvement to the removal of administrations and forbids changing the basis or form of government.

FURTHER INFORMATION

Constitution for Workers Control: www.marxists.org/archive/reed/works/1919/10days/ch3.htm#1n
Paris Commune: www.marxists.org/archive/marx/works/1871/civil-war-france
Recall campaign in Britain: www.iniref.org
Recall provisions, USA: www.ncsl.org/programs/legman/elect/recallprovision.htm
Simultaneous Policy for global democracy: www.simpol.org

DEREGULATION is the process by which governments remove certain restrictions – sometimes referred to as 'red tape' – from the operation of business in general and **CORPORATIONS** in particular. In the northern hemisphere, the term is often used interchangeably with liberalization and privatization, as these are names for similar policies that are intended to promote free-market economies. Supporters of **NEOLIBERALISM** and the traditions of **LAISSEZ-FAIRE**, for example, believe that the removal of regulations encourages the efficient operation of a **MARKET** by raising competitiveness and ultimately lowering prices – especially wages. Deregulation of economic activity was a major trend in Britain, Europe, Japan, New Zealand and the USA towards the end of the twentieth century. For the most part, these processes have been encouraged and even required by international institutions like the European Union, the **INTERNATIONAL MONETARY FUND** (IMF), the **ORGANIZATION FOR ECONOMIC COOPERATION AND DEVELOPMENT** (OECD) and the **WORLD TRADE ORGANIZATION** (WTO). Prescriptions usually involve deregulation of financial and labour markets, the privatization of public industries and services, the weakening of environmental protection and are accompanied by reductions in welfare provision as means of keeping public spending within narrow limits.

There is a general tendency among advocates to emphasize the benefits of trade liberalization, but the liberalization of capital or financial markets produces particularly severe consequences. Financial deregulation, for example, includes allowing banks and corporations to borrow abroad and invest without any government controls or coordination and without adequate bank supervision. When combined with advances in communications technology used in the international monetary system, these developments increased the speed with which capital could be transferred in and out of countries and led to an increase in the number of countries involved in financial market transactions. In December 1997, for example, over seventy countries signed the WTO's agreement on opening banking, insurance and securities markets to foreign firms – as was the intention of the OECD's stalled MULTILATERAL AGREEMENT ON INVESTMENT.

Encouraged by the IMF, the OECD, and western governments, banks and firms, Asian governments undertook radical financial deregulation in the 1990s. In the case of South Korea, the OECD made financial deregulation a condition of membership and so the government abolished the Economic Planning Board, the main body for economic strategy, and increased the importance of its Finance Ministry. As a consequence of allowing the free movement of unregulated finance between countries, Asian corporations in general were granted large short-term, unhedged dollar loans. This resulted in widespread financial crisis once some of the loans were called in and other lenders panicked and followed suit – developments that are covered by Kwame S. Jomo in *Tigers in Trouble* (1998) (also see CAPITAL FLOWS).

While the effect of labour market deregulation may appear to be less dramatic than national economic collapse, the impact on individuals and families has been no less painful and both have served to compound existing deprivation. Deregulation has taken the form of curtailing employment and trade-union rights, reducing job security by increasing employers' freedom to hire and fire, abandoning controls on the hours worked each day and week, removing allowances for working shifts and unsocial hours, and lowering standards of health and safety protection. In the name of flexibility, a living wage, equal pay between men and women, equality of opportunity and the elimination of discrimination have become empty slogans compared to experiences in the real world. As a consequence, more people have temporary jobs and more have to work overtime or take several part-time jobs in order to take home enough money to live on.

Meanwhile, free-market orthodoxy prescribes changes to the tax and welfare systems to make low-paid work more attractive or even compulsory as an antidote to unemployment. Ironically, however, CHILD LABOUR is not yet permitted in the industrialized world, though many of its corporations take advantage of it in the developing world, especially in MAQUILADORAS

67

and **EXPORT-PROCESSING ZONES**. Likewise, corporations are able to exploit different national circumstances by moving investment and production, but open migration is opposed by national governments, so that people cannot enjoy the same advantages.

A significant factor in labour market deregulation has been the privatization – cut-price sale to private-sector corporations – of industries and services that had been state-owned and therefore under government control. Wages, working conditions and job numbers have all been cut in areas that have been sold off or threatened with the process of deregulation. Areas particularly affected include transport – airlines, air traffic control and railways – national energy production and supply – electricity and gas, telecommunications and state-owned **MEDIA**. The mere threat of deregulation therefore poses a stark choice between the fulfilment of public service missions, competing with private corporations by concentrating on the provision of profitable services, or effectively privatizing and becoming companies motivated by profitability. Privatization amounts to a different form of regulation that requires competition between private and public sectors to provide the lowest priced services, reduce democratic accountability by removing ultimate responsibility from elected authorities, and supposedly provide an increased choice in services, by reducing standards of service provision and employment.

As Michel Chossudovsky, *The Globalisation of Poverty* (1997), clearly articulates, the deregulation process not only affects people but has also had a negative impact on environmental standards in an effort to encourage investment and expansion. Examples include relaxing restrictions on harmful emissions that pollute the atmosphere and the dumping of toxic waste and other hazardous substances. Even the **KYOTO PROTOCOL** – the imperfect attempt to address the consequences of emitting carbon dioxide into the atmosphere – has been resisted by industrialized nations like Australia, Japan and the USA. Deregulation also includes moves to allow exploration for oil and gas in nature reserves and exploitation of natural resources – such as logging – in delicately balanced ecosystems. In areas of technological advance, such as genetic testing, reproductive cloning and **GENETIC ENGINEERING**, corporations resist regulation, except where it allows them to establish intellectual property rights over their 'discoveries'.

Advocates of regulation see it as a compromise between prohibition and no control at all and an attempt to balance commercial interests, such as profit maximization or tendencies towards monopoly or oligopoly, and the interests of employees, consumers and the environment. It can take the form of public statutes, standards or statements of expectations and can involve registration or licensing and inspection to ensure compliance and acceptable continuation of the activity itself within specified limits. Supporters of regulation, as diverse as the Association for the Taxation of Financial Transactions for the Aid of Citizens (ATTAC) and Rainforest Action Network, argue that such processes provide a basis to establish and respect human rights – civil and political as well as economic, social and cultural. They also argue that deregulation is dependent on a form of regulation that is overseen by bodies like the OECD and WTO; one that undermines national sovereignty and DEMOCRACY in monetary and development matters, including fiscal, wage, financial and social policies, and increases the likelihood of social instability.

In addition, deregulation and privatization are seen as increasing the power and legitimacy of multinational corporations by allowing them to operate without limits. In Britain, for example, the Regulatory Reform Act 2001 gives ministers the power to reform legislation which imposes burdens on people in the practice of any activity and these decisions are implemented with scarcely any public debate. ATTAC argues for a TOBIN TAX to regulate short-term borrowing by commercial banks and unregulated flows of short-term international capital, so that national taxpayers do not end up footing the bill for bankruptcies and financial crises. In contrast, however, socialist critics of regulation, like Johannes Agnoli (1925–2003), argue that regulation merely legitimizes the exploitation of LABOUR and, by extension, the environment, whereas the solution to such problems requires the overthrow of CAPITALISM.

FURTHER INFORMATION

Environmental issues: www.edwardgoldsmith.com/page47.html
Financial deregulation: www.france.attac.org/a2550
Arguments for regulation: www.globalexchange.org/campaigns/alternatives/americas

DEVELOPING COUNTRY is one of a series of terms that are used to categorize those nations that have not reached a certain level of industrial and technological advance relative to the size and growth of population and therefore exhibit a low standard of living. Other designations include least developed, lesser-developed or less (economically) developed; non-industrialized; the South; the third world; and underdeveloped or undeveloped. The criteria used to make such evaluations are questionable for a variety of reasons, not least because of the difficulties involved in classifications that ignore vast variations in cultural, economic, political and social circumstance. Although the terms are usually associated with the continents of Africa, Asia and Latin America – especially when extrapolated into 'developing world' – Asia, for example, includes Hong Kong, Japan, South Korea, Singapore and Taiwan, as well as the nuclear powers of China, India and Pakistan. Other countries that defy simple categorization include the oil-producing states that are resource-rich but are not generally industrialized.

The origin of such differentiation is usually traced to the 'Three Worlds, One Planet' article published by Alfred Sauvy (1898–1990) in 1952, where he compared certain countries to the 'Third Estates' of the French Revolution. The practice of dividing countries into the three broad categories of first, second and third world was accepted in capitalist countries during the 'cold war'. During this time, allies of the USA – including members of the North Atlantic Treaty Organization (NATO)– Japan and ex-British colonies like Australia, Canada, New Zealand and South Africa were afforded the affirmative status of the 'first world'. Although little used, the term 'second world' referred to the allies of the Soviet Union (the Warsaw Pact members) and other centrally planned economies described as communist. With the disintegration of the Soviet bloc in the last decade of the twentieth century these two terms became redundant. Hence, the adjectives 'advanced', 'developed' and 'industrialized' are now used to describe capitalist countries. The synonym 'North' is also used to refer to such countries, but ignores the geographical location of Australia, New Zealand and South Africa.

By way of contrast, 'third world' was used to refer to non-aligned countries, such as those represented at the Bandung Meeting of 1951 and first Summit Conference in 1961. Members were often courted by either superpower or both, covertly and overtly, as they attempted to extend their spheres of influence. Such attempts often involved the allocation of loans to favoured governments – now identified as a major factor in crises associated with INTERNATIONAL DEBT – and the destabilization and overthrow of unfavourable regimes. Even so, countries like Eire, Finland, Sweden and Switzerland chose to be neutral but were not described as 'third world'. Today, the term is largely a media label and carries pejorative overtones that reflect the perspective of the user, not least because the countries it refers to were the victims of past colonization by Europeans. Juxtaposing the categories of developed and developing countries also im-

70

plies that capitalist industrialization and western values are the inevitable consequence of progress.

The *World Fact Book* published annually by the Central Intelligence Agency, for example, lists countries it considers to be developed nations, while it and the UNITED NATIONS distinguish between 'least developed countries' and 'less developed countries'. Similarly, the INTERNATIONAL MONETARY FUND (IMF) provides a list of advanced economies that excludes South Africa and Turkey, but others include parliamentary democracy as an indicator of 'development'. Thus Bulgaria, Estonia, Latvia, Lithuania, Romania and Slovenia are considered, by academics and others, to be developed nations, due to their level of industrialization, infrastructure and technology coupled with free-market and democratic structures.

The *Report of the Independent Commission on International Development Issues* (1980), known as the Brandt Report, represents an early attempt to adopt a new form of categorization, reflected in the inclusion of 'North–South: A Programme For Survival' in its title. Some organizations also prefer to use less derogatory terms like 'lesser' or 'least developed', while 'fourth world' is sometimes used to refer to nationalities without representation at the United Nations, like Kurdistan, where INDIGENOUS PEOPLE live across national boundaries or lack exploitable resources. Depending on the starting point, the classification of least developed country is now applied to around forty countries and includes many that have experienced foreign occupation and years of conflict: Afghanistan, Botswana, Chad, Laos, Lesotho, Mali, Sierra Leone, Sudan, Somalia and Yemen.

Many of the concerns expressed by today's anti-capitalists regarding the relationship between multinational corporations and international institutions and poorer countries have echoes of earlier analyses. These include the underdevelopment theses outlined by Paul Baran in *Political Economy of Growth* (1957) and dependency theory as articulated by, among others, Kwame Nkrumah (1909–1972), *Neo-colonialism* (1965) and André Gunder Frank, *The Underdevelopment of Development* (1966). The conclusions drawn by Yilmaz Akyuz, *Developing Countries and World Trade* (2003), for example, are similar to arguments that production for export coupled with low wages means that there is an absence of domestic demand to fuel economic growth. Multinational corporations, the IMF, the WORLD BANK, foreign aid programmes and the free-trade agenda are also accused of working to create economies that depend on industrialized countries and exerting indirect political control to ensure that they and their corporations benefit.

FURTHER INFORMATION

CIA World Fact Book: www.cia.gov/cia/publications/factbook/
Focus on the Global South: www.focusweb.org
Third World Network: www.twnside.org.sg

DIGGERS, THE Also known as True Levellers, the Diggers were a group of radicals during the English Revolution who advocated the cultivation of common wasteland, rejected PRIVATE PROPERTY in favour of a 'community of goods', and viewed the earth as a 'common treasury'. In response to food shortages and increases in the cost of living between 1647 and 1650, a small group of people started to cultivate the common wasteland at St George's Hill, Surrey, on 1 April 1650. Although this community is the best known, Digger groups were also established at Barnet in Hertfordshire, Bosworth in Leicestershire, Cox hall in Kent, Enfield in Middlesex, Dunstable in Bedfordshire, Iver in Buckinghamshire, Wellingborough in Northamptonshire, as well as in Gloucestershire and Nottinghamshire. These communities faced harassment from local landlords who sought to confiscate and enclose the commons for their own benefit. The St George's Diggers, for example, moved to Cobham Heath in response to legal action and mob violence, orchestrated by local landowners. By April 1650 their community had been dispersed by force, and buildings burned; participants were later tried at Kingston.

Whereas the LEVELLERS proposed a new political order, Christopher Hill (1912–2003) in *The World Turned Upside Down* (1972) identifies the Diggers' desire to question all institutions and beliefs, their proposal of a new economic system and their subversion of the existing social order. They were consistent republicans whose proposals and practice constituted a form of agrarian communism – although the term had not entered usage at that time. Like the Levellers, they looked forward to a new form of society, in contrast to groups like the Fifth Monarchists, but whereas the Levellers included constitutional and more radical elements, the Diggers appear to have advocated a more coherent programme. This is due, in part, to the fact that Gerrard Winstanley (c. 1609–1660) was their leading theorist, though William Everard (c. 1575–1650) was also a spokesperson during the early stages of the movement. Winstanley wrote a number of pamphlets including *The True Levellers' Standard Advanced* (1649), a Digger manifesto, and *The Law of Freedom in a Platform* (1652), a draft constitution. Among other things, he advocated universal free education and health care, annual elections for parliaments and all officials, abolition of the standing army and its replacement with a militia.

Just as the name of the eighteenth-century ENRAGÉS was resurrected in 1960s' France, so too the name of the Seventeenth Century Diggers reappeared in the 1960s, this time in the USA. In the Haight-Ashbury district of San Francisco, an anarchist guerrilla theatre group founded by Peter Berg, Peter Coyote and Emmet Grogan adopted the name. Funded by donations to their Free City Bank they distributed free food, established a free medical clinic, organized free concerts as works of political art and opened shops in which everything was free. These and other exploits are recorded by Coyote in *Sleeping Where I Fall* (1998) and by Grogan in *Ringolevio* (1972). The street theatre and DIRECT ACTION tactics of the Haight-Ashbury Diggers are practised by today's anti-capitalists as a means of drawing attention to their cause. They also set up a communication company to produce manifestos and leaflets that were distributed by hand on Haight Street, whereas today's movement uses Indymedia and the Internet to bypass corporate media censorship.

FURTHER INFORMATION

On-line Digger documents: www.bilderberg.org/land/true
Twentieth Century Diggers: www.diggers.org

DIRECT ACTION can be any form of proactive tactic, an act of PROTEST or of resistance, and is often favoured by activists, organizations and movements that campaign for social change, including animal rights, environmental and peace campaigners. The spectrum of examples ranges from the comparatively passive such as a BOYCOTT of commodities, tourism, cultural and sporting events, through participation in forms of industrial action including a general strike, to acts of kidnap, sabotage and assassination. William Mellor, *Direct Action* (1920), for example, saw direct action as a tactic used in struggles between worker and employer, including lockouts and the formation of cartels. The principal aim of any form of direct action is to exert pressure on a specific target like CORPORATIONS, lending institutions and governments, but is often designed to persuade participants and observers in the hope that a particular cause will develop into a mass movement that ultimately achieves its goals.

In an attempt to focus attention on issues and ensure that events are not ignored by the corporate media or by the public, activities are often particularly vocal, dramatic or entertaining and accompanied by press releases for local and national radio, television and newspapers. As already noted, direct action can be either violent or nonviolent, which in the latter case means not physically or verbally assaulting anyone, not resisting arrest or contributing to escalating violence by the police, management or bystanders. The tactics of nonviolent direct action are perhaps most often associated with the CIVIL DISOBEDIENCE campaigns led by the likes of Mohandas Gandhi (1869–1948) and Martin Luther King (1929–1968). Examples of violent direct action – that is, acts of violence against the person as opposed to property – are normally attributed to small groups acting on the fringes of movements and generally portrayed as TERRORISM by the MEDIA and those against which such acts are directed.

While direct action includes activities like letter-writing and forms of litigation – appeals, requests for restraining orders, lawsuits and testifying at hearings – public demonstrations are designed to show strength of feeling and encompass a variety of activities. In the early 1980s, for example, there were mass rallies and peace camps outside military bases throughout Europe to protest against the presence of nuclear weapons. Activities also included climbing, cutting or decorating security fences, a tactic still used today by peace activists. Campaigners also mount human rights camps outside embassies, vigils, lobbies of parliament and sometimes hunger strikes in order to get their message across. Blockades and pickets whereby a group of people physically block the entrances to an office or building or occupy it in a sit-in are also used to express convictions, obstruct activities and publicize causes. In an extension of this tradition, the tactics of trespass and blockade are now applied to the virtual realm of the Internet as a form of electronic direct action known as HACKTIVISM.

Organizing, collecting and presenting petitions can also attract media publicity and allow issues to be explained to the general public. Likewise, informative handouts, street stalls, press releases, radio and television interviews, articles in newspapers and magazines, presentations and video showings to schools and universities, public meetings and debates serve promotional and educational purposes. Direct action as a form of art practice – exhibitions, street theatre, video and alternative forms of advertising – does likewise. Street theatre, for example, involves members of a group acting and re-enacting a compelling and concise story in a public location – on a pavement or sidewalk, in a park or perhaps a hallway – to alert passers-by about the group's work and to draw attention to a particular issue.

Costumes, props, satire and skit are often employed to catch attention and illustrate a point and are accompanied by leaflets and activists to explain the issue addressed and to promote related events.

Sabotage is also a form of direct action that, while it is considered to be nonviolent because it is aimed only at inanimate objects and the wallets of those targeted, is also a step beyond civil disobedience. Examples include billboard bandits who deface advertising hoarding, activists who damage industrial equipment and infrastructure, groups that break into laboratories and remove animals to prevent experimentation, and others that target military hardware and infrastructure such as Trident Ploughshares group. The LUDDITES are a historical case of industrial sabotage and an analogy can be drawn between their activities and that of ecotage – the practice of damaging property to prevent ecological damage – which, as Christopher Manes, *Green Rage* (1990), explains, includes monkeywrenching, road reclamation, tree sitting, tree spiking and tyre slashing. In most cases, targets are picked for their strategic value, like the direct action taken against genetically modified crops by activists in Europe and by farmers in Operation Cremation Monsanto in India.

FURTHER INFORMATION

Environmental cyberactivist community: http://act.greenpeace.org/aboutus
Nonviolent direct action resource: http://ruckus.org/resources/nvda/index.html
Peace group: www.tridentploughshares.org

E

ECOLOGY has three different meanings. It can be the study of the interaction between living things (biocenose) and their environment (biotope),
the system that embodies interrelations between species, or the movement
to prevent ecological devastation by creating a degree of harmony between
human activity and nature. Ernst Haeckel (1834–1919) first used the term
'oekologie' in *Generalle Morpholigie* (1866). The word is derived from the
Greek *oekos*, 'house', and *logos*, 'to study'. Although the impact of human
activity on other species' conditions of life and chances of survival has
long been known, only from the 1960s were popular concerns raised about
the detrimental impact of industrial activities such as pollution, intensive
agriculture and fishing. As a consequence the **UNITED NATIONS** launched
the Man and Biosphere programme in 1971 to study the interrelationship
between humans and the environment, and, in 1972, held the first international conference on the human environment in Stockholm, Sweden. By
1992, the Earth Summit held in Rio de Janeiro in Brazil accepted that
BIODIVERSITY was threatened, and in 1997 the Kyoto conference acknowledged similar implications for the **BIOSPHERE**.

In general terms, an ecological crisis occurs if the environmental conditions upon which one or more species depend for life are disturbed in
some way. This can happen with or without human involvement and can
be specific and reversible. At the local level, for example, an oil spill can
endanger ecology, or a nuclear disaster, as occurred at Chernobyl in 1986,
can have catastrophic consequences for the environment and the life systems
it supports. Similarly an increase in the number of predators, overpopulation
or the disappearance of prey can threaten the existence of a species and be
the result of human action or other events. On a global scale, changes in
temperature, rainfall or sea level can have an adverse affect on habitat, as is
considered to be the case with **GLOBAL WARMING** and depletion of the ozone
layer due to the use of chlorofluorocarbons (CFCs).

While some dispute the relevance of human behaviour to global warming
or even the reality of the phenomenon, there is little doubt that the destruction caused by dam building (like the Arcediano dam in Mexico), clearance

of ancient forest in Daintree, Australia, and wars are human endeavours. Deforestation occurs as a consequence of increasing human population and associated agricultural practices (see Jan Maarten Dros, *Managing the Soy Boom*, 2004), as a result of imperial colonization and through stripping forests for paper-making, fuel and furniture production. Even where attempts have been made to regulate these and other practices, as in Costa Rica's National Institute for Biodiversity, there are still concerns about the efficacy of such schemes. Elsewhere, negative consequences are more apparent and evidenced by an increase in areas affected by desertification due to soil erosion and mineral leeching associated with deforestation, the disappearance of species, and an increase in the number of refugees affected by drought and famine. Among other things, the injudicious use of technology is considered to have had a significant affect on the human environment and on the quality of and prospects for life in the form of epidemics, air quality, food crises, reduced living space and the dumping of toxic or non-degradable waste.

A variety of analyses and solutions have been proffered for these problems, and the term 'ecology movement' has been introduced as a collective term to describe the diverse range of groups and individuals who support remedial or proactive approaches to ecological issues. In 1979, James Lovelock published *Gaia*, in which he compares the earth to a single living macro-organism that is self-sustaining and not threatened by human activity. He does contend, however, that humans can and should modify their behaviour in order to enhance the chances of surviving as a species. In contrast and at odds with the approach and outlook of many environmentalists, 'deep ecology' offers a BIOCENTRIC view of the world that attributes equal intrinsic value to all living things. 'Shallow ecology', on the other hand, is considered to be anthropocentric and concerned with preserving the earth and its resources for human use. Introduced by Arne Naess and explained in *Ecology, Community and Lifestyle* (1989), the deep ecology thesis has supporters around the world and is promoted by groups like Earth First, who consider mainstream groups like Planet Ark, for example, to be compromised by corporate association.

The formation of Green political parties to contest elections in a variety of industrialized countries during the 1970s evidenced another schism, as supporters chose to work within existing constraints in an attempt to mitigate problems associated with exhaustion of natural resources, industrialization, nuclear energy, pollution and population growth. A primary aim of the move is to encourage consideration of the ecological consequences of policy decisions. Others, such as Green economists and scientists, prefer lobbying through official channels, but engage in research that provides evidence to be used in support of the campaign goals of other groups. Activist groups like Greenpeace also fund or undertake research and join others like the Anarchist Golfing Association, Earth Action and Sea Shepherd who use DIRECT ACTION to prevent disasters and raise public awareness of issues. Despite their differences, however, most groups recognize the need for fundamental change at the levels of individual, community and societal activity and in the primary motivations that drive CAPITALISM and treat nature as little more than a resource to be acquired and a utilized in the pursuit of PROFIT.

Among others, Theodor Adorno (1903–1969) and Max Horkheimer (1895–1973), *Dialectic of Enlightenment* (1947), consider the Judaeo-Christian myth, as outlined in Genesis 1:26 and 9:1–3, to be a source of the anthropocentric approach. Namely that humanity is superior to other species, able to exploit them and is separate from and essentially in conflict with its natural surroundings. This compares to the view that other organisms are more than objects to be used, but belong to a larger, coherent system imbued with an intrinsic value of its own. Nevertheless, there is a central paradox in the view that humanity is somehow separate from nature and therefore impacts upon it, usually negatively, when in reality there is no passive harmony in which humans coexist with nature, because humanity is nature and vice versa.

FURTHER INFORMATION

International forum: www.resurgence.gn.apc.org
News and Issues: www.theecologist.org
Lists of links: www.politicalindex.com/sect10.htm; www.broadleft.org/greens.htm

ECOSYSTEM is a contraction of the term 'ecological system' and is attributed to the botanist and ecologist Arthur Tansley (1871–1955), *The Use and Abuse of Vegetational Concepts and Terms* (1935), to refer to the interactive system between organisms (biocenose) and their environment (biotope). The concept is used to refer to any situation – from the microbial world to the whole planet – where life forms display interdependence in terms of energy, food and matter recycling, which has established a form of perennial self-regulation and balance.

EMPIRE originates from the Latin *imperator*, meaning a supreme leader, and has since been used to describe a territorial realm ruled with exclusive authority by a sovereign person, an empress/emperor, or a government. This also translates into the domination or control by one country or group of people over another. Examples of pre-capitalist empires are plentiful, span human history and include the Roman Empire, the Holy Roman Empire in Europe, the Ottoman Empire in the Near East and the Mughal Empire in India. Perhaps not surprisingly, given its etymological origin, the term is now closely associated with imperialism, but also has a connection with colonialism. All of these are symptomatic of an extension of control beyond national borders and the use or threat of force, the absence of which is equated with the formation of alliances or federation.

Apart from the fact that 'colonia', from the Latin, means 'country estate' and was subsequently used to refer to territory deliberately settled on foreign soil, the modern-day differentiation between colonialism and imperialism rests largely on a periodization of history. According to such a schema, old colonialism refers to the pre-capitalist practice of the Iberian powers – Portugal and Spain – in Latin America, for example, where conquest was motivated by prestige, ideas of racial superiority and securing payment of tribute. In contrast, the new colonialism or imperialism is associated with the birth, development and expansion of West European capitalism and a restructuring of appropriated economies, particularly towards the end of the nineteenth century.

The creation of empire – as countries formed by colonization or conquest and subject to the authority of the conqueror – had also been justified as a means of spreading civilization, exporting a way of life or political project, as was the case with Napoleonic France. Whereas such projects required some element of direct control as a form of integration, the main, original imperial power, Britain, favoured the use of chartered companies to colonize and administer territories, which included Canada, Kenya, Nigeria and Rhodesia. Although ultimately sustained by naval and therefore military supremacy, their preferred means of control relied on settlement, control of technology, the IDEOLOGY of cultural superiority and the principles of free trade; this also entailed RACISM and xenophobic justification. Towards the end of the nineteenth century, competition between European powers for territorial conquest led to greater direct rule and the creation of more singular political units. This also contributed to an increase of European military intervention in Africa, Indochina, Manchuria and Northern China, while Japan and the USA, respectively, pursued similar objectives in Formosa and Korea and in the wider Pacific.

In an apparent attempt to offset strategic threats, territories were conquered that did not fit with the previous practice of administering and developing less developed countries primarily for the purposes of TRADE; that is, the acquisition of markets for mass-produced goods, together with cheap sources of labour-power and raw materials. Colonial or imperial state structures were employed more overtly as instruments of domination over indigenous populations and a preponderance of monoculture developed solely to service metropolitan requirements. Originally employed in plantations and extraction industries as slaves, colonized people were subsequently emancipated in order to supply sources of cheap labour-power for labour-intensive light manufacturing industries and a limited purchasing power for commodities.

Anti-capitalist explanations developed in the early twentieth century tended to emanate from the Marxist tradition and saw economic factors driving the search for investment opportunities, new markets and sources of raw materials. Leading theorists fell into two categories. Those like Vladimir (Ulyanov) Lenin (1870–1924), *Imperialism* (1916), for example, saw capitalist expansion as a consequence of the remorseless drive for accumulation and therefore increased value, whereas Rosa Luxemburg (1871–1919), *The Accumulation of Capital* (1913), premissed her arguments on the notion that domestic production exceeded demand. Later discussions around this subject include contributions from Michael Barratt Brown, *The Economics of Imperialism* (1974), and Bill Warren (1935–78), *Imperialism: Pioneer of Capitalism* (1980).

While former colonies achieved independence in the years that followed World War II, usually as a consequence of trenchant national liberation movements, the globe still bears the scars of colonialism, most evidently in the division between industrialized and developing countries. Consequently, the term 'imperialism' is now largely used to refer to exploitative and oppressive relations between the two parties, while André Gunder Frank and Kwame Nkrumah (1909–1972) developed respective theories of dependency and neocolonialism to explain the postcolonial experience (see DEVELOPING COUNTRY). Meanwhile, Robert Blauner, *Racial Oppression in America* (1972), and Michael Hechter, *Internal Colonialism* (1975), have used similar theories to explain processes at work within the USA and the British Isles.

Present-day groups and organizations like CorporateWatch, Earth First, Free Burma Coalition and Mulinational Monitor link the practices of multinational and transnational corporations to imperialism, an asymmetric distribution of economic power and an integration of countries into a system of global markets and trade. Michael Hardt and Antonio Negri in *Empire* (2000) take this analysis further, conceptualizing the existence of a new form of empire that neither has a territorial centre of power nor relies on fixed barriers or boundaries. On the contrary, it is epitomized by a new form of sovereignty that is located in the regulation of global exchanges by supranational powers that include the G8, INTERNATIONAL MONETARY FUND, UNITED NATIONS, WORLD BANK and WORLD TRADE ORGANIZATION.

Beneath are two more layers. First are the networks of monetary regulation, resource distribution and exchange that are the preserve of nations and multi-national corporations. Next come the mechanisms of democratic and popular representation, of cultural, MEDIA and non-governmental organizations that manage communications networks and the dissemination of knowledge. Hardt and Negri see the creation of Empire as a response to working-class struggle and national independence, which moves decision-making and power networks to the supranational level so that they are beyond autonomous national institutions, state apparatuses and therefore traditional strategies of resistance. A corresponding feature of this process, they contend, is the move from material, factory-based production to affective production based on communication, cultural and leisure activities, and services.

These developments are, in turn, considered be the source of a new revolutionary subject, the multitude, which supersedes the proletariat as agent of human emancipation. The amorphous nature of the multitude, defined by diverse desires but integrated through the development of communicative, cultural networks of production and POWER, is seen as its strength. As communication produces and regulates public discourse and opinion, so access to and control over knowledge, information, communication and affects is proposed as the means to global democracy and LIBERATION. Instead of institutional workers' organizations that can be combated or co-opted, a strategy of withdrawal is proposed, based on non-compliance and refusal that does not aid the development of counter-strategies and structures of control. Although such themes are introduced in *Empire* and developed by the same authors in *Multitude* (2004), they bear analogy with the concepts and categories of the AUTONOMIA in which Negri played a leading role.

While similarities can also be drawn with Giorgio Agamben, *The Coming Community* (1993), and Nick Dyer-Witherford, *Cyber Marx* (1999), not everyone agrees with the premises and conclusions of *Empire*. Examples of dissent can be found in contributions to Jodi Dean and Paul Passavant's *The Empire's New Clothes* (2003), and Hardt and Negri engage in dialogue with some critics in Gopal Balakrishnan, *Debating Empire* (2003). More recently, Atilio Boron's *Empire and Imperialism* (2005) builds on criticism that the notion of Empire is focused on Northern, industrialized countries and ignores the significance of national economies, together with capital and multinational corporations that have national bases. The hegemonic role played by some countries and supranational institutions appears to have been allowed to obscure the reality of uneven development and the contradictions that still beset capitalism, even as a supposedly universal system.

FURTHER INFORMATION

Cyber Marx: www.fims.uwo.ca/people/faculty/dyerwitheford/index.htm
Nkrumah on neocolonialism: www.marxists.org/subject/africa/nkrumah/neo-colonialism
Lenin on imperialism: www.marxists.org/archive/lenin/works/1916/imp-hsc

EMPLOYMENT RIGHTS see WORKERS' RIGHTS.

ENRAGÉS, LES A radical movement that emerged during the French Revolution in response to the catastrophic effects – especially food shortages – of the Girondins' decision to wage war on Britain, the Netherlands and Spain in 1793. In contrast to Girondin idealism, which equated the experience of liberty with the existence of constitutional legal rights, Enragés viewed the concept in more practical terms – as freedom from hunger. They therefore advocated practical resolutions to immediate problems, such as economic controls. They also sacked the Paris food stores in February and March and demanded the execution of anyone profiteering from food shortages. Their aims were supported by the all-women Republican Club and put into practice during the early months of the Terror that accompanied the Jacobin overthrow of the Girondins – a move that also saw the arrest of prominent Enragés, including Claire Lacombe (1765–c. 1795), Jacques Roux (1752–1794) and Jean Varlet (1764–1837). For a fuller account, see Robert Rose, *The Enragés* (1966).

Just as opponents attempted to discredit Enragés as harbingers of anarchy and therefore chaos and disorder, government ministers and the MEDIA reintroduced 'Enragés' as a term to describe a group of Nanterre students who participated in the protests that engulfed France in May 1968. Analogies can be drawn between the tactics adopted by the latter Enragés, who were associated with the SITUATIONIST INTERNATIONAL, and those of present-day anti-capitalists, particularly the use of street theatre as a form of protest and attempts to synthesize art and POLITICS. Theatrical slogans were, for example, one aspect of the approach favoured by the Enragés and included such proclamations as 'Never Work' (*Ne travaillez jamais*), which is analogous to 'Refusal of Work' (*Il rifiuto del lavoro*), favoured by the AUTONOMIA of 1970s' Italy.

FURTHER INFORMATION

Present day: www.enrager.net

ENVIRONMENTALISM is quite literally a concern about the importance and influence of surroundings within and for society. The concept developed in the nineteenth century as Charles Darwin (1809–1882), *On the Origin of Species* (1859), noted the effect of environment on the development and evolution of species and German geographers introduced the notion of *umwelt* as an explanation for economic and cultural differences between peoples. Not until the 1960s and 1970s, however, was the term used to describe concern about the fragility of the environment in ecological terms and to describe a critique of policies and practices deemed to have a detrimental impact on human society. In its broadest sense, this involves a recognition that the ultimate survival of humanity and that of other species are interdependent and require the conservation and protection of all our environs; an approach that is related to ECOLOGY.

Rachel Carson (1907–1964), *Silent Spring* (1962), and the advent of campaigning around issues like the hydroelectricity scheme at Lake Manapouri, New Zealand, in 1969 helped foster public awareness of such concerns. The creation of organizations like Friends of the Earth and Greenpeace in the early 1970s and the subsequent formation of political parties – variously using the appellation GREEN – similarly enhanced the development of public knowledge and interest. Issues that inspire environmentalists cover a diverse spectrum that includes animal and human rights, controlling and preventing or eliminating pollution – up to and including matters related to GLOBAL WARMING – industrial democracy, liberalization of private morality and the eradication of endemic diseases, hunger and poverty through SUSTAINABLE DEVELOPMENT. John Whitelegg, *Critical Mass* (1996), for example, explores such issues in relation to transport and an overwhelming reliance on the motor car in Europe and North America. Opposition to the nuclear industry and its involvement in the production of energy, weapons and waste is also consistent with a generally pacifist outlook, the protection of BIODIVERSITY and safeguarding the provision of clean, public water.

Present-day participants include non-governmental organizations like Action Network and Earth Action, as well as activist-based groups such as the Campaign Against Depleted Uranium, which organizes in Britain. Causes related to the enhancement, preservation and restoration of the natural environment range from those that see human population as an impediment to nature to those that focus primarily on the detrimental impact of unchecked industrial activity. The latter is associated with the depletion of natural resources, the destruction and exploitation of GLOBAL COMMONS, and the development and use of untested technologies. Concerns about GENETIC ENGINEERING, for example, relate issues of animal and human welfare through the production and consumption of modified food and medicine. At the same time, perceived tensions between economic growth and quality of life translate into advocacy of simpler, less materialistic lifestyles that consume fewer resources and eschew the values of CONSUMERISM. Similarly, vegetarianism is advocated as using less land, nutrients and water in the production of foodstuffs than the growth of fodder to feed animals that are then eaten by humans.

Whereas today's mass media are wont to present genetics as the sole explanation for the behaviour and illnesses that afflict animals and humans, an equivalent myopia of environmental determinism prevailed during the nineteenth century. In other words, there was a tendency to view a person's environment as more important than other factors in influencing personal development, health and well-being. William Morris (1834–1896), *News from Nowhere* (1890), and the arts-and-crafts movement, for example, placed great import on the beauty and utility of surroundings, including domestic utensils, furniture and architecture. In a more functional way, a similar view feeds into the modern-day concern with environmental health – defined by the World Health Organization as aspects of health and disease determined by constituents of the environment. Understood in such general terms, relevant factors can range from physical pollutants, which include biological, chemical and radioactive agents emitted as waste, to aesthetic, psychological and social factors related to architectural design, housing, land use, transport and urban development. Of course, the control of such activities is denigrated as REGULATION by advocates of NEOLIBERALISM, as is the promotion of environmental parameters and encouragement of environmentally friendly activity and technology.

FURTHER INFORMATION

Campaign groups: www.cadu.org.uk, www.foei.org; www.greenpeace.org/
   international
Resources: www.envirolink.org

EQUALITY and egalitarianism are conventions associated with the proclamations of the eighteenth-century American and French Revolutions. The
United States Declaration of Independence (1776), for example, asserts: 'We
hold these truths to be self-evident, that all men are created equal' – even
though it excluded slaves, women and other groups. Hence, the fourteenth
amendment to the United States Constitution was introduced in 1868 and
requires that: 'No State shall ... deny to any person within its jurisdiction
the equal protection of the laws' – albeit that the privilege was granted to
CORPORATIONS before Southern blacks! Similarly, Article 6 of the Declaration of the Rights of Man and of the Citizen (Déclaration des Droits de
l'Homme et du Citoyen) (1789) states: 'All the citizens, being equal in its
eyes [the law], are equally admissible to all public dignities, places and
employment, according to their capacity and without distinction other than
that of their virtues and of their talents.'

Such principles are today preserved through political and legal structures
and procedures that mask and therefore exacerbate the reality of widespread
inequality, upon which CAPITALISM depends. Abstract equality between
people as legal citizens is nothing more than a principle of procedural fairness that guarantees all relevant similar cases will be treated according to
the same rules. The UNITED NATIONS and European statements on human
rights are, for example, formal, procedural documents rather than substantive practices. Likewise, the official yardstick of democratic and political
equality – one person, one vote – is applied to citizens only at elections and
no other time. In each instance, however, the daily experience of inequality
is manifested as hierarchy, prestige, wealth and associated life chances that
include educational and employment opportunities; all of which serve to
contradict espoused ideals. Not only does wealth offer influence through
political donations; money also buys the best defence lawyers and access to
elite educational institutions.

Equality of opportunity is presented as an attempt to redress socio-
economic circumstances that impede equal access to education, employment,
health care or welfare on the grounds of disability, ethnicity, race, RELIGION,
sex or sexual orientation in the name of distributive justice. In the 1960s and

85

1970s, Britain and the USA established commissions to promote equality of opportunity in employment, including guaranteeing that people receive the same pay for doing the same job, but this is the only aspect of equal treatment or material equality they purport to address. Progressive taxation and welfare provision are designed to ameliorate inequality of outcome rather than eliminate it, so that, beyond meeting basic human needs that will allow people to fulfil their capacity to work, material inequality is permitted. Some neoliberals even suggest that everyone be taxed at the same percentage rate as a form of equality.

At the opposite end of the spectrum, the doctrines of ANARCHISM and COMMUNISM propose that advances in technological production create a potential for abundance that makes material equality possible. They differ over the use of the STATE as a means of transitional redistribution, however, with the latter arguing that material inequality under capitalism makes some form of coercive power necessary, albeit a democratic body with limited powers to prevent abuse. According to liberal notions, such circumstances are undesirable as they undermine the economic incentive to work and reduce the FREEDOM of the few to benefit from familial wealth and PRIVATE PROPERTY. John Rawls (1921–2002), *A Theory of Justice* (1971), for example, justifies economic and social inequality on the basis that opportunities to acquire elite positions are open to all as an incentive for seeking well-paid jobs that benefit society as a whole.

Many of the activists and groups that are included in MEDIA definitions of modern-day anti-capitalism advocate some or all of the ideals referred to above. Advocates of FAIR TRADE, for example, seek procedural fairness in international trade agreements between rich and poor. Similarly, others demand that all countries should honour human rights conventions and that the developing world be afforded equality of opportunity in its dealings with its advanced capitalist counterparts and corporations. See also JUSTICE and TRADE.

FURTHER INFORMATION

UK Commission for Equality and Human Rights: www.cre.gov.uk/about/cehr. html

US Equal Employment Opportunities Commission: www.eeoc.gov

EXCHANGE RATE refers to the differences between the worth of one national currency and another, and is also known as the foreign exchange rate, Forex or FX rate. Taking the currencies of the European Union (EU) and the USA as an example, a hypothetical exchange rate of two euros (€) to one US dollar ($) means that you can buy €2 with US$1, or US$0.50 with €1. According to orthodox economic theory, dealers acquire supplies of a particular currency in order to finance TRADE with the country to which it belongs. The comparative worth of a currency depends on demand for it, which rises with external demand for commodities and services produced in countries that use that particular currency. Furthermore, if the EU imports more commodities and services from the USA than it exports to them, it would risk a currency crisis. In other words, the EU would have to use its US dollar reserves to pay for some imports or use gold or other currency reserves to buy US dollars and risk devaluing those currencies it sells by increasing their supply on the international currency markets. Thus, one of the reasons why the US dollar is one of the stronger world currencies is because oil is priced in US dollars and other nations need to acquire dollars in order to purchase it. Consequently, the US economy is heavily dependent on oil because it does not need to acquire foreign currency in order to purchase it.

Exchange rates are also affected by CAPITAL FLOWS, which make supplies of currency available for loans and investment. When capital crosses national boundaries, for example, it has to be changed into the currency of the target country. Where such movement is long-term, any consequent fluctuations in the value of respective currencies is evened out over time. If such movements are short-term, however, the result can be instability as a currency rises and falls quickly and banks and other financial institutions are panicked into selling reserves in order to minimize short-term losses. From 1973 onward, exchange rates have increasingly been a free-market operation, due to a process of financial deregulation – including floating exchange rates – encouraged by the INTERNATIONAL MONETARY FUND (IMF), the ORGANIZATION FOR ECONOMIC COOPERATION AND DEVELOPMENT and western governments, banks and firms. This culminated, in the 1990s, in a decade that witnessed a series of financial crises and the 1997 agreement on liberalizing financial services, supervised by the WORLD TRADE ORGANIZATION.

Contributors to *Global Finance* (2000), edited by Walden Bello and others, see the deregulatory process – often imposed through STRUCTURAL ADJUSTMENT PROGRAMMES administered by the IMF and WORLD BANK – as the root cause of the problem. In particular, the policy of free-floating exchange rates means that currencies are traded as commodities on financial markets around the world. This variability facilitated the development of foreign-exchange options – also known as derivatives, forward transactions, futures and financial swaps – that, in turn, permit the transformation of 'long trading' into 'short trading' with significant repercussions. The volume of such transactions has, for example, grown rapidly to account for a substantial share of all foreign-exchange transactions and has been associated with the increase in short-term capital flows and consequent financial crises. Furthermore, foreign-exchange markets and therefore decision-making are concentrated in the countries of the G8, with large trading centres in Frankfurt, London, New York, Paris and Tokyo. This has been interpreted as indicating that the policy of DEREGULATION has operated almost exclusively in the interests of the industrialized world and at the expense of developing nations.

There are several solutions to the problems and concerns discussed above. One of the most popular, among campaigning organizations like the Association for the Taxation of Financial Transactions for the Aid of Citizens, is the idea of a tax on foreign currency exchanges – the TOBIN TAX – to deter speculation. Alternatively, the European Union gave the European Central Bank a primary role in deciding monetary policy and abolished national exchange rates with the introduction of a single currency – the euro – in an attempt to eliminate speculation on currency exchange among participating nations. The scheme does not prevent speculative transactions between the euro and other national currencies, however, but it does mean that the adjustment of real exchange rates pertaining to trade between participating countries is achieved through flexible relative prices – that is, by lowering wages and increasing unemployment.

A third solution involves the introduction of exchange controls to restrict the freedom of traders to buy and sell a particular currency or currencies. As Bruno Jetin, *Utility of the Tobin Tax* (2000), records, Malaysia introduced a series of unilateral measures in September 1998 to counter international speculation and prevent its currency collapsing. These included pegging the exchange rate for the ringgit against the US dollar and only allowing convertibility for commercial as opposed to financial activities. Delays were also introduced for the return to Malaysia of ringgits circulating abroad and for the sale of securities and bonds bought in Malaysia by foreign investors. The selling and buying of securities or bonds issued in ringgits were also restricted to the Kuala Lumpur stock market, new foreign credits were banned, and payments abroad only permitted with prior authorization. In contrast to IMF and World Bank prescriptions, the measures adopted by the Malaysian authorities stopped its exchange rate from collapsing and prevented the need to raise interest rates in an attempt to protect the ringgit. They therefore helped prevent bankruptcies, redundancies, increases in the prices of food and cuts in public services.

FURTHER INFORMATION

A case for capital controls: www.attac.org/fra/toil/doc/witwatersrand.htm

EXPLOITATION, in a comparatively neutral and therefore general sense, means making use of something – an object, a situation or a resource – in order to realize potential benefits. The concept is more contentious when it is understood as taking advantage of something, especially if the advantage has been derived unfairly or is detrimental in some way. For this to be the case, a value system is necessary in order to denote a sense of fairness or JUSTICE and thereby understand how an action or process is deemed to be exploitative. Depending on the point of view and the circumstances in which it takes place, taking advantage of a natural resource, an animal or human being – as happens in HUMAN TRAFFICKING, PATRIARCHY and the SEX INDUSTRY – is considered to be exploitation.

Environmentalists object to practices, such as industrial logging or strip mining, that damage local ecosystems, threaten BIODIVERSITY and risk the extinction of flora and fauna and, ultimately, the future of all life on the planet. Likewise, animal rights activists draw similar conclusions to Peter Singer, *Animal Liberation* (1990), and oppose, as exploitative, the industrial farming of animals in intensive units – such as battery hens – and vivisection for medical research or the testing of cosmetics by the 'beauty' industry. Perhaps for slightly different reasons, both environmentalists and animal rights activists consider genetic experimentation to be wrong, while the possible dangers for humans and animals of genetically engineered plants is a cause for wider concern. Animal rights activists, for example, see a clear abuse of power by humans over animals and a moral hypocrisy whereby donations to animal welfare charities exceed all others, while species cherished as pets – birds, dogs, rabbits and so on – are also used in vivisection and food production.

The question of whether human beings are inevitably exploited as a consequence of capitalist social relations raises similar issues. On one side, there is the liberal argument that in the absence of physical coercion individuals enter into free, equal and consensual contracts as employer and employee. In contrast is the anti-capitalist, Marxian view that exploitation takes place, not least because the situation in which contracts are made between employer and employee is not equal, free or fair. A prospective worker without access to means of production necessary to create an income, for example, has no other choice but to sell her or his labour-power in order to live. As a consequence, an employer is able to pay the worker the going hourly rate, while extracting a VALUE in the production process over and above the price paid to the worker, and this makes the very process of profit-making exploitative.

The prime example of such practice involves the exploitation of cheap labour through globalized production circuits whereby MULTI-NATIONAL CORPORATIONS produce famous brand products in sweatshops in the developing world. Not only are the workers paid at the local hourly rate and granted minimal employment rights, but the commodities they produce are also sold in the developed countries for amounts far greater than the cost of production. Although this process often involves practices outlawed in the developed world – like the employment of children – and therefore constitutes an example of moral hypocrisy, an issue explored by Jeremy Seabrook in *Children of Other Worlds* (2001), labour practices do not have to be extreme in order to be exploitative. The simple fact that employees have to work more hours to achieve a living wage indicates a greater rate of profit for the employer.

In moral terms, the very fact that people are treated as mere objects in the production process is evidence enough that they are being exploited. Similarly, the production of a surplus over and above that needed to meet the minimum requirements for the survival of the population can also be considered to constitute exploitation of people and resources. So too, the fact that one section of the population is engaged in producing the said surplus, while another section takes exclusive ownership and advantage of it. A similar analysis is extended in underdevelopment and dependency theses that see relations between developed countries, multinational corporations and developing countries as little more than a continuation of colonial exploitation. See also DEVELOPING COUNTRY.

FURTHER INFORMATION

Marx's theory of exploitation: www.marxists.org/archive/marx/works/1847/wage-labour/index.htm; www.marxists.org/archive/marx/works/1865/value-price-profit/index.htm

EXPORT CREDITS take the form of government-backed guarantees, loans and insurance to underwrite the activities of national **CORPORATIONS** so that they can secure contracts abroad – often in the developing world. In practice, export credits amount to a public subsidy – paid by taxpayers – to compensate corporations when a contract fails and reimburse banks for the loans they made on the basis of the contract. The scheme is usually operated by government agencies such as Coface in France, Ducroire-Delcredere in Belgium, Hermes in Germany, the Export Development Corporation in Canada, and the Export Credit Guarantee Department in Britain. These bodies tend to shun public attention, however, even discouraging discussion about the projects they cover. Their lack of **ACCOUNTABILITY** and **TRANSPARENCY** at home and abroad inevitably raises concerns about democratic practice. Such disquiet is highlighted when export credits are granted to schemes that contradict minimum standards of environmental protection and human rights obligations that are outlined in agreements and treaties, in accordance with which governments and their aid agencies are supposed to abide.

Corporations involved in the construction of the Ilisu dam in Turkey and the Three Gorges dam in China, for example, are supported by export credits. Opponents of such schemes point to the fact that environmental destruction results from the flooding of valleys and agricultural land, that sites of archaeological and cultural significance will be lost, and that the forced relocation of people is a flagrant violation of their human rights. Similarly, credits are often used as part of the **ARMS TRADE** to underwrite the export of armaments and military equipment to governments – such as those of Burma, Indonesia and Israel – that have records of human rights abuse and of conducting military campaigns against civilians. The sale of non-productive hardware to governments in the developing world also exacerbates their debt levels by diverting funds away from **SUSTAINABLE DEVELOPMENT** projects that have the potential to enhance – as opposed to destroy – the lives of local people and to facilitate debt repayment through the generation of foreign exchange.

FURTHER INFORMATION
International campaign: www.eca-watch.org

EXPORT-PROCESSING ZONES, also referred to as enterprise or free-trade zones, are designated parts of a country where governments offer incentives for firms to locate and produce commodities for export – usually clothing and electronics. They are found across Asia and in developing countries where governments contribute to the cost of establishing production facilities, and relax planning regulations and environmental protection. Other inducements include exemptions from paying duties and taxes, minimum standards of health and safety, and an absence of regulations covering working conditions, hours worked, rates of pay and rights of employees to organize. In this way, developing countries and their impoverished populations compete with each other for investment, while CORPORATIONS profit from the cheap costs of production by selling commodities produced in the zones to consumers in Europe and the United States at developed-world prices. See also SWEATSHOP.

FAIR TRADE requires that a number of minimum standards be satisfied in the production and exchange processes. These include sustainable development initiatives that facilitate social and welfare provision – education, health care and social security – together with conservation and protection of the environment. Working conditions must comply with International Labour Organization agreements and other human rights. In return, purchasers undertake to pay a price for goods that covers the cost of production; agree long-term, transparent contracts that make advance payments to finance future production; provide security necessary for long-term planning and operation of sustainable projects. A fair trade label is therefore an indication of quality produce which consumers in the industrialized world can buy to help establish independent production in developing countries, thereby alleviating reliance on foreign aid or loans and the terms and conditions they entail. See also TRADE.

FEMINISM, the way of interpreting the world from the perspective of women, is not a homogenous doctrine, but shares the central, defining goal of achieving women's economic, political and social equality with men. At its most progressive and anti-capitalist, the liberation of women from exploitation and oppression is identified as a necessary aspect of human liberation and is usually associated with anarchist, communist and socialist thought and action. In contrast, the democratic, liberal focus emphasizes domestic, marital and reproductive rights, and particular attention is paid to EQUALITY and equal opportunities in the workplace and social policy provision – childcare, maternity leave and so on – so that women can pursue careers. Male domination – as PATRIARCHY – is not specific to CAPITALISM, though feminism is largely a western or industrialized-world movement, and the authoritarian, hierarchical, militaristic and violent characteristics feminists attribute to men permeate capitalist society. See also LIBERATION.

FLOODNET is a URL-based software device used to block websites. The idea started as a proposal from the Anonymous Digital Coalition for a virtual sit-in on targeted websites in support of the ZAPATISTA uprising in Chiapas,

93

Mexico. The original method involved a manual blockade of a website by a coordinated, simultaneous and collective action of people repeatedly request-ing the targeted website to reload. The Electronic Disturbance Theatre consequently developed the Floodnet device as an automated version of the process. In essence the tactic transfers the civil disobedience activities of trespass and blockade to the Internet. Whereas protesters might hold a vigil or sit-in, or try to blockade, occupy or picket an office, building or workplace, Floodnet constitutes an electronic form of DIRECT ACTION that replicates such tactics in the virtual environment without activists having to leave home or work. Unlike some forms of HACKTIVISM, Floodnet is not about placing messages on websites, but aims at inconveniencing targeted organizations and relies on the publicity achieved by such actions to promote a particular message or cause.

FURTHER INFORMATION
Electronic civil disobedience: www.thing.net/~rdom/ecd/ecd.html

FOREIGN EXCHANGE see EXCHANGE RATE.

FREE TRADE AREA OF THE AMERICAS (FTAA), under nego-tiation since 1994 and originally scheduled for implementation in January 2005, is a treaty designed to eliminate or reduce trade barriers between some thirty-four countries of the Caribbean and the whole of the American continent, excluding Cuba. In practice this would mean: opening all public services and public purchases to international corporations; governments guaranteeing foreign investment; the monopolization and PRIVATIZATION of intellectual property rights; and giving CORPORATIONS the right to sue national governments. If implemented, it will extend the scope of the NORTH AMERICAN FREE TRADE AGREEMENT and raise fears that it will have an equally detrimental impact on the environment and populations of those countries that join with Canada, Mexico and the United States. Although FTAA negotiations appeared to stall in October 2003 and the January 2005 deadline passed, negotiations were concluded with Costa Rica, El Salvador, Guatemala, Honduras and Nicaragua with the signing of a Central American Free Trade Agreement (CAFTA) in May 2004. Opponents therefore see the CAFTA as part of an incremental approach towards the introduction of a FTAA and continue their campaigns against ratification of CAFTA and FTAA negotiations.

FURTHER INFORMATION

Opposition: www.stopftaa.org; www.ftaaresistance.org; www.citizen.org/trade/cafta
Official viewpoint: www.ftaa-alca.org; www.usembassy.or.cr/Cafta/cafta.html

FREEDOM in standard liberal terms is the absence of coercion or interference that restricts options open to people. This involves a narrow definition of constraint as deliberate interference, so that people are free to do what others do not prevent them from doing. John Stuart Mill (1806–1873) in *On Liberty* (1859) developed such notions to include the right of the individual to do whatever they want so long as they do not cause harm to others or infringe their rights to act accordingly. The emphasis here is always on individual as opposed to collective choice and autonomy. Hence, the paradox of eulogizing personal freedom at home while subjecting distant populations to the constraints of colonial or corporate domination and EXPLOITATION.

The French Revolution of 1879 proclaimed liberty – along with EQUALITY and fraternity – as virtuous ends, worthy of constitutional and therefore legal protection. Consequently, freedom interpreted as individualism – the idea that individual people pursue independently conceived goals – became enshrined as civil, economic and political rights. In terms of capitalist business and enterprise, this translated into the doctrine of LAISSEZ-FAIRE and the view that CORPORATIONS should not be subject to governmental, institutional or regulatory constraint. Primacy of the individual was thus identified with the corporation – albeit a collective organization – over and above the right of employees to organize and act collectively. According to this way of thinking, the will of the individual is expressed as free competition between equals in the marketplace and a consumer's right to choose what to buy.

In the sphere of civil as distinct from economic society, freedom of assembly, association, belief, conscience, movement and speech are protected as liberties or RIGHTS according to national constitutions, bills of rights or human rights conventions and acts. Unless limited by law or other obligations, for example, people are allowed and expected to act autonomously in each sphere. Following the English tradition of Thomas Hobbes (1588–1679), John Locke (1632–1704) and Mill, Isaiah Berlin (1909–1997), *Four Essays on Liberty* (1969), uses the term 'negative freedom' to describe the absence of external constraints. In this sense, interference or impediment can take the form of legal or regulatory provisions implemented by government, or social mores that prevent or demand certain forms of behaviour. This definition of constraint is based on the relevance of human agency – human action limiting another human – and therefore excludes the role of nature interpreted as natural ability.

Despite the perception and presentation of civil liberties and rights as ubiquitous, there are numerous ways in which they are limited. Freedom of speech or thought – as holding, communicating or expressing views without hindrance or punishment – for example, is subject to censorship and therefore restricted. Such impediments include laws on blasphemy, conspiracy, defamation, incitement, libel, obscenity, sedition and slander; which according to the liberal tradition do not prevent freedom of speech, but merely deter or punish those who exercise the right in an unacceptable way. Similarly, laws covering obstruction, public nuisance and picketing curtail freedom of association and movement. In the early twenty-first century the undefined threat of TERRORISM and the need to protect against it have also been used to justify the restriction of liberties and rights.

Freedom of the press is associated with free public speech, through the gathering, reporting and dissemination of news information. Here, however, governments license cinema, radio and television activity and can influence the news agenda through the staging of press conferences, giving misleading or false information as 'spin' and PROPAGANDA, or by restricting access to 'classified' records regardless of freedom-of-information legislation. Corporate ownership of the MEDIA has also been accused of distorting or preventing the expression of alternative points of view; a charge that can also be levelled at publishing companies that are only interested in commercially viable products. Concerns about press freedom are explored by Richard Barbrook, *Media Freedom* (1995), and monitored by groups like Reporters Without Borders (Reporters Sans Frontières), while initiatives like the Censoware Project are committed to identifying and removing surreptitious forms of censorship on the Internet, which block access to and receipt of information.

Negative liberty fails to differentiate between the formal freedom to do something – defined as an absence of physical impediment like imprisonment or slavery – and the substantive ability or capacity to act. In contrast, the concept of positive freedom has a European lineage represented by Baruch Spinoza (1632–1697), Jean-Jacques Rousseau (1712–1778), Immanuel Kant (1724–1804), Georg W.F. Hegel (1770–1831), Karl Marx (1818–1883) and Herbert Marcuse (1898–1979). For such thinkers, freedom is associated with the possibility of self-determination, implies a wider notion of restrictions and options beyond what people conceive or choose to do, and is linked to the processes of emancipation and LIBERATION. According to this tradition, cultural, economic, historical, political and social forms – such as ALIENATION – represent obstacles to the realization of the manifold potential of human beings as individuals through the cultivation of their abilities in whichever direction they choose.

In the case of wage labour, for example, creative activity is conditioned, constrained and mediated by the fact that an employee has little or no control over their activities at work. The need to work in order to live forms the basis of this relation and is similarly perceived to constitute a constraint on activity. Freedom of speech is also mediated by the threat of legal retribution, social disdain and campaigns to limit the use of language, as in the media and political attempts to rename French fries in the USA, because France opposed the invasion of Iraq in 2003. Similarly, interpreting debate as a 'marketplace of ideas' reinforces a narrow, commercial interpretation of freedom as the right to buy and sell and equates free speech with ADVERTISING. While such conceptions restrict the options for self-expression to the consumption of commodities, a more positive approach, advocated by organizations like Information for Social Change, Statewatch and War on Want, sees freedom from mediations like deprivation, discrimination, oppression, POVERTY and want as prerequisites of self-determination and expression.

Ultimately, the concepts of negative and positive liberty are inter-dependent, in the sense that each recognizes the impact of constraints on the ability to act and advocates their transcendence. Any differentiation therefore rests on the definition of constraint, while ANARCHISM and other progressive theories argue that a truly free society must embody both nega-tive and positive aspects. Accordingly, any enforced law that does not have individual consent is considered to be a limitation of freedom, hence the idea of restricting activity in order to protect DEMOCRACY is incongruous and inimical to the concept of ACCOUNTABILITY. Limitations on the use of ecosystems, deforestation and pollution must therefore be consensual, and the minimization of the time people are required to work in order to live subject to democratic, human control of the social conditions of production. Similar conditions apply to the use of animals, although organizations like People for the Ethical Treatment of Animals consider animals to have inher-ent rights of their own.

FURTHER INFORMATION
Exposing Internet censorship: http://censoware.net
Reporters Without Borders: www.rsf.org
Uncensored Internet use: http://freenetproject.org

G

G8 see GROUP OF 8 INDUSTRIALIZED NATIONS

GENERAL AGREEMENT ON TARIFFS AND TRADE (GATT)

was approved during the negotiations that also resulted in the BRETTON WOODS SYSTEM and was signed in Geneva, Switzerland, in 1947 by twenty-three states. Originally adopted as an interim accord between signatories on rules for TRADE, GATT was operated through a specialized agency of the UNITED NATIONS. This oversaw rounds of negotiation to manage world trade and oversee a progressive lowering of barriers, reduction in tariffs and discrimination – such as the British Imperial Preference or subsidizing the exports of domestic corporations – and an opening of economies among signatories. A particular aspect of the accord was the status of unconditional 'most favoured nation' that was afforded to all members, which meant that the least restrictive trade policy or any trade concession – such as cuts in tariffs – between any members had to be applied to all signatories. The ultimate goal of world free trade was to be achieved via consultation and was considered to be the best way of raising employment levels, income and living standards. Membership of GATT rose to seventy countries by 1979, and ten years later the countries of the former Soviet Union and its allies were allowed to join for the first time.

The focus of GATT signatories on reducing tariffs on manufacturing products, as opposed to agriculture and textiles, led to the charge that is was nothing more than a 'rich man's club'. In other words, because the manufacturing sector of the economy in developing countries was usually weak, they had little to gain from a free-trade agreement that focused on that sector. Not only did tariffs remain relatively high on the main exports of developing countries, agriculture and textiles, but their biggest markets – the European Union, Japan and the USA – give large subsidies to domestic agricultural production. This also restricted the ability of developing countries to acquire, through trade, the currencies they needed in order to import manufacturing products, and industrialized nations were accused of being interested in free trade when it was in their interests, but not when it had a detrimental effect on domestic producers. It also raises the question of whether or not regional trading arrangements like the European Union are really compatible with the GATT principle of 'most favoured nation' status, because it discriminates against non-members.

As Graham Dunkley demonstrates in *The Free Trade Adventure* (2000), the GATT was ultimately amended as part of the Uruguay Round of negotiations to extend its remit to the service sector of the economy: transportation, communications systems and so on, intellectual property and some aspects of agricultural trade. This round of negotiations also agreed to replace the provisions of GATT through the creation of the WORLD TRADE ORGANIZATION (WTO) with effect from 1 January 1995. Despite the WTO's status and role, GATT still forms the basis of the world trading system and remains in force.

FURTHER INFORMATION

Original treaty and amendments: www.wto.org/english/docs_e/legal_e/final_e. htm

GENERAL AGREEMENT ON TRADE IN SERVICES (GATS) is a multilateral accord that came into effect in January 1995 and was negotiated as part of the talks to establish the WORLD TRADE ORGANIZATION (WTO). Under its auspices, all national governments that are WTO members are obliged to draw up lists of services that foreign corporations can run. The accord covers all internationally traded services such as banking, tourism and film production and includes public services such as education, health care, post and telecommunications, as well as natural monopolies like energy supply, rail and water. Although governments choose what to include in the schedule, only services that exercise an element of governmental authority or relate to air traffic rights are automatically excluded from GATS.

Opponents like Friends of the Earth and the World Development Movement contend that GATS pressurizes governments to privatize public services and allows multinational corporations to cherry-pick the most profitable opportunities. Furthermore, they argue that democratic rights are undermined because elected governments are prevented from regulating the way services are provided. In certain circumstances, for example, regulations designed to prevent corporations from damaging the environment could be challenged as a barrier to trade. Similarly the Disputes Panel hearings are held behind closed doors and therefore beyond public scrutiny. January 2000 saw the start of a new round of negotiations aimed at expanding the remit of the accord by allowing countries to identify service sectors they would like other countries to include. A deadline for the completion of negotiations was set for January 2005, but the failure of the Ministerial Meeting in Cancún, Mexico, in September 2003 made the date unworkable.

FURTHER INFORMATION
WTO trade topics section: www.wto.org/english/tratop_e/serv_e/serv_e.htm
Criticism: www.gatswatch.org
www.wdm.org.uk/campaign/GATS.htm

GENETIC ENGINEERING is also known as genetic modification, as in 'genetically modified organism' (GMO) and less commonly as genetic manipulation and gene splicing. Stated briefly, it refers to the process of altering the genetic material and make-up of a bacterium, plant or animal outside the normal process of reproduction. Examples include some commercial strains of wheat modified by irradiation since the 1950s and microscopic organisms altered for the purposes of genetic research. Using genes from different organisms is referred to as 'recombinant' and the product described as 'transgenic'. Although the genes of plants and animals can be altered by viral infection, changes to cells infected by the virus are usually eliminated by the immune system.

The permanent substitution of genes from other species into whole animals has so far been accomplished in the OncoMouse for research into cancer. This involves genetically modifying a mouse embryonic stem cell, implanting it into an early embryo (blastocyst) and implanting that into a female mouse. The offspring contains unmodified and modified cells. By selecting mice whose sperm or egg-producing cells developed from the modified cell and interbreeding them, mice that contain the genetic modification in all of their cells are harvested. This process is akin to cloning, whereby identical transgenic animals can be produced for commercial use.

The stated aim of such experimentation is to introduce new genetic characteristics to an organism in order to improve its usefulness for things like research into the mechanisms of diseases. Products in use or in development include forms of gene therapy, whereby diseases caused by defective genes are treated using viruses to supply a normal copy of the genes. Other examples of medicines and vaccines include the use of bacteria to produce human insulin and experiments to grow bananas and other forms of fruit that contain oral vaccines. Attempts have also been made to develop strains of rice with enhanced vitamin A and other qualities, such as the 'golden rice' developed by the International Rice Research Institute. Research into the viability of transgenic animals is also aimed at the introduction of human genes so that they produce human proteins in their milk or provide body parts and organs suitable for XENOTRANSPLANTATION.

In the production of food, ingredients and animal feed, genetic engineering is claimed to enhance taste and quality, help crops and animals grow faster and bigger to improve nutrition, and enhance harvests through greater resistance to disease, pests and herbicides. Examples include fish that mature more quickly, fruit and nut trees that provide fruit earlier, and plants that produce new forms of plastic. Along with increased production of meat, eggs, milk and wool, animal health and the diagnosis of disease are also targeted as improvements. The first commercial genetically modified food was the Calgene FlavrSavr tomato, which was approved in 1994 by the United States Food and Drug Administration as not threatening public health and not needing identification as genetically modified (GM). Other genetically modified food crops included virus-resistant squash, a potato that included an organic pesticide called Bt, as well as strains of canola, soybean, corn and cotton. Other crops grown commercially or field-tested include virus-resistant sweet potato and plants able to survive weather extremes and flourish in otherwise harsh growing conditions.

All in all, BIOTECHNOLOGY is believed to revolutionize agricultural, industrial and pharmaceutical production through a more efficient processing that increases profitability and the security of food supplies for the world population. The use of modified herbicides and insecticides is also believed to aid soil conservation, water purity and natural waste management. As Brian Tokar, *Redesigning Life* (2001), demonstrates, however, opposition to genetic engineering encompasses many sections of society and a diverse range of concerns from ethical objections to playing 'God' and tampering with nature, through welfare issues relating to the health, rights and welfare of animals and humans. Consequently, demands from a variety of groups, which include Friends of the Earth, Green parties, Greenpeace and the safe trade movement, range from complete bans, to moratoria and raising public awareness through labelling. Effective and informed public participation in decision-making processes governing the introduction and use of genetic technologies is also a common requirement. Thus, with experimentation on animals still in its infancy and equated with suffering, the imprecise nature and knowledge of the long-term results of genetic engineering inform calls for products to be tested in a wide variety of environments to determine what, if any, dangers they pose.

Concerns also include the possible development of human allergens, the transfer of antibiotic resistance markers and the long-term effects of genetically modified crops that are pest-resistant or designed to tolerate certain forms of pesticide. Unforeseen side effects are, for example, feared as a result of interactions in the environment or between proteins that will be difficult to trace back to genetic engineering. Although the rapid sequencing of the human genome is possible, comparatively little is known about the interaction of proteins. Protein and molecular engineering for medicinal purposes has therefore been subject to calls for its restriction to the relief of serious human suffering where there is an absence of alternatives. Knowledge of the human genome has also raised fears about the misuse of information by insurers and employers to discriminate against prospective policyholders and employees, and has resulted in demands for strict, independent regulation of genetic testing and genetic databases. On the science fiction fringes, talk of human reproductive cloning and the modification of the human genome through augmentation and the potential use of genetics in warfare add to existing fears.

Genetic engineering of plants is much more common and raises questions about their impact on humans due to the practice of feeding modified crops to animals that are destined for the dinner table. In broader terms, research into the transfer of transgenes through cross-pollination, the effect on other organisms and therefore on flora and fauna, is inconclusive and therefore fuels support for the precautionary principle advocated by Stephen Nottingham, *Genescapes* (2002), and others. In Australia, for example, the parasite of the cotton plant, which was supposed to be killed by the GM cotton Ingard, proliferated. Transgenic insecticide has also been correlated with heavier selective pressure on insects, which encourages resistance and thereby reduces the effect of the pesticide.

In 2003, farm-scale studies in Britain recorded similar findings with GM sugar beet and GM oilseed rape. There are also fears that genetically engineered crops could jeopardize BIODIVERSITY if herbicide-tolerant crops contribute to the elimination of wild plants, and toxic plants like Bt corn, cotton and potatoes have a similar impact on insects. Potential knock-on effects up the food chain on birds and other animals that feed on seeds and insects are incalculable. Recombinant technology also involves the danger of cross-pollination, whereby genes can pass to wild and domestic varieties of the same plant, thereby modifying the original gene pool. The expansion of new croplands into areas currently too harsh to grow crops is also likely to disturb the wildlife balance that currently exists in those areas.

Biodiversity would be similarly threatened by a reduction in seed stocks and strains that form the basis of traditional agricultural practice. Especially in developing countries, farmers develop crop varieties that suit their local conditions through selective breeding and seed retention. The results are the product of collective efforts over generations without ownership, but, in a process termed BIOPIRACY, CORPORATIONS like Cargill, Monsanto, Novartis and Pioneer modify and patent traditional strains, which means that the original owners are prevented from using the new product without permission. In some cases, the manufacturer can stop original seeds from being grown to avoid cross-pollination and thereby oblige farmers to use the new variety. Monsanto even experimented with plants that produce sterile seeds, ostensibly to protect against cross-pollination, but also to protect their intellectual property rights; despite the implications for developing nations where seed saving is an integral aspect of subsistence farming. In view of the corporate preoccupation with patenting, it is somewhat ironic that when addressing safety concerns the corporations argue that genetically engineered crops are not significantly different from those modified by nature or humans.

Food safety is a pertinent issue in Europe, where a variant form of Creutzfeldt–Jakob disease in humans has been linked to bovine spongiform encephalopathy (BSE), which affected cattle in Britain during the 1990s, after DEREGULATION allowed herbivores to be fed processed animal remains. In Britain, France and Germany, there is therefore a public predisposition against genetically modified food and demands for labelling and consumer choice. European regulations require labelling of all food and animal feed containing more than 0.5 per cent genetically engineered ingredients, and a deoxyribonucleic acid (DNA) marker so that contaminated crops, feed or food can be identified, withdrawn and their origins traced. China and Japan also employ labelling and documentation safeguards and require government approval of imports. Japan even set up a processing facility for non-GM soybeans in the USA, because of fears that the mixing of genetically engineered and normal crops could undermine Japanese labelling requirements.

Genetic modification of food is also considered to represent a further industrialization of agriculture and corporate domination of food supply under the guise of trade liberalization agreements. Not only does the WORLD

103

TRADE ORGANIZATION (WTO) consider the refusal to accept genetically modified food imports as an unnecessary obstacle to international trade, but the American Agriculture Department offers training to developing countries on WTO rules and the benefits of biotechnology. Likewise, industry groups fund initiatives that promote biotechnology regulation based on 'scientific' findings, while simultaneously promoting intellectual property protection within the WTO. In contrast, groups like Compassion in World Farming advocate public involvement in decisions about research. They also recognize that addressing lifestyle, social, economic and environmental health factors can also help to prevent disease, poverty and hunger; as does Roy Burdon, *The Suffering Gene* (2003), when exploring the impact of environment on human genes. In short, the idea that problems can be solved by technology alone is analogous to the marginalization of alternative social, economic and political solutions by those who push NEOLIBERALISM as the only option.

FURTHER INFORMATION

Contamination issues: www.grain.org/research/contamination.cfm
Guide to GM and non-GM products: www.geneticfoodalert.supanet.com
Opposition: www.greenpeace.org/international/campaigns/genetic-engineering

GENUINE PROGRESS INDICATOR is, like the Index of Sustainable Welfare, a method of assessing economic growth that takes into account costs and benefits in an attempt to measure well-being and the potential for sustainable development. See also GROSS DOMESTIC PRODUCT.

GLOBAL COMMONS can be areas that, like the high seas, fall outside the control of any single nation, but they also include information commons such as the Internet, the human genome and traditional knowledge and are anathema to private and intellectual property rights. The global commons are also those parts of the earth's BIOSPHERE that do not belong to any particular country or individual and are therefore held in common. These include things that affect the climate system, such as air space, forests, the open oceans and BIODIVERSITY in general. They are also commonly owned land and water, as well as the resources contained therein, such as much of the Arctic and Antarctica. As commons, especially natural resources – such as air, fisheries, forests, gas, oil, public land, water and wildlife – are not inexhaustible, the Global Commons Institute and others argue that they should be protected for the benefit of all, including future generations, and not left to the mercy of the profit motive.

Economic and legal constraints on use and abuse exist in the form of quotas and limited entry for fisheries, tax and royalty regimes for gas, oil and forests, and other regulations that attempt to manage common resources. REGULATION can be national, regional or global such as the UNITED NATIONS (UN) convention on the use and exploitation of the ocean and its resources, Law of the Sea (1982). Similarly, there are UN conventions intended to protect: marine and terrestrial ecosystems, Biological Diversity (1992), species categorized as endangered, threatened or listed, International Trade in Endangered Species of Wild Fauna and Flora (1973); and the global climate, Framework Convention on Climate Change (1992). Difficulties faced by authorities charged with managing and protecting global commons are manifold. They include the need to coordinate action between states, as well as ensuring that resource users understand and practise a necessary level of interdependence in terms of collecting and sharing information so that the economic, environmental and social impacts of management regimes can be evaluated. As demonstrated by the case studies compiled by Michael Goldman, *Privatizing Nature* (1998), authorities also need to establish mechanisms that secure the participation of nations, national and regional governments, INDIGENOUS PEOPLE, CORPORATIONS and local residents if measures are to be effective. Such difficulties are exacerbated where there is no clear distinction between local, regional and global commons.

Multilateral trade and financial institutions like the WORLD TRADE ORGANIZATION and the WORLD BANK are also supposed to help national governments work together to protect global commons. There would appear to be a conflict of interest, however, especially where structural adjustment programmes prescribed by the INTERNATIONAL MONETARY FUND and World Bank encourage minimum regulation. In contrast, implementation of agreements and treaties intended to protect global commons – be they voluntary or binding, bilateral, regional or global – is up to the individual signatory countries. Mechanisms for monitoring and enforcing agreements vary and penalties for non-compliance are no more serious than whatever political and financial pressure more committed signatories desire to exert.

FURTHER INFORMATION

Global Commons Institute: www.gci.org.uk
Project to create international commons: www.thisisthepublicdomain.org
Response to the 'Tragedy of the Commons' thesis: www.infoshop.org/faq/sec16.
  htm

GLOBAL WARMING refers to an increase in the average temperature of the atmosphere, land and oceans. The Intergovernmental Panel on Climate Change (IPCC), *Climate Change 2001*, for example, estimates that the global average surface temperature has increased by 0.6 ± 0.2°C since records were first kept in 1860. The phenomenon of global warming is not one-dimensional, however, as it involves interconnected changes in cloud cover, precipitation levels and patterns, sea levels, weather formation and other elements of the atmospheric system, all of which affect each other. Although the examination of ice cores suggests that global temperatures fluctuate, they have been comparatively consistent over a 10,000-year period since the end of the last ice age – Medieval Warm Period *circa* 1000–1300 CE and Little Ice Age *circa* 1350–1850 CE excepted. This makes the rise in temperature of 0.4°C since 1980 all the more unusual and potentially alarming.

While the IPCC represents a consensus of scientific opinion, which accepts that temperatures are rising, there is less agreement about why this is so. Variations in climate and temperature are influenced by a number of factors, including changes in the levels of volcanic activity and emissions, and the amounts, types and geographic and temporal distribution of solar energy that reaches earth. In the latter case, for example, changes in the solar orbit and axial tilt of the earth – known as Milankovitch Cycles after Milutin Milankovitch (1879–1958) – influence the amount of solar radiation striking different parts of the earth at different times of the year and are considered to affect climate. Meanwhile, Willie Soon, in *Solar Variability and Climate Change* (2000), correlates change in sunspots and temperature.

A third explanation originated with Svante Arrhenius (1859–1927), who is credited with theorizing the importance of atmospheric levels of carbon dioxide (CO_2) for the climate. Stated briefly, levels of CO_2 and other gases – methane (CH_4), nitrous oxide (N_2O), hydrofluorocarbons (HFCs), perfluorocarbons (PFCs) and sulphur hexafluoride (SF_6) – change processes that regulate the amount of water vapour in the atmosphere. Concentrations of these gases are therefore indicated in the amount and distribution of cloud, increases in which are considered to effect climate by producing a 'greenhouse effect' that prevents radiant energy from the sun being re-radiated back into space and leads to an increase in average temperature over time. The IPCC, *Climate Change 2001*, attributes increases in the concentrations of these gases to human activity: the burning of fossil fuels – coal, oil and gas – for domestic consumption, industrial production and the generation of energy. Other factors include increased use of cars, aerosols and changes in land use such as deforestation, which releases CO_2 into the atmosphere and makes it less likely to be absorbed as part of the natural carbon cycle.

While there is no consensus that any individual theory is comprehensive enough to provide an adequate account, there is a growing recognition that a combination of factors represents the most likely explanation, a view supported by Peter Stott et al., *External Control of 20th Century Temperature by Natural and Anthropogenic Forcings* (2000), among others. Despite such conclusions, Bob Burton and Sheldon Rampton, *The PR Plot to Overheat the Earth* (1998), describe how vested interest groups like Access to Energy, Competitive Enterprise Institute, Cooler Heads Coalition and Global Climate Coalition dispute the validity of predictions. Such groups are therefore reluctant to countenance increased energy efficiency or investment in renewable energy sources and are vehement in their opposition to the KYOTO PROTOCOL.

In contrast, environmentalist groups like Friends of the Earth, Greenpeace, the Worldwatch Institute and Worldwide Fund for Nature join concerned governments and individuals in highlighting existing dangers and promoting solutions. These include IPCC estimates that the global sea level will rise by up to 1 metre by 2100 due to warmer water expanding and melting the polar ice caps, sea ice and glaciers, thereby endangering the existence of Pacific Ocean island nations like Tuvalu. Paradoxically, global warming could also lead to colder conditions in Europe as melting ice interrupts the conveyance of warm water from the Gulf Stream across the Atlantic Ocean. Fluctuations in La Niña and El Niño oscillations in the Pacific are also correlated with the growing incidence of extreme weather patterns, with cyclones, floods, hurricanes and typhoons that result in increased financial costs and human suffering as infrastructure, food and water supplies are disrupted. Additional consequences include changing ecosystems, with a potential reduction in biodiversity as smaller numbers of species flourish at the expense of others, and the spread of infectious disease as conditions favourable to malaria, dengue and yellow fever develop in new areas. A broader account of these and other developments is provided by Dinyar Godrej, *The No-nonsense Guide to Climate Change* (2001).

Nevertheless, the governments of George W. Bush in the USA and John Howard in Australia oppose the Kyoto Protocol that resulted from the United Nations Framework Convention for Climate Change (1992). There is probably no coincidence between these positions and the fact that, as Hal Turton, *Greenhouse Gas Emissions in Industrialized Countries* (2004), records, the USA has the largest emissions in absolute terms and the second largest per capita behind Australia. What is more surprising, however, is the fact the Bush government appears to ignore the concerns expressed by the National Academy of Sciences, the American Geophysical Union and the American Meteorological Society. In contrast, the European Union, which with North America is estimated to be responsible for 85 per cent of the man-made CO_2 in the atmosphere today, launched a Climate Change Programme in March 2000. See Joyeeta Gupta, *Our Simmering Planet* (2001), for a discussion of the political and other machinations that surround such anomalies.

FURTHER INFORMATION

European Climate Change Programme: http://europa.eu.int/comm/environment/climat/eccp.htm

Intergovernmental Panel on Climate Change: www.ipcc.ch

Union of Concerned Scientists: www.ucsusa.org/global_environment/global_warming/index.cfm?pageID=27

United Nations Framework Convention on Climate Change: http://unfccc.int

GLOBALIZATION is a generic term used by academics, activists, media commentators and others to imply that the emergence of MULTI-NATIONAL CORPORATIONS, the predominance of multilateral institutions and negotiation of regional and international trade agreements represent an erosion or even the end of national borders and sovereignty. Some, like Paul Hirst and Grahame Thompson, *Globalisation in Question* (1996), however, think that closer inspection reveals a more complex picture of reality. Immanuel Wallerstein, *Geopolitics and Geoculture* (1991), for example, agrees that there is nothing unique about the search for new markets and cheaper sources of labour-power to exploit – facilitated by new and improved methods of production and communication. Such activities are age-old characteristics of CAPITALISM and are associated with earlier stages of development, particularly the use of the gold standard between 1871 and 1932. According to such views, a number of factors – commercial, cultural, economic and social – have been taken at face value and assumed to demonstrate that TRADE, investment, people and information now cross international borders with unparalleled ease and without exception.

While it is undeniable that a revolution in information and communications technologies (ICT) – communications satellites, the Internet and telephony – has enhanced the ability of traders to 'annihilate space by time', the new markets and cheap labour-power that they now access are distinctly regional in character. The economies of the former Soviet bloc – Russia and the countries of central and Eastern Europe – for example, have been reintroduced into the international orbit of capitalism. Similarly, the rapid growth of economies in East and South East Asia and the enlargement of the European Union and treaties like the NORTH AMERICAN FREE TRADE AGREEMENT give the impression of a new dimension to the international economy. Ultimately, however, these developments failed to alter significantly the concentration and therefore the share of trade, investment and GROSS NATIONAL PRODUCT between Japan and those countries that inhabit North America and Western Europe. Likewise, the proportion of trade accounted for by international exchange has remained fairly constant and, regardless of perceptions, manufacturing and service sector corporations are not truly global or transnational entities. Instead they prefer to operate from indigenous national bases – even if the ubiquitous corporate images that appear on television and in films suggest otherwise.

There has been an increased interdependence and integration of economic activity across national and regional boundaries in the area of foreign direct investment (FDI) – especially the expansion of international financial market activity. This particular development was fuelled by the reformulation of the BRETTON WOODS SYSTEM in the 1970s, the abolition of fixed exchange rates in 1973, the removal of capital controls, the DEREGULATION of financial markets in the 1980s and concomitant advances in ICT. The resultant explosion of cross-border lending and the ease with which CAPITAL FLOWS move across national borders therefore create the impression that we live in a truly global community – even though twelve countries in East Asia and South America received 80 per cent of North–South capital flows in the 1990s. As George Caffentzis, *Notes on the Antiglobalization Movement 1985–2000* (2000), argues, however, the perception of globalization owes much to the universal application of neoliberal prescriptions in the form of STRUCTURAL ADJUSTMENT PROGRAMMES required by the INTERNATIONAL MONETARY FUND (IMF) and the WORLD BANK.

Opposition to the practical consequences of the policies promoted by these bodies and the WORLD TRADE ORGANIZATION (WTO) – exemplified by the round of protests that started in Seattle, November 1999 – has heightened the public profile and helped hasten acceptance of the idea that globalization is a real process. Similarly, the apparently ubiquitous presence of commodities and corporate values is perceived as a form of cultural imperialism that reduces diversity and is opposed by those who prefer to embrace and celebrate indigenous and other ways of living. The term 'anti-globalization', coined to categorize groups and individuals that protest against aspects of contemporary capitalism that they find distasteful, is therefore a misnomer. Paradoxically, opposition and resistance to the excesses of capitalism that are experienced around the globe have fostered new levels and means of international cooperation. Perhaps this process – considered as part of a wider study by Michael Hardt and Antonio Negri, *Empire* (2000) – should be seen as 'pro-' rather than 'anti'-globalization.

Moreover, Ulrich Beck, *What is Globalisation?* (2000), recognizes that the processes that really do not respect national borders are by and large negative: pollution and environmental devastation – see GLOBAL WARMING – and increasing POVERTY, which generates migration and facilitates the EXPLOITATION of illegal immigrants in employment and transportation and in the use of RACISM by conservative and reactionary thinkers. Additional concerns stem from the view that CORPORATIONS and national governments are increasingly unaccountable and therefore beyond the control of ordinary citizens. Domestic policies are therefore seen as designed to attract corporate investment or meet the demands of the IMF, the World Bank, the WORLD INTELLECTUAL PROPERTY ORGANIZATION or the WTO, which in turn are viewed as promoting a corporation-friendly agenda. Consequently, voter demands are deemed to be ignored, thereby bringing into question the true nature and worth of democratic institutions at the national level. As part of this trend, regulations designed to provide safe working conditions, safeguard living standards and protect the environment are abandoned or prohibited at the behest of organizations like the IMF and the WTO, while property rights are strengthened and investors and speculators indemnified against loss.

FURTHER INFORMATION

Links, information and resources: www.globalissues.org; www.aworldconnected.org

GREEN is the name and colour adopted by political parties within the broader ecology and environmental movements. The MEDIA use the term to refer to these broader concerns, to identify the related policy agenda within established political parties, and it has also been appropriated by advertisers and corporate marketing strategists in an attempt to sell certain commodities. At first, different names were used, such as the Values Party formed in New Zealand in 1972 and the Ecology Party founded the following year in Britain. The advent and electoral success of the Greens (Die

Grünen) in Germany, following their formation in 1980, encouraged others to adopt the name either as new parties or as a change of an existing title – the Ecology Party changed its name in 1985, for example. The formation of parties to contest elections and seek to influence policy is seen by supporters as a necessary compromise, whereas activist groups who see the movement as a broader cultural, radical social force refuse to compromise with institutions, people and processes that epitomize values that they detest. Examples of compromise include so-called Red–Green alliances with left or social-democratic parties for elections and, as in Germany, in order to form a federal government in 1998.

During the 1980s, European Green parties sought to identify and promote their common values through the adoption of the 'Four Pillars' of ecology, grassroots democracy, nonviolence and social justice. The Green Party of the USA incorporated these into Ten Key Values in 1984, adopted by their Canadian counterpart and by others during the 1990s. The additional criteria can be broadly defined as community-based economics, decentralization, FEMINISM, personal and global responsibility, respect for diversity and sustainability. A Global Greens Charter was agreed in 2001 at a meeting of 800 Green Party delegates from seventy countries in order to commit themselves to a global partnership based on the Four Pillars and two other guiding principles taken from the Ten Key Values: respect for diversity and sustainability. The Charter also proposes key areas of political action designed to put the principles into practice. See also ECOLOGY and ENVIRONMENTALISM.

FURTHER INFORMATION

Global Green Charter: www.global.greens.org.au/charter.htm
Green parties around the world: www.greens.org.
Key values in more detail: www.gp.org/documents/tenkey.html

GROSS DOMESTIC PRODUCT (GDP) is the total or aggregate monetary VALUE of all commodities and services produced by CORPORATIONS in a given nation. The figure takes into account inputs involved in the process of production – capital, LABOUR, land and entrepreneurship – regardless of ownership, but does not take the value of the final product at face value. In other words, the profits made by producers of component parts are deducted from the cost of the final output. As well as calculating (nominal) GDP as the total amount of money spent, a 'real' GDP figure is adjusted to take account of inflation. In comparative terms, figures are used to measure economic growth between and within economies. Here again, different methods produce different results, according to whether the EXCHANGE RATE or purchasing power of each currency is used to calculate parity against a selected standard. The measure of national output, including investment and production abroad, is called GROSS NATIONAL PRODUCT.

Paradoxically, however, using the monetary value of commodities and services produced as a measure of economic growth fails to discriminate between activities that pollute the environment and those that repair the damage. Similarly, income distribution and the depletion of natural resources are not taken into account, whereas attempts to tackle crime, prosecute marital divorce and manage social breakdown are counted as economic growth. In the final analysis, GDP is little more than a balance sheet of commodities and services that are bought and sold and therefore fails to distinguish between transactions that contribute to human welfare or environmental well-being and those that undermine them. Moreover, GDP does not take into account illegal or informal economic activity, volunteer work or domestic labour. Even though it is designed to measure the quantity as opposed to the quality of growth, it falls short on that count too.

Using GDP as an indication of growth in the economy implies that all economic activity is beneficial, when it is clearly not – cigarette production and arms manufacturing being two of many examples. No account is taken of how the functioning and organization of society and the economy – from working conditions to road safety – affect the happiness, health and well-being of individuals, families and communities. Likewise the quality of education and the causes and consequences of the inequalities of income distribution remain anonymous. In its present form, GDP is obsolete as a mechanism for identifying and measuring progress towards goals that are compatible with SUSTAINABLE DEVELOPMENT.

Attempts have therefore been made to devise an alternative measure that counts the costs of crime, family breakdown, loss of farmland and wetlands, ozone and resource depletion and pollution. Clifford Cobb, Ted Halstead and Jonathan Rowe, *The Genuine Progress Indicator* (GPI) (1995), for example, worked with the Redefining Progress group to devise and use one such method in relation to the USA. Similarly, Friends of the Earth attempted to devise an Index of Sustainable Economic Welfare (ISEW) for Britain. Their work in this field is based on the ideas of Herman Daly and John Cobb, *For the Common Good* (1989); Clifford and John Cobb, *The Green National Product*

(1994); and Tim Jackson and Nic Marks, *Measuring Sustainable Economic Welfare* (1994).

FURTHER INFORMATION
ISEW: www.foe.co.uk/campaigns/sustainable_development/progress
GPI: www.redefiningprogress.org/projects/gpi/updates/gpi1999.html

GROSS NATIONAL PRODUCT (GNP) is a measure of the total or aggregate monetary value of the output – final product sold to the consumer – of all industries and, in contrast to gross domestic product, includes output and income achieved by investment abroad. For a critique that applies to both forms of measurement see GROSS DOMESTIC PRODUCT.

GROUP OF 8 INDUSTRIALIZED NATIONS (G8) involves policy research and economic and political meetings between governmental representatives – elected and appointed – from Britain, Canada, France, Germany Italy, Japan, Russia and the USA to discuss policymaking by and for bodies like the ORGANIZATION FOR ECONOMIC COOPERATION AND DEVELOPMENT. Of course, these are not the only industrialized nations, but – with the exception of Russia – they represent the largest economies measured in terms of GROSS DOMESTIC PRODUCT. Established as the Group of 6 in 1975, it became the Group of 7 with the admittance of Canada and the Group of 8 (G8) when Russia joined in 1998. Since the disintegration of the Soviet bloc in the 1990s, the group has become increasingly important in determining aspects of world governance that feed into bodies like the WORLD TRADE ORGANIZATION (WTO) and stands accused of secrecy and an absence of direct ACCOUNTABILITY and TRANSPARENCY.

Whereas during the cold war developing countries tried to coordinate their interests through the non-aligned movement, the 'Group of 77' (G77) now plays a similar role. Originating in 1967 under the auspices of the United Nations Conference on Trade and Development, the G77 now includes China and has an overall membership of 132. Small island countries like Samoa and the Marshall Islands have also established the Alliance of Small Island States in an attempt to force the international community to address the impact of GLOBAL WARMING and rising sea levels that threatens their very survival. At the WTO talks held at Cancún, Mexico, in 2003, twenty-two developing countries also formed an informal alliance in order to protect their interests against the more economically powerful countries and corporations that sought access to markets while retaining subsidies to agricultural production in Europe and the USA. Those involved – Argentina, Bolivia, Brazil, Chile, China, Colombia, Costa Rica, Cuba, Ecuador, Egypt, Guatemala, India, Indonesia, Mexico, Nigeria, Pakistan, Paraguay, Peru, the Philippines, South Africa, Thailand and Venezuela – account for half of the world population. They also include nearly two-thirds of the world's farmers, who produce one-fifth of global agricultural output and supply more than a quarter of global farm exports.

G8 meetings are also attended by the presidents of the European Council, the European Commission and the European Parliament. They also form a focus for anti-capitalist protesters. Meetings are hosted annually by member countries and follow the same sequence. The 2005 summit took place at Gleneagles in Scotland between 6 and 8 July.

FURTHER INFORMATION

Canadian opponents: www.g8.utoronto.ca
French protests 2003: www.nadir.org/nadir/initiativ/agp/free/evian
US opposition: www.nog8.org
British opposition: www.dissent.org.uk

H

HACKTIVISM refers to a term and practice that came to prominence in 1994 during the **ZAPATISTA** uprising. It represents the combination of the words and worlds of computer hacking and political activism; as discussed by the Electronic Disturbance Theatre, *Hacktivism* (2003), and Tim Jordan and Paul Taylor, *Hacktivism and Cyberwars* (2004). In other words, acts of **CIVIL DISOBEDIENCE** and **DIRECT ACTION** are carried out in the virtual realm of the Internet, where the ability to invent, modify and refine computer systems is exercised for political ends. Hacktivists therefore exhibit adroit hacker skills together with an understanding of the tactics, purpose and efficacy of political protest. Knowledge is then used to sabotage the websites of institutions – be they government, multilateral trade organizations or **CORPORATIONS** – the policies and practices of which the saboteur disapproves.

A variety of motivational goals include achieving social and political change by drawing attention to a specific cause, provoking debate about certain issues, and the desire to protect free access to information in the face of corporate or government attempts to impose control over Internet use and content. Corporations, for example, are viewed as attempting to exploit the virtual environs by imposing their notions of **PRIVATE PROPERTY**, restricting access and dominating the ownership and control of computer technology. In the process, the Internet is appropriated as an advertising medium, thereby occupying the time and space of other users. Likewise governments and other organizations that use the World Wide Web to promote their ideas inevitably become targets for hacktivists who disagree with their official version of events.

As the organizational defences against hacktivism develop, so the objectives and tactics of the latter evolve and innovate in order to be effective. Examples therefore range from disruption by computer break-ins, through 'bombing' whereby keywords are used to alter Internet search engines results, to denial of service. More specifically, they include posting banned or censored material on the Internet; distributing email bombs, viruses and worms to selected targets; altering, defacing, hijacking and leaving messages on websites; and electronic blockade and trespass. The last example is epitomized by **FLOODNET** and the 'virtual sit-in' organized by the electrohippies to coincide with street-based demonstrations occurring in Seattle against the **WORLD TRADE ORGANIZATION** in November 1999. In addition to public participation in blockades and trespasses, similarities between hacktivism and civil disobedience are also evident in the practice of painting slogans on walls, defacing advertising posters and placing messages or altering information on a website.

FURTHER INFORMATION

Theory and practice: www.thehacktivist.com
Technical assistance for activists: www.hacktivismo.com

HAYMARKET MARTYRS were a group of anarchists who agitated in favour of a shorter working day, in the USA, towards the end of the nineteenth century. The campaign for a legally enforceable eight-hour working day, with effect from 1 May 1886, began with the Federation of Organized Trades and Labor Unions in 1884 and was taken up by the Knights of Labor trade union in Chicago. On 3 May 1886, police officers shot, killed and wounded strikers who were supporting the campaign at Chicago's McCormick Reaper Works – actions that precipitated the call for a demonstration in Haymarket Square the following evening.

At the subsequent protest, a bomb was thrown at police officers as they dispersed the remnants of an otherwise orderly meeting and resulted in the death and injury of police officers and of protesters; the number of deaths and injuries was increased by the fact that police officers fired indiscriminately into the crowd. Despite Rudolph Schnaubelt being identified as the person who threw the bomb, six Germans – George Engel (1836–1887), Adolf Fisher (1858–1887), Louis Lingg (1864–1887), Oscar Neebe (1850–1916), Michael Schwab (1853–1898) and August Spies (1855–1887) – and an Englishman, Samuel Fielden (1847–1922), were arrested. Although Schnaubelt was also arrested, he was released without charge amid allegations that he acted as an agent provocateur.

Having addressed the 4 May meeting, with Fielden and Spies, Albert Parsons (1848–1887) was also sought by the police, but managed to avoid capture until he gave himself up on the morning of the trial, to face charges of conspiracy to commit murder. Because witnesses would testify that none of the defendants threw the bomb on 4 May, the case rested on the charge that they made speeches and wrote articles that encouraged the use of violence for political purposes and therefore motivated an unnamed person to throw the bomb. The jury, chosen by a court bailiff instead of being selected at random, which included a relative of one of the police victims, found the defendants guilty as charged. As a consequence, Engel, Fisher, Parsons and Spies were executed in 1887; Lingg committed suicide in prison after being sentenced to death; and Fielden, Neebe and Schwab were pardoned in 1893.

To commemorate the Haymarket Martyrs, the founding congress of the Second International, held in Paris in 1889, agreed to make 1 May – MAY DAY – an international working-class holiday. See also Philip Foner, *The Autobiographies of the Haymarket Martyrs* (1969).

FURTHER INFORMATION

Primary sources: www.chicagohs.org/hadc
List of secondary sources: www.chicagohistory.org/dramas/overview/resource.htm

HEGEMONY stems from the Greek for leader, *hegemon*, and therefore refers to leadership and predominance. The first use of the term in an anti-capitalist context is attributed to Georgi Plekhanov (1856–1918) writing on relations between the Bolsheviks and proletariat in the aftermath of the 1905 Revolution in Russia. The concept was later developed by Antonio Gramsci (1891–1937), *Prison Notebooks* (1929–35), to explain how liberal democracy is able to maintain the dominance of capitalist interests through the use of consent plus force. In other words, intellectual and moral leadership is exercised through CIVIL SOCIETY as POLITICS, education, CULTURE and RELIGION to shape perception, understanding and knowledge, while the overt use of force is reserved for crisis situations. This web of beliefs, as IDEOLOGY, is cultivated through institutional and social relations that serve to socialize oppression and therefore the acquiescence of the subordinated. In this context, the predominance of corporations and the interests of consumer capitalism in general can be compared to a form of hegemony. See also the STATE.

FURTHER INFORMATION

Selections from the *Prison Notebooks*: www.marxists.org/archive/gramsci/editions/
  spn/contents.htm

HOT MONEY refers to short-term capital movement involving indirect foreign investment in bonds, real estate, speculation and stocks by corporations, investment firms, individuals and governments. See also CAPITAL FLOWS.

HUMAN TRAFFICKING is defined by Article 3, paragraph (a) of the Protocol to Prevent, Suppress and Punish Trafficking in Persons (2000), which is a supplement to the United Nations Convention Against Transnational Organized Crime (UNCATOC). At the crux of this definition are the recruitment, transportation, transfer, harbouring or receipt of people, by coercion, abduction, fraud, deception, abuse of POWER or exchanging payments or benefits to achieve the consent of a person having control over another person, for the purpose of EXPLOITATION. The protocol also defines exploitation as forced labour, including prostitution and other forms of sexual employment, servitude, slavery and related practices, and the removal of organs.

Although the protocol makes reference to making or receiving payments and benefits, the fact that people are moved against their will distinguishes trafficking from smuggling. Thus, Article 3, paragraph (a) of the Protocol against the Smuggling of Migrants by Land, Sea and Air – also a supplement to UNCATOC – defines smuggling as procuring, for financial or other material benefit, the illegal entry of people into countries where they are neither a national nor a permanent resident. Other differences include the fact that smuggled migrants arrive at their expected destination and this always involves crossing national borders. Trafficking, on the other hand, is a means of generating ongoing, illicit profit for traffickers and can occur within or between countries.

The fact that migrants are smuggled by criminal syndicates means that their illegal status when they arrive in a country can be used by their smugglers to coerce them into working in the SEX INDUSTRY or in SWEATSHOP conditions. This is especially the case for poorer migrants, who are forced into a form of debt bondage whereby they work in the illegal labour market to pay off exorbitant debts supposedly incurred during their transportation. As part of this exploitative process, their travel or identity documents are taken away and they are threatened with violence, prosecution or deportation if they do not cooperate. Syndicates can also extort money from relatives by threatening to harm or kill their hostages. The richer the migrant the more chance they have of surviving the trip and avoiding exploitative practices.

Victims of trafficking are mostly women and children who have been abducted or exchanged in settlement of disputes, with Afghanistan now a major source of trafficking in girls and women. Victims can also be acquired through fake advertisements for well-paid employment, marriage agencies or through offers of assisted migration. Once under the control of criminal gangs, people are forced into domestic service, illegal sweatshop factory work and prostitution. Insanitary travelling conditions, the sinking of vessels that are not seaworthy, and suffocation in overcrowded or sealed lorries also compromise the safety and welfare of people.

International migration is not new, but the international division of labour equated with GLOBALIZATION and levels of POVERTY in Asia, Africa, South America and Eastern Europe encourage millions of vulnerable people to seek a better standard of living in Australia, Western Europe and North America. Migrants from Asia travel through Kazakhstan, Kyrgyzstan, Uzbekistan, Tajikistan and Turkmenistan to Russia, and then to Ukraine, Slovakia or the Czech Republic before reaching Western Europe. Alternatively, people from Asia travel through Iran and Turkey to the Balkans and on to Western Europe. People from the Middle East and Southern Asia travel to Australia through Malaysia and the southern Indonesian islands of Bali, Flores or Lombok. The USA and Canada are accessed via Central and South America where migrants move through Mexico to North America. Asian migrants, particularly Chinese nationals, also travel to South Africa with fraudulent documents or to Swaziland, Lesotho or Mozambique and continue their journey to the USA and European countries by plane.

Compared to drugs and arms smuggling, criminals involved in human trafficking and smuggling benefit from weak legislation and a relatively low risk of detection, prosecution and arrest. Governments of liberal democracies appear to be more concerned about the perceived security threat of migration than the cost of human suffering that includes denying people the right to freedom of movement, the right to own property and a fair wage. Paradoxically, more restrictive immigration policies and technology used to monitor border-crossing increases the power of smugglers and panders to prejudice, while exacerbating RACISM and social divisions by reinforcing stereotypical ideas about migrants.

Trafficking and smuggling are considered to represent a contemporary form of slavery; see, for example, Christen Van Den Anker, *The Political Economy of New Slavery* (2004), for a discussion of this issue. Organizations like Anti-slavery International, Foundation Against Trafficking in Women, Global Alliance Against Traffic in Women (GAATW) and Payoke campaign against trafficking and offer support to its victims. The GAATW *Human Rights Standards for the Treatment of Trafficked Persons* (1999), for example, is used by interested groups to lobby governments at national, regional and international levels in an attempt to secure human rights protections for trafficked persons and to promote their basic rights.

FURTHER INFORMATION

European legal resource for trafficked women: www.femmigration.net

GAATW: www.gaatw.org

UN information on trafficking: www.unodc.org/unodc/en/trafficking_human_ beings.html

I

IDEOLOGY was first used as a term to describe the study of ideas by Antoine Destutt, Comte de Tracy (1754–1836) towards the end of the eighteenth century. As part of his approach, de Tracy advanced a critique of the social functions of religious thought, building on the materialist perspectives of Claude Helvétius (1715–1771) and Paul Thiry, Baron d'Holbach (1723–1789). These and later developments are analysed by Jorge Larrain, *The Concept of Ideology* (1979), to distinguish between ideology as a positive concept – the science of ideas – and a pejorative term. The first negative use of the term is attributed to Napoléon Bonaparte (1769–1821), who referred to 'ideologists' as those preoccupied with ideas, thereby placing the satisfaction of an ideal above material interests. Karl Marx (1818–1883) and Friedrich Engels (1820–1895) developed the negative connotation, adding a critical character by asserting that ideology is a distortion of thought that stems from, conceals and misrepresents social contradictions.

CULTURE as high art and religion, for example, offers idealized answers to the question of contradictions in a purely abstract manner that misrepresents the nature of the problem and its materialist solution. Similarly, the ideals of EQUALITY, FREEDOM and property are projected onto the legal and political institutions and processes of the STATE. According to this perspective ideology is more than mere false consciousness, because it refers not to all errors, but only to those involving the misrepresentation of societal contradictions. In the late nineteenth and early twentieth centuries the term was given new meanings by thinkers as diverse as sociologists Émile Durkheim (1858–1917) and Max Weber (1864–1920), the revisionist Eduard Bernstein (1850–1932) and revolutionaries Karl Kautsky (1854–1938) and Vladimir (Ulyanov) Lenin (1870–1924). These new meanings lost the critical aspect posed by Marx and interpreted the term variously as a dominant consciousness or way of looking at things, a world-view (*Weltanschauung*) or a complete and self-consistent set of attitudes, beliefs, ideas, logic, science, values and views.

In this respect, Antonio Gramsci (1891–1937), *Prison Notebooks* (1929–35), considered ideology to be a conception of the world that is implicit in art, law, economic activity and individual and collective life. This all-encompassing sphere of influence, through educational institutions and the MEDIA, is considered to be the source of HEGEMONY whereby dominant ideas are inculcated as 'public opinion' or 'common sense'. Bernstein, Kautsky and Lenin, on the other hand, understood MARXISM as ideas and theory about the political practice of class struggle and party organization and therefore an ideology that opposed BOURGEOIS or ruling-class ideology. For Lenin, *What Is To Be Done?* (1902), there is also a link between material experience and the state of class consciousness. Louis Althusser (1918–1990), *Lenin and Philosophy* (1971), therefore offers a distinction between ideology in general, which attempts to unify society, and individual ideologies that have a particular goal, such as the domination of one class.

As a doctrine that combines ideas and theory, ideology is now used to refer to most 'isms' including ANARCHISM, COMMUNISM, fascism, liberalism, MONETARISM, Nazism, NEOLIBERALISM, SOCIALISM and so on. Conversely, however, modern-day anti-capitalism encompasses many theories and traditions and is therefore irreducible to such a conception. Nevertheless, some of its constituents adopt positions and address issues in a manner consistent with some of the definitions outlined above. Ecologists, environmentalists and Greens, for example, seek to raise awareness and consciousness of humanity's role in ecological relationships and advocate solutions to perceived problems. Similarly, opponents of GENETIC ENGINEERING seek to challenge dominant scientific paradigms that prevent challenges and alternative theories or experiments from being heard and conducted. Moreover, governments and the media equate the term 'science' with the right or only viable option, as a means of stifling critical inquiry and thereby concealing contradictory findings.

FURTHER INFORMATION

Anti-capitalist 'belief system' challenge to 'ideology' of free market: www.foei. org/trade/activistguide/index.html

Marx and Engels, *The German Ideology*: www.marxists.org/archive/marx/works/ 1845/german-ideology/index.htm

INDEX OF SUSTAINABLE WELFARE is, like the Genuine Progress Indicator, a method of assessing economic growth that takes into account costs and benefits in an attempt to measure well-being and the potential for sustainable development. See also GROSS DOMESTIC PRODUCT.

INDIGENOUS PEOPLE, communities and nations are defined by José Martinez Cobo, *Study of the Problem of Discrimination Against Indigenous Populations* (1987), as 'those which, having historical continuity with pre-invasion and pre-colonial societies that developed on their territories, consider themselves distinct from other sectors of societies now prevailing on their territories or parts of them'. The International Labour Organization, *Convention Concerning Indigenous and Tribal Peoples in Independent Countries* (1989), also lists social, cultural and economic conditions, customs, traditions, special laws and regulations as defining characteristics.

The terms 'aboriginal', 'first', 'native' and 'tribal' people are used as synonyms for 'indigenous', as are 'first nation' and 'Indian'. Usage varies according to time and place, however, with first nations defined in Canada as people who are registered under An Act Respecting Indians, which was adopted in 1876 and amended in 1985. In the USA, the term 'Native American' is used together with 'Amerindian', while the latter is also applied to indigenous people throughout the continent, as are their Portuguese and Spanish equivalents. Meanwhile, colonists have used the word 'Aboriginal' since the eighteenth century to categorize Australian people, although the Koori and others prefer names that reflect their language.

There is hardly a modern country that does not include at least one group of indigenous people. In addition to the examples referred to above, Basque people live in Spain and France, Celts in the British Isles, Frisians in Germany and the Netherlands, the Komi and Sakha people control autonomous republics within Russia, Sami live across Scandinavia, and Wends in Germany and Poland. On the African continent, Maasai people inhabit Kenya and Tanzania, Ogiek are also in Kenya, and the Nuba live in Egypt and Sudan. In Asia, examples occur in India, Indonesia, Irian Jaya, Japan, Malaysia, Papua New Guinea and Tibet, while in Latin America Argentina, Bolivia, Brazil, the Caribbean, Chile, Guatemala, Paraguay, Peru and Venezuela share a variety of indigenous populations. Elsewhere, Kurds are to be found within the boundaries of Georgia, Iran, Iraq, Syria and Turkey.

Each people have their own history, language, laws, traditions and values that govern decision-making, land use, medicine, property ownership, religious ceremonies, social responsibilities, water rights and work. The survival of these distinguishing features has faced a variety of challenges, which generally began with military conquest and colonization, as described by Ken Coates, *A Global History of Indigenous Peoples* (2004). In the USA during the nineteenth and early twentieth centuries, for example, military force

123

was used to confine Native Americans in reservations, a process of domination and marginalization that continues to be reinforced in the twenty-first century with the naming of military hardware after native people and their weapons. Indeed, observers noted the irony, during the war on Serbia in 1999, that hardware named after people who had themselves been ethnically cleansed was used to prevent similar atrocities in Kosovo. Across the Americas, the effects of genocide and massacre were also exacerbated by the introduction of new diseases, which had similarly devastating effects on indigenous people.

The development of cattle and sheep stations in Australia also served to destroy indigenous ways of life that were closely associated with the land and seasons. Similar processes are still at work today in the Andean highlands and the Amazon, where the introduction of industrial agriculture and BIOTECHNOLOGY is threatening generations of coexistence with the environment, as is creeping, corporate control of the food supply through BIOPIRACY. Actions such as the government of Botswana expelling people from the Kalahari in 2002 are often justified in the name of economic progress, processes explored by Blaser, Feit and McRae, *In the Way of Development* (2004). More often, the real reason is to allow mining and extraction corporations to gain access to mineral and oil deposits, or logging to take place, and the financial backer of such projects is quite often the WORLD BANK.

Attempts at assimilation and discrimination take many forms and include the practices of Christian missionaries, conservationists and guerrilla armies. Governments have also outlawed native languages and religion and implemented drastic initiatives, some of which are discussed by David Wallace Adams, *Education for Extinction* (1995), and Rosalie Fraser, *Shadow Child* (1999), and include forced adoption, sterilization and termination. Alternatively, building on the concept of Terra Nullius – that lands not recognized as having a form of government compatible with European standards were eligible for colonization – Britain effectively ignored the RIGHTS of native Australian people by not including them in census counts until 1967. On a commercial level, native art, including carving, painting, pottery and weaving, has since been commoditized and so the original mythic and other purposes have been subsumed into the world of capitalist value.

A number of movements and organizations are involved in struggles to combat the negative effects of invading and prevailing societies, especially the denial of indigenous people's right to self-determination – that is, how and where they live. The National Liberation Zapatista Army (Ejército

Zapatista de Liberación Nacional) or ZAPATISTAS, for example, frame their campaign in terms of combating discrimination against the people of Chiapas and the neoliberal agenda represented by the NORTH AMERICAN FREE TRADE AGREEMENT. Likewise the National Liberation Army (Ejército de Liberación Nacional) of Bolivia encompass a number of indigenous interests, most recently the campaign to renationalize Bolivian gas reserves. Other campaigning groups include the Convergence of Peoples of the Americas, the aims of which include empowerment of indigenous people and changing policy related to development, militarization and peace. Similar aims are shared by the Confederation of Indigenous Nationalities of Ecuador, which also campaigns for plurinational government.

On the Internet GreenNet provides services to indigenous networks in Africa and Asia. On the ground, groups like Genetic Resources Action International, Food First, Rainforest Action Network, Survival International and Third World Network support struggles to guarantee land and develop ecologically sustainable initiatives based on traditional knowledge and practices. Though the Brazilian Landless Rural Workers' Movement (Movimento dos Trabalhadores Rurais Sem Terra) is not overtly an indigenous movement, the issues it addresses include the inequities of corporate monopolization of agriculture that impacts upon people in the region.

FURTHER INFORMATION

Resources and facts: www.cwis.org; www.elandnet.org; www.ghostchild.com; www.nativeweb.org; www.survival-international.org

INTELLECTUAL PROPERTY is equivalent to the physical form of PRIVATE PROPERTY in so far as it is designed to allow people to own aspects of their mental creativity and innovation – images, inventions, literary and artistic work, names, symbols and so forth – and therefore trade them as commodities. In this way, an individual can apply for an idea to be registered as their property and thereby have their ownership protected in the form of an intellectual property right. Broadly speaking, intellectual property falls into two groups: industrial property and COPYRIGHT. The former includes geographical indications of source, industrial designs for commodity appearance, patents for inventions, trademarks for brand identity and trade secrets. Whereas copyright covers literary and artistic work such as architectural design, drawings, films, music, novels, paintings, photographs, plays, poems and sculpture.

The precise timing of the introduction of intellectual property rights is unclear but probably originated with the granting of patents in the fifteenth century. In England, for example, Henry VI granted John of Utynam a monopoly on his method of making stained glass in 1449, and the Venetian Statute of 1474 made provisions to grant similar privileges to manufacturers and traders. Similarly, the English Statute of Anne, 1710, is usually recognized as the basis of copyright, while the Designing and Printing of Linen Act of 1787 is considered to have introduced the concept of industrial design rights. Meanwhile, the term 'intellectual property' is variously attributed to Alfred Nion, *Droits Civils des Auteurs, Artistes et Inventeurs* (1846).

The concept of intellectual property is a distinct form of private property since, if the notion is taken at face value, it does not require physical capital – other than the creator's actual existence – in order for an idea to be created. The rights to it are not regarded as fundamental and available to every citizen, however, but are granted by some authority so that a person has an exclusive right to sell or license the right to use their creation. As the only seller of that particular commodity, they then benefit from a government-granted monopoly. In reality, ideas are not produced in a vacuum; rather, they are inspired and produced from other concepts. How far, for example, can or should an individual or CORPORATION appropriate traditional knowledge and folklore and why should a corporation be recognized as the creator and owner of the creative work of their employees?

Critics like Michael Perelman, *Steal this Idea* (2004), see the ownership of ideas as inhibiting creativity and ask the question whether a truly civilized society would value human creativity as an end in itself rather than presenting financial gain as the only tangible reward. Controversy rages, therefore, over the practice of pharmaceuticals corporations that use patents to protect price levels of certain drugs, so much so that governments and people in the developing world cannot afford them. Likewise, corporations involved in GENETIC ENGINEERING are accused of BIOPIRACY for using patents to own seeds, plants and genetic codes that farmers and traditional communities previously held in common, while ownership of the human genome is set to remain a live issue.

While there is an element of irony in the categorization of Barbie and Disney as examples of intellectual property, Carlos Correa, *Intellectual Property Rights* (2000), argues that international treaties like TRADE-RELATED INTELLECTUAL PROPERTY RIGHTS (TRIPS) exist in order to make sure that countries like China and India conform. Furthermore, corporations adopt a collectivist approach that they normally deny to others, when they join with similarly interested parties, as in the case of the Business Software Alliance and the Recording Industry Association of America. In this way, they regulate the market in ideas to protect prices, while the market in people – the labour market – is deregulated in order to keep the cost of labour, in the form of wages, to a minimum.

FURTHER INFORMATION

Brief history and associated links: www.boycott-riaa.com/article/print/9699
Civil liberties and digital information: ipjustice.org
Resource guide: www.eldis.org/ipr

INTERNATIONAL BANK FOR RECONSTRUCTION AND DEVELOPMENT see WORLD BANK.

INTERNATIONAL DEBT, also known as external or third world debt, is largely a problem faced by developing countries. Roughly speaking, the Debt Channel locates the origins of the current crisis in the 1970s when banks flush with petro-dollars – following increases in the price of oil in 1973 – began lending to developing countries. Today, lenders fall in to three categories: international institutions like the INTERNATIONAL MONETARY FUND (IMF), the WORLD BANK and regional development banks; governments like those of the USA, Britain, Japan and France – the Paris Club; and international commercial institutions like Citibank. Around 45 per cent of developing countries' debt is multilateral and therefore falls in the first category. A further 45 per cent belongs to the second and is classed as bilateral debt. The remaining 10 per cent is commercial. Initially, money was borrowed by developing countries (ostensibly) to finance development programmes. More recently borrowing became necessary in order to finance the repayment of existing debt. In 2000, for example, the Dakar Conference issued a Declaration, which estimated that since 1988 65 per cent of the increase in the sub-Saharan African debt was due to arrears on amortization and capitalized interests.

Much of the original lending took place during the years of the cold war between the Soviet Union and the capitalist West, when securing and cementing allegiances was considered to be more important than the moral standing or creditworthiness of recipients. This means that some countries are now saddled with debt accrued by previous despotic and dictatorial regimes that used the money to undertake symbolic projects designed to glorify themselves and bought military equipment to use against their subjects and neighbours. In South Africa, for example, the Campaign against Neoliberalism in South Africa notes that an external debt of US$18 billion was inherited from the apartheid regime. Other cases like Iraq, the Philippines and Zaire – now the Democratic Republic of Congo – saw money siphoned off by corrupt leaders and officials for personal gain, often with the complicity of lenders. Campaigners like DATA, 50 Years is Enough, the Jubilee Debt Campaign and World Development Movement consider such debt immoral – due to the way it was accumulated and because repayments are made at the expense of addressing fundamental human needs like shortfalls in health, literacy, education, nutrition and food security.

Even today, military spending and ethnic and civil conflicts are maintained by foreign loans at the expense of social spending and productive investments. Susan George, *The Debt Boomerang* (1991), for example, sees the issue of debt as a human, political and social problem that impacts on industrialized and developing countries, as opposed to a financial or technical issue for creditors. According to War on Want, governments in Africa spend nearly three times more on external debt than they do on health services and thereby transfer more resources to developed countries than they receive in the form of aid. External debt is therefore considered to represent the largest obstacle to growth and SUSTAINABLE DEVELOPMENT and an impediment to governments that want to address the AIDS crisis with schemes that prevent infection, care for those who are ill or help sustain affected communities. In broader terms, repayment of original loans and accrued interest limits a willing government's ability to spend on health, education, welfare and development projects and therefore exacerbates existing levels of POVERTY and environmental devastation. Thus, even where an amount equivalent to or greater than the original debt has been paid, repayment of interest remains an important mechanism for transferring assets and wealth from the people of sovereign indebted nations to international creditors in the developed world.

For some campaigners, debt is an integral part of a neoliberal framework that includes multilateral trade and financial agreements administered by the IMF, the World Bank and the WORLD TRADE ORGANIZATION (WTO) in the interests of the G8 countries and multinational corporations. With debt structure beyond the control of developing countries, creditors use the burden of debt as a mechanism to impose policies consistent with their interests and therefore exert control over developing countries in a new form of debt bondage, indenture, peonage or slavery. In this respect, it is not in the interests of the World Bank, the IMF and G8 governments to cancel debt, but instead to offer the prospects of refinancing or limited debt relief to those countries that are prepared to accept conditions. Invariably, this means STRUCTURAL ADJUSTMENT PROGRAMMES (SAPs) and euphemistic Poverty Reduction Strategy Papers (PRSPs), which exacerbate socio-economic problems through the imposition of deflationary economic policies that elevate the RIGHTS of foreign creditors over those of citizens and remove policy autonomy from sovereign governments. Debt campaigners therefore add their voices to calls for the democratization and transformation of the World Bank and the IMF to make them and the international financial activities of sovereign governments more transparent and accountable to citizens. They also join demands to promote a framework of JUSTICE for relations between sovereign debtors and international creditors by scrapping SAPs and PRSPs and creating multilateral agencies that serve the interests of social and economic justice as opposed to those of international financial institutions and MULTINATIONAL CORPORATIONS.

Cancellation of debt is proposed as a first step towards developing policies for financing development in a more self-reliant way, without recourse to dependency on foreign donors and creditors, and building equitable and just relationships between and within different parts of the world. Nevertheless, there are different opinions over how this should take place, questions that are addressed by Damien Millet, Eric Toussaint and Vicki Briault Manus, *Who Owes Who?* (2004). Proposals range from debt cancellation without conditions to an insistence that cancellation be dependent on clear, budgeted programmes approved by CIVIL SOCIETY in the indebted countries so that money previously allotted to debt repayment is used to fight poverty, advance social and economic justice and fund sustainable development projects. Proposals for funding such a process include using positive net capital and assets held by those institutions that supervised and benefited from lending, and using the proceeds of a TOBIN TAX. Other proposed contingencies include taking account of the ecological impact of debt, such as the effect of projects funded by loans and environmental damage incurred in order to finance repayment, as well as other ecological debts identified as part of the KYOTO PROTOCOL. Campaigners therefore advocate repayment of the North's ecological debts to countries of the South either in the form of debt

129

cancellation or in kind by developing and funding retrospective action as well as environmentally sustainable policies and projects for the future.

FURTHER INFORMATION

Global portal: www.debtchannel.org
Global resource: www.debtlinks.org
Jubilee Framework: www.jubileeplus.org/analysis/reports/jubilee_framework.html

INTERNATIONAL MONETARY FUND (IMF) was set up as a specialist agency of the UNITED NATIONS following the Bretton Woods conference of 1944, is sometimes referred to as 'the Fund' and is based in the US capital, Washington DC. Together with the WORLD BANK, the IMF is responsible for implementing the BRETTON WOODS SYSTEM, the terms of which serve as its charter. Originally covering 39 countries, membership now stands at 184 and each country is represented on a board of governors that meets once a year. While an International Monetary and Finance Committee consisting of 24 governors meets twice each year, the day-to-day operation is undertaken by a 24-member Executive Board and a staff of around 2,700 people. The IMF is funded by it members on a quota basis that is designed to reflect the economic strength of individual contributors, and contribution size determines voting rights. As the world's largest economy and the IMF's largest contributor, for example, the USA controls about 20 per cent of the votes. The main role and responsibilities of the IMF relate to the regulation of the international monetary and financial system and are set out in its Articles of Agreement. These can be summarized as promoting a cooperative international monetary system by monitoring national economic policies to avoid conflicts of interest and overseeing monetary relations between nations to ensure stability in private financial flows, balance of payments, multilateral payments and exchange rate systems. The overriding aim of this global mechanism is to ensure that a balanced and stable growth of international trade can take place in perpetuity.

Three main devices are employed by the IMF, supposedly, to prevent economic crises. The first is called 'surveillance' and involves appraising member countries' economic situation, their policies relating to exchange rates and growth, combined with regular dialogue and policy advice. A *World Economic Outlook* and a *Global Financial Stability Report* are also published twice a year and assess global and regional developments and prospects. Technical assistance and training are similarly provided to member countries so that they are able to adopt 'suitable' fiscal, monetary and exchange rate policies, operate appropriate supervision and regulation of banking and financial systems, and collect and publish relevant statistics.

Perhaps the most obvious function, or the best known, is the IMF's lending role in making resources available to member countries that experience balance-of-payments difficulties. Bridging finance is provided so that problems can be corrected through a policy programme agreed between national authorities and the IMF, and further financial support is only given on condition that the programme is implemented. Perhaps less well known is the Fund's provision of financial support through concessional lending – the Poverty Reduction and Growth Facility – and a debt relief initiative for Heavily Indebted Poor Countries. As of June 2003, for example, loans outstanding amounted to US$107 billion, involved 56 countries – 38 of which enjoyed concessional terms. Such financial support is often accompanied by Poverty Reduction Strategy Papers that are agreed between national governments, CIVIL SOCIETY and external development partners and implemented to provide a comprehensive economic, structural and social policy framework that is intended to produce growth and thereby reduce poverty.

Although this general description of the IMF's role and responsibilities gives the impression of consistency, it conceals important changes in approach that broadly correspond to a shift from KEYNESIAN to neoliberal prescriptions. Until the 1976 Jamaica Conference, when the Articles of Agreement were changed, the Fund's role as the main source of liquidity to facilitate international trade had been based on a fixed exchange rate mechanism. This meant that short-term loans made in US dollars were granted if a country was experiencing balance-of-payments problems and was short of foreign exchange, so as to avoid a disruption in domestic macroeconomic policy, international monetary instability and protectionism. Although national governments were free to adopt deflationary policies designed to reduce domestic demand, the main goals of technical assistance and training involved fiscal tightening and devaluation at moderate socio-economic cost, but not removal of capital controls.

A change from fixed to floating exchange rate policy took place in the 1970s and was accompanied by the use of high real interest rates to protect national currencies on foreign exchange markets and attempts to improve balance of payments by encouraging export-led growth. In other words, the DEREGULATION of a country's trade regime – removing trade-related subsidies and import licensing that favour domestic corporations – and reduction of WORKERS' RIGHTS to create flexibility are intended to attract foreign investment. This process is also combined with financial sector deregulation, which includes opening capital accounts to allow the free inflow and outflow of investment and removing or loosening controls on companies' foreign borrowings – thereby abandoning the coordination of borrowings and investments. Further measures include the PRIVATIZATION of state-owned assets and a reduction in government spending, particularly on social and welfare programmes, in order to dampen domestic demand and to restore the capacity to repay foreign debts.

Critics like David Felix, *IMF Bailouts and Global Financial Flows* (1998), argue that this change in direction has created self-perpetuating problems. Removing controls on CAPITAL FLOWS, for example, is considered to contradict the thinking behind Bretton Woods and to have contributed to financial crises that, in turn, exposed a level of underfunding that left the IMF unable to make loans necessary to cover the volume of capital flows it had encouraged. The IMF has therefore been charged with being incapable of meeting its responsibilities outlined in Article One, because it actively flouted Article Four of its own Articles of Agreement – which, among other things, forbade lending to cover capital flight. As a consequence, the Fund relied on the support of international banks so that it was able to lend to countries in trouble, and the banks demanded financial deregulation as a condition of their cooperation. What is more, because loans are made in US dollars, the interests and preoccupations of American banks and the US Treasury are equated with such policy developments. From the 1980s onward, therefore, the IMF has been seen as a debt management agency, coordinating lending to allow debt repayment. The Fund also stands accused of using its influence with prospective foreign investors as a lever to introduce STRUCTURAL ADJUSTMENT PROGRAMMES (SAPs) and impose other conditions on borrowers – also known as 'conditionalities' – in the guise of technical assistance and training.

Operating in this way, the IMF is viewed as directing economic policies – especially in developing countries that have a historical dependence on loans – and therefore undermining national sovereignty by elevating the RIGHTS of foreign creditors over those of citizens, overriding democratic mandates, and removing policy autonomy from sovereign governments. Perhaps the most damning are allegations that the IMF is no longer involved in preventing crises, but only in controlling them once they have occurred. Critics therefore point to a contradiction, whereby the idea of market infallibility is promoted, but the logic of this argument is not allowed to run its course when the markets inevitably fail. In other words, IMF bail-outs do not allow markets to balance, but have the effect of absolving international financial markets and banking of responsibility by providing a security net to investors and speculators – as in Southeast Asia in 1997 and Argentina at the start of the twenty-first century. Preventing market sanctions from taking effect is therefore considered to encourage speculation, the granting of risky loans and unsustainable behaviour, while remedial SAPs penalize otherwise innocent citizens.

FURTHER INFORMATION

Argentinean crisis: www.fpif.org/papers/argentina2.html
Critical Network: www.50years.org
Official site: www.imf.org

INTERNATIONALISM, although usually associated with ANARCHISM, SOCIALISM and COMMUNISM, the principle of international fraternity, rather than sorority, was proclaimed during the first period of the French Revolution 1789–91 and reflected themes popular during the Enlightenment. In general terms, the ideal recognizes that people have common interests as human beings regardless of nationality and promotes solidarity as a means of realizing those interests. If nationalism is defined as principles or programmes based on a devotion to nation, then internationalism can be understood as a devotion to humanity that places shared identity among individual human beings over and above national identities. Such ideas range from the 'world society' view that advocates the elimination of nation-states and nationalities, to the view that the long-term mutual interests of greater economic and political cooperation between nations outweigh individual short-term needs. The latter stance recognizes all nations as equal and that each has a right to self-determination. The success of either is premised on a maximum level of openness and interdependence, and examples of international cooperation include regional subsystems like the European Union, postcolonial associations like the British Commonwealth and the UNITED NATIONS.

Although an Anarchist international existed 1872–81 and the Anarcho-Syndicalist International Workers Association has survived from 1922 until the present day, Karl Marx (1818–1883) and Friedrich Engels (1820–1895) are credited with the development of 'proletarian internationalism' and thereby adding a class base to the idea of human brotherhood. Established in 1864,

133

the International Working Men's Association (IWMA) constitutes the first attempt to unite international opponents of capitalism. The body included followers of Louis Blanqui (1805–1881), Ferdinand Lassalle (1825–1864), Marx, Giuseppe Mazzini (1805–1872), Robert Owen (1771–1858), Joseph Proudhon (1809–1865), as well as Chartists and Irish and Polish nationalists. The General Rules of the IWMA, written in 1871, stated that it was founded 'to afford a central medium of communication and cooperation between working men's societies existing in different countries'. The purpose was to counteract the divisive nature of nationalism that allowed capitalists to act in their own interests as they competed for resources, a process considered a root cause of war and imperialism. Although a universal system, CAPITALISM is considered to use nationhood as a form of divide and rule to prevent the development of worldwide opposition. In idealist terms, the alternative was to leave the borders and divisions of nations behind and move forward to a truly global and united humanity, without bigotry, war and class division.

The absence of a shared vision of how society should be organized, let alone the method of achieving societal change, resulted in sectional infighting, the expulsion of Mikhail Bakunin (1814–1876) and his followers in 1872 and the disbanding of the organization in 1876. A resurrected IWMA, reformed in 1889, eventually foundered when some of its constituents elected to support national efforts during the build up to World War I, though a descendant still exists today as the Socialist International. The Communist International, formed in 1919, adopted a list of conditions for membership and argued that the interests of proletarian struggle in any one country should be subordinated to the interests of the struggle worldwide; as outlined by Vladimir (Ulyanov) Lenin (1870–1924), *Theses on Fundamental Tasks* (1920). Under Stalin's leadership, the Communist Party of the Soviet Union (CPSU, Kommunisticheskaya Partiya Sovetskogo Soyuza) replaced internationalism with the policy of 'socialism in one country'. Jonathan Valdez traces these and other developments in *Internationalism and the Ideology of Soviet Influence* (1993), including the exercise of autocratic, centralized control over affiliated parties that resulted in a series of contradictory U-turns in the struggle against Fascism and Nazism during the 1930s.

A Fourth International founded by Leon (Lev Bronstein) Trotsky (1879–1940) in 1938 is still in existence, but is blighted by doctrinal sectarianism and bears little comparison to today's anti-capitalist coalitions. The Communist International was abandoned in 1943. Although the CPSU maintained the pretence of proletarian internationalism, from the late 1960s it once again became a reason for allied Communist parties to practise an uncritical acceptance of Soviet policies and activities. Such activity left some disillusioned, but a 'new internationalism' was developed by the Communist Party of Italy (Partito Communista Italiano) and Eurocommunists in general. This new movement advocated establishing links with other progressive organizations, such as communists, socialists, social democrats, liberation movements in the developing world and wider sections of world opinion around the defence of 'universal human values' – a concept and practice that is not dissimilar to those of the SOCIAL FORUM, which forms part of today's anti-capitalist movement.

Internationalism is also a feature of a wider movement that is not opposed to globalization per se, but one in which participants recognize that the realization of ends and goals different to capitalist GLOBALIZATION requires links between activists and causes in and between nations in the industrialized and developing worlds. The Global Greens Conference held in 2001 is a prime example. Opposition to the globalization of corporate culture and practice through the use of branding, patents and trade agreements that destroy local traditions and autonomy is also based on a mutual solidarity between those seeking alternatives. Some activists propose that the United Nations constitutes the basis of a new form of world government that is not dominated by the interests of multinational corporations and banks. Others like the Tax Justice Network call for the creation of a democratic global forum to investigate specific issues, and 50 Years is Enough call for the reform of unaccountable institutions like the INTERNATIONAL MONETARY FUND and the WORLD TRADE ORGANIZATION.

Moreover, the advent of the Internet has allowed activists and organizations across the globe to NETWORK and communicate in ways and at speeds that were previously impossible, a development partially explored in *The Labour Movement and the Internet* (1996) by Eric Lee.

FURTHER INFORMATION

Anarcho-Syndicalist International: www.iwa-ait.org
Fourth International: www.wsws.org
Global Greens Conference: www.global.greens.org.au/entrance.html
Socialist International: www.socialistinternational.org

J

JUSTICE is usually defined as a standard of fairness or balance within a society or collective and, as such, constitutes an ethical or moral code for the evaluation and determination of benefits and burdens, punishment and reward. John Rawls (1921–2002), *A Theory of Justice* (1971), for example, provides the classic twentieth-century liberal definition of the concept. As with any value judgement, however, the criteria used to define or measure what counts as justice vary from epoch to epoch and society to society. Similar differences in interpretation pertain to the understanding of what is meant by the subdivisions of criminal, distributive, economic, environmental, natural and social justice; so too the distinctions between their procedural and substantive applications.

The notions of due process, criminal and natural justice are inextricably linked as juridical principles, even though the standards of natural justice are held to pertain regardless of whether legal and political institutions exist to administer them. Where such arrangements are present, legal procedures are only considered to be fair if certain requirements are met. These include: a separation of the state apparatuses that make and administer laws; impartial judicial personnel and proceedings; notification of the charges faced; the right to cross-examine witnesses; the right to legal representation and to challenge the composition of a jury. Such proceedings are expected to take place in public and, because they apply to all involved, all are considered to be afforded equality before the law.

In contrast, the notions of distributive, economic and social justice exist because people are treated unequally in everyday life. There are also examples where due process does not apply and the reality of criminal justice as an instrument of social control is laid bare. These include the British Diplock courts in the province of Northern Ireland ('the North' to the Republican movement) during the latter third of the twentieth century and the prisoners held by the USA at Guantánamo Bay. Various countries have also passed legislation in the wake of the atrocities that took place in New York in September 2001, to allow people suspected of **TERRORISM** to be held indefinitely, without charge or being informed of the accusations against them.

At a procedural level, the rights of EQUALITY and justice are prescribed in the UNIVERSAL DECLARATION OF HUMAN RIGHTS, but this does not guarantee that its principles are put into practice, or that there will be a degree of consistency where they are applied. Similarly, the ideal of distributive justice – 'to each their due' (*suum cuique*) – possesses a potential for disagreement about what constitutes a fair and proper division of desert, entitlement, needs and rights. Once again, the criteria used to decide what represents a fair distribution of goods are selected according to a value system and such expectations are conditioned by the capitalist mode of production. Thus Rawls argued that wage differentials were necessary incentives that encouraged people to serve a social good, whereas anarchists and communists see ideals of fairness, in relation to the distribution of wages and profits, as mediated by the ownership of the productive forces and by practical concerns like conflict and scarcity.

Ideas about compensation as a means of restoring balance through the punishment of offenders are founded on the principle of distributive justice, but have been used recently to justify legal claims for financial recompense, thereby implying that the allocation of money provides a solution to all ills. A broader understanding of the ways in which distributive justice is and can be practised informs the concept of social justice. The introduction of the term is attributed to Luigi Taparelli d'Azeglio (1793–1862) in 1840 and promulgated by Antonio Rosmini-Serbati (1797–1855), *The Constitution of Social Justice* (*La costitutione civile secondo la giustizia sociale*) (1848). As all forms of justice are a social convention, the term is something of a misnomer and is therefore sometimes referred to as civil justice.

While distributive and social justice are both concerned with just outcomes, the latter associates the virtue of justice with pursuit and realization of common good in material terms – which is explored by David Cohen, Rosa de la Vega and Gabrielle Watson, *Advocacy for Social Justice* (2001). Understood thus, the concept forms the basis of a social contract whereby people accept and are accepted for membership of a social group knowing that they will contribute to and benefit from conditions of social cooperation that ensure the functions of common existence are fulfilled and balanced. In other words, all persons are entitled to satisfy their basic human needs for food, clothing and shelter, as opposed to a simple redistribution of consumer goods, as the basis for healthy personal development and self-realization. As a form of due process that meets the requirements of fairness and balance, entitlement is universal and therefore excludes divisions based on age, CLASS, disability, ethnicity, gender, race, **RELIGION** or sexual orientation in the goal of eliminating **POVERTY** and illiteracy.

As with other notions of justice, however, the definition of need is open to interpretation; so too questions of how to distribute surplus. Criteria used as measures of justice in the economy also range from the abolition of all forms of **EXPLOITATION** and oppression to minimum wage demands and the acceptance of wage differentials as incentives and rewards for some form of merit. As the International Labour Organization, *Organizing for Social Justice* (2004), demonstrates, however, expectations and goals can also reflect perceptions of what can be achieved according to circumstance. The concept therefore covers both capitalist and anti-capitalist demands, the latter of which seek collective ownership and distribution of all wealth generated by industries and services of society based on the open, democratic, participatory and accountable organization of society as a defence against tyranny, prejudice and the abuse of **POWER**.

In environmental terms, the Four Pillars of the Green Party and organizations like Earth Island Institute and People *&* Planet portray ecological sustainability and social justice as inextricably linked. This involves the establishment of sound environmental policy and the formation and promotion of cultural, economic and social structures that can be sustained without knowingly damaging ecosystems; local examples of which are surveyed by Paul Wolvekamp, Ann Usher, Vijay Paranjpye and Madhu Ramnath, *Forests for the Future* (1999). Other groups like 50 Years is Enough see the elimination or reform of the **INTERNATIONAL MONETARY FUND**, the **WORLD BANK** and the **WORLD TRADE ORGANIZATION** as a precondition of the realization of global economic, political and social justice. Meanwhile, Food First and the Trade Justice Movement see the area of **TRADE** as fundamental to the goal of realizing a fair distribution of wealth and resources between the developing and industrialized worlds.

FURTHER INFORMATION

Information, analysis and research: www.datacenter.org
Centre for Economic Justice: www.econjustice.net
Socialist Alliance statement on social justice and ecological sustainability: www.cpgb.org.uk/worker/254/lg_statement.html

K

KEYNESIAN is a term that is used to refer to the economic and social theory advocated in or derived from the works of John Maynard Keynes (1883–1946) – whether directly or through other thinkers like J.K. Galbraith, Joan Robinson (1903–1983) and Piero Sraffa (1898–1983). In his principal work, *General Theory of Employment, Interest and Money* (1936), Keynes promotes government intervention in the economy, at a macro-economic level, in order to avoid slumps and inflationary booms. Among other things, this involves injecting money into the economy during a slump through lower taxes and interest rates, together with expanded credit and public works in order to increase purchasing power and stimulate demand. During inflationary periods the opposite measures would be adopted in order to curtail demand. As part of this strategy full employment – as a means of perpetuating demand and social stability – and a stable EXCHANGE RATE were considered to be integral factors in securing sustained economic growth and the perpetuation of CAPITALISM.

Aspects of Keynes's approach were implemented in response to the 1930s' depression in the USA as part of the Roosevelt administration's 'New Deal' programme; the success of which led to their acceptance and practice in most capitalist countries after World War II. In contrast, those economists considered by Andrew Gumbel, *How the War Machine is Driving the US Economy* (2004), refer to the Bush administration's attempts to stimulate the economy through the MILITARY–INDUSTRIAL COMPLEX as 'military Keynesianism'. The reluctance of CORPORATIONS to increase productive investment contributed to economic stagnation and higher inflation during the 1970s, however, thereby creating the appeal of MONETARISM, or at least aspects of it, for governments and institutions in industrialized countries from the 1980s onward.

FURTHER INFORMATION

The General Theory: www.marxists.org/reference/subject/economics/keynes/
   general-theory

KYOTO PROTOCOL, adopted in December 1997, is the main international agreement on how to deal with climate change (GLOBAL WARMING). The Protocol represents the culmination of a process that began in 1979 with the first World Climate Conference and included the creation of the Intergovernmental Panel on Climate Change (IPCC) in 1990. Based on the United Nations Framework Convention on Climate Change (UNFCCC) – signed at the 1992 Earth Summit in Brazil – signatories agree to start reducing greenhouse gas emissions – carbon dioxide (CO_2) methane (CH_4), nitrous oxide ($N_{2}o$), hydrofluorocarbons (HFCs), perfluorocarbons (PFCs) and sulphur hexafluoride (SF_6). In the first instance, signatories are expected to show that they have made 'demonstrable progress' by 2005. After that, developing countries are not obliged to take any action, but industrialized countries are required to reduce their carbon emissions between 2008 and 2012 by an amount equal to 5.2 per cent of their 1990 emissions.

By setting different standards for developing and industrialized countries the Protocol recognizes that developing nations have lower per capita emissions than their industrialized counterparts and therefore would have to sacrifice economic growth to achieve the same level of cuts. Likewise, this involves a recognition that industrialized countries have contributed to the present problem in terms of past emissions. For the Protocol to be activated, however, 55 Parties to the Convention had to ratify it and that number had to include enough industrialized nations listed in Annex One to account for 55 per cent of CO_2 emissions in 1990. Problems arose because the USA, which accounted for 36 per cent of the emissions in 1990, opposes ratification, as does Australia. The USA and some other countries are even opposed to non-binding targets for increasing the use of wind and solar power, while the European Union and some developing countries favour targets. In September 2004, the Russian government started the process of ratification, which once completed saw the protocol become effective for the 141 signatories on 16 February 2005.

The Protocol consists of three main mechanisms that allow industrialized countries to purchase emission credits from other countries and therefore avoid reducing levels of emissions at home. Article 17, for example, makes provision for International (carbon) Emissions Trading (IET), so that a country that has achieved emissions reductions over and above those required by their Kyoto target can sell their excess to countries with emissions levels that are over target. Article 6 covers Joint Implementation (JI) programmes whereby a country can obtain emission credits for projects they undertake to reduce emissions in another. Finally, Article 12 promotes Clean Development Mechanisms (CDMs) as a way of industrialized countries investing in clean technology projects to reduce greenhouse gas emissions in developing countries. Both the JI and CDM mechanisms include the concept of 'carbon sinks' as systems in the BIOSPHERE, such as forests and oceans, which are the reverse of emission sources because they store CO_2, the main greenhouse gas. Industrialized countries can therefore obtain credits by assisting in reforestation schemes or similar projects, while countries with large forests or those willing to plant forests can count their carbon-storing capacity when calculating their emissions and thereby meet targets without actually reducing carbon emissions in their own countries. Russia, for example, has been given a large forest management sinks allowance.

Environmentalists, Friends of the Earth (FOE), Greenpeace and like-minded organizations have expressed serious reservations about the efficacy of the Protocol's provisions. Some consider the 5.2 per cent target for emissions reductions to be too little to avoid global warming and argue that it will merely slow the rise in average world temperature. By 2010, for example, FOE, *The Politics of Climate Change* (2000), expect levels of CO_2 in the atmosphere to have increased by 8 per cent on 1990 levels and only be around half a percentage point lower even if all the Kyoto targets were achieved. Furthermore, the fact that emissions are rising makes the Protocol targets harder to achieve, with the developed countries as a whole needing to reduce emissions by about 20 per cent. Critics therefore consider the Kyoto agreement to be a political deal rather than a real attempt to address the issue of climate change, arguing that emission reductions in the order of 80 per cent are needed to counter global warming and climate change. Thus, the Earth Summit on Sustainable Development held in Johannesburg, South Africa, in September 2002 is accused of voting for a compromise declaration that was acceptable to pro-Kyoto countries and to those that oppose it. Furthermore, Kevin Baumert, *Building on the Kyoto Protocol* (2003), argues that, in the long term, alternative measures need to be developed.

The value of balancing reductions in emissions with the natural carbon cycle, whereby a figure is calculated for the amount of CO_2 absorbed and stored from the atmosphere in agricultural land, forests, grasslands and oceans, is also challenged by environmentalists. Whereas carbon in the form of fossil fuels – coal, gas and oil – can be left unused or untapped, critics of the Kyoto Protocol argue that calculating the amount of CO_2 stored in sinks is arbitrary and difficult due to the complexity of reporting and accounting for sinks' activities. Not only does it take years for new sink developments to mature, but changes of land use, fire, deforestation, decomposition or ploughing of agricultural land all release CO_2 into the atmosphere. Without adequate reporting mechanisms for sink credit activities, conducted within a universally agreed framework, FOE and others argue, credits will be allowed in error and thereby lead to higher fossil fuel emissions and unknown amounts of CO_2 entering the atmosphere. In other words, if a tonne of carbon counted as a sink is calculated in error, but traded with an industrialized country to allow them to emit a tonne of CO_2, then an equivalent increase in emissions has been allowed.

While the Johannesburg Earth Summit of 2002 agreed to enforceable rules on reporting, monitoring and verification of emissions and ways to verify the geographical location of areas of land claimed for sink credits, other concerns remain. These include reservations about the development of cheap monoculture plantations as carbon sinks, instead of developing technology to produce energy without fossil fuel emissions. Industrialized countries can fund large-scale monoculture and fast-growth forests in developing countries under Articles 6 and 12 of the Kyoto Protocol, for example, but such initiatives are not guaranteed to meet targets. Likewise, reforestation and monoculture have the potential to damage BIODIVERSITY through the replacement of old growth trees and plants by alien varieties and by farming single crops in an unsuitable environment through the use of chemical fertilizer and insecticides. Instead of burning less fossil fuel, therefore, industrialized countries are expected to avoid changing patterns of consumption, industrial structure and energy technology. In contrast, environmentalists contend, more should be done to encourage the development of renewable energy, sustainable patterns of production and consumption, and the protection of biological diversity, local examples of which are provided by Margie Orford, *Climate Change and the Kyoto Protocol's Clean Development Mechanism* (2004).

FURTHER INFORMATION

Kyoto Protocol: unfccc.int/resource/docs/convkp/kpeng.html
Intergovernmental Panel on Climate Change: www.ipcc.ch
UN Framework on Climate Change: http://unfccc.int

L

LABOUR in general refers to any kind of productive activity, whereas 'useful labour' can be defined as productive activity of a definite kind and exercised with a definite aim. For economists labour (human effort) is a factor of production together with capital (commodities used in the production of other commodities, such as machinery, tools and buildings) and land (naturally occurring resources such as minerals, ore and soil). These categories were defined by classical economists: Adam Smith (1723–1790), David Ricardo (1772–1823) and James Mill (1773–1836), although more recent theories of macro- and microeconomics have attempted to distinguish between imitative aspects of labour as instructional capital and creative or inspirational aspects as individual capital. Either way, the conception of labour in general form – as labour as such – can refer to any form of productive activity at any time. As part of his critique of political economy, however, Karl Marx (1818–1883) distinguished wage labour from labour in general, precisely because it is the form of productive work that is specific to CAPITALISM. This distinction is significant, because wage labour is an exploitative process whereby the labour-power of a person is used to create articles that can be sold for more than they cost to produce, but the labourer receives less than an equal share of the proceeds.

Wage labour is therefore that mode of production in which the labourer sells their combined mental and physical capabilities for use in production; their labour-power or capacity to work is sold as a COMMODITY in exchange for money. Employers not only buy labour-power as a commodity at a fixed price or wage for a particular set of capabilities, but also own the labour process and the end product, which they sell in order to realize PROFIT. No rational person would consent to such a process, so its continuation depends on the 'dull compulsion of the economic': the fact that people are forced to work because they have no other means of production or survival other than the sale of their labour-power. This reality is obscured by orthodox economists, who recognize labour in general as a factor of production, while measuring it in terms of hours worked or total wages. Labour-power is a commodity, because it is sold for a definite period, otherwise it would be the labourer who is the commodity, in which case they would sell themselves into slavery. There is, however, a point of disputation as to whether wage labour constitutes a form of slavery to the extent that the product of the labourer's work belongs to the employer and the fact that the employer seeks to use the labour-power bought in whatever way they see fit.

The minimum price of labour-power is the cost of human subsistence and the social labour-time necessary for it to be produced and reproduced. In other words, the capacity or power of each person to work has to be replenished and refreshed each day, and because human beings are mortal they have to be replaced by their own progeny. The cost of subsistence therefore includes rearing children and also the cost of domestic labour-power – historically provided by the wife and mother. Some feminists, for example, argue that domestic labour should be remunerated separately, while Bridget Anderson, *Doing the Dirty Work?* (2000), describes a trend towards remuneration that is based on EXPLOITATION. As the division of labour between productive activities involves varying degrees of complexity, the cycle of reproduction in generational terms can vary, from basic schooling to a doctoral university education. Of course, these variances apply more to industrialized nations, where the gains of organized labour have increased the cost of labour-power and of reproduction. In the developing world and particularly in SWEATSHOP industries, subsistence wages continue.

As the production process is totally dependent on human labour-power there are differences of opinion over what constitutes the real value of a commodity. According to the labour theory of value, for example, the VALUE of a commodity is equal to the quantity of socially necessary labour-time required for its production, so comparative value depends on the amount of labour-power expended in the production of commodity A against commodity B. Of course, this would also have to include costs of reproduction and so on. In chapter 5 of *The Wealth of Nations* (1776), Adam Smith argued that the value of any commodity exchanged for other commodities is the quantity of labour-power that it enables the owner to purchase or command. Understood thus, the real price, or worth, of a commodity is the amount and duration of labour-power required to produce and acquire it, because this allows the owner to benefit from the time and effort of other people; time and effort s/he has not had to waste!

The basic point here is that without human labour-power, the other factors of production – factories, machines and raw materials – are worthless; it

takes human labour-power to make or acquire these things and to turn them into something else. Employers and capital are therefore totally dependent upon human labour-power, but that labour-power is used to create more value (profit) than is paid in wages. This unequal practical relation between capital and labour is the source of exploitation and therefore grievance for those who sell their labour-power in order to survive.

In the nineteenth and early twentieth centuries, trade unions, communist, social-democratic and socialist parties and other organizations were formed to campaign for the interests of working people. Known collectively as the labour movement, these groups and individuals were motivated to varying degrees by a desire to reform or abolish the exploitative capitalist employment process; they have achieved a level of amelioration in the industrialized world that includes statutory WORKERS' RIGHTS, paid holidays and welfare benefits. Many of these are now the target of NEOLIBERALISM, and issues and causes that motivated earlier activists, such as Mary 'Mother' Jones (1830–1930) and her efforts to end CHILD LABOUR in the USA, are now taken up by today's anti-capitalist movement.

Although many of the old organizational forms, tactics and dogma are now discredited, the issues remain. They are now approached from a perspective that rejects conventional political parties and strategies for the capture of the STATE, in favour of more fluid, autonomous approaches. These range from the SOCIAL FORUM that is held on global, continental and regional levels, to international groups like United Students against Sweatshops that focus on a specific cause. Wherever the labour process occurs, it involves human endeavour to effect a change of form in the material worked on. In fact, this is the very point where the immediate struggle within and against capitalism takes place, as workers seek to exert more control over their own activities during worktime and to minimize the exploitative effects of the unequal employment relations. In keeping with the principles of INTERNATIONALISM, present-day anti-capitalists, whether in a TRADE UNION or other groups, campaign for employment and other human rights so that the exploitation of unprotected workers employed by western corporations on subsistence wages in developing countries does not go unchallenged.

FURTHER INFORMATION
Labour theory of value: www.marxist.com/Economy/theory_of_value_1.html

LABOUR RIGHTS/STANDARDS see WORKERS' RIGHTS.

LAISSEZ-FAIRE *Laissez faire et laissez passer* – let everyone do as they please and everything takes its course – is the dogma of economic individualism associated with nineteenth-century capitalism. A modern-day version of the doctrine is largely a response to the 'stagflation' of the 1970s and has become synonymous with monetarist and neoliberal ideas. These schools of thought hark back to earlier treatises, like those of Adam Smith (1723–1790), *The Wealth of Nations* (1776), the perfect competition theories of David Ricardo (1772–1823) and Alfred Marshall (1842–1924), and Thomas Malthus (1766–1834), *Essay on the Principle of Population* (1798), to justify DEREGULATION. The promotion of free trade can also be traced back to the French Physiocrats of the late eighteenth and early nineteenth centuries, even though they considered agricultural and peasant production to be the main source of societal wealth. Whereas Malthus – a Christian minister – believed he had identified natural forces beyond human control, Smith and Marshall advocated regulation in certain circumstances. The policies promoted by the WORLD TRADE ORGANIZATION and prescribed by the INTERNATIONAL MONETARY FUND and WORLD BANK are the practical outcome of contemporary laissez-faire thinking. The day-to-day realities of these proposals can be found in EXPORT-PROCESSING ZONES, for example, where the theoretical equality in bargaining power between employer and employee is laid bare. See also MONETARISM and NEOLIBERALISM.

LEFT, or left-wing, is a term that – when used in a positive or affirmative sense – indicates a propensity towards progressive or radical thought and action. In this sense it encompasses modern-day anti-capitalism, as opposed to conservatism and reaction on the right. The meaning is attributed to the seating arrangements in the Estates General that preceded the French Revolution and the assemblies that succeeded it, whereby supporters of the monarchy and the status quo sat to the right of the speaker and their egalitarian opponents to the left. This is, in turn, explained in reference to the feudal convention of affording nobility and honour to those who sat at the king's right hand.

Those described as being on the 'left' are therefore usually opposed to the established order of things – existing power relations and distribution of wealth, for example; hence the term is normally used when referring to supporters of ANARCHISM, COMMUNISM and SOCIALISM. All usage of the left–right dichotomy relies on an oversimplification of reality and is employed by those in the MEDIA and by establishment figures in a pejorative sense to indicate that a person or an idea is extreme, is revolutionary and therefore dangerous, irresponsible and not to be trusted. As with all generalizations, the term is used as a form of shorthand and therefore serves only to conceal variations in schools of thought and action that would otherwise be difficult to categorize on a day-to-day basis.

FURTHER INFORMATION
Redefinition of the dichotomy: www.politicalcompass.org

LEVELLERS, THE A radical tendency, rather than a united disciplined movement or party, that emerged during the English Revolution and flourished until its suppression at Burford in May 1649. During the period 1645–49 John Lilburne (1615–1657), Richard Overton (c. 1625–1664), John Wildman (c. 1621–1693) and William Walwyn (1600–1681) led a constitutionalist wing until their imprisonment in the Tower of London. Leveller demands included: adult male suffrage based on property qualifications; annual elections; abolition of the monarchy, aristocracy and House of Lords; religious freedom; trial by jury; an end to censorship; abolition of taxation and church tithes on annual earnings below £30 and a maximum interest rate of 6 per cent. Christopher Hill (1912–2003), *The World Turned Upside Down* (1972), also notes that a tradition of physical-force Levellers made a range of demands that included: forms of agrarian communism; a republic of equals; opposition to enclosures and rejection of the principle of PRIVATE PROPERTY.

The contemporaneous clergyman Nathanael Homes (1599–1678) was therefore moved to refer to 'a levelling anarchy', while some historians consider the Leveller movement to have involved the first expressions of anti-capitalist sentiment – in so far as the English Revolution presaged the Industrial Revolution. Such sentiment was often backward-looking, however – seeking a return to an imaginary halcyon period – and yet for others, such as the DIGGERS or True Levellers, the revolutionary period offered the opportunity to forge a new society based on egalitarian principles. There is therefore often confusion of the two groups, not only because of the similar names, but also through the interchange of people and ideas. Today, the tradition is still celebrated each year on Leveller Day.

FURTHER INFORMATION
Leveller Day: www.levellers.org.uk
Original Leveller texts and commentary: www.bilderberg.org/land/index.htm; www.constitution.org/lev/levellers.htm; www.tlio.demon.co.uk/leveller.htm

LIBERALIZATION is used largely as a euphemism for DEREGULATION and privatization.

LIBERATION is the act of setting free or the realization of FREEDOM from bondage, coercion, domination, interference, oppression or slavery, in whatever form. The notion is akin to emancipation, though the term 'liberation' is normally preferred when describing a movement that aims to secure freedom for a group of people, such as black liberation, national liberation, liberation theology and women's liberation. Some people are also concerned with the freeing of animals from industrial farming and vivisection; hence the term 'animal liberation'. Johannes Agnoli (1925–2003), *Transformation of the Left (Die Transformation der Linken)* (2000), however, defines the 'categorical imperative of human emancipation' as democratic self-determination of the social individual, social self-organization and autonomy based on the overthrow of institutions and relations through which people are debased, dominated and enslaved. In other words, the manifold development of human powers requires a form of association worthy of human nature, which is, in turn, controlled by people and not institutions or things.

Not all liberation movements, their supporters or advocates are anti-capitalist; though some colonial and national liberation movements adopted the rhetoric, if not the practice, of SOCIALISM. In addition to socialism, ANARCHISM and COMMUNISM are critical of capitalist social relations like wage labour, because they are considered to obviate individual control over the conditions of existence, life and work. The solution is seen as a collective process that involves the social cooperation of individuals in replacing the capitalist mode of production with one that places the conditions of human development, movement, nature and production under democratic and therefore social control. This approach juxtaposes the idea of personal freedom as each individual having the means to cultivate their gifts in all directions with that of free competition based on the ownership of PRIVATE PROPERTY and the domination of capital as ALIENATION and a preclusion of other freedoms.

Some liberation movements espousing anti-capitalism emerged from within radical campaigns, as did the Black Panther Party from the civil rights movement in the USA. Others, like the Christian tendency of liberation theology, developed within the citadels of conformity. Associated with the Second Vatican Council, which lasted from 1962 to 1965, the movement found expression in the decision of the Second Latin American Bishops Conference at Medellín, Colombia, in 1968, to take 'a preferential option for the poor'. This pronouncement was based on an already existing NETWORK of grassroots basic communities (*comunidades de base*) that were seeking to address and interpret issues of dictatorship, oppression, POVERTY and the plight of INDIGENOUS PEOPLE in Brazil, Chile, El Salvador, Nicaragua and Uruguay through biblical study and practice.

Evinced by Paulo Freire (1921–1997), *The Pedagogy of the Oppressed* (1970), and Gustavo Gutiérrez, *A Theology of Liberation* (1971), among others, the movement depicted poverty as a sin and equated the Christian mission of liberation from sin with the goal of economic, political and social justice. This approach was in stark contrast to the traditional role of the Catholic Church, which was perceived as defending the status quo and vested interest. As Christopher Rowland, *Radical Christianity* (1988), recognizes, these differences are reflected in the focus of Church leaders on the interpretation of biblical text, abstracted from real life, and the concern of liberation theology with the role of human agency in realizing the reign of God on earth. The latter takes as its exemplar the work of Jesus of Nazareth described in the first half of the Gospel of Mark, while the former concentrates on the remainder of that text and therefore advocates martyrdom and suffering as the road to salvation.

The Vatican under John Paul II sought to curb the influence of liberation theology and excommunicated many of its advocates, often on the basis that they were involved with guerrilla movements and the view that calls for the redistribution of land and wealth amounted to communism. The focus on praxis, in South and Central America, was also equated with MARXISM, perhaps with some justification, by the Congregation for the Doctrine of Faith in 1984. Nevertheless, in South Africa the following year, the authors of the Kairos document adopted a similar approach to that of their brethren in the Americas when devising an analysis of and solution to the system of apartheid.

In the second half of the twentieth century, the subjugation of women as housewives was challenged by Betty Friedan (1921–2006), *The Feminine Mystique* (1963), and others, who called for women to liberate themselves from domestic drudgery and strive for personal fulfilment as whole human beings. Kate Millett, *Sexual Politics* (1969), took this critique a stage further arguing that PATRIARCHY was reinforced by literature, philosophy, POLITICS and psychology and urging an end to the institutions of the family and marriage. Using the model of socialist revolution, Shulamith Firestone, *The Dialectic of Sex* (1970), advocated a feminist revolution to eliminate sexual

149

classes and therefore distinction based on sex. The practice of such ideas took the form of consciousness-raising activism, exhibitions, demonstrations and meetings, as well as the formation of alliances with others engaged in similar struggles.

The conclusion drawn by Dale Spender, *Man Made Language* (1980), that men define the world through language is still valid today, but involves new ways of co-opting and subordinating women. ADVERTISING, MEDIA and music industries, for example, portray stereotypes of liberated women as bitch, girl power and successful career woman. The focus is on girls rather than women, who are free to choose clothes, cosmetics, image and jobs with equal wages; thereby obscuring the alienating, exploitative and oppressive nature of commercialism and wage labour and thus mystifying the goal of liberation from capitalist relations per se.

Women's liberation is a multiple agenda, however, that also includes self-determination in terms of a woman's right to control her own body; as in the case of abortion, contraception and freedom from violence in both private and public life. Also women were frequently treated as second-class citizens in male-dominated revolutionary movements, while Teresa Ebert, *(Untimely) Critiques for a Red Feminism* (1995), offers a critique of postmodern feminism asserting that the struggle for emancipation has to address more than cultural oppression, but economic exploitation as well. This is epitomized by the division of domestic labour involved in capitalist reproduction through the family and social relations of production that require women to work a double shift of paid employment and unpaid housework. Uniquely, the Cuban family code requires the latter to be shared equally between men and women.

FURTHER INFORMATION

Black Liberation: www.marxists.org/history/usa/workers/black-panthers
Feminist theory resource: www.cddc.vt.edu/feminism
Kairos document: www.bethel.edu/~letnie/AfricanChristianity/SAKairos.html

LUDDITE is a term used, generally, as a pejorative description of anyone who objects to new ideas, technology, working practices or 'progress' in general, especially where change has a detrimental impact on their circumstances. The name Ludd – originally a Celtic deity whose epithet was Silver Hand (*Llaw Ereint*) – appeared as the signature 'King Ludd' or 'Ned Ludd' on public letters in England between 1811 and 1818. These were written and issued on behalf of a secret organization of rioters who wrecked machines that made hand-workers redundant in the hosiery and woollen industries and forced down wages. Although their actions are misrepresented as attempting to halt 'progress', Eric Hobsbawm, *Primitive Rebels* (1972), used the phrase 'collective bargaining by riot' to describe a process whereby machine breakers targeted industrialists who refused to guarantee jobs and wages. E.P. Thompson (1924–1993) expounds a similar view in *The Making of the English Working Class* (1963).

M

MAOISM refers to economic, political and social theories that are derived from or are claimed to relate to the works or thought of Mao Zedong (1893–1976). As a radical version of **COMMUNISM** and **MARXISM**, it appealed to and was therefore influential among radical elements of the anti-Vietnam War and **STUDENT MOVEMENTS** of the 1960s in France, Germany and the USA. Of particular significance are the anti-elitist rejection of hierarchy, the idea that a communist party should not be immune from criticism, and the mass line theory of leadership, which assigned importance to direct involvement with those outside the party. Similarly, a stress on the creation of consciousness over organization envisaged a two-way process of agitating and listening, albeit within limits and under party guidance.

Maoism in theory and practice has been adopted as an alternative to Marxism–Leninism as applied in the Soviet Union under Joseph (Dzhugashvili) Stalin (1879–1953) and his successors. In Maoism, for example, emphasis is placed on the role of the commune in the small-scale organization of social and economic units; as earlier described by Thomas Kirkup (1844–1912), *A History of Socialism* (1892). With a focus on village-level industries and rural development, this approach rejects the Soviet development of heavy industry at the expense of the peasantry and involves the argument that class struggle constitutes an essential part of the development of **SOCIALISM** as a means of guarding against excessive bureaucratization. Similarly, the mass line theory of leadership is an implicit critique of the practice of democratic centralism by the Communist Party of the Soviet Union (CPSU, Kommunisticheskaya Partiya Sovetskogo Soyuza). Ironically, however, Mao Zedong's thought as the official doctrine of the Communist Party of China (Zhongguo Gongchandang) has since lost its radical aspects and reverted to a more democratic centralist model of practice.

Today, Maoism remains one of the most enduring tactics of communist revolution through its focus on the practice of guerrilla warfare, mobilization of peasantry, setting up guerrilla organizations, establishing rural base areas and transition to conventional warfare. Its main presence and influence are in the predominantly agrarian and non-industrialized societies of the developing world, particularly in Asia. In India, for example, Maoist organizations are active in Andhra Pradesh, Bihar, Chhattisgarh, Jharkhand Maharashtra, Orissa, Uttar Pradesh and West Bengal, while the Communist Party of Nepal (Maoist) (Nepal Kamyunist Parti) controls large swathes of the country. Other examples include the Communist Party of the Philippines (Partido Kommunista ng Pilipinas) and New People's Army (Bagong Hukbong Bayan) and the Communist Party of Peru (Partido Communista de Peru), also known as Sendero Luminoso (the Shining Path).

FURTHER INFORMATION
Maoist Internationalist Movement: www.etext.org/Politics/MIM
Communist Party of Nepal (Maoist): www.cpnm.org
Communist Party of the Philippines: www.philippinerevolution.org/index.shtml

MAQUILADORA is the Spanish name for a light-assembly factory, usually producing clothing, electronic goods and other commodities. In Mexico, the term is used to describe the assembly of imported component parts for re-export, usually by women at poverty wage rates, without environmental and labour regulations. Similar conditions are to be found in Asia and other Central American countries, especially in **EXPORT-PROCESSING ZONES**. The term has therefore become synonymous with **SWEATSHOP**.

FURTHER INFORMATION
www.maquilasolidarity.org

MARKET in economic theory is the mechanism or place through which buyers and sellers come together to exchange or **TRADE** commodities, finance and **LABOUR**. The concept is of fundamental importance to the operation of **CAPITALISM** and constitutes the means by which most resources are supposed to be allocated. This can involve direct contact, as in the case of wholesale produce markets where retailers buy perishable foodstuffs like fish, fruit, meat and vegetables, or be indirect when a broker or factor mediates between buyer and seller; as happens on the stock and foreign exchange markets. Brokers arrange contracts for commodities they do not possess, like shares, insurance from underwriters and cargo space on aircraft and ships. A factor, on the other hand, is an agent who mediates between producer and retailer, has possession of the items sold and delivers them; as in the case of 'spot markets' where something is delivered as soon as payment is made.

153

A free or perfect market is a theoretical situation in which a large number of buyers and sellers are needed to ensure maximum competition and prevent domination by one party. For this to be the case, buyers are expected to carry out transactions with any trader, have a perfect knowledge of all matters – price, quality and so forth – and neither suffer discrimination nor receive preferential treatment. Furthermore, the STATE is barred from the provision of commodities and services and should seek to minimize 'friction' in the form of REGULATION, subsidy, tariff and TAXATION. Although advocates of LAISSEZ-FAIRE and NEOLIBERALISM are wont to eulogize the virtues of the free market, there is little likelihood of such conditions being achieved, even in financial or metal markets where a share in a corporation or a carat represents a uniform category.

For one thing, all capitalist markets are regulated in some way or another, if only because they are based on state-supported private property rights and assurances that contracts will be honoured. The labour market is also 'distorted', according to free-market theory, by the provision of social security, health and safety regulations and trade unions that create an artificially high price for labour-power. Likewise, the public provision of education and health care is considered to be interference by the state and requires price-adjusting taxation to fund it. If only prices and the provision of services were left to the laws of supply and demand that operate in the marketplace, capitalism would be able to work perfectly. There would be no need for environmental regulation to protect the immediate future of species or the long-term survival of the planet, and consumers would not need to be protected by laws governing product safety.

The real world involves a multiplicity of variables, however, not least of which is the fact that people are not just economic actors, but political and social animals as well. Knowledge about commodities is therefore often imperfect and those in the know can take advantage of their privileged position by, for example, indulging in insider trading on stock where information about losses or mergers is about to be published. Markets are similarly distorted by the activities of speculators who take advantage of futures, hedging and options to buy a COMMODITY for which they have no use, other than hoping that they can secure a PROFIT due to changes in demand, supply and therefore price. Futures and terminal markets, for example, involve contracts for the trade of assets at some future date and allow manufacturers to draw up a specification for future work based on stable prices, whereas a producer might sell projected output now to 'hedge out' the risk of future price changes. This type of transaction is known as a 'derivative instrument' and these also include 'options' to buy or sell a contract without obligation. Speculators, however, seek to influence price by selling stock to induce a 'bear market' with the aim of buying back at lower prices.

The advent and rapid development of information communications technology in the last quarter of the twentieth century meant that financial markets dealing in bonds, currency, insurance and stock became global phenomena exchanging huge sums of money in almost instant transactions. Much of this activity was speculative, targeted at developing countries and involved CAPITAL FLOWS that had the effect of destabilizing national currency and causing local and regional economic crises. Unlike trading in manufactured commodities, such transactions were unhindered by geography or transaction costs and, with the exception of massive losses incurred by Barings Bank, did not require purchasing power to be backed up with hard cash as profits made far outweighed the costs involved.

Markets are also compromised by monopolistic and oligopolistic practices, such as the formation of cartels, that constitute a form of economic coercion designed to inflate prices; a practice associated with ADVERTISING, branding and patenting. Demand is also likely to vary according to the purchasing power of people, hence the likelihood that expensive medical care will not be available to the majority. This is due, in part, to the fact that the distribution of purchasing power depends on how individuals fare in the labour market, but also relates to family wealth, inheritance and gifts. With reference to the labour market, for example, the purchasing power of CORPORATIONS dwarfs that of individual workers. Even though they meet as theoretical equals in the market place, a corporation is able to exert a greater influence on wage levels than a single worker; as demonstrated by Allan Engler, *Apostles of Greed* (1995). According to free-market theorists, however, the combination of workers into a TRADE UNION acts to distort the function of the market.

Evidence of attempts to establish some form of free-market practice is available in Prem Shankar Jha, *The Perilous Road to the Market* (2002), who considers prescriptions advocated by the INTERNATIONAL MONETARY FUND (IMF), WORLD BANK and WORLD TRADE ORGANIZATION (WTO) in relation to China, India and Russia. More often than not these take the form of a STRUCTURAL ADJUSTMENT PROGRAMME, which can be summarized as DEREGULATION, free trade, PRIVATIZATION and reductions in public spending to facilitate the redeployment of economic resources. Paradoxically, the state is needed to introduce such changes into the market, but it is not supposed to interfere in the economy for any other reason. In market parlance, developing countries can be seen as hedging risk by their acceptance of conditions proposed by the IMF, multinational corporations, the World Bank and the WTO before help or investment is forthcoming, but again this is not an equal, let alone perfect, market situation in which the buyer and seller meet.

In the aftermath of World War II, a consensus developed among West European capitalist countries that accepted the need to balance protection of the individual with the pursuit of free enterprise self-interest in the marketplace. Variously referred to as **KEYNESIAN**, mixed economy, social democracy and social market, this approach involved state intervention to define and enforce economic rules, guide economic performance through interest rates and redress inequality through welfare reforms. These attempts to mitigate the excesses of the market were undoubtedly influenced by a desire to lessen the appeal of self-described socialist states to the east. The description of this approach as socialist or **SOCIALISM** is, however, a misnomer and, as David McNally, *Against the Market* (1993), argues, so too is market socialism.

While attempts to integrate markets and socialism were tried in Bulgaria, China, Hungary, Poland, the Union of Soviet Socialist Republics (USSR) and Yugoslavia, **ANARCHISM** and **COMMUNISM** reject the role of the market in deciding distribution, exchange and production. For communism, the maxim of 'from each according to their ability, to each according to their needs' can be understood as using the potential for abundance to provide free, universal access to lifelong education, health care and personal development and fulfilment. Maximizing the use of available resources for such purposes is consistent with prescriptions for **SUSTAINABLE DEVELOPMENT**, which shun the production and sale of disposable commodities designed to be replaced and therefore generate more profit. Opinions differ over how this could be achieved, but proposals usually involve forms of direct democracy, such as workers' control, as a bulwark against corruption.

FURTHER INFORMATION

List of free-market advocates: www.stockholm-network.org/weblinks.cfm
Social Market Foundation: www.smf.co.uk

MARXISM is a broad category that can refer to any social, political or economic theory that derives from or is claimed to relate to the works of Karl Marx (1818–1883); whether directly or through other thinkers like Friedrich Engels (1820–1895) or Vladimir (Ulyanov) Lenin (1870–1924).

The term was not used in Marx's lifetime and there is a question as to whether Marx would have approved of a school of thought or comprehensive 'world-view' – the principles and practices of which are considered to be universal – being ascribed to him. An indication that he would disapprove is evident in his remark about the phraseology of Paul Lafargue (1842–1911) and other French socialists, attributed to him by Engels in a letter dated 5 August 1890: 'All I know is that I am not a Marxist.' Furthermore, the word 'critique' also appears in the title or subtitle of many works by Marx, including *Capital: A Critique of Political Economy* (1867), a fact that appears to have been disregarded by those who seek to use the findings of such works as a blueprint for a Marxist economics.

Before the Bolshevik Revolution in 1917 and the construction of Marxism–Leninism after the death of Lenin, attempts to apply or interpret Marx's approach, method, findings or theory were comparatively widespread. These include, but are not restricted to, the Austro-Marxism of Max Adler (1873–1937), Otto Bauer (1881–1938), Rudolf Hilferding (1877–1941) and Karl Renner (1870–1950). Likewise, the Spartacus League (Spartakusbund) of Rosa Luxemburg (1871–1919) and Karl Liebknecht (1871–1919), the Council Communism of Antonie Pannekoek (1873–1960) and Herman Gorter (1864–1927) and the reformism of Eduard Bernstein (1850–1932). As demonstrated by the diversity of entries in Tom Bottomore (1920–1992), *A Dictionary of Marxist Thought* (1991), this process was varied and continued throughout the twentieth century. Nevertheless, the question of whether Marxism refers to Marx's analysis or models based on it became important due to the imposition of Marxist–Leninist orthodoxy by and through the Communist Party of the Soviet Union (CPSU, Kommunisticheskaya Partiya Sovetskogo Soyuza) and the Third International, especially under Joseph (Dzhugashvili) Stalin (1879–1953).

Although Georgii Plekhanov (1856–1918), *In Defence of Materialism* (1894), is credited with describing Marxism as a whole world-view, the process of creating a Marxist discipline started two decades earlier. The catalyst for this development was the experiences of the Social Democratic Party (Sozialdemokratische Arbeiterpartei) in Germany, which included government repression under Otto von Bismarck (1815–1898), their own political ineffectualness, and the consequent attempt to develop and consolidate a culture of working-class organization through education. Partly to assist the German Social Democrats in this process Engels wrote *Anti-Dühring* (1878), in which he sought to counteract the growing influence of positivism and to derive a universal and scientific law from the joint and individual work of Marx and himself. Karl Kautsky (1854–1938) also interpreted Marx and Engels as providing a universal science of history, nature and society – a deterministic reading adopted by Plekhanov. In view of the repressive conditions experienced by the fledgling working-class movement in tsarist Russia, the development of Marxism as a world-view there served similar purposes to the German process. The emergence and rise to power of a Bolshevik vanguard, determined to bring its world-view to the proletariat as class consciousness, had the effect of taking the process in a specific direction that saw the creation and imposition of a rigid dogma of orthodox Marxism.

Marxism–Leninism was developed as the official state and party doctrine of the Union of Soviet Socialist Republics (USSR) and defined by Stalin in *The Foundations of Leninism* (1924) as 'the theory and tactics of the proletarian revolution in general, the theory and tactics of the dictatorship of the proletariat in particular'. Accordingly, the Communist Party of a particular nation was depicted as the vanguard and representative of the working class and considered to be the only means by which a socialist revolution and the conquest of power could be accomplished. After the revolution had been effected, the vanguard was expected to act as the sole representative of the working class, while the STATE acted on behalf of the whole people. Marxism–Leninism therefore represented a dogmatic stricture that the conditions and principles of practice that were particular to Russia at the beginning of the twentieth century applied to all countries in perpetuity. The prospects of the world proletariat were consequently subordinated to the interests and survival of the USSR and the orthodox line policed by national communist parties – including the former Eastern European governments that occurred more as a consequence of Soviet occupation than hitherto prescribed theory and tactics of proletarian revolution.

Leninism was presented as the correct theory and practice of Marxism and as the theory of scientific communism, incorporating the dictatorship of the proletariat and democratic centralism. The conclusions of Marx's critique were also reformulated as societal laws of development that fed into the study of class relations, their correspondence to the mode of production and the level of productive forces. Other developments that were inconsistent with Marx's method, theory and practice included the development of dialectical and historical materialism, originally formulated by Nikolai Bukharin (1888–1938), *Historical Materialism* (1921), as methods of analysis and their application to societal studies, to the natural sciences and to art and literature. In practice, this meant that Leninism amounted to little more than a materialist ideology of legitimation that resembled Marx's description of RELIGION as an expression of unfree social and political conditions.

As Herbert Marcuse (1898–1979), *Soviet Marxism* (1958), concluded, Marxism–Leninism even contrived to transform Lenin's view that socialism could only exist on an international scale into justification for Stalin's theory of 'Socialism in One Country'. Ultimately and perhaps inevitably, Nikita Khrushchev (1894–1971) and his successors completed the negation of Marxism–Leninism as a form of anti-capitalist praxis by developing the conclusion that because the Soviet Union was economically stronger than the capitalist world, it would inevitably prevail. The international struggle between workers and capitalists was therefore deemed to be redundant and peaceful coexistence was portrayed as an inherent aspect of class struggle.

Until their expulsion or execution in the 1930s, Leon (Lev Bronstein) Trotsky (1879–1940) and the Left Opposition developed alternatives to and critiques of this brand of Marxism in the USSR. Trotsky accepted the primacy of party in revolutionary action and Lenin's method, but advocated a theory of permanent revolution that rejected the concept of socialism in one country and recognized that social, political and economic upheavals occurred on various levels and in diverse social structures. Similarly, Mao Zedong (1893–1976) did not seek to challenge the basic tenets of Marxism–Leninism, but sought a degree of tactical flexibility that would allow approaches to vary according to national conditions and experiences. In China, for example, Marxism–Leninism was developed to include military and guerrilla strategies and an economic focus on rural as opposed to urban development. Developments in Yugoslavia also took their own form, this time under the auspices of the Praxis group and experiments in workers' control.

Similarly, José Mariátegui, *Seven Interpretative Essays on Peruvian Reality* (1928), rejected the Eurocentric emphasis that ignored conditions in Latin America; a process enhanced by the practice of revolution in Cuba and adaptation of Marxism–Leninism by Fidel Castro and Che (Ernesto) Guevara (1929–1967). In practice, however, Guevara's unsuccessful attempts to export a Cuban model of revolution to Africa and Latin America suffered from the same limitations as the notion that the experiences of Russia were applicable to other countries. The problems of dogma and party lines have not only had the effect of fragmenting Marxism into Leninism, MAOISM and TROTSKYISM, but have also atomized each wing into small factional parties that all proclaim themselves the sole representative of Marx's legacy.

In contrast, Antonio Gramsci (1891–1937), *The Prison Notebooks* (1929–35), Georg Lukács (1885–1971), *History and Class Consciousness* (1923), and Karl Korsch (1886–1961), *Marxism and Philosophy* (1923), attempted to pursue a critical aspect while considering themselves to be orthodox Marxist–Leninists. Perhaps inevitably, given the adoption of factory practices in the USSR based on Frederick Taylor (1856–1915), *The Principles of Scientific Management* (1911), the Third International opposed the interpretation of Marxism as the abolition of political economy and therefore as LIBERATION from the rule of the economy. Any attempt to subvert the categories of political economy and the economic domination that they entail was inimical to the role of Marxism–Leninism in the USSR as preserving philosophical truths as opposed to transforming them into reality through REVOLUTION.

The critical tradition was also represented and continued by those associated with the Frankfurt School or Institute for Social Research (Institut für Sozialforschung). Theodor Adorno (1903–1969), Walter Benjamin (1892–1940), Max Horkheimer (1895–1973), Marcuse and others, for example, undertook critical studies of CULTURE, music, philosophy, art, psychoanalysis and consciousness. Gramsci is also renowned for his contributions on the role of cultural and political hegemony, but unlike members of the Frankfurt School he worked with the Third International before his imprisonment, though critical of Bukharin's approach. Dissatisfaction with Marxist–Leninist orthodoxy, epitomized by Hungary under Imre Nagy (1896–1958) in 1956 and Czechoslovakia under Alexander Dubček (1921–1992) in 1968 and the the military repression that followed, contributed to the emergence of the NEW LEFT in the 1950s and 1960s. Similarly, Louis Althusser (1918–1990) attempted a reformulation with *For Marx* (1969) and *Reading Capital* (1970). More recently, Antonio Negri, *Marx Beyond Marx* (1984), and Werner Bonefield and Richard Gunn, *Open Marxism* (1991, 1992, 1995) have sought to maintain the critical anti-capitalist tradition of Marx. Alfredo Saad-Filho, *Anti-capitalism* (2003), and others have also attempted to maintain the relevance of Marxism to present-day anti-capitalist ACTIVISM and thinking.

FURTHER INFORMATION

Marxists Internet Archive: www.marxists.org

MAY DAY was originally celebrated as Beltane (*Beltain*) by the Celts, as *Walpurgisnacht* by the Teutons and *Floralia* by the Romans. These festivals took place on the Eve of May and 1 May and were a joyful celebration of the beginning of summer and of fertility in general. The festival was banned by the Catholic Church and by the Puritans in seventeenth-century England, due to its association with witchcraft and pagan rites. Nevertheless, the occasion continued to be celebrated and consequently acquired increasingly subversive overtones. One example is the character of Robin Goodfellow (the Green Man), considered to be akin to Robin Hood; he was elected as the 'Lord of Misrule' or as a King, Priest or Fool for the day, as part of a process whereby local authorities, lords and priests were ridiculed. In keeping with attempts to suppress the festival, the London May Fayre was abolished in 1708 and the site developed into present-day Mayfair – the epitome of wealth and privilege.

Towards the end of the nineteenth century 1 May was adopted as a holiday by the international labour movement, when in July 1889 the founding congress of the Second International, held in Paris, decided to commemorate the sacrifices of the HAYMARKET MARTYRS. From 1 May 1890, the day was marked by demonstrations and strikes to raise the profile of the movement and its causes, celebrate its traditions and express international solidarity. In the USA and Canada, however, the governments chose the first Monday in September as their preferred date and called it 'Labour Day'. The same name is also associated with the campaign for an eight-hour working day by some Australian states and by New Zealand and is therefore celebrated on dates that have particular significance for that cause.

During the twentieth century, the strictures of the cold war resulted in May Day being institutionalized in both the East and the West. In the Soviet bloc and other self-proclaimed communist states, the day was celebrated with military parades and orchestrated displays. In capitalist countries annual marches were organized by official labour movement bodies and attended by officials and some activists, but often lacked spontaneity or appeal to the broader public. Meanwhile, in the USA the authorities sought to appropriate 1 May for their own purposes, naming it 'Loyalty Day', and in the 1950s the Roman Catholic Church dedicated the day to 'Saint Joseph the worker'.

In the last decade of the twentieth century, May Day was rejuvenated as a celebration of alternative culture – due in part to it being freed from association with the Soviet bloc and being invigorated by a resurgence of anti-capitalist activism. Nowhere has this been more evident than in the English capital, London. In 1999, for example, activists from Reclaim the Streets joined with local anarchist and other groups to oppose PRIVATIZATION of the London Underground. For May Day 2000 a four-day Festival of Anti-Capitalist Ideas and Action took place and involved a Critical Mass cycle ride and a demonstration involving several thousand protesters. Anti-capitalist protests took place around the world on May Day 2001, while in London a May Day Monopoly board was used by protesters to select targets such as McDonald's, Mayfair and Coutts Bank, and a party was held against CONSUMERISM in Oxford Street. May Day 2002 and 2003 have been quieter in London, but in France over 1 million protesters took to the streets to march against the 2002 presidential candidacy of the far-right politician Jean-Marie Le Pen, including around 800,000 protestors at an anti-Le Pen carnival in Paris – at that time the largest demonstration since the 1968 uprising.

FURTHER INFORMATION

Anti-capitalist view: www.riseup.net/ourmayday/mayday/index03.html
New Zealand history: www.nzhistory.net.nz/Gallery/Labour/index.html

MEDIA, THE – often referred to as mass media – are channels of communication through which information and news are distributed in society. These include STATE and privately owned broadcasters who use radio, television and film as their media of communication and printed matter such as books, journals, magazines and newspapers. In the twentieth century, technological advances facilitated the mass production of printed material at minimal cost; a process that was accompanied by the electronic duplication of film, music, radio and television content. Such developments resulted in the mass circulation of newspapers and magazines and the introduction of national and international radio and television networks. Towards the end of the century advances in computer operating systems meant that the Internet was more easily available to individuals and groups with the financial and technological means to produce a site that has the potential to be viewed by a global audience.

As increases in production and circulation became easier, these processes were accompanied by the concentration of ownership into the hands of individuals and multinational media corporations. In the modern era, media monopolization is associated with people like Silvio Berlusconi, who owns Telemilano and Fininvest, and Rupert Murdoch and his News Corporation. Earlier examples include William Randolph Hearst (1863–1951) in the United States, whose legacy continues as the Hearst Corporation, and

William Aitken (1879–1964) in Britain. Where individuals are not identified with ownership, the costs involved in running a mass media operation still prohibit access to such activities by the majority of the population; realities and alternatives that are considered by Robert McChesney, *Rich Media, Poor Democracy* (1999). Even in the case of the Internet, access requires subscription to an Internet Service Provider (ISP) and profit-making search engines, while the flooding of server space by commercial interests and attempts at ISP and state censorship limit freedom of use.

In spite of the demographics of ownership, the media and the information it circulates are still presented as value-free, balanced and independent. Together with other critics, Edward Herman and Noam Chomsky, *Manufacturing Consent* (1988), argue that structural constraints mean that dissenting activities and views do not get fair coverage in the mass media. Only a token amount of space is therefore afforded to seriously challenging journalists and journalism. Stated more specifically, it is not in the interests of a profit-seeking corporation to give a platform to people and ideas that represent its antithesis. The state and corporately owned media have neither questioned the thesis that the process of GLOBALIZATION is pursued primarily on behalf of the poor, nor publicized the existence of viable alternatives and analyses. The effects of free-trade agreements on national sovereignty, corporate profits and the living and working standards of those who sell their labour-power in developing countries receive similarly scant attention. Media managers, editors and journalists present information about 'celebrities', stock markets and the activities of politicians as news, while PROTEST and DIRECT ACTION are marginalized and distorted.

Storylines also reflect the interests of governments and CORPORATIONS, reducing the reality of human suffering – POVERTY, human rights abuses, war – and environmental degradation – including pollution and climate change – to an uncritical sound bite. The predominance of commercial messages and the focus on entertainment represent a form of censorship, by which information is controlled or mediated in a manner that influences the expectations of people, setting limits on what they see as possible and providing trivial subject matter as the basis for social interaction. See, for example, the account offered by Richard Hoggart, *Mass Media in a Mass Society* (2004).

A dependence on television for entertainment and information, coupled with the fact that television viewing is largely undertaken in the home, constitutes ideal circumstances for the practice of ADVERTISING. Newspapers and broadcasters also portray their opinions as mainstream and project a vision of the world that limits public perceptions of what is, what ought to be and what is possible. Wholehearted support for the 'war on terror', for example, uses warnings of possible terrorist atrocities and the fear of violence to promote popular passivity and obedience. By and large, readers and viewers are told that you either support free markets and trade, multinational corporations, PRIVATIZATION and war or you side with the terrorists. Was it really just a coincidence that Walt Disney decided not to distribute the Michael Moore film *Fahrenheit 9/11* in 2004?

Although small-scale projects like public access stations, underground radio and newspaper publishing have a long history, the advent of the Internet has seen the formation of groups dedicated to promoting diversity of opinion and offering grassroots, non-corporate, radical coverage of events. These include AlterNet, whose site provides links to sources of information with public interest content and policy analysis for use by activists, researchers, independent journalists and the public. Perhaps the largest initiative is the Independent Media Centre (IMC), or Indymedia, network that originated in November 1999 as the initiative of independent and alternative media organizations and activists to provide grassroots coverage of the protests against the WORLD TRADE ORGANIZATION meeting in Seattle. Indymedia centres, run by activists, act as a clearing house of information for journalists by producing and disseminating reports, photos, audio and video footage through websites. Examples include centres formed to cover the Biodevastation Convergence in Boston, the A16 protests against the WORLD BANK and INTERNATIONAL MONETARY FUND in Washington DC, the Israel–Palestine IMC and others in Italy, Melbourne in Australia, Chiapas in Mexico, and Prague in the Czech Republic.

Whereas Protest.Net and the above examples work to create their own media, groups like Media Lens, set up in 2001, and Fairness and Accuracy In Reporting engage in media monitoring of mainstream news stories to highlight bias, omission and distortion. Likewise, Media Workers Against War reformed in September 2001, to promote pluralism in debate, the free flow of information and the public scrutiny of official pronouncements. This is achieved by collating and disseminating facts and arguments about war as a means of exposing and resisting attempts at censorship and disinformation. In addition to the common aims of raising public awareness of the failings of existing media institutions, ensuring that the public has access to independent news reports, and engaging in struggle to democratize the media and communications infrastructure, these and other groups have other practical similarities.

All are run collectively by unpaid volunteers who include journalists and media activists, eschew allegiance to individual political parties and organizations, and fund their activities through donations and grants while rejecting corporate finance. They also operate email lists, chat rooms to provide the opportunity for discussion, feedback and thereby meaningful dialogue. The IMC News Wire, for example, embodies the principle of 'open publishing', allowing independent journalists, organizations and individuals to publish their own articles, analysis and information on globally accessible bases. Anyone can publish and, although duplicate posts and commercial messages are relocated, all articles remain publicly accessible.

FURTHER INFORMATION
Links to IMC websites: www.indymedia.org

MILITARY–INDUSTRIAL COMPLEX refers to the powerful alliance between the military, CORPORATIONS involved in the manufacture of arms and defence industry procurement, and government agencies including the civil service. President Dwight Eisenhower used the term in 1961 to warn of the associated political and commercial concerns that have (illegitimate) financial or strategic interests in expanding the state arms budget at the expense of the civil interests of society. Noam Chomsky also uses the term 'Pentagon system' to describe the way high-technology industry receives public subsidy for research and development, thereby socializing cost, stimulating economic growth and minimizing management decision-making risks by providing a guaranteed market and profitability through company ownership of marketable spin-offs.

In *Mandate for Change* (1993), for example, Chomsky describes how the Department of Energy and the National Aeronautics and Space Administration were used by the Kennedy administration to subsidize advanced industry through the production of nuclear weapons and rockets as part of the arms and space races. Similarly, in the 1980s, Ronald Reagan (1911–2004) sought to fund and develop a Strategic Defense Initiative – commonly referred to as 'Star Wars' – that was promoted as using space-based systems to intercept nuclear missiles. In reality, however, the main achievement of this programme was economic growth among industries producing aviation, computer and associated electronic equipment. A scaled-down programme

continued under the Clinton administration, until George W. Bush resurrected the idea of developing ground, high-altitude, sea and space-based
missile defence systems in December 2002, under the pretext of deterring
or guarding against nuclear attack by terrorists and 'rogue states'. The cost
of this programme was estimated as US$53 billion between 2004 and 2009
– bigger than any other single item of Pentagon spending.

FURTHER INFORMATION

Chomsky article: www.chomsky.info/articles/199302–.htm
Official reasons for resurrecting star wars: www.fas.org/irp/offdocs/nspd/nspd-23.htm
Text of Eisenhower speech: wikisource.org/wiki/Military-Industrial_Complex_Speech

MONETARISM does not appear in technical economic discourse, but
the term 'monetarist' was used by Karl Brunner (1916–1989), *The Role of
Money and Monetary Policy* (1968), to refer to a set of economic theories that
consider the demand for and supply of money as the main factors determining economic activity. While advocates disagree about exactly how much
influence money has, the shared central principle is that controlling inflation
is a fundamental requirement for stable economic growth and that inflation
is a response to the growth in the supply of money. Other shared beliefs are
reminiscent of the principles of LAISSEZ-FAIRE, such as the emphasis placed
on the importance of minimal government intervention in the economy and
the free play of market forces. Monetarism is essentially a resurrection of the
'quantity theory of money' that originated with David Hume (1711–1776)
and John Locke (1632–1704) and was economic orthodoxy before John Maynard Keynes (1883–1946) outlined his ideas on demand management in *The
General Theory of Employment, Interest and Money* (1936).

Similarly, although Milton Friedman, *Capitalism and Freedom* (1962), George
Stigler (1911–1991) and other economists at the University of Chicago are
considered to be the main exponents of monetarism, the work of Irving
Fisher (1867–1947), *The Purchasing Power of Money* (1911), is a forerunner.
Whatever their origins, monetarist ideas gained credibility during the years
of 'stagflation' following the oil crises of the early 1970s when production
slumped and inflation reached double figures in the USA and Western Europe.
Since 1976, for example, governments in Britain have sought to influence the
rate of price inflation by controlling the supply of money. This approach was

also adopted by the USA in the 1980s and enshrined in the European Union Treaty of Maastricht 1992, in accordance with which the control of inflation appears as the key objective of European macroeconomic policy. This means that because inflation is believed to result from 'too much money chasing too few goods', economic policy is geared to ensuring that the level of national income (measured in current prices as GROSS NATIONAL PRODUCT and GROSS DOMESTIC PRODUCT) is not exceeded by the rate of growth of money. Nevertheless, there are differences of opinion over the appropriate definition – whether it should include notes and coin in circulation, balances in bank accounts, overdraft facilities and other forms of credit – and about how it should be controlled.

Adjusting levels of TAXATION is one way of controlling the levels of money available, for example, but this is dismissed by monetarists as government interference in the realm of the free market. The preferred method of control is therefore interest rates – the price of borrowing money – even though this is also influenced by government debt financing services and central banks. If government spending exceeds income from taxation, for example, a government needs to borrow new money and therefore increases money supply. As an answer to such problems, monetarists advocate a balanced budget – whereby spending is equivalent to income raised from taxation – and that interest rates are set by a central bank that is independent of government – as is the case in Britain, Europe and the USA. Another way of controlling the supply of money is through a 'non accelerating inflation rate of unemployment' (NAIRU). Unemployment is therefore used to encourage greater 'flexibility' in the labour market, which in practice means lowering wages and social standards to reduce the cost of labour-power and therefore reducing demand and inflation. In this way, it is argued, government can avoid direct intervention to control prices and incomes.

There are a number of inconsistencies and problems that plague monetarist prescriptions. While government is not allowed to interfere in the running of the free market, for example, its direct involvement in the form of legislation is required to restrict the right of employees to form and join a TRADE UNION and engage in free collective bargaining. Similarly, although taxation is eschewed as a means of reducing the supply of money, tax cuts are, conversely, a preferred method of increasing money supply, raising the level of income and therefore demand for commodities and services. There is also a circularity of reasoning in the proposition whereby interest rates (the price of money) and wages (the price of labour-power) are used to control

167

the price of commodities and services. What this means in practice is that human welfare and well-being become subservient to the calculations of accountants and economists.

Economies that use rates of unemployment and interest charges to control price inflation are also vulnerable to any number of domestic and international variables. A sharp increase in unemployment, for example, leads to a reduction in tax revenues and therefore requires reductions in public spending, at the very time that demand for welfare payments increases. Likewise, relying on interest rates as a policy instrument, while international financial markets are unregulated, means that national economies can be devastated by CAPITAL FLOWS linked to foreign currency speculation. Using the control of inflation as the main policy objective implies that stable growth, production, employment, income and welfare are incidental aims – while the environment is completely disregarded. There are obvious analogies that can be drawn between monetarism and NEOLIBERALISM.

FURTHER INFORMATION

History of monetarism: www.j-bradford-delong.net/Econ_Articles/monetarism. html

European critique: www.uni-giessen.de/fb03/seminar/online/europa99/text2.htm

MULTILATERAL AGREEMENT ON INVESTMENT (MAI) was an unsuccessful initiative of the ORGANIZATION FOR ECONOMIC COOPERATION AND DEVELOPMENT (OECD), for a proposed treaty to govern trade and investment. Negotiations took place with little public debate under the auspices of the OECD between 1995 and 1998 when the treaty was all but abandoned in the face of mounting public opposition. Proposals were designed to extend the rights of investors, already guaranteed under the WORLD TRADE ORGANIZATION (WTO), by removing all direct foreign investment restrictions and requiring signatory governments to treat foreign and domestic corporations equally. Furthermore, instead of governments challenging 'barriers to trade' through the WTO, as happens at present, CORPORATIONS would have been allowed to sue national governments that were 'guilty' of introducing regulations to protect consumers, the environment, public health and workers.

The MAI would therefore have given corporations more power than democratically elected national governments in international law, in order to facilitate the free movement of capital worldwide. Such measures would have had profound implications for sovereignty, DEMOCRACY and the social and economic well-being of local populations. The different levels of economic development and the varying standards of monitoring exhibited by participating countries would also have posed problems to the smooth operation of the system. Although this attempt to allow investors to move capital easily in and out of countries was defeated by popular pressure, some of its prescriptions are included in regional accords like the NORTH AMERICAN FREE TRADE AGREEMENT and the proposed FREE TRADE AREA OF THE AMERICAS.

FURTHER INFORMATION

Arguments against: www.wdm.org.uk/cambriefs/wto/MAI.htm; www.oxfam.org.uk/what_we_do/issues/trade/maidec98.htm
Declassified documents: www1.oecd.org/daf/mai

MULTINATIONAL CORPORATION (MNC) is a term used to describe a corporation that has its headquarters in one country – normally in the industrialized world – and manufacturing or distribution facilities in others – usually in the developing world. The term became popular after World War II, but MNCs appear to have enjoyed disproportionate success as a result of the policy agendas of the INTERNATIONAL MONETARY FUND, WORLD BANK and WORLD TRADE ORGANIZATION over the last thirty years or so. Such developments give the impression that a new process of GLOBALIZATION has taken place, especially through the growth of financial markets and the EXPLOITATION of cheap raw materials and labour resources in developing countries. See also CORPORATIONS.

N

NEOLIBERALISM is a political, social and economic agenda that is promoted as orthodoxy by the **INTERNATIONAL MONETARY FUND** (IMF), **WORLD BANK, WORLD TRADE ORGANIZATION** (WTO) and the multilateral agreements administered by the last. Some governments, like those of Britain, the USA and the European Union – in accordance with the terms of the Maastricht Treaty – support this agenda; as do international banks, multinational corporations and the **MEDIA**. The central neoliberal tenet is that markets are inherently efficient and that the **STATE** and public sector have no essential role to play in economic development apart from facilitating the expansion, intensification and primacy of market relations.

Policies that are designed to allow businesses to operate as freely as possible and reduce the economic functions of the state form the core of neoliberalism. These include the **DEREGULATION** of domestic and international financial systems to stimulate saving and allow free-floating exchange rates to reduce the cost of currency, stimulate exports and increase domestic competition. The principles are also applied to the labour market where reduced employment and trade-union rights are designed to stimulate job creation by lowering wages and producing a flexible labour force. In the arena of international trade, treaties like the **NORTH AMERICAN FREE TRADE AGREEMENT** and **TRADE-RELATED INVESTMENT MEASURES** aim to remove or lower tariffs and other barriers like environmental and quality standards to help create free trade. **PRIVATIZATION** of government-owned industries and services like banks, railways, education, telecommunications, gas, electricity, water and post are also designed to enhance the operation of the **MARKET**. A third defining feature is the use of monetarist mechanisms to control inflation, such as reducing the money supply by lowering public expenditure through cuts in welfare spending – thereby lowering social standards and demand – and increasing the cost of borrowing money by raising interest rates.

Although these features are all contemporary, their advocacy and practice are not especially new. Ultimately, they draw on eighteenth-century antecedents like Adam Smith (1723–1790), but have a more direct association with neoclassical economic traditions of the nineteenth century. This involves the attempt to restate 'classic' liberal economics in a more precise mathematical form and the French Physiocrats who promulgated the concept of LAISSEZ-FAIRE. There are also strong twentieth-century influences, particularly the 'New Right' movement epitomized by Friedrich von Hayek (1899–1992), *The Road to Serfdom* (1944), which advocated self-regulating, free markets without constraint by government or CIVIL SOCIETY to achieve growth, social justice and political freedom.

Milton Friedman, *Free to Choose* (1980), and other advocates of MONETARISM also form an important aspect of neoliberalism. Practitioners of the approach that proposed control of the money supply to manage inflation include the 1980s' governments of Margaret Thatcher in Britain, Ronald Reagan (1911–2004) in the USA and David Lange in New Zealand. These examples are variously associated with the diminution of trade-union rights, high levels of unemployment, cuts in welfare spending and the privatization of government assets to finance tax cuts. Furthermore, the recent George W. Bush government in the USA is closely linked to supporters of neo-conservatism – a term attributed to Michael Harrington (1928–1989) – who are sceptical about the economic role of government, and support deregulation and the minimization of welfare provision.

The term 'neoliberalism' is used pejoratively by the anti-capitalist movement and forms a particular focus for organizations like the Association for the Taxation of Financial Transactions for the Aid of Citizens and the Zapatista Army of National Liberation (Ejército Zapatista de Liberación Nacional). Common themes are evident in the criticism levelled by these and others, including Noam Chomsky, *Profit over People* (1999). First and foremost is the argument that the reliance on market forces to organize economic relations ignores the role of political and social processes in the economy and leads to an increased inequality in wealth and POWER within and between countries. Allowing market forces to decide which industries survive, for example, has adverse effects on populations such as the destruction of jobs and livelihoods (particularly in the manufacturing sector), the creation of structural unemployment, POVERTY, marginalization and social exclusion. A process exacerbated – according to Susanne Soederberg, *The Politics of the New International Financial Architecture* (2004) – by the increase in short-term capital flows and currency crises that accompanied the deregulation of financial markets and introduction of floating exchange rates.

The belief that established industries will be replaced by the spontaneous growth of new ones has not materialized, but has contributed to balance-of-payments crises due to an increased dependence on imported products. Meanwhile, measures to deregulate the labour market and control inflation result in lower wages, worse working conditions and job insecurity for those in work and are therefore considered to undermine the social role of paid work – treating human beings as mere tools for profit-making in globalized production circuits. Targeting the control of inflation as a key objective of economic policy means that growth, employment, income and welfare are relegated to subsidiary aims, even though economic stability is concomitant with stable production, employment and a sustainable environment.

As IDEOLOGY, neoliberalism also contains a central contradiction in so far as the professed opposition to state control and reliance on market forces is dependent on the existence of a repressive, strong state to implement prescriptions and contain any social conflicts that might result. State intervention does take place, for example, to push through programmes of deregulation and privatization, to reduce the legal rights of trade unions and those of consumers. The state also plays a central role in establishing and maintaining institutional and regulatory authorities that oversee the operation of markets, including laws governing property rights, accounting conventions and the collection of taxes. Even where it is not directly involved in building roads or providing education, transport and other forms of infrastructure, the state is still responsible for establishing regulatory bodies to oversee provision, for setting educational standards in general and for vetting qualifications in particular.

Moreover, if the role of the state is merely regulatory – intervening to encourage economic growth over the welfare of its citizens – the political agenda is moved away from the economy and therefore lessens democratic control over CORPORATIONS, financial institutions and other economic agencies. Colin Leys examines such phenomena in *Market Driven Politics* (2003). Similarly, neoliberalism's reliance on the legal protection of property rights as the basis of the social order, and the replacement of collectivist notions of public good, solidarity and social responsibility with a belief in individual action and ambition, are considered to undermine DEMOCRACY. Although there are inherent problems in formulating and popularizing a coherent alternative to neoliberalism, steps are being taken in this direction with the promotion of people-centred initiatives for SUSTAINABLE DEVELOPMENT.

FURTHER INFORMATION

A short history: www.globalexchange.org/campaigns/econ101/neoliberalism.html

NETWORK understood in general means a system of interconnections. Translated into a societal context, the term is used to imply a process of connecting individuals via acquaintances, friends and relatives, and therefore as a form of mediation through which the singular relates to the multiple. This can range from a small group of individuals where each knows the other, through to a social circle, a local community and on to an international scale when it will be impossible for an individual to know all members or even appreciate the extent of those participating. Examples within such a range might include dining clubs, interest groups, social movements and those who perceive a connection to others according to what they buy, as in some aspects of CONSUMERISM.

On another level, associations between certain groups of people have a considerable impact on the structure of society, the way it is run and therefore in maintaining the status quo. Ralph Miliband (1924–1994), *The State in Capitalist Society* (1969), for example, argued that those who occupy the higher echelons of banks, civil and diplomatic services, CORPORATIONS, government, judiciary, military and police are likely to share similar educational backgrounds. More recently, www.theyrule.org notes that many of the 500 largest companies in the USA share directors, with some individuals holding up to seven different directorships. These personnel also swap jobs between government appointments and the employ of the INTERNATIONAL MONETARY FUND, WORLD BANK, WORLD TRADE ORGANIZATION and other international institutions. Such networks are cultivated and maintained by transnational actors that crisscross nations and include entities like the CORPORATE LOBBY GROUP and the WORLD ECONOMIC FORUM. Power networks are also apparent at the national level in the shape of the MILITARY–INDUSTRIAL COMPLEX.

There are also many examples of alternative forms of network that constitute relationships of mutual support for those who are opposed to CAPITALISM per se or aspects of it. These include groups, organizations and parties associated with ANARCHISM, COMMUNISM and SOCIALISM, together with newer varieties of opposition. The last cover groups founded in the final third of the twentieth century and still going strong today, like People and Planet started in 1969, the World Development Movement founded in 1970, the Transnational Institute set up in 1974 and Earth First! in 1979. The 1980s also saw the emergence of Witness for Peace in 1983 and the Earth Island Institute, together with its Rainforest Action Network, International Rivers Network and Urban Habitat projects.

Networks of non-governmental organizations also exist, as in the case of the International Forum on Indonesian Development, established in 1985, and Jobs With Justice in 1987. An indication of the many issues covered by networks formed since 1990 can be gleaned from a small sample. This includes the Association for the Taxation of Financial Transactions for the Aid of Citizens, Central America Women's Network, Clean Clothes Campaign, Convergence of Peoples of the Americas, Export Credit Agency Watch, Genetic Engineering Network, Globalize Resistance, Independent Media Centre, Jubilee Debt Campaign, Labour Behind The Label, Maquila Solidarity Network, McInformation Network, Tax Justice Network and Ya Basta!

Developments in information communications technology (ICT) have been embraced and enhanced by such groups as a means of building continental and intercontinental networks to complement existing local, grassroots equivalents. Evolving from the US-government-sponsored Advanced Research Projects Agency Network (ArpaNet) and Unix User Network (Usernet) in the 1970s, for example, ICT innovations resulted in the sharing of information, messages, news and opinions as part of open-source and shareware initiatives over direct dial-up networks. Commonly referred to by the generic term 'discussion groups', ICT used by today's movement includes bulletin boards, chat rooms, forums, electronic mailing lists and newsgroups. Thus, the term 'Internet' or 'Net' now represents a variety of local and global electronic computer communications networks.

Indymedia, among others, operates a News Wire as a clearing house to allow for the instant and globally accessible publication of information, and thereby enables ideas to be shared, solutions and tactics innovated, as well as the organization of events. In keeping with the principle of open publishing, anyone with access to the Internet can publish news or opinion and posts are not edited. Commercial material, duplicates and posts that infringe guidelines are removed, however, but remain accessible on other areas of the site. Using ICT in this manner also allows an almost immediate international interaction of individuals, exchange of information and research, and therefore facilitates online debates, discussions and meetings.

Other sites, like Action Network, use the Internet and email to motivate, activate and communicate with activists and decision-makers. Email lists are used to distribute action alerts, campaign updates, general information, newsletters and press coverage and invite people to become involved by modifying and sending template emails, faxes and letters to decision-makers that include corporate executives and elected officials. Various forms of software are used for these purposes, one example being the Working Assets' 1995 Flash Activist Network rapid response programme.

A number of initiatives were also developed to allow the international use of ICT for progressive and radical purposes, in countries in both North and South, without the threat of censorship by state or corporate providers, examples of which are provided by Liberty, *Liberating Cyberspace* (1999). These include the Institute for Global Communications (IGC) and Green-Net, both of which began in 1987 and became co-founders of the Association for Progressive Communications (APC) in 1990. Envirolink Network was created in 1991 and, in common with IGC networks AntiRacismNet, EcoNet, PeaceNet and WomensNet, provides website and domain name hosting, automated mailing lists, interactive bulletin boards and email accounts. Like the APC networks LabourNet and LaNeta, these services are focused on particular groups and interests. Similar initiatives are also undertaken by Global Knowledge Partnership, One World, Tao Organization for Autonomous Telecommunications and the Intercontinental Network of Alternative Communication (Red de Intercontinental Comunicacion Alternativa) project against NEOLIBERALISM.

FURTHER INFORMATION

Association for Progressive Communications: www.apc.org
GreenNet: www.gn.apc.org
Institute for Global Communications: www.igc.org

NEW LEFT is the name given to the upsurge in radicalism that emerged in Europe and the USA towards the end of the 1950s and persisted throughout the 1960s and into the 1970s. The origin of the term is attributed to C. Wright Mills (1916–1962), *Letter to the New Left* (1960). In Europe, the movement is associated with the critique of Stalinism that followed the speech made by Nikita Khrushchev (1894–1971) to the Twentieth Congress of the Communist Party of the Soviet Union and the military invasion to crush the Hungarian reform movement in 1956. The critical process was assisted by the appearance of alternative ideas and practices offered by China under Mao Zedong (1893–1976) – see MAOISM – and in Cuba under Fidel Castro and Che (Ernesto) Guevara (1929–1967).

Michael Kenny, *The First New Left* (1995), records how the New Left developed new ways of understanding the theoretical importance of CULTURE, history and radical politics. The movement coalesced around Stuart Hall,

Edward Thompson (1924–1993), Raymond Williams (1921–1988), Raphael Samuel (1934–1996), Ralph Miliband (1924–1994), John Saville, Perry Anderson, Robin Blackburn, Tom Nairn and Richard Hoggart, among others. In France, Louis Althusser (1918–1990) was also engaged in a critical reassessment that was to question the authority and integrity of the Communist Party of France (Parti Communiste Français). A similar process was instigated in Italy by people like Antonio Negri, Sergio Bologna, Mario Tronti and Alberto Asor Rosa and groups to the LEFT of the Communist Party of Italy (PCI, Partito Communista Italiano), resulting ultimately in the AUTONOMIA.

On both sides of the Atlantic, authority structures were called into question, in society as a whole but especially the methods of radical political organization, practice and theory. In a similar fashion to today's anti-capitalist movement, the New Left challenged and rejected establishment party politics – bureaucracies, manipulation, party leadership, tactics and forms of hierarchical organization. Favouring decentralization, participatory democracy and lay control over decision-making, the movement embraced diverse goals, opinions and antagonistic tendencies – black liberation, women's liberation, anti-war action, ECOLOGY and so on – an approach that bears comparison to today's anti-capitalism.

There was also an attempt to engage with popular culture, but in the 1960s, especially in Europe, the New Left still focused on a radical critique of the capitalist system itself – commodity production, wage labour and so forth – in search of an alternative to Marxism–Leninism and reformist social democracy. In some cases this led to the rupturing of Communist parties, as in Britain where people left to join Trotskyist organizations like the International Socialists, the International Marxist Group and later offshoots the Militant Tendency, Socialist Workers Party and Workers Revolutionary Party. Defectors also joined the syndicalist Solidarity UK or the Independent Labour Party, while parties in France, Italy and Spain dedicated themselves, with varying degrees of commitment, to Eurocommunism during the 1970s.

In Britain New Left activism is associated with the Campaign for Nuclear Disarmament, attempts to expose the hypocrisy of the Soviet Union and its allies, and working with popular-front organizations to campaign for peace, disarmament and global justice. The influence of the movement is presented as having a disproportionate effect on intellectual life and the universities, with the introduction of new academic disciplines like Cultural Studies and the practice of writing 'history from below'. The *New Left Review*, formed by the merger of the *New Reasoner* and *Universities and Left Review*, was considered to be the journal of a movement, sponsoring the English translation and publication of Althusser, Jürgen Habermas, Georg Lukács (1885–1971), Theodor Adorno (1903–1969) and Antonio Gramsci (1891–1937).

Nevertheless, the upsurge in industrial militancy, the emergence of the shop stewards' movement, anti-war demonstrations and university unrest were all symptomatic of a general social upheaval, which was mirrored on the continent of Europe and culminated in the students' uprising of May 1968 in Paris. Likewise the civil rights movement and armed conflict in the province of Northern Ireland resemble developments in the USA – where the civil rights movement began with campaigns and demonstrations against segregation. The period also witnessed the emergence of the Black Power movement and the formation of the Black Panther Party led by Stokely Carmichael (1941–1998), Huey Newton (1942–1989) and Bobby Seale, among others.

In the USA, Students for a Democratic Society (SDS) became synonymous with New Left activism – due in part to the national profile it attained as a leading organization of campus opposition to the Vietnam War. The war provoked mass resistance, however, which involved the burning of draft cards, refusal to be inducted into the armed forces, stopping trains and buses that carried military personnel, and other demonstrations held by the Peace Movement. The SDS Port Huron Statement, written by Tom Hayden in 1962, for example, called for 'participatory democracy' based on nonviolent civil disobedience. Other student groups included the Southern Student Organizing Committee and the Free Speech Movement of 1964, which opposed the imposition of restrictions on campus political activity at the University of California, Berkeley, with demonstrations, sit-ins and student strikes.

John McMillan and Paul Buhle, *The New Left Revisited* (2003) offer an account of the diversity of the New Left in the USA; a variety that included the counterculture. Combining the culture of the hippies and radical activism, for example, Abbie Hoffman (1936–1989), Jerry Rubin (1938–1994) and others formed the Youth International Party (Yippies), which aimed to use the 'Festival of Life' as a form of PROTEST – in similar fashion to the SITUATIONIST INTERNATIONAL. Along with the Motherfuckers and the DIGGERS, they sought radicalization through the staging of events such as standing a pig for president in 1968 and invading New York Stock Exchange in 1967 to perform a 'money drop' – an act resurrected outdoors as sabbath economics by evangelical Christians in 2002. Anticipating modern-day anti-capitalist distrust of the corporate media, Yippies sought to promote their ideas by making their own news and grabbing media attention.

The counterculture also included the Weather Underground, an offshoot from the SDS that adopted a form of urban terrorist strategy based on the shock value of 'doing something is better than doing nothing'. They adopted the slogans of the Black Panthers and disparaged Yippies for not being serious. In reality, both groups advocated a revolution in daily life, with the Yippies focusing on romantic individualism and the Weathermen adopting a militarized lifestyle in an attempt to create the Weather Machine. This preoccupation with 'lifestyle' developed into urban communes and collectives that rejected work, school and the nuclear family as enforcing societal roles and values. By trying to reproduce themselves until the dominant society was outnumbered, they aimed to instigate social change, while protecting their members and developing new ways to live. Ultimately, they succumbed to the contradiction of trying to live outside the society they wished to transform.

FURTHER INFORMATION

New Left Review: www.newleftreview.net
Weather Underground and New Left: www.counterpunch.org/jacobs0726.html

NON-GOVERNMENTAL ORGANIZATION (NGO) refers to tax-exempt, non-profit, social and cultural groups whose primary goal is not commercial – like those working in international development such as Oxfam and Médecins Sans Frontières in humanitarian aid – but also includes campaigning groups like Amnesty International and Greenpeace. Some NGOs like those that advocate women's rights or trade unions exist to further the interests of their members, but their defining characteristic is their independence from any governmental entity. The term is included in Article 71 of Chapter 10 of the United Nations Charter to allow the Economic and Social Council to make arrangements for consultation with international and national representatives of CIVIL SOCIETY. The term 'Private Voluntary Organization' is also used to identify NGOs that obtain funding from private sources and voluntary contributions in the form of financial donations, activity and support from employees, members and the public in general.

FURTHER INFORMATION

International NGO alliance: www.solidar.org
Information Communication Technology support for NGOs: www.gn.apc.org

NORTH AMERICAN FREE TRADE AGREEMENT (NAFTA) was introduced on 1 January 1994, with the intention of eliminating tariffs on commodities and services traded between Mexico, Canada and the United States. The accord also makes provision for the DEREGULATION of investment, the reduction of travel restrictions for entrepreneurs and white-collar workers and for the protection of intellectual property rights between the three signatories. As Noam Chomsky, *Mandate for Change* (1993), notes, consultation between the architects of the agreement and bodies like the Canadian British Columbia Teachers Federation and the US Labor Advisory Committee were subject to deliberately imposed time constraints that made effective scrutiny, evaluation and comment impossible.

Opposed by trade unions, farmers and environmental groups in all three countries, the agreement has neither improved wages and working conditions nor protected the environment; as David Bacon, *The Children of NAFTA* (2004), records. On the contrary, northern CORPORATIONS have chosen to move operations to Mexico where garment workers receive around one-tenth of the wages earned by counterparts in the North and to take advantage of unenforced labour and health-and-safety laws, sparse union organization, negligible industry scrutiny and lax environmental regulations. Any attempt by democratically elected bodies to implement or raise standards could now be challenged by corporations as a restraint of TRADE. Nevertheless, government subsidies to farmers in the USA give them an unfair advantage over their Mexican counterparts, who cannot afford to undercut prices and therefore go out of business.

FURTHER INFORMATION

NAFTA Secretariat: www.nafta-sec-alena.org
Critical review: www.citizen.org/trade/nafta/index.cfm

O

ORGANIZATION FOR ECONOMIC COOPERATION AND DEVELOPMENT (OECD) was formed in 1961, when the Organization for European Economic Cooperation decided to admit non-European members at the close of Marshall Plan reconstruction. Today, the OECD acts as a forum through which representatives – some elected, some not – from thirty member countries meet to discuss and agree domestic and international socio-economic policies covering agriculture, the environment, investment and finance, the labour market, structural adjustment, TAXATION and TRADE. Deliberations usually produce one of three outcomes: legally binding codes; simple agreements; or guidelines for governments and CORPORATIONS, typically involving some form of neoliberal prescription.

To this end, the OECD was involved in the abortive Multilateral Agreement on Investment negotiations and participates in the implementation of agreements reached and overseen by the WORLD TRADE ORGANIZATION and likewise works in partnership with the G8, the INTERNATIONAL MONETARY FUND, regional development banks and the WORLD BANK. As an organization that represents countries that account for two-thirds of the world's economic output, the OECD appears to have as one of its main functions a less than equal engagement with developing countries in an attempt to re-create the latter in an image of its own choosing.

FURTHER INFORMATION
Official site: www.oecd.org
Critical view: www.tuac.org

P

PATRIARCHY is rule or government by the father. Associated with the theory of the divine right of kings as expounded by James Stuart, King of England and Scotland (1566–1625) in *Royal Gift (Basilikon Doron)* (1599), whereby the power of a king is bestowed by their male god and they are therefore only answerable to it. Robert Filmer (1588–1653) sought justification for male domination in *Patriarcha* (1680) – published posthumously – by tracing male authority through the Judaeo-Christian myth of Adam being granted absolute power and **PRIVATE PROPERTY** over the whole world. This was supposed to have descended through a process of primogeniture – sole inheritance by the first-born male – through the kings of Israel to European monarchs; although Filmer acknowledged that lineage could not be traced directly.

More generally, the term is used to refer to societal institutions and processes that afford primacy and powers of **EXPLOITATION** to fathers, sons and men over mothers, daughters and women. This logic was refuted by Mary Wollstonecraft (1759–1797), *A Vindication of the Rights of Woman* (1792). Although not exclusive to capitalist society, male dominance in the institutions of government, **CIVIL SOCIETY** and **CORPORATIONS** forms the subject of feminist critique. Even though domination is generally achieved through a subtle process, overt examples are evident in hierarchical religious organizations such as orthodox Judaism, Roman Catholicism and Orthodox Christianity. See also **LIBERATION**.

POLITICS refers, in the broadest sense of the term, to the nature, distribution and dynamics of private and public forms of **POWER** – who has it, who does not, where it originates, who wants it, what they do with it and what they will do to acquire it. Understood this way, politics is a pervasive and ubiquitous societal phenomenon, the essence of which involves the emergence, practice and resolution of human conflict in cultural, economic, 'political' and social spheres. Power and domination are, for example, evident in all aspects of **SOCIAL RELATIONS** and at inter-social and societal levels – in any hierarchical organization where authority and the exercise of power exclude a free exchange of ideas associated with participatory, democratic decision-making.

Even if understood as the art or science of government – whether it be the realpolitik of Niccolò Machiavelli (1469–1527), *The Prince* (*Il principe*) (1532), or *Utilitarianism* (1863) advocated by John Stuart Mill (1806–1873) – politics is not the sole preserve of the STATE. On the contrary, it involves the employment of any decision-making power that has at least the potential for the use of coercion, force or violence. The perception that politics is a discrete societal realm can be traced to the nineteenth-century drive by marginalist economists like William Stanley Jevons (1835–1882), *The Theory of Political Economy* (1871), to establish their discipline as a separate and distinct branch of science as opposed to classical political economy.

Today, this arbitrary, artificial and misleading distinction is reinforced by NEOLIBERALISM, is popularized and confirmed by the media's exclusive categorization of certain processes, institutions and issues as 'politics', and is confirmed by academic disciplines that focus on the psephological measurement of public opinion. Political activity, according to such a schema, is reduced to membership of and campaigning for parties and pressure groups, and the behaviour of lobbyists and of voters at elections. Likewise political processes are reduced to the conduct of elections, the practice of government, the performance of party leaders, governmental policy and decision-making procedures and the efficacy of decisions and policy.

Political institutions are equated with the machinery of government – the voting procedures of the legislature and executive – and the public administration of crime, immigration, TAXATION and welfare by civil servants. Political issues are also confined to questions of civic rights and responsibilities, suffrage, methods of electing representatives and the exercise of regulatory state power – though the armed forces, police and other employees of the state are said to be non-political. Consequently, organizations like the environmental group Planet Ark in Australia claim to be non-political because they do not align themselves with political parties and will work with any government.

In the real world, however, the tangible effects of financial and economic power mean that no such dichotomy can be drawn between economics and politics – as anarchists, communists and syndicalists argue. The fortunes of political parties have, for example, long depended on funding from wealthy individuals, CORPORATIONS or trade unions. More and more, they appear to rely on wealthy individuals and corporations to enable them to purchase advertising time and space and therefore electoral success. The degree to which wealthy donors are able to influence certain aspects of public policy debate and influence decisions in their own interests is therefore a concern, as is the extent to which those without financial resources are excluded, alienated or choose to refrain from the democratic process.

In the second half of the twentieth century, the attempt to separate politics from the practice of everyday life was challenged by a current in radical thought and action that focused not on changing governments or winning elections, but on mobilizing people based on common interests or identity. Examples of movements that adopted this type of approach include the struggles for recognition of rights for blacks, gays, women, young people and those whose lives are affected by AIDS; causes and issues that also motivated the NEW LEFT.

This view or manifestation of politics brings us back to the general definition outlined earlier, whereby the microcosm of human conflict is founded on interpersonal relations that involve power, domination and the authority of one person or persons over others. Following on from ideas promulgated by Michel Foucault (1926–1984), for example, forms of oppression, identity and struggle are not believed to be the immutable product of human nature, but consequences of the social and cultural interactions between people in institutions like the family, church, school, corporations and TRADE UNIONS. Such factors are perceived to be just as important, perhaps even more so, than state apparatuses – the police, judiciary and military – that are associated with the exercise of overt oppression. In this sense, politics constitutes the ultimate social activity – embodying the feminist maxim that 'the personal is political' and its anarchist counterpart that 'everything is politics' – and thereby encompasses the importance of various sources of power. An important consequence of such conclusions is the possibility that new forms of social consciousness and social relations can be forged through struggles against authority, discipline and oppression wherever it arises.

The latest manifestation of anti-capitalism represents a movement in which various groups and interests seek alliances to resolve issues by targeting areas of CIVIL SOCIETY as sites of struggle. The ZAPATISTAS and the SOCIAL FORUM, for example, represent a new practical politics based on ACTIVISM and the mobilization and motivation of people to build civil resistance, not through political parties or the capture of state institutions, but through the practice of their daily lives. In this way, the current anti-capitalist movement has the potential to transcend the narrow focus of orthodox politics

183

and achieve the emancipation of humanity through a multiplicity of social action that culminates in the realization of human rights – social, economic, cultural, civil and political. Such goals are at odds with an orthodox political process that Bernard Crick, *In Defence of Politics* (2000), acknowledges has degenerated into cynical zero-sum games of semantics and statistics. The process is typified by the use of focus-group-based marketing strategies that formulate party programmes to appeal to a majority of voters, thereby treating them as consumers of political products.

Perhaps this development is an inevitable consequence of establishing special institutions and procedures for the discussion and resolution of issues and conflicts – like class struggle – in an attempt to avoid the risk of social disruption that would threaten the existence of the present political, economic and social system. Instead of addressing such matters as part of everyday life, they are ignored or their relevance denied and this has resulted in a growing distrust of politicians, falling voter turnout, the rise of neo-fascism and a questioning of the ACCOUNTABILITY, justification, legitimacy, TRANSPARENCY and purpose of government in general. This process, termed *Legitimation Crisis* (1973) by Jürgen Habermas, has been enhanced by a growth in the power and number of transnational actors like multinational corporations and the WORLD TRADE ORGANIZATION. See also DEMOCRACY.

POVERTY is a descriptive term that denotes inequalities of wealth, and, as with the subcategories of absolute and relative poverty, usually involves some form of comparison. Absolute poverty, for example, implies a level at which the minimum requirements of a healthy existence are not met. People and Planet (www.peopleandplanet.org) estimate that 1.2 billion people fall into this category, because they do not have access to safe water supplies, enough food, shelter and basic health care. Similarly, Jan Vandemoortele, *Are We Really Reducing Global Poverty* (2002), reports that the number of people below the international poverty line fell from 1.3 to 1.1 billion between 1990 and 1999. Relative poverty, on the other hand, is measured as the comparative wealth of groups and individuals. Globally, for example, the 1998 United Nations *Human Development Report* stated that the richest 225 people in the world had an income equivalent to 47 per cent of the world's population – 2.5 billion people, while the World Development Movement estimates that the poorest 57 per cent earn as much as the richest 1 per cent.

At the national level, poverty can be defined in terms of a person's or group's standard of living in relation to the rest of society – their level of access to goods and services available to others. This can also be measured in terms of their income and access to capital, money, material goods, savings and other resources that will enable them to live a 'normal' life for that society – like being able to raise a healthy family and make full use of cultural and educational facilities. Such standards necessarily vary depending on which nations and which parts of the world are being considered. An income of less than US$1 per day is generally used to indicate poverty in developing countries.

In reality, poverty is more complex and is irreducible to a universal standard, because not only does the cost of living vary within and between nations, but institutions and nations also choose to set different targets according to their own objectives. Thus, the ORGANIZATION FOR ECONOMIC COOPERATION AND DEVELOPMENT chooses to exclude the richest sections of society from its calculations by drawing its poverty line at 60 per cent of the median equalized net household income, thereby comparing the poorest in each society with those in the middle. Other factors included in such calculations can involve the domestic circumstances of individuals, like parenthood, age or marital status. Likewise an ability to enjoy leisure activities might be counted, where poverty is relative to the lifestyle enjoyed by the majority.

A poverty line is used by some progressive governments to judge the efficacy of welfare and other measures designed to ensure that no one has a net income below the minimum required for an acceptable standard of living. These standards are arbitrary, however, as an increase in median incomes would mean that the minimum standard becomes higher. Hence, there are contentious debates in industrialized countries as to whether pensions, social security and welfare payments should be adjusted for inflation or average earnings. If the lowest incomes – including those that depend on such payments – do not keep pace with average income growth in real terms, for example, then relative poverty will grow. Ironically, those who advocate increasing pensions in line with price inflation conveniently ignore the fact that earnings are really no more than the price paid to workers for their labour-power.

Indicators are also arbitrary because there will be little qualitative difference between the standards of living of people who are marginally above or marginally below the cut-off point. The negative aspects of poverty are also continuous, which means that increased crime rates in poor communities affect everyone regardless of the marginal differences in their incomes. Similarly, an absence of safe and stable homes, adequate clothing and regular meals is considered to impair children's ability to concentrate and therefore learn effectively while at school regardless of parental income. The fight against poverty is therefore perceived to be primarily a social goal that involves highlighting and tackling the interrelationship between the causes, effects and trends of poverty and social inequality.

KEYNESIAN economists consider a large percentage of citizens without disposable income to be an impediment to economic growth, because that means less demand for consumer goods. Paradoxically, societies with welfare systems ensure that social security benefits are set at a level or paid in a way that does not deter people from taking the lowest-paid jobs; hence statutory minimum wages are intended to make low-paid work more attractive, as are working tax credits. Even so, if means-tested assistance is reduced as income rises, recipients will be no better off and stuck in what has been called a 'poverty trap'.

The entire developing world provides an example of relative poverty in comparison to the wealth of industrialized nations and multinational corporations. There are also specific features of deprivation at the regional, national and local levels – AIDS, environmental degradation, illiteracy, marginalization, social injustice and denial of human rights being symptomatic. Various campaigning organizations argue that such conditions are exacerbated or perpetuated by the INTERNATIONAL MONETARY FUND and the WORLD BANK through the imposition of STRUCTURAL ADJUSTMENT PROGRAMMES and their refusal to countenance the cancellation of INTERNATIONAL DEBT. Multilateral trade agreements implemented under the auspices of the WORLD TRADE ORGANIZATION are also considered to be an integral part of the problem by giving ever more power to multinational corporations to challenge national regulations such as labour standards.

Poverty in the developing world is particularly associated with the experience of children, as demonstrated by David Gordon et al. in *Child Poverty in the Developing World* (2003). The fact that women and children suffer disproportionately (People and Planet estimate that women account for 70 per cent of the world's poor) indicates that unequal power relations – including class, caste, disability, sex and race – are a major determinant of poverty. Organizations like Oxfam campaign to alleviate poverty within CAPITALISM by promoting the right to a livelihood, services, security, participation and diversity, while seeking change at global, national and grassroots levels to address the needs of real people by empowering them to enforce changes in policies and practices. Others see SUSTAINABLE DEVELOPMENT as part of the answer, while anarchists, communists and socialists consider poverty to be endemic to capitalism.

FURTHER INFORMATION

Global poverty: www.undp.org/poverty/docs/arewereally-reducing-gobal-poverty. pdf

Poverty Lines: aspe.hhs.gov/poverty/papers/relabs.htm

UNDP's Human Development Report: hdr.undp.org/reports/global/1998/en

POWER is a form of relation between actors, be they institutions or people, in economic, political and social spheres, and involves a real or perceived ability to change or influence activity, behaviour and preferences. In other words, people or things are made to do something that they would not have done without external constraint or pressure; hence, Michel Foucault (1926–1984), 'The Subject and Power' (1982), argued that power permeates and distorts all social relationships. Defined thus, power involves the related categories of authority, coercion, force, manipulation and persuasion. Coercion, for example, implies the threat of force, while persuasion involves the capacity to manipulate. Likewise, authority understood as legitimacy can be a resource for power that gives the right to act in a particular way, as in the idea that only the STATE has the right to employ physical force.

In capitalist society, this prerogative is linked to the theory of DEMOCRACY whereby elected representatives make laws on behalf of voters, enforce them on their behalf and citizens are therefore expected to comply, whether they have the right to vote or not. An integral aspect of this reasoning involves the assertion that tyranny or abuse of power by an individual or group is militated by the separation of executive, judicial and legislative functions. Such safeguards clearly failed in the twentieth century in those countries where fascist and military dictatorships were installed or where the populace called the authority of the state into question. Nevertheless, C. Wright Mills (1916–1962), *The Power Elite* (1956), and others have argued that certain groups seek to dominate political, economic and military institutions and networks to control and manipulate policy areas in their own interest; see MILITARY–INDUSTRIAL COMPLEX.

David Hume (1711–1786), *Of the Original Contract* (1748), considered all hitherto existing governments to be founded on the use of force, violence and usurpation, without any pretence of consent or voluntary subjection. In contrast, the systems of CAPITALISM and liberal democracy are presented

187

as enduring traditions, the validity of which no right-minded person would seek to question. This IDEOLOGY conceals the reality that government is still practised by those able to accumulate, access and expend vast wealth; that it is normally maintained through the management and manipulation of knowledge or, as a last resort, through the exercise of physical force by the police and military. The preferred options for social control involve the use of ADVERTISING, censorship, MEDIA, PROPAGANDA and education systems to influence and shape beliefs, ideas, opinions and perceptions. Through the selective presentation of information, for example, a particular way of seeing the world is portrayed as 'common knowledge' or 'common sense' and approved lifestyles are depicted as the norm.

Those who own and control the means of production, distribution and exchange are able to exert an influence over the behaviour and outlook of people at work. The power to hire, fire and discipline employees for errant behaviour are forms of coercion, whereas opportunities for better pay, conditions and promotion are ways of persuading workers to perform according to expectations. In turn, these rewards afford greater purchasing power and the opportunity to demonstrate success to others through the purchase of status symbols. Where more resources are available, as demonstrated by Paul Ginsborg, *Silvio Berlusconi* (2004), whole markets are manipulated through the use of advertising, the monopolistic control of prices and other means. Such influence can be mediated by macroeconomic conditions, however, as levels of (un)employment can affect demand for commodities and the bargaining power of a TRADE UNION. Perhaps the most extreme examples of corporate power involve the SWEATSHOP and the ability to influence government policy through the decision whether or not to invest in a particular country.

The last example refers to the international power of the MULTINATIONAL CORPORATION, some with an annual turnover that exceeds that of entire industrialized sovereign countries. Ironically, however, only countries are normally referred to as economic, national or state powers, not the corporate concerns that dwarf most of them. The United States of America, for example, is known as a superpower, while Australia, China, India and Israel are variously considered to be regional powers as a direct consequence of their economic and military strength. Where dominance is disputed or contested by an equivalent or rising regional interest the relationship is referred to as a balance of power. In cases of relative economic and military capability, a deciding factor might involve the cultural influence of corporate brands, the acceptance of values associated with 'democracy' or the appreciation of particular forms of art and literature. Michael Hardt and Antonio Negri, *Empire* (2001), for example, consider ideological influences to be exerted by the INTERNATIONAL MONETARY FUND, WORLD BANK, WORLD TRADE ORGANIZATION and UNITED NATIONS.

Institutions often seek to shape opinion through the pronouncements of 'experts' and other figures vested with authority by the radio and tele-communications media. From a feminist perspective, for example, the predominance of men in positions of power, whether it be in churches, CORPORATIONS, courts or governments, indicates and reinforces the power relations of PATRIARCHY and associated relations of EXPLOITATION. Symptomatic relations of domination and oppression are also evidenced in the prejudicial beliefs and practices of heterosexism, homophobia, RACISM and sexism, through which the options for autonomous human aspiration and behaviour are deliberately restricted.

At the official level, protective charters like the UNIVERSAL DECLARATION OF HUMAN RIGHTS and consequent domestic legislation are intended to curtail the assumption and practice of absolute power. In reality, however, power relations are constituted through the practice of resistance and struggle. This involves the extent to which people are prepared to accept the authority of others or subjugate themselves to the threat or use of physical force. Resistance and struggle are ways in which people seek to assert autonomy and rights to self-determination, whether in the factory, family, office or society at large and thereby constrain the actions or power of would-be oppressors. Understood this way, power is a process – a social relationship – in which people prefer to assert their power to do that which they choose as opposed to exerting their desires, expectations or wishes over others. For Hardt and Negri, as well as for John Holloway, *Change the World without Taking Power* (2002), this involves the practice of 'anti-power': the refusal to participate in or withdrawal from centres of existing power relations and the counter-power of oppositional organizations and social movements. The dilemma they posit is a not a simple choice between withdrawal and participation, or even revolutionary strategy focused on the seizure of the state, but finding and taking to its logical conclusion the most effective way of moving against and beyond existing power and therefore SOCIAL RELATIONS.

FURTHER INFORMATION

Analysis of Black Power: www.marxists.org/archive/james-clr/works/1967/black-power.htm

PRIVATE PROPERTY is not unique to CAPITALISM, as each mode of production exhibits specific property forms, relations and rights. Anthropological studies, dating back to Lewis H. Morgan (1818–1881), *Ancient Society* (1877), for example, define tribal societies according to a collective ownership of land and egalitarian practices that exclude the existence of classes, state, hereditary status, EXPLOITATION and economic stratification. In order for a system of private property to exist, therefore, it requires some form of human justification, which in the case of capitalism occurs under the guise of the legal system and, curiously enough, as Article 17 of the UNIVERSAL DECLARATION OF HUMAN RIGHTS.

As a general category, property is defined in terms of a relation between a person and a thing, whether that is a concrete object – an animal, building, land or machine – or something abstract such as bank deposits, INTELLECTUAL PROPERTY or financial market mechanisms, such as bonds, derivatives, futures, options and stock. In either case, that which is owned by a legal person is considered to constitute property, and under capitalism a legal person can be a natural person – a human being – a CORPORATION or the STATE. The abstract notion of the corporation as an 'artificial' or 'moral' person masks the reality that it is a collective enterprise that exercises POWER over the lives and professional activities of its employees. In other words, only by conceiving of the corporation as an individual in legal terms is it made compatible with the principle of individualism that underpins the notion of capitalist property ownership and ensuing relations.

Corporations therefore enjoy the same property rights as real people to buy, enjoy, own, possess, sell, transfer or use a given thing – and, at the same time, exclude all others from exercising such RIGHTS. All such privileges exist according to legal process, which confers contractual obligations on buyer, seller and user so that a particular thing can be traded as a COMMODITY. Moreover, such rights confer the ability to derive PROFIT from ownership, as in the case of royalties in lieu of use or possession, whether that is by lease or licence. Hence, the assertion made by Pierre-Joseph Proudhon (1809–1865), *What is Property? (Qu'est-ce que la Propriété?)* (1840), that all property is theft, because the legal construct of private property denies people equal access to the rights and benefits of ownership, possession and use, and therefore compromises individual FREEDOM, even when they are supposed to be legal equals.

Stated briefly, capitalist property ownership equates to a right to derive profit and is therefore the consequence of and has implications for the economic, legal and political system. Thus, the manner in which property is recognized and methods by which it is distributed and redistributed affect the concepts and practice of JUSTICE and power within a given society. Laws governing inheritance, for example, impact on intergenerational justice by compromising the principles of EQUALITY among men, women and the population as a whole; the interrelations of which are explored by Jeremy Waldron, *The Right to Private Property* (1988). In the case of primogeniture, only the first-born male is allowed to inherit a family's wealth. More generally, inherited wealth undermines the concept of equality of opportunity by privileging those who can afford to buy private education, health care and a better standard of nutrition. This also applies on an international scale, where the industrialized world and the CORPORATIONS based there enjoy an unparalleled advantage over developing countries and industries in terms of the ownership and control of financial and physical collateral.

In capitalist society, the ultimate determinant of such advantages is ownership of the means of production, distribution and exchange – factories, transport, shops and money. A distinguishing feature of which is the fact that the vast majority of people do not have access to means of production that would enable them to produce their own goods and thereby reproduce themselves. Without access to such facilities, they are forced to sell their labour-power to employers in return for a wage. In this manner, ownership of property in capitalist society affords employers the power of hiring and firing employees, determining the relations of production and therefore the CLASS and social strata of society.

Even where property is held collectively or in common as joint ownership, by a community or cooperative, the capitalist legal system interprets ownership in terms of individual entities. Where industries have been nationalized or taken into public ownership within the context of capitalist society or mixed economy, for example, they are generally run by the same people and in the same way as before. Essentially, the social relations of production remain unchanged, because those who own it in theory – the populace at large – have no immediate control over how it is used. Similar problems were faced in the Soviet Union and other self-proclaimed socialist systems where property was held by the state in the name of the whole people, but run and managed by a bureaucracy.

According to such analyses, personal possessions – cars, clothing, entertainment equipment, food, and so on – constitute a separate category, lacking the ability to exert significant impact on the economy at large, but indicated in the processes of **ALIENATION** and **REIFICATION**. Similarly, the principle of self-ownership implies that each individual has ownership of and sovereignty over their own body and therefore the right to exercise labour-power and talents, to express views and values according to their personal desires. Nevertheless, the integrity of the human body is subject to exigencies where pharmaceuticals corporations seek to patent human deoxyribonucleic acid (DNA) or others benefit from bonded labour employed in **SWEATSHOP** and other exploitative conditions that restrict individual autonomy during the working day.

While the concept of **GLOBAL COMMONS** is anathema to private property relations, **ANARCHISM**, **COMMUNISM** and **SOCIALISM** represent the main anti-capitalist traditions that advocate abolition of private ownership. In the case of socialism, this involves communal ownership in the form of the state, while anarchism and communism theorize the absence of state and therefore a system of communal ownership based on direct democratic participation and decision-making in all sectors of society. To a certain extent, the concept and practice of **COPYLEFT** is consistent with these traditions as improvements to a document or computer programme are made by individuals and shared with others on the basis that ownership cannot be privatized. As Roy Vogt, *Whose Property?* (1999), and Calestous Juma and J.B. Ojwang, *In Land We Trust* (1996), recognize, there is a fundamental conflict of interest where property rights permit pollution and environmental degradation over the well-being of community and environment and are therefore inimical to **SUSTAINABLE DEVELOPMENT**.

FURTHER INFORMATION

Friedrich Engels, *The Origin of the Family, Private Property and the State*: www.marxists. org/archive/marx/works/1884/origin-family

Pierre-Joseph Proudhon, *What is Property?*: www.marxists.org/reference/subject/economics/proudhon/property/index.htm

PRIVATIZATION see DEREGULATION.

PROFIT is subdivided into several categories in textbooks written by economists and others, such as Richard Lipsey and Alec Chrystal, *Principles of Economics* (1999). Normal profit, for example, is the difference between the direct cost of producing items sold and the revenue achieved through the selling price, but is also known as the average rate of profit, and for conventional accountancy purposes is referred to as the gross margin or gross profit. In contrast, the category of normal profit is based on the assumption that a 'rational' person would not continue in business unless they can achieve a return that exceeds costs of production. According to this way of thinking, profit is the payment to which entrepreneurs are entitled as a reward for having made available the capital to enable a particular project to take place and for taking the risk of losing out on their investment.

'True profit' is the name given to the reward for enduring risks, which might include the volatility of the MARKET, the competition of other producers, advances in technology or legal, financial and political uncertainties. Another category familiar to economists is 'net profit', which takes into account rent paid to the owners of land and property, the costs of ADVERTISING, distributing and marketing products by wholesalers and retailers, together with interest paid on loans to banks, TAXATION and wages paid to workers. This is said to include manual and mental work, but does not take account of the fact that every manual procedure involves mental exertion in order to put it into practice. Finally, there are two more types of profit. The first is known as 'supernormal profit' and accrues from interest charges that are higher than the standard rate; they can be associated, in anti-capitalist terms, with INTERNATIONAL DEBT and the generation of short-term CAPITAL FLOWS. The second is 'abnormal', 'economic' or 'extraordinary' profit, and derives from any innovation that limits competition or from monopoly conditions created by copyrights, patents and brands that allow producers to charge more.

The 'profit motive' – the desire to acquire and maximize profits through business enterprise(s) – is seen by advocates as a dynamic force in capitalist society that promotes economic growth, encourages investment and thereby facilitates the satisfaction of consumer wants. As an added and unplanned bonus, it also helps create enough wealth to be redistributed through taxation in the form of social and welfare provision. Those less enamoured with CAPITALISM see the unfettered pursuit of economic growth as endangering the environment – through the exhaustion of natural resources, for example – and ultimately threatening the existence of life on the planet (see ENVIRONMENTALISM). Others see advertising, marketing and other social pressures – such as ALIENATION – as creating a vicious circle of spurious needs that result in a perpetual demand for new commodities, while generating unecessary waste in the form of discarded purchases. Ironically, such factors are not included in risks that economists identify as justifying corporate rewards in the form of profit and are therefore excluded from the calculation of GROSS DOMESTIC PRODUCT.

Critiques of corporate practice such as that outlined by Joel Bakan, *The Corporation* (2004), or critiques of capitalism in general – based on ANARCHISM and MARXISM – also point to the connection between profit and the EXPLOITATION of people. As part of this analysis, it is acknowledged that money is paid to buy certain means of production – factories, machinery, materials and so forth. The point of disputation, in brief terms, relates to the purchase of labour-power – without which the means of production would be useless and worthless – and the fact that it is human beings that produce the commodities that are subsequently sold for more than they cost to produce – that is, for profit. Here the rate of profit is calculated by taking into account the value of components and materials used in production and the ratio of surplus to necessary labour-time.

Karl Marx (1818–1883), *Theories of Surplus Value* (1863), for example, calculated this ratio according to the amount of time worked by an individual compared to the amount s/he would need to work in order to have enough wages to meet the cost of living. Following this line of reasoning, profit can only be made if a process of exploitation happens at work and at home. In other words, the monetary worth of unpaid labour is expropriated from workers; and at the same time domestic, family and household labour required to replenish the worker for another day also goes unpaid. This process is most obvious in the form of the SWEATSHOP and is evident in any circumstance where profits are not shared equally with workers, but distributed among directors, investors and others – as dividends to shareholders, for example.

FURTHER INFORMATION

Theories of Surplus Value: www.marxists.org/archive/marx/works/1863/theories-surplus-value

PROPAGANDA originally meant the propagation of a set of principles or doctrine, as in the Roman Catholic Congregation for Propagation of the Faith (Congregatio de Propaganda Fide) established in 1622 by Pope Gregory XV to manage missions. In modern usage, it refers to the subordination of knowledge to state policy and was therefore used pejoratively by Western capitalist countries to denigrate the educational and public information policies and practice of the Soviet Union and its allies during the cold war. This simplification ignored the Soviet distinction between agitation (*agitatsii*) as the formation of public opinion and propaganda (*propagandi*) as the dissemination of revolutionary ideas and Marxism–Leninism in an attempt to overcome the culture of the tsarist regime. The National Socialist government in Germany between 1933 and 1945 pursued similar aims through the Ministry for Public Enlightenment and Propaganda, which vetted the output of artists, journalists, musicians, writers and the press, and productions in film and theatre as well as on radio and television.

In 1917, US president Woodrow Wilson (1856–1924) set up the Committee for Public Information – otherwise known as the Creel Committee. This body employed George Creel (1876–1953), Edward Bernays (1891–1995) and Walter Lippman (1889–1974), among others, to produce favourable publicity for their government during World War I, a practice now known as white propaganda. Similarly, Britain created a Ministry of Information in the 1930s to promote state policy and counteract Nazi propaganda using film, print, radio and the spoken word. During the cold war both sides attempted to influence their own citizens and the populations of other states. The United States Information Agency operated the Voice of America, Radio Free Europe and Radio Liberty, while the Soviet Union ran Radio Moscow and Radio Peace and Freedom. Even today, Cuba and the USA bombard each other with broadcasts, as do the two Koreas, with each attempting to block the transmissions of the other.

In the sense that propaganda constitutes misleading information in support of a political campaign or the presentation of government policy, the most obvious example in recent times was the case for war on Iraq. As the contributors to David Miller, *Tell Me Lies* (2004), testify, the argument was based on 'a real and imminent threat' posed by weapons of mass destruction and the unspecified danger of TERRORISM, linked to the atrocities committed in New York in September 2001, thereby tapping into public fears. In fact, the whole 'war on terror' is a prime example of propaganda through the simplification of complex subjects and use of an undefined yet ever-present enemy and threat to manufacture uncritical acceptance of government policy and practice. This is achieved through the management or manipulation of the news media through government announcements and the publication of reports and public information documents – such as how to survive a nuclear or terrorist attack. The frequency of such messages is designed to affect public perceptions, and this process is reinforced by radio and television broadcasts, as the 'news' agenda influences the content of current-affairs or talk-show programmes. On a subtler level, a climate of insecurity is also maintained with the production of films about alien invasion, natural disasters and foreign invaders.

In typically euphemistic fashion, the US Information Agency uses the term 'public diplomacy' to describe its activities, while the use of vague words and phrases that everyone understands in their own way – such as 'common knowledge' – is the point at which propaganda overlaps with IDEOLOGY. In this sense, propaganda is normally used to refer to the political agenda of governments and parties, even though there are obvious analogies between the skills and techniques employed in ADVERTISING, marketing and public relations. Both involve the partial presentation and use of factual information to influence perceptions and behaviour in a manner designed to benefit those who transmit the message. Nevertheless, the term 'propaganda' is normally used pejoratively to imply deception, while 'advertising' is equated with persuasion – a dubious distinction explored by Anthony Pratkanis and Elliot Aronson in *Age of Propaganda* (2001).

FURTHER INFORMATION

Encyclopaedia of propaganda: www.disinfopedia.org
Advocacy of 'public diplomacy': www.publicdiplomacy.org

PROTEST is a generic term that can be used to refer to any form of activity that is intended to put pressure on or persuade a government, bank, lending institution, corporation or some other authority or organization to change their policy and practice. It can take the form of violent or peaceful action, which can be either direct, as in the case of CIVIL DISOBEDIENCE, or include flag-burning, the writing and publication of zines, satire, song, dance, music, street and other forms of theatre in its indirect form. Public demonstrations usually involve rallying existing support to show strength of feeling and have a dual purpose of publicizing a cause while attempting to change or galvanize public opinion.

An act of protest therefore has limited intentions and does not form part of a programme to overthrow the STATE, though a revolutionary movement can emerge from or participate in a protest movement and stage protests as a tactic to raise their own profile. More usually, protest forms part of a campaign, is a response to an event or situation intended to demonstrate resistance, or expresses opposition to someone else's activity or policy. Protesters often have preferred alternative policies and practices or solutions, but these are usually diverse and not necessarily compatible. The common ground for protesters is therefore what they are against, what they are protesting about, as opposed to what they are for.

Campaign groups, causes and movements that involve or focus on a single issue are usually termed 'protest politics' or a 'protest movement'. Examples include the Campaign for Nuclear Disarmament and those anti-war movements that opposed attacks on and involvement in Vietnam, Serbia, Iraq and elsewhere. Such movements are characterized by a focus on the tactic of protest, in the hope that a groundswell of support and public opinion will help realize their goal, without necessarily challenging or changing the existing socio-economic interests and power relations; though this might be an inevitable consequence of success. Historical examples of movements that have engaged in acts of spectacle include Chartists and suffragettes, who campaigned for an extension of the franchise; trade unionists in pursuit of recognition, employment rights or wage increases; and civil rights campaigners. Many student organizations and the causes they promote are also categorized as protest movements, but this ignores the diverse aims and viewpoints of participants and is often applied in a pejorative sense to imply a lack of serious intent or accurate analysis.

The MEDIA adopt this approach to the modern-day anti-capitalist movement partly out of ignorance, partly as a consequence of superficial media coverage that focuses on spectacle over serious analysis, and partly out of deliberate intent to misrepresent the significance of the movement. While there have undoubtedly been some spectacular demonstrations, these are not the whole picture. Those who demonstrated against the WORLD TRADE ORGANIZATION (WTO) in Seattle in November 1999, for example, were exercised by a variety of causes that included labour-law abuses, WORKERS' RIGHTS, environmental destruction, human rights, and the erosion of wages and social benefits in the USA. This and other protests also included people who oppose CONSUMERISM and campaign to make CORPORATIONS accountable.

The protests against the INTERNATIONAL MONETARY FUND and the WORLD BANK during their annual meeting held in Prague in the Czech Republic during the final week of September 2000 also involved counter-conferences as well as DIRECT ACTION and mass demonstrations organized by the Initiative Against Economic Globalization. The SOCIAL FORUM usually involves or culminates in huge demonstrations and is further evidence of the development of a movement, the strategies and aims of which involve and represent more than mere protest. Furthermore, the efficacy of the movement is demonstrated by the failure of governments to agree on measures to privatize trade in services at the Fifth Ministerial meeting of the WTO held in September 2003 in Cancún, Mexico, and the choice of increasingly remote or inaccessible venues for meetings to avoid protests. The G8 meeting held in 2004, for example, was held on an island off the coast of Georgia in the USA and known as the Sea Island Summit.

FURTHER INFORMATION

Annual reports on protests in developing countries:
2000: www.globalpolicy.org/socecon/bwi-wto/imf/2000/protest.htm;
2001: www.wdm.org.uk/cambriefs/debt/Unrest2.pdf;
2002: www.wdm.org.uk/cambriefs/debt/States%20of%20Unrest%20III_04.03.pdf

Q

QUISLING is a generic term or synonym for traitor and an eponym for any leader of an enemy-sponsored regime. It derives from the actions and reputation of Vidkun Abraham Lauritz Jonssøn Quisling (1887–1945). A major in the Norwegian army, Quisling served as minister of war 1931–33, until he decided to form the fascist National Unity Party (Nasjonal Samling). Quisling adopted the role of party Führer (*Fører*), established links with Germany through their naval attaché in Oslo and introduced a pro-German and anti-Semitic party policy from 1935 onwards. In 1939, Quisling visited Hitler to suggest how Germany could assist the establishment of a sympathetic government in Norway. After the German invasion of 1940, he was minister president of Norway, 1942–45, until his trial, conviction and execution.

R

RACISM involves the holding of prejudicial views and the practising of discrimination against individuals and groups based on their race, usually involving projections of inferiority and superiority. This is in contrast to the narrower doctrine of racialism, which seeks to posit a causal connection between race and behaviour; though one often informs the other. The concept of race as a distinguishing feature of human beings is a fairly recent phenomenon, however, as the term means a group of common origin and was used in this broad sense prior to the nineteenth century. Application of the concept to humanity is attributed to Robert Knox (1791–1862), *The Races of Men* (1850), and Joseph Arthur, Comte de Gobineau (1816–1862), *The Inequality of Human Races (Essai sur l'inegalitie des races humaines)* (1855). Knox had earlier achieved notoriety as an anatomist for his acquisition of cadavers from Burke and Hare in Edinburgh.

Interest in differentiating human beings coincided with the growth of international interaction that accompanied expansion of European imperialism and EMPIRE in Africa, the Americas and Asia; with racial superiority used as one of the justifications for conquest. Some, like Houston Stewart Chamberlain (1855–1927), *The Foundations of the Nineteenth Century (Die Grundlagen des neunzehnten jahrhunderts)* (1899), depicted western civilization as the consequence of a struggle between races. His focus on Aryans and Jews found a particular resonance in Nazi racial theories, which considered Roma, Slavs and Jews to be subhuman and ultimately led to the carnage and crime of the Holocaust.

In the aftermath of World War II, the United Nations Educational, Scientific and Cultural Organization issued proclamations that refuted the validity of biological differentiation between races: *Statement on Race*, Parts 1 and 2 (1949–51). The idea that there are subspecies of *Homo sapiens* has also been rejected by studies of mitochondrial deoxyribonucleic acid (DNA), which suggest that *Homo sapiens* evolved from a common ancestor. Despite the absence of a scientific basis for racial theories based on biology, prejudice and discrimination continue to be justified on the bases of ignorance, language, religion, skin colour and other differences between people that are constituted by cultural, economic, institutional and social factors.

In this sense, there is little difference between the categories of ethnicity, nationality and race. Some forms of nationalism and ethnic chauvinism, for example, are premissed on the distrust or fear of that which is different and unknown, while CULTURE, history, language and territory are combined to create a sense of collective consciousness or identity. Similar notions have been used as a tool to establish and maintain minority control, as in the Hindu caste system, or the racial segregation in the south-eastern states of the USA from the abolition of slavery to the 1964 Civil Rights Act. Daniel Malan (1874–1959), Hendrik Verwoerd (1901–1966) and Johannes Strijdom (1893–1958) devised a similarly justified system of apartheid that operated in South Africa from 1948 to 1991.

More usually, racism is directed against minorities, as in the treatment of Acholi and Lango indigenous people and the expulsion of Asians from Uganda in 1972. In Malaysia, Chinese citizens suffer discrimination, as do the Roma in central and Eastern Europe. Postcolonial migrants like Asians and West Indians in Britain, Indonesians and Surinamese in the Netherlands, central Africans in Belgium, and North and West Africans in France are also victims of racism. Whereas European countries sought to associate domestic interests with national identity and empire during the nineteenth century, neo-fascist and neo-Nazi groups like Combat 18, the British National Party and National Front in Britain, and the Front National in France, now exploit socio-economic depravation and fears of TERRORISM to promote racist scape-goating. In Australia, One Nation employs similar tactics to blame social ills on immigrants from Asia.

While some of these groups and individuals persist with the fatuous notion that abilities, aptitudes and behaviour are determined by some uni-dentified biological difference, Étienne Balibar, *Is there a Neo-racism?* (1991), argues that cultural and sociological differences now form the main bases for racism. Likewise, Michael Hardt and Antonio Negri, *Empire* (2001), see social separation of groups in terms of dress, interests, locality and music as a two-way process that has replaced fears of the unknown with prejudice based on proximity and visible difference. Paradoxically, therefore, subordinated people develop a common consciousness and a set of interests that are cemented by the very factors that mark them as different.

These and other variables are evident in the articulation of struggles that arise around distinct and differentiated types of EXPLOITATION and attempts to advance the interests and status of groups. Levels of crime, education, employment, POVERTY and representation, for example, are all indicative of years of discrimination and exploitation and typify the way capitalism contrives to distinguish and exploit groups of people in a variety of different ways. In the European Union, all mainstream political parties promote fear and anxiety about refugees and asylum-seekers, as recorded by Alana Lentin, *Racism and Anti-racism in Europe* (2004), and this in turn fuels the problem of HUMAN TRAFFICKING and results in the imprisonment, deportation and vilification of all migrants including refugees. Fatal arson attacks on refugee hostels in Rostock, Solingen and Moln in Germany during the early 1990s are indicative of the policy of scapegoating and of electoral strategies that appeal to prejudice rather than promoting inclusivity.

In Britain, the murder of Stephen Lawrence and his family's struggle for justice helped to highlight the level of institutional racism in the Metropolitan Police. Meanwhile, organizations like the Campaign against Racism and Fascism and Searchlight work to highlight and combat stereotypical media images and reports on Africa and Asia, the activity of neo-Nazi and fascist organizations and the exploitative practices of CORPORATIONS and other large organizations in developing countries. This latter point is explored by Frank Furedi, *New Ideology of Imperialism* (1994). Across the industrialized world, the so-called 'war on terror' has also led to the identification and distrust of Arab males, described by Elaine Hagopian, *Civil Rights in Peril* (2004), and resulted in Islamophobia that is fed by MEDIA frenzy and political strategies that use fear to secure popular acceptance of repressive measures.

FURTHER INFORMATION

AntiRacismNet: www.antifa.net
Campaign Against Racism and Fascism: www.carf.demon.co.uk
Searchlight: www.searchlightmagazine.com

REFUGEE is defined by the United Nations, Convention Relating to the Status of Refugees (1951), as a person who is living outside their country of nationality or usual residence because of a fear of persecution due to their race, RELIGION, nationality, political opinion or membership of a particular social group. They have therefore sought sanctuary or asylum in a second country and cannot or do not want to return home. As a consequence, the person will have lost their home, livelihood, community, even family and are in need of help to re-establish their lives; 80 per cent are women, children or elderly. Of course, such circumstances are not confined to individuals, but can affect any number of people; as in the case of Albanians and Bosnians in the former Yugoslavia, Afghans who fled the Taliban and subsequent war; Congolese, Eritreans, Rwandans and Sierra Leoneans in Africa; and Kurds in Iraq and Turkey.

This definition of a refugee is anomalous, as Patricia Tuitt, *False Images* (1996), demonstrates, however, as it excludes the millions of displaced people who suffer similar privations without leaving their home country. People who flee their homes due to civil war, but remain within the same national borders, for example, are not recognized as refugees and therefore are not eligible for associated relief or protection. Similarly, people who are recognized as facing persecution or severe social and economic deprivation as a group within the country of their birth are not granted formal recognition as refugees. Palestinian refugees dispersed throughout Jordan, Lebanon, Syria, the West Bank and Gaza Strip as a consequence of the 1948 war are also excluded because they are covered by the United Nations Relief and Works Agency for Palestine Refugees in the Near East (UNRWA). Conversely, however, the UN High Commissioner for Refugees (UNHCR) has covered Palestinians not covered by UNRWA since 2002.

Although many refugees wish to return home, there are only about twelve states that are willing to accept refugees for permanent resettlement on a regular basis when there is no realistic possibility of return. There is now a trend for governments – especially in Europe – to introduce tough laws to deter refugees from seeking asylum in their country. Such measures are often introduced in a misguided attempt to placate domestic prejudice that is cultivated by racist political parties and politicians and in contravention of the 1951 Convention, which requires asylum to be granted to refugees and forbids forcible return to nation of origin. Deterrents increasingly include the indefinite detention of refugees in purpose-built centres and even in prisons, together with attempts to withdraw or restrict access to welfare entitlement and provision. Those detained include people awaiting a decision on their application for asylum or leave to stay, an appeal hearing or deportation. They include children, single women, the elderly and people with special medical or psychological needs, such as torture victims; the implications of which are explored by John Wilson and Boris Drozdek, *Broken Spirits* (2004).

In addition to the offices of the UNHCR, national and local organizations – campaign groups, trade unions, political and religious groups, advice centres and community organizations – work to protect the RIGHTS of refugees and provide advice, support and legal representation. Among other things, refugees are helped to access services, challenge refusal of asylum, offered training and employment courses to develop their skills and qualifications and provided with appropriate accommodation. Non-governmental organizations like Refugees International also campaign for the fair treatment of refugees and for fairer asylum, immigration and refugee policies – including the abolition of detention – to build public support and awareness of these issues and make sure that they remain on the political agenda and are therefore discussed in the MEDIA. Assisted by the No Borders Network, activists and organizations also work to ensure that, in line with the UNHCR principle of refoulement, nobody is returned involuntarily to a country where they have reason to fear persecution, and point out that the ARMS TRADE helps fuel the conflicts that create refugees. Likewise the urgency with which governments and multilateral trade agencies promote the free flow of commodities and services across borders is contrasted with the same institution's efforts to deny any such right to people who fear persecution; a point made by Jeremy Harding, *The Uninvited* (2000).

FURTHER INFORMATION

Issues, reports, statistics and analysis: www.refugeecouncil.org.uk
Convention relating to the Status of Refugees: www.unhchr.ch/html/menu3/b/
    o_c_ref.htm

REGULATION is a limit or limits placed on the operation of CORPORATIONS, governments, markets and the provision of public services. In capitalist society, regulations are considered necessary in order to mediate the conflict of interests between those seeking to maximize profits and the interests of consumers, the environment and workers. This translates into publicly imposed rules that govern the behaviour of a firm or industry, in terms of minimum standards for the safety of employees, people who live near factories and those who buy or use the end product, especially food and electrical and gas appliances. Examples in the area of employment practices include trade-union recognition rights, the right to strike, collective bargaining arrangements and minimum wages, and are overseen by bodies like the Advisory, Conciliation and Arbitration Service (ACAS) in Britain and the National Labor Relations Board in the USA. Regulations are therefore intended to balance the interests of the public and corporations – employers and investors – so as not to discourage the effective functioning and development of business activity.

In Britain regulation was first introduced in the form of the Regulation of the Railways Act 1844, which recognized the need to place limits on the activities of monopolies in general and natural monopolies where options for competition were limited. In the USA a number of regulatory bodies were established as part of the presidency of Franklin D. Roosevelt (1882–1945) in response to severe economic depression. Existing agencies include the Securities and Exchange Commission to regulate stocks and shares, the Environmental Protection Agency, the Federal Communications Commission and the Trade Commission. In Britain the process of PRIVATIZATION, started in the 1980s, resulted in the creation of a number of regulatory offices to oversee the operations of public utilities, including communications, electricity, gas, railways and water. Sanctions for breaching regulations variously include fines, de-licensing – where an organization or person is banned from continuing operations – and imprisonment.

Regulation normally involves a requirement of registration or licensing to allow a named organization or person to operate and is applied through inspection and other means of policing compliance. In a more general conception, theorists like Michel Aglietta, *A Theory of Capitalist Regulation* (1976), use the term to explain the way capitalist society organizes and reproduces itself despite and because of its contradictions, crises and social struggles. In addition to examples cited earlier, these include the provision and regulation of credit, social security and other forms of welfare provision. With the advent and dominance of bodies like the INTERNATIONAL MONETARY FUND and the WORLD TRADE ORGANIZATION, however, national processes and procedures are undermined, paradoxically, by an international regulatory agenda that demands DEREGULATION at the local level; a development that exercises many of today's anti-capitalist individuals and organizations.

REIFICATION is the mistaking of an abstraction, idea or concept for a real or concrete thing. Georg Lukács (1885–1971), *History and Class Consciousness* (1971), developed the term to mean a relation between human beings that appears as a relation between things that have been produced by humans, are separate from us and affect the way we live our lives. In capitalist society, for example, commodities are imbued with human qualities – fetishized – take on a life of their own, and appear to be independent of the conditions of their production. Relations between producers, on the other hand, are only visible as a characteristic of their product, which is mistakenly considered to be inherent. Exchange value is one such characteristic, and as the form in which a commodity's value is expressed it serves to hide the reality of the production process as a social relation between people. Consequently, whatever impression people have of their situation – i.e. their consciousness – the truth of the matter is that repetitive, restrictive forms of thought and action that are the conditions of production serve to enslave people.

In this respect, Theodor Adorno (1903–1969), *The Culture Industry* (1991), identifies reification as a social category that indicates the way consciousness is determined. In Adorno's analysis of contemporary culture this process of reification is shown to have an ideological purpose through its effect on interpretation in everyday life. He argues that through the commercialization of the standardized 'Culture Industry' individuality, FREEDOM and the capacity for critical thinking are eroded. Expressions of creativity, for example, are neutralized when artworks are offered for sale, because in the market place VALUE is equated with price and thereby reduced to exchange value. In contrast, Adorno's theory of aesthetics promotes the struggle to understand art, philosophy and so on as the way of establishing real value. See also ALIENATION, COMMODITY and CONSUMERISM.

FURTHER INFORMATION

Lukács chapter on 'Reification and the Consciousness of the Proletariat': www.marxists.org/archive/lukacs/works/history/index.htm

RELIGION as a general category refers to a belief system that involves the worship of supernatural, transcendent beings. In common with all forms of myth, this usually involves a metaphysical dimension based on mystical contemplation and revelation rather than empirical inquiry. Paradoxically, this process of explaining and understanding truth is represented in terms of a deity, ritual and symbolism and therefore conflates appearance and reality. The role of organized religion in Europe, as a source of governmental authority and wisdom, was challenged from the seventeenth century by advocates of a free-thinking rationalism, initially concerned more with materialist inquiry than maintaining social order.

Forms of religion other than Christianity, such as Hinduism and Islam, perform similar legitimizing roles, as Debiprasad Chattopadhyaya, *Indian Atheism* (1969), and Ernest Gellner (1925–1995), *Muslim Society* (1981), have argued. Although the relationship between capitalism, Hinduism and Islam is disputed, there has long been an argument that an inextricable link exists between CAPITALISM and Christianity, especially in its Protestant form. Prominent exponents of this view include Max Weber (1864–1920),

The Protestant Ethic (1905), and Richard Tawney (1880–1962), *Religion and the Rise of Capitalism* (1926). E.P. Thompson (1924–1993) in *The Making of the English Working Class* (1963) describes a connection with Methodism, in particular, while Christopher Hill (1912–2003), *The World Turned Upside Down* (1972), also explores the religious origins of radicalism.

Although the American and French revolutions of 1776 and 1789 introduced the notion of religion as a personal matter through the separation of church and state, the function of religion in capitalism continued to be criticized. Features like misogyny, PATRIARCHY and PRIVATE PROPERTY, for example, are not unique to capitalism, but are consistent with certain tenets of Christianity, Hinduism, Islam and Judaism. In anti-capitalist terms, Karl Marx (1818–1883), Friedrich Engels (1820–1895) and others viewed religion in general as an expression of imperfect self-awareness – a form of ALIENATION – and monotheism in particular as an attempt to personify the abstract idea of humanity through the incorporation of all other deities into one.

According to this way of thinking, religion constitutes a form of IDEOLOGY that serves to mask the irrationalities of society through a focus on ideas that exclude reality. Interestingly, however, a similar process has been identified in secular society and associated with positivism by Theodor Adorno (1903–1969) and Max Horkheimer (1895–1973), *Dialectic of Enlightenment* (1947), and with industrial technology by Herbert Marcuse (1898–1979), *One Dimensional Man* (1964). Some aspects of religion are also equated with criticisms of capitalism, as in the case of theoretical opposition to usury espoused by Judaism and Islam and the *Vix Pervenit* encyclical issued by Pope Benedict XIV in 1745. Of course, such practices are not unique to capitalism, and religious opposition to capitalism per se is not necessarily progressive.

The Christian Democracy movement, for example, has overwhelmingly been a conservative force in Austria, Belgium, France, Germany, Italy and the Netherlands, since World War II. Nevertheless, some Christians advocate a form of SOCIALISM based on cooperation, EQUALITY, fraternity, pacifism and the rejection of competition, hierarchy and POWER. Typified by the promotion of industrial reconciliation based on morality as opposed to CLASS, this movement includes the potent mix of LIBERATION and theology evident in Latin America towards the end of the twentieth century. Present-day anti-capitalism also involves Christian groups campaigning for the cancellation of INTERNATIONAL DEBT as part of the Jubilee initiative, which takes its name from Leviticus:25 and the command that debt should be abolished and land returned to original owners. Likewise, Ched Myers, *The Biblical Vision of Sabbath Economics* (1998), and a myriad of organizations also work with secular and other groups in pursuit of their vision of social justice.

FURTHER INFORMATION

Christian Socialism: www.christiansocialist.org.uk
Marx and Engels on religion: www.marxists.org/archive/marx/works/subject/religion/index.htm
Sabbath economics: www.sabbatheconomics.org

REVOLUTION had an original meaning of a turning around of POWER so that a previously existing state of affairs was re-established. The present-day understanding, as the overthrow of an existing order and consequent change in the distribution of state power and structure of social and economic relations, followed the French Revolution of 1789. In a broader sense, the term is also applied to a process of social or technological change, as in industrial or second industrial revolution, sexual revolution and scientific revolution. By way of contrast, a *coup d'état* or the current euphemism of 'regime change' involves the replacement of one set of rulers with another, without effecting any real or significant change to the distribution of power or to existing socio-economic structures and relations.

The revolution of 1789 was also the first to be interpreted in terms of a class dimension, initially by French commentators in the early nineteenth century; a theme subsequently adopted and developed by Karl Marx (1818–1883) and Friedrich Engels (1820–1895). This thesis postulates the deliberate and intentional overthrow of one CLASS by another – of a ruling class by a subordinate one – and of the economic, political and social interests associated with the dominant class and their mode of production. While the specific nature of class interest, motivation and participation has proved difficult to demonstrate in the French and English cases, the implications of the idea that revolution and therefore class conflict constitute the 'locomotive of history' have had far-reaching consequences.

On the one hand, some historians and other commentators have sought to neutralize the significance of certain events by using the term 'civil war' as opposed to 'revolution'. The English Revolution of 1642, for example, is stylized as civil war in spite of the fact that it involved the execution of the king and the creation of a republic. Likewise the American Revolution of 1776 established a republic, independent from Britain, but is more often referred to as a war of independence. More recently, the failed revolution in

Spain between 1936 and 1939 is also referred to as a civil war, perhaps to obviate the significant role played by anarchists in the struggle to establish a republic and defeat fascism. Revolutionary changes in former Soviet bloc countries like Hungary 1953–56 were also referred to as uprisings, and in the case of Czechoslovakia in 1968 the 'Prague Spring'.

The theorization of the process and reasons for revolution was an integral aspect of the deliberate creation of revolutionary organizations to provide leadership and strategy for revolutionary forces. Thus, the failure of revolutionary movements in Europe in 1848 led Marx and Engels to develop a theory of permanent revolution. This involved the separate organization of militant workers to ensure that liberal or bourgeois democratic reforms were carried out in full, before proceeding immediately to the creation of working-class power and socialism. Although Marx and Engels later abandoned this idea, it was reformulated by Leon Trotsky (Lev Bronstein) (1879–1940), *The Permanent Revolution* (1919). Various advocates of ANARCHISM, COMMUNISM and SOCIALISM have, for example, considered revolution to be a necessary step to break down existing societal structures and replace them with new forms of economic and social relations.

More often than not, such attempts have involved armed insurrection, as in the case of the Russian Revolution of 1917, the Chinese Revolution of 1949, the Cuban Revolution of 1959, as well as in Angola and Mozambique in 1975, and Nicaragua in 1979. Although the actual seizure of power is not necessarily a violent act, conflict usually occurs between the forces for progress and those resisting changes to existing power structures; hence the convenient reference to civil war. These wars have also been characterized by foreign powers intervening on one side or the other, recent examples of which are explored by Ivan Molloy, *Rolling Back Revolution* (2001), and the use of 'terror' as a means of securing popular compliance. In Russia between 1918 and 1920, for example, atrocities committed by opponents of the revolution were described as 'white terror' and those by the revolutionary forces known as 'red terror'.

While anarchism, anarcho-syndicalism and syndicalism foresee revolution as a necessary strategy for the transformation of society, there is no such unity of thought concerning the transition from CAPITALISM to socialism. Revolutionary strategy forms a central tenet of Leninism, MAOISM and TROTSKYISM, while the possibility of gradual, incremental change became synonymous with social democracy following the creation of the Communist International in 1919. More recently, social democracy has come to be equated with an agenda of social reform, but this differs from the concept of reformism as a programme for the creation of a different social order through existing executive and parliamentary institutions and their eventual replacement by new forms of popular administration.

For the most part, Marx and Engels expected transformation to involve struggle and crisis that resulted in a decisive revolutionary moment, but conceded that contemporary democratic structures in Britain and the USA could be used to facilitate transformation. Engels also came to the conclusion that advances in military hardware and technology made the possibility of a successful armed uprising less likely. In the late nineteenth and early twentieth centuries, there were several contributors to debates on the issue. These included Eduard Bernstein (1850–1932), *Evolutionary Socialism* (1899); Rosa Luxemburg (1871–1919), *Social Reform or Revolution* (1899); Karl Kautsky (1854–1938), *The Road to Power* (1909); and Vladimir (Ulyanov) Lenin (1870–1924), *The Proletarian Revolution and Kautsky the Renegade* (1918).

Questions about the viability of reformism continued to be raised in the twentieth century, especially about the tendency towards incorporation – see Leo Panitch, *Social Democracy and Industrial Militancy* (1976), for example – and in response to the military overthrow of the elected government of Salvador Allende (1908–1973) in Chile. Similarly, the reduction of revolutionary strategy to the interests of the Soviet Union raised doubts about its own efficacy. Towards the end of the century radical Eurocommunists and social democrats sought a third way based on struggle within and outside the structures of the STATE in order to win elections and introduce direct democracy and self-management bodies – Nicos Poulantzas (1936–1979), *State, Power, Socialism* (1978). In Italy, meanwhile, Antonio Negri and other supporters of the AUTONOMIA argued that developments in productivity, infrastructure and consequent welfare provision facilitated an immediate transition to communism. Questions of revolution and transformation in terms of modern-day anti-capitalism are evident in the theory and practice of the SOCIAL FORUM, the ZAPATISTAS and are considered by John Holloway, *Change the World Without Taking Power* (2002), and Michael Hardt and Antonio Negri, *Empire* (2000).

FURTHER INFORMATION

Reform or revolution polemics:
Daniel DeLeon: www.marxists.org/archive/deleon/works/1896/960126.htm
Rosa Luxemburg: www.marxists.org/archive/luxemburg/1900/reform-revolution/index.htm

RIGHTS involve legal recognition or other forms of safeguard and protection that afford the provision of choices and the freedom to act or exercise particular interests to individuals or groups – otherwise know as positive rights. Negative rights, on the other hand, usually imply a protection from outside interference and prevent others, especially the STATE, from undertaking acts that might be discriminatory or injurious to the interests, welfare and well-being of others. To this extent, the rights of some involve the limitation of other peoples' freedom to act. Examples include the holding and accumulation of PRIVATE PROPERTY, as not everyone has the means to exercise their rights, mainly as a consequence of the existing ownership of property in the hands of the few. Laws or codes that prevent discrimination on the basis of age, race, religion, sex and sexual orientation also limit the activities of others in order to protect people who belong to these groups. Alternatively, a right to act can also involve the absence of legal constraint. A variety of prefixes are used when referring to rights, including 'civil', 'equal', 'human', 'natural' 'property' and 'welfare', with the last implying an obligation for the state to provide people with minimum resources. The term 'civil liberties' is also often used interchangeably with 'civil rights'.

These and other legal rights are often listed in constitutional or other documents. The USA, for example, has the Bill of Rights, Canada has the Charter of Rights and Freedoms and Europe has the Convention on Human Rights and the Social Charter. Internationally, there is also the UNIVERSAL DECLARATION OF HUMAN RIGHTS (UDHR), International Covenants on Civil and Political Rights and on Economic, Social and Cultural Rights (both 1966) and the United Nations (UN) Convention on the Rights of the Child (1989). While these documents and national legislation, like the British Human Rights Act 1998, variously extol the virtues of inherent human dignity and of the equal and inalienable rights of all human beings, their existence does not guarantee that individuals, groups or even states abide by them. Different emphasis is placed on different rights, with the International Labour Organization, *Declaration of Fundamental Principles of Rights at Work* (1998), being ignored by CORPORATIONS that use SWEATSHOP labour and by those states that permit their existence. Furthermore, Caroline Dommen, *Trading Rights?* (2002), examines the impact of the WORLD TRADE ORGANIZATION and the treaties it administers.

A number of legal rights are also defined as 'qualified rights'. This means that a government or public authority can infringe rights where they can show that they were justified in doing so. After the atrocities committed in the USA on 11 September 2001, for example, a number of countries declared a state of emergency to allow the indefinite detention without trial of those suspected of involvement with TERRORISM; see Elaine Hagopian, *Civil Rights in Peril* (2004). The introduction of compulsory identity cards, databases and technology to create comprehensive files on individuals that integrate information from closed-circuit television, facial recognition systems and mobile phone location services represents a threat to Article 12 of the UNDR and the right to privacy. Identity cards were used in Britain during both world wars, but were subsequently abandoned amid widespread public resentment that law-abiding people who objected to them were forced to become law-breakers.

To insist that rights are 'inalienable' therefore appears to have little practical value if they cannot be bestowed, granted, limited, bartered away or sold, but they can be and are violated as a matter of expediency. The distribution of POWER within and between countries often dictates which rights are considered to be most important; hence in capitalist society the interests of private property, guaranteed by Article 17, appears to be regarded as more important than Article 25 and the right to an adequate standard of living. In such circumstances 'inalienable' rights have to be secured by those to whom they are supposed to apply. Civil rights and liberties fall into this category as legal rights granted by the state and include the right to vote and anti-discrimination laws that are intended to afford equal protection for minorities from discrimination and its vestiges. In the province of Northern Ireland during the 1960s, for example, campaigners demanded an end to the gerrymandering of electoral districts whereby the distribution of electors was manufactured to ensure the election of unionist candidates and to allocation procedures for local authority housing in favour of unionist communities. Here issues were also complicated by views about the freedom to practise religion and reflect concerns that one form of religion impinges on other faiths. Ultimately, Irish civil rights activism was influenced by developments in America, but both have a longer, shared history, the nature of which is explored by Brian Dooley, *Black and Green* (1998).

In the USA, the 13th Amendment to the Constitution outlawed slavery in 1865; the 14th Amendment, passed in 1868, afforded citizenship and EQUALITY before the law to all people born in the USA; and the 15th Amendment provided the right to vote to all citizens, regardless of race, in 1870. Nevertheless, many states adopted laws that enforced racial segregation, and treated African Americans as second-class citizens; voter registration boards used discriminatory practices to limit the number of eligible black voters. In response, a primarily nonviolent civil rights movement developed to secure full civil rights and equality under the law for all Americans and was epitomized by the struggles that took place between 1945 and 1970. The movement was diverse, involved thousands of people and was led by Martin Luther King, Junior (1929–1968). Organizations included the National Association for the Advancement of Colored People (NAACP), founded in 1909; the National Urban League, founded in 1911; the Congress of Racial Equality (CORE), founded in 1942; and the Southern Christian Leadership Conference (SCLC), founded in 1957. The American Federation of Labor was also involved in campaigning for civil rights in the workplace.

Many individuals were involved in several organizations, such as CORE's leader James L. Farmer (1920–1999), who became executive secretary of the Student Non-violent Coordinating Committee (SNCC), which was formed in 1957. Similarly, Bob Moses of SNCC created the Council of Federated Organizations (COFO) to coordinate the work of the SCLC, the SNCC and other civil rights groups. They also shared tactics, such as DIRECT ACTION strategies that included bus boycotts, sit-ins and freedom rides. Some groups and individuals within the civil rights movement like the Black Panther Party, formed in 1966 by Huey Newton (1942–1989) and Bobby Seale, advocated armed resistance.

Stokely Carmichael (1941–1998), who later changed his name to Kwame Ture, and Charles Hamilton elaborated their views in *Black Power* (1967), while black separatism was advocated by the Nation of Islam and Malcom X (1925–1965), or El-Hajj Malik El-Shabazz, as he became known. The overall campaign achieved certain victories such as the Civil Rights Act of 1964, which required equal access to public places and outlawed discrimination in employment. The Voting Rights Act of 1965 also suspended literacy and other voter tests and authorized federal supervision of voter registration in states and individual voting districts where such tests were being used. These and other gains are often eroded, however, as in the state of Florida in 2000, and it is only through the vigilance of activists and bodies like the American Civil Liberties Union that they are enforced.

The concept of human rights follows from European traditions associated with Jean-Jacques Rousseau (1712–1778), *The Social Contract* (1762), and Thomas Paine (1737–1809), *The Rights of Man* (1792). Ironically, however, some of the worst human rights abuses stem from European colonization and the practice of slavery. Such examples include, but are not restricted to, the

213

practice of apartheid in South Africa and the treatment of indigenous peoples throughout Africa, in Australia and in North and South America. These are issues of discrimination that are still occurring and therefore unresolved by human rights declarations. Similarly other struggles for human rights include the women's and gay liberation movements – considered in an American context by David Richards, *Women, Gays and the Constitution* (1998) – the disabled rights movement and many class-based movements.

FURTHER INFORMATION

International Labour Organization declaration: www.ilo.org/dyn/declaris/
    declarationweb.indexpage
European documents: http://conventions.coe.int
International Law documents: www.ohchr.org/english/law
International organizations: www.amnesty.org; http://globalexchange.org

S

SEX INDUSTRY consists of transactions that can involve children, men and women in the payment of money for sexual gratification. Often referred to in euphemistic terms as adult entertainment, such activities involve films, lap dancing, magazines, massage, photography, prostitution, striptease and premium-rate telephone lines. The term 'pornography' is also used to refer to anything that is designed to encourage sexual arousal without emotional attachment and therefore considered to be obscene; the Greek roots are *porne*, meaning 'harlot', and *graphein*, 'to write'. In contrast, literature, painting, photography and sculpture that deal with sexual love are termed erotica; while in a psychoanalytic context, eroticism refers to direct, perverted, physical, psychical and sublimated forms of love.

According to Herbert Marcuse (1898–1979), *Eros and Civilisation* (1955), CAPITALISM is responsible for emphasizing genital sexuality and gratification, because the processes of production need bodies that are desensitized of erotic energy. This amounts to a repression of libidinal freedom, which is considered to be a natural human desire, constitutes a form of ALIENATION, and is therefore an imperative aspect of how and why the sex industry prospers. Understood thus, the sex industry exploits not only people who work in and for it but also those who use it, due to the dehumanizing effects of capitalism.

Accompanying this process, the people who provide sexual services and parts of their anatomy are presented as objects that are solely intended for sexual gratification. As the overwhelming majority of customers are heterosexual men, it is the female body that is usually objectified for male pleasure, a message that is reinforced by the fashion and film industries, through the use of sex in ADVERTISING and in the MEDIA in general. In the sex industry, the modes of EXPLOITATION and oppression by the male sex are also indicative of PATRIARCHY and typically involve acts of abuse, degradation and violence.

The exploitation of women as prostitutes usually involves vulnerable young people who have left home, having been abused as children, and are addicted to drugs; they are generally subject to the violent control of

215

a pimp. Anna M. Agathangelou, *The Global Political Economy of Sex* (2004), also demonstrates how prostitution is a common consequence of HUMAN TRAFFICKING whereby criminal gangs offer women help in dealing with immigration processes. They are subsequently coerced into sexual slavery through the withholding of passports and travel documents and because they are unable to pay off debts supposedly accrued as travel and other costs. In cases where the women are illegal immigrants, they do not have recourse to the law for fear of expulsion. Sexual slavery has also been linked to military conflict. Examples include the government of Japan establishing brothels in occupied countries during World War II and South Korea doing the same during the Korean and Vietnam wars.

In some South Asian countries children are abducted by criminal gangs and sold into prostitution; a fear raised over the fate of the many children orphaned by the tsunami disaster of 2004. This form of exploitation is often equated with sex tourism, whereby men from industrialized countries travel to Brazil, Cambodia, the Caribbean, Eastern Europe and Thailand for the sole purpose of sexual activity. Not all sex tourists are paedophiles, but they nevertheless take advantage of the conditions of POVERTY that drive women into prostitution and may be drawn by ethnicity and subservience; as revealed by Jeremy Seabrook, *Travels in the Skin Trade* (1996). The United Nations Convention for the Suppression of the Traffic in Persons and of the Exploitation of Prostitutes and of Others (1949) therefore deems prostitution to be incompatible with human dignity and calls for its abolition.

Australia, Germany, the Netherlands, Nevada in the USA, New Zealand and Switzerland have introduced various forms of legality and regulation in an attempt to minimize abuse, criminality and slavery, while providing health-care facilities. Groups like the Bayswan, International Prostitutes Collective, International Sex Worker Foundation for Art, Culture and Education, the Sexual Freedom Coalition and the Sex Work Cyber Resources Centre variously advocate decriminalization and recognition of prostitution and sex work as legitimate professions. Aims also include making the benefits of health care and social security available, and the formation of self-help organizations and trade unions like the International Union of Sex Workers, affiliated to the GMB trade union in Britain.

FURTHER INFORMATION

Prostitution Research and Education: www.prostitutionresearch.com
United Nations convention: www.ohchr.org/english/law/trafficpersons.htm

SITUATIONIST INTERNATIONAL originated in 1957 as a group dedicated to the revolutionary realization of art and POLITICS, through the transformation of art from a separate activity into a part of everyday life. The Situationist critique of society identifies a modern-day trend that is devoted to the mediation of CULTURE and experiences through a commodification of appearances in order to conceal the dominant interests in society. Thus, according to Guy Debord, *Society of the Spectacle* (*La Société du spectacle*) (1967), the spectacle is a social relation among people mediated by images. This involves what the Situationists call a process of 'recuperation', whereby radical or revolutionary ideas are neutralized through their representation as a saleable commodity. In response is advocated *détournement*, the alteration and subversion of images so that their meaning is changed from one that supports the status quo into one that challenges it – the synthesis of art and politics.

As revolutionaries, the Situationists were active in the occupation movement, during the revolutionary uprisings of May 1968 in Paris, but refused to lead it or speak for it and acted only in their own name. As René Viénet, *Enragés and Situationists* (1992), recalls, there was cooperation between the ENRAGÉS and Situationists, while neither belonged to nor claimed to represent the other. This took the form of the Enragés–Situationist International Committee and the participation of both groups in the Council for Maintaining the Occupations. The Situationist influence was also evident in the theatrical nature of the activities, posters and slogans of the uprising.

Although the Situationist International dissolved in 1972, their ideas and practices impacted on the counterculture, the NEW LEFT, and are evident in today's anti-capitalist movement. Their influence, for example, appears in the activities of the DIGGERS guerrilla theatre group in San Francisco and persists today in the DIRECT ACTION and protests of groups like Earth First and the Art and Revolution collective. Together with the Movement of the Imagination, Art and Revolution also share the Situationist goal of combining art and politics, whereas adbusters and certain hacktivists employ the practice of *détournement* when they alter adverts and websites in a manner which inverts the original message.

FURTHER INFORMATION

Situationist International Online: www.cddc.vt.edu/sionline
Viénet's *Enragés and Situationists*: www.cddc.vt.edu/sionline/si/enrages.html

SOCIAL FORUM forms part of a permanent process that was conceived and implemented by a committee of Brazilian groups as a means of building alternatives to NEOLIBERALISM, a world dominated by capital, MULTINATIONAL CORPORATIONS and the governments and institutions, whether national or international, that serve their interests. The first World Social Forum (WSF) was held in Porto Alegre, Brazil, 25–30 January 2001, to coincide with the WORLD ECONOMIC FORUM in Davos, Switzerland, and adopted the slogan 'another world is possible'. As part of an annual process, regional, continental and thematic initiatives are also convened to precede and feed into the annual WSF.

In keeping with the spirit of present-day anti-capitalism, organizers describe the Social Forum as a process rather than an organization. The central purpose of each forum is to create new and strengthen existing national, continental and global links among organizations, movements, activists and local mobilization committees. In a deliberate break with established political organizational practice, each forum is not a locus of POWER to be controlled; instead, as Jai Sen and Anita Anand, *World Social Forum* (2004), show, there is an emphasis on debate and information sharing rather than decision-making. The approach is therefore inclusive as opposed to exclusive, thereby allowing alternative methods of interrelation and action between participants. Likewise, those attending are not committed to a particular form of action, as the Forum does not adopt positions as a whole, nor claim to speak on behalf participants, although those attending are encouraged to return to their communities and effect change.

Each Forum aims to bring together organizations and movements of CIVIL SOCIETY that are engaged in concrete action – from local to international levels – to create a global society based on fruitful relationships among humanity and between it and the earth. Participation is therefore open to any SOCIAL MOVEMENT, any kind of NETWORK, association and organization, that wishes to be part of the process, accepts the charter of the Social Forum and does not seek to speak for civil society as a whole. The aim, identified in the *Charter of Principles* (2001), is to provide 'an open meeting place for reflective thinking, democratic debate of ideas, formulation of proposals, free exchange of experiences and inter-linking for effective action'.

An indication of the issues that motivate those who participate can be found in *Another World Is Possible* (2003), edited by William F. Fisher and Thomas Ponniah. These include but are not limited to: alternative media, citizen rights, community and local development, ENVIRONMENTALISM, farming, FEMINISM, gay, lesbian, transgender and human rights, immigration, international solidarity, peace, popular education, RELIGION, social economy based on solidarity, social exclusion and trade unionism. Formal representatives of governments, legislative assemblies, political parties and military organizations are not allowed to participate in the Forum, but all individuals who accept the commitments of its charter can participate in a personal capacity.

For some the concept and practice of the Social Forum represent a change in focus for the anti-capitalist movement from a force of opposition and PROTEST to one of constructive proposals and a growing maturity of political theory and analysis. As well as aiming to increase the capacity for nonviolent social resistance, for example, participants are encouraged to act in public and private life, at local, national and international levels, to develop and promote issues of planetary citizenship and promote change-inducing practices to build a new world based on solidarity. While opposing dehumanization and state violence as a means of social control, action is advocated to advance respect for the environment and the human rights of all citizens — regardless of sex and ethnicity — in all nations.

Operating in a representative, open way, which allows for a transparent and decentralized democratic decision-making process, each Forum constitutes a practical opposition to 'totalitarian and reductionist views of economy, development and history'. Likewise its condemnation of all forms of domination or subjection of one person, or groups of people, by others is evident in its own organizational practice as 'a forum for debate... that prompts reflection ... on the mechanisms and instruments of domination by capital'. Support for the creation of democratic international systems and institutions to engender EQUALITY, peaceful relations, solidarity, social justice and real participatory democratic sovereignty is premissed on economic activity and political action that meet the needs of people and respect nature, for present and future generations. Describing itself as 'plural, diversified, non-confessional, non-governmental and non-party', the Social Forum works to identify means and actions to resist and overcome domination and to discover alternatives to the problems of environmental destruction, social exclusion, inequality, RACISM and sexism.

FURTHER INFORMATION

Asian Social Forum: www.wsfindia.org
European Social Forum: www.fse-esf.org
World Social Forum: www.forumsocialmundial.org.br

SOCIAL MOVEMENT is a term used by academics interested in the interaction between popular movements, institutionalized political processes, the formation of new political parties and influences on the agenda of established political parties. Although the term is associated with Manuel Castells's studies of *The Urban Question* (1977) and *City, Class and Power* (1978), there is no precise definition of what constitutes a social movement. At best it is a somewhat nebulous reference to a loose alliance of organizations and activists who participate at local, national and international levels to advance transnational and ethical issues that embody an alternative way of thinking through which to understand the world. Some examples exhibit a formal structure while others do not; the characteristics of which can depend on the particular movement's stage of development and transformation.

Beginning with public concern about a particular issue, social movements are believed to evolve through the holding of loosely connected actions and demonstrations. At this stage, there is a lack of formal programme, structure or rules. These features are associated with the expansion of the movement and the development of groupings and organizations that begin to formulate their own agenda according to their particular concerns. Depending on one's point of view, a social movement has either achieved its purpose or been neutralized when its aims have been adopted by the mainstream political parties and become 'common sense'. Understood thus, a social movement can have a finite lifespan, which concludes with fragmentation along party lines.

The labour and socialist movements of the nineteenth century fit this description, leading as they did to the formation of communist, socialist and social-democratic political parties and organizations. During the second half of the twentieth century a number of new social movements arose, including campaigns for peace and nuclear disarmament, civil rights, gay rights, women's liberation and those concerned with environmental issues. Interestingly, however, although the last case has resulted in the formation of Green parties, the movement has by no means been incorporated into or neutralized by establishment politics and forms part of the anti-capitalism and anti-globalization movements that emerged in the 1990s.

Both can be considered to constitute a social movement, in line with the above definition, because they consist of groups and movements in loose alliances that seek to resolve economic, political and social problems through forms of struggle that are not aimed at the capture of state power. Defined in such general terms, modern-day anti-capitalism can be categorized as an autonomous movement that is united not so much by the support of a particular ideal but by a common foe. The broad association of anti-capitalists is therefore based on their opposition to specific characteristics of, or issues connected with, the operation of capitalism that might or might not be in the immediate material self-interest of activists.

While anti-capitalism and anti-globalization both involve campaigns to address moral and practical issues that motivate people regardless of CLASS or socio-economic background – like CHILD LABOUR and GLOBAL WARMING, for example – they also embody forms of critique, be they anarchist, communist or socialist, that strike at the very basis of capitalist society. This presents a conundrum for those who see social movements as being distinguished by their desire to achieve their aims within the confines of existing society. Similarly, it is also difficult to decide when a movement based on class, nationality, race or RELIGION becomes a social movement.

FURTHER INFORMATION
African list: www.nu.ac.za/ccs/?6,20
European list: www.euromarches.org/english/02/esfo3.htm
Global directory: www.social-movements.org/en/
Latin American Social Movements on the Net (2001): www.alainet.org/publica/
    msred/en/index.html

SOCIAL RELATIONS refer to the way people interact with each other in a given context or situation – at home, in school or at work, for example. The way people relate to each other on a day-to-day basis influences the behaviour of others, so when somebody becomes a boss they behave towards others the way they think a boss should. Nevertheless, people's perceptions, values and behaviour are changed through new experiences and interaction and therefore offer the opportunity for individuals – as activists, friends or otherwise – to exercise a fundamental transformation in the lives of others through their own conduct of social relations.

SOCIALISM, like COMMUNISM, refers to an ideal conception or theory of society, to the political movement that advocates and agitates for the creation of such a society, and to the self-described states that existed in the twentieth century and those that persist in Asia and Cuba. Adjectives like anarchist, Arab, Christian, democratic, guild, libertarian, scientific and utopian are all used to distinguish different brands of socialism. The

221

distinction between communism, socialism and social democracy is largely a twentieth-century convention, however, as the three terms had been fairly interchangeable during most of the nineteenth century. According to Karl Marx (1818–1883), *Critique of the Gotha Programme* (1875), and Vladimir (Ulyanov) Lenin (1870–1924), *The State and Revolution* (1917), socialism was the first or lower phase of communist society. The term 'social democracy', on the other hand, was adopted towards the end of the nineteenth century by a number of European socialist parties to indicate their desire to extend DEMOCRACY to all areas of social life including that of work.

Regardless of semantic differences, socialism is associated with one or more of the following values: cooperation, fraternal and sororial solidarity, INTERNATIONALISM and mutualism. In organizational terms, socialization or common ownership of the means of production, distribution and exchange of goods and services is considered to be a prerequisite of greater material equality. Prescriptions for how this might be achieved range from centralized state control and planning, through decentralized decision-making in public boards, trusts, municipalities and self-governing communities, to workers' control involving directly elected planning boards. Underpinning each approach is the eradication of material poverty through universal provision of means that guarantee adequate living standards, defined as clothing, education, food, health, housing, leisure and transport. Consequent to such standards is the absence of discrimination based on race, gender, nationality, sexuality, RELIGION and bodily or mental ability and the elimination of EXPLOITATION. Nevertheless, advocates of MONETARISM and NEOLIBERALISM use 'socialism' and 'socialist' as terms of derision.

The idea that goods should be held in common and that all men and women should be equal can be traced back to earlier movements, including the DIGGERS and ENRAGÉS. The Online Etymology Dictionary attributes the first use of the word 'socialist' to 1827 and the followers of Claude Henri de Rouvroy, Comte de Saint-Simon (1760–1825), and socialism to 1837 and Robert Owen (1771–1858). Saint-Simon, *Social Organisation* (1825), advocated a society based on science, technology and industrialism and run by experts and technicians as the 'administration of things'. In contrast, François-Marie Charles Fourier (1772–1837) promoted the creation of model, self-governing communities named 'phalanx' (*phalansteres*) based on harmony, love and sexual equality as opposed to coercion, commerce and competition; sentiments shared by Étienne Cabet (1788–1856), *Travels in Icaria* (*Voyages en Icarie*) (1839). Meanwhile, Robert Owen, *A New View of Society* (1813), supported the cooperative control of industry and set up ideal settlements based on rational enlightenment in Scotland and the USA.

Other approaches to the realization of socialism included the unsuccessful plot and *coup d'état* attempts of Louis Auguste Blanqui (1805–1881), whose practice and post-revolutionary dictatorship strategy owed much to François Noel (Gracchus) Babeuf (1760–1797). Louis Blanc (1811–1882), *Organization of Labour* (*L'Organisation du Travail*) (1839), propounded a theory of equal wages based on state ownership schemes and advocated a nationally coordinated system of autonomous national workshops (*ateliers sociaux*) managed and elected by workers to guarantee employment. There was also a crossover between the ideas of socialism and ANARCHISM, represented by Pierre-Joseph Proudhon (1809–1865) and Mikhail Bakunin (1814–1876), whose followers were expelled from the International Working Men's Association in 1872.

Karl Marx (1818–1883) and Friedrich Engels (1820–1895) had a prodigious impact on the development of socialist ideas in particular and the movement in general through their direct involvement and the emergence of MARXISM. Marx and Engels, for example, sought to distinguish between scientific and utopian formulations of socialism based on the latter's prescription of class reconciliation and amelioration of socio-economic privations (see UTOPIA). Such conclusions were the consequence of critical investigation, but these processes have since been neglected by those who have sought to turn findings about class struggle, PRIVATE PROPERTY and wage labour into immutable laws; as in the case of Nikolai Bukharin (1888–1938), *Historical Materialism* (1921). Their influence was initially manifested through the formation of social-democratic parties in Europe; a prime example being the German Social Democratic Workers Party (Sozial demokratische Arbeiterpartei). As indicated earlier, such parties represented a broad alliance that covered reformist and revolutionary socialists. The German Party, formed in 1869, included the non-proletarian socialism of Ferdinand Lassalle (1825–1864) as well as the Marxists August Bebel (1840–1913) and Wilhelm Liebknecht (1826–1900).

Elsewhere, Jules (Basile) Guesde (1845–1922) founded the Workers Party (Parti Ouvrier) in France in 1876, the Socialist Labour Party was formed by Daniel De Leon (1852–1914) in the USA (1877), a social-democratic party was formed in Denmark (Det Socialdemokratiscke Forbund) (1878) and a Social Labour Party in Spain (Partido Laborista Social) (1879). Similar parties were also formed in Belgium (1885) Norway (1887) and Sweden (1889); in 1889 an Austrian party was founded by Viktor Adler (1852–1918). The

223

following decade saw the emergence of parties in Hungary (1890), Bulgaria (1891), Italy under Filippo Turati (1857–1932) and Poland (both 1892), Romania (1893) and the Netherlands (1894). In Russia the Emancipation of Labour Group (Osvobozhdenie Truda) was formed in 1883 by Georgii Plekhanov (1856–1918) and became the Social Democratic Labour Party (Sotsial-Demokraticheskaia Rabochaia Partiia) (1898). The early twentieth century witnessed the formation of a party in Japan (1901), a Socialist Party under Eugene Debs (1855–1926) and Norman Thomas (1884–1968) in the USA (1901) and in Finland and Serbia (1903). The year 1905 witnessed the French merger of the followers of Guesde, Blanc, Blanqui and Proudhon under Jean Jaurès (1859–1914) and Léon Blum (1872–1950).

The shared characteristics of such parties include their use of Marxist terminology and divisions about how best to achieve socialist transformation. This latter aspect is perhaps best illustrated in reference to the debates between Karl Kautsky (1854–1938), *The Road to Power* (1909), Eduard Bernstein (1850–1932), *Evolutionary Socialism (Die Voraussetzungen des Sozialismus und die Aufgaben der Sozialdemokratie)* (1899), and Rosa Luxemburg (1871–1919), *The Mass Strike, the Political Party and the Trade Unions* (1906). Similar disputes led to the emergence of the Bolshevik and Menshevik groupings at the Second Congress of the Russian Social Democratic Labour Party in 1903. Although these divisions centred on the nature of party organization appropriate to the repressive regime in Russia, they also encompassed the general disagreements between those who advocated a gradual implementation of reforms to achieve socialism and those who saw REVOLUTION as a prerequisite of transformation.

The exceptions to this rule were the trade-union-based Labour parties formed in Britain (as the Labour Representation Committee in 1900 and Labour Party in 1906) and in the dominions of Australia (1901), South Africa and New Zealand (1913). Although preceded by the Social Democratic Federation, founded in 1881 by Henry Hyndman (1842–1921), the Socialist League (1885) of Edward Aveling (1849–1898), Eleanor Marx (1855–1898) and William Morris (1834–1896) and comprising affiliate organizations like the Independent Labour Party (1893), the programme of the British Labour Party was consistently gradualist. This was due in part to the role played by the Fabian Society (1884) and members like the Webbs – Sidney (1859–1947) and Beatrice (1858–1943) – and George Bernard Shaw (1856–1950). The Society's outlook was typified by the Fabian Essays Series, which adopted a conception similar to that of Saint-Simon to the extent that both favoured a society organized and run by experts. Leading figures like James Kier Hardy (1856–1915) also attributed their socialism to Christian values. These were linked to non-conformist movements like Methodism in nineteenth-century Britain and the Christian socialist movement of Frederick Denison Maurice (1805–1872), *The Kingdom of Christ* (1838), Thomas Hughes (1822–1896) and Charles Kingsley (1819–1875) – see LIBERATION.

Alternative theories were promoted within the Labour Party, such as the guild socialism of George Douglas Howard Cole (1889–1959), *The World of Labour* (1913) and *Self-Government in Industry* (1917). Sharing with anarcho-syndicalism, Industrial Workers of the World and syndicalism an antipathy to the wage system and to production and a distrust of the STATE, supporters proposed producers' control through cooperatives, municipal government, trade unions or guilds. Broader differences between nationalist reformist and internationalist revolutionary factions within social democracy and the Second International (1889–1914) became untenable when, with the advent of World War I, the former chose to support their respective national war efforts. These divisions were concretized further, following the Bolshevik Revolution of 1917 and the creation of the Communist International in 1919, as a split between those who accepted subordination of proletarian struggle to national interests and those who equated worldwide struggle with the interests of the USSR.

In the USSR, all means of production were taken under state control and a system of government based on soviets introduced. Under Joseph (Dzhugashvili) Stalin (1879–1953) and the doctrine of 'socialism in one country' the communist party was extolled as the sole representative of the working class and the state was presented as acting on behalf of the whole people. With the collectivization of agriculture after 1929 and rapid industrialization equated with five-year plans, the victory of socialism was declared by Stalin in 1936; 'advanced socialism' was later proclaimed by Leonid Brezhnev (1906–1982). Critics of this approach include Leon (Lev Bronstein) Trotsky (1879–1940), *The Revolution Betrayed* (1937), while adherents to TROTSKYISM, in general, argue that bureaucratization stalled the transition to communism. Mao Zedong (1893–1976), *A Critique of Soviet Economics* (1977), on the other hand, considered the absence of class struggle in soviet-type societies to imply a return to CAPITALISM. Others, like Tony Cliff (Ygael Gluckstein) (1917–2000), *State Capitalism in Russia* (1974), considered the development of bureaucracy and the emphasis on massive economic growth to constitute a hybrid socio-economic system.

Socialist ideas and organizations also informed and participated in the struggle against colonialism and as part of national liberation movements in Africa, Asia and Latin America. Leading advocates in Africa, for example, included Ahmed Ben Bella in Algeria, Habib Bourguiba (1903–2000) in Tunisia, Léopold Sédar Senghor (1906–2001) in Senegal, Ahmed Sékou Touré (1922–1984) in Guinea, Julius Nyerere (1922–1999) in Tanzania, and Kenneth Kaunda in Zambia. Their various attempts to incorporate African traditions – communal land ownership and egalitarian tribal practices – with European ideas about socialism have been termed African Socialism, though this masks differences in approach. In North Africa, the Arab Socialist Renaissance Party (Hizb al-Ba'ath al-'Arabi al-Ishtiraki) was formed in Damascus, Syria, in 1943 by Michel Aflaq (1910–1989), Salah al-din Bitar (1912–1980) and Zaki al-Arsuzi (1908–1968) to oppose colonialism. Parties also appeared in Iraq, Jordan, Lebanon, Libya, Saudi Arabia and Yemen. In 1958, Syria joined with Egypt under Gamal Abdel Nasser (1918–1970) to form the United Arab Republic (UAR), but Syria withdrew from the project in 1961 because of the failure to address domestic social and economic problems.

In Latin America, the struggle against Spanish and Portuguese colonialism took place largely in the nineteenth century and was succeeded by struggles against dictatorship and military *coup d'état* orchestrated and maintained by the USA. Richard Gott, *Rural Guerrillas in Latin America* (1973), provides a comprehensive account of developments in Guatemala, Venezuela, Colombia, Peru and Bolivia. In Chile, Salvador Allende (Gossens) (1908–1973), a founder of the Socialist Party in 1933, was elected president in 1970 on behalf of the Popular Unity coalition (Unidad Popular), an alliance of socialists, communists, left Christian Democrats and others. His government was overthrown in a US-sponsored coup in 1973. The failure of the 'Chilean road to socialism' prompted debate over the efficacy of a gradualist or parliamentary strategy.

By way of contrast, successful wars of LIBERATION were waged against US-backed dictatorships in Cuba (1959) and Nicaragua (1979), led by Fidel Castro and the Sandinista National Liberation Front (Frente Sandinista de Liberación Nacional), respectively. In Asia, socialist revolutions also took place in China (1949) and in North Vietnam (1954), a process extended to South Vietnam in 1973 through the successful war of liberation. Elsewhere, governments in Burma, Ceylon, India, Indonesia and Singapore variously claimed to be socialist at one time or another, but the disparity between such pronouncements and practical achievements reflects questions levelled against gradualist attitudes in Europe and its dominions.

Social-democratic or labour parties, for example, first participated in or formed a government in Australia (1904), Russia (1917), Germany (1919) Britain (1924) and Sweden (1932). In France (1934) and Spain (1936), they also participated in united or popular front governments against fascism. During the second half of the twentieth century such parties have also held office in these and other countries, but their manifestos and programmes have generally focused on legalizing collective bargaining rights and improving social security and working conditions. Towards the end of the last century, therefore, social democracy had become synonymous with prescriptions for a mixed economy that involved public control of natural resources, utilities and ailing industries, economic planning and the provision of social benefits in the form of a welfare state. Reformist party programmes were now restricted to a redistribution of wealth that involved extending or defending the welfare state and progressive taxation policy as opposed to transforming or overthrowing capitalism. These are historical processes reviewed by Donald Sassoon, *One Hundred Years of Socialism* (1997), and Willie Thompson, *The Left in History* (1997).

Paradoxically, the second half of the twentieth century also witnessed experimentation in market socialism in soviet-style and Asian socialist societies: Bulgaria, Czechoslavakia, the German Democratic Republic, Hungary, Poland, the USSR, Yugoslavia, China and Vietnam. In something of a parody of social-democratic and Eurocommunist programmes and echoing the warnings of Mao and Trotsky, varying attempts were made to utilize market forces – previously considered inefficient – to determine levels of distribution, exchange, LABOUR and production. Advocates of such an approach include Oskar Lange (1904–1965), *On the Economic Theory of Socialism* (1938), Abba Lerner (1905–1982) and David Miller, *Market, State and Community* (1990). These and other views relating to such societies also faced criticism from the NEW LEFT in the last quarter of the twentieth century (see MARKET).

More recently, social-democratic parties in Europe have eschewed use of the word 'socialism' – notably in Britain and Germany – as they attempt to reconcile the conflicting goals of neoliberal balanced budgets, DEREGULATION and free trade with desires to achieve full unemployment, stimulate growth and institute liberal social reform. Nowhere, more than here, is the neoliberal paradox of advocating that governments do not intervene to subsidize or otherwise influence various sectors of the economy more apparent. Fringe groups that advocate anarchism, MAOISM and Trotskyism form part

227

of current anti-capitalist criticism of such processes, as do myriad other groupings that coalesce around the SOCIAL FORUM. Mirroring trends within the anti-imperialist struggle, however, the ZAPATISTAS (Ejército Zapatista de Liberación Nacional) have sought to subordinate western socialist notions to the communitarian culture of indigenous peoples.

FURTHER INFORMATION

British Christian Socialist Movement: www.christiansocialist.org.uk
Members of the Socialist International: www.socialistinternational.org/2Members/
who.html

STATE, THE Defined by Max Weber (1864–1920), *Politics as a Vocation (Politik als Beruf)* (1919), as those associations that have a monopoly of physical violence in a given geographical area and are concerned with legitimizing existing societal practices. The fact that the state exercises supreme authority over a particular territory has resulted in the assumption that state and 'country' are one and the same thing. Similarly, 'state' and 'government' are used interchangeably and therefore obscure the fact that a government is in fact the mouthpiece of the state, its public persona. The positions of prime minister and president are officers of the state but no more. Ralph Miliband (1924–1994), *The State in Capitalist Society* (1973), equates the state with society as a whole and the distribution of POWER within it. The concept of the state should not be confused, however, with what constitutes a nation under international law or a political subdivision of a country organized along federalist lines.

Nor is the state a single entity; it should be seen as a variety of institutions, the interaction of which constitutes the state system. In addition to the legislative and executive functions of government, these include the administrative arm or civil service that runs public corporations, including television, radio, banking and TAXATION systems and other regulatory bodies. They also comprise organizations like the military and police forces that are concerned with national security and ensuring social order. Meanwhile, the judiciary oversees the legal system, while the institutions of sub-central government carry out a variety of functions, including the provision of education, transport systems and welfare services. A central feature of these functions is the direction and control of economic and social affairs by the state through the regulation of employment and private property rights, investment, TRADE and commodity markets.

The exercise of power to control, order and organize society takes place in a number of ways, but happens essentially through an interaction between the various apparatuses of the state and those of CIVIL SOCIETY. Examples include the MILITARY–INDUSTRIAL COMPLEX, which consists of links between private-sector firms, civil servants and the military involved in the procurement and provision of equipment, the funding of research, and support of the domestic arms industry in international trade through EXPORT CREDITS. In the education sphere, CORPORATIONS are also responsible for funding academic research and providing sponsorship and endowments, not to mention their involvement in the running and sponsorship of private and state-sector schools. Government spokespeople also brief media organizations, commission reports and inquiries that become news, and organize events that are reported daily. These include the Iraq War-related Hutton and Butler inquiries in Britain in 2003–04 and the American Senate investigation into the atrocities that occurred on 11 September 2001.

Public broadcasters also present their views as independent and therefore mainstream opinion, thereby reinforcing existing belief systems and the status quo. Similarly, privately owned MEDIA are presented as free and independent, even though much of their funding derives from corporate advertising and their ownership requires vast wealth. Equally subtle is the inculcation of acceptable ideas and forms of behaviour through the education system, where the principles of discipline and obedience necessary for factory and office work are instilled, as is the idea that the only purpose of university education is to enable students to acquire better jobs. In the USA during the 1960s, for example, the Southern Student Organizing Committee and the Free Speech Movement opposed the imposition of restrictions on campus political activity. Michel Foucault (1926–1984), *Discipline and Punish* (1977), considered these forms of state activity to amount to the cultural regulation of daily lives through the projection of acceptable norms, such as the description of welfare payments as a 'benefit'. Others see state-approved institutions like marriage as legitimizing PATRIARCHY, while organizations like the military and police have been accused of institutionalized racism.

Antonio Gramsci (1891–1937), *The Prison Notebooks* (1928–37), also concluded that the state was not only involved in presenting coercion in the form of police action as legitimate but also manufacturing consent through CULTURE and IDEOLOGY, a process he referred to as HEGEMONY. State institutions therefore employ a number of strategies aimed at securing a domination of 'common interest' in their particular territorial remit. Political parties, RELIGION, monarchy, elections, universal suffrage, tradition and the concepts of nationalism as national interest and security over people and firms from other countries help constitute a particular idea of inclusivity and self-perception. Constitutional government, law and order, and PRIVATE PROPERTY are equated with FREEDOM. For a society to be free we are told that there has to be free enterprise and therefore an acceptance of existing economic, social and political arrangements. According to this form of reasoning, alternative types of society cannot therefore be free.

The revolutionary principle of universal human equality is preserved through political and legal state structures that mask the real inequalities that pervade society. In specific terms, the formal legal relations between the supposedly equal parties of employer and employee disguise the reality that in selling the 'right of disposition' over labour-power, a worker forfeits the right to self-determination, to liberty, during the period of work. As the guarantor of abstract equality between people – as electors and legal citizens – the state serves to legitimize EXPLOITATION as a social relationship of formal freedom and EQUALITY. In order to preserve the appearance of equality, areas of potential conflict and decision-making processes are removed from society. The political and legal structures of the state perform this function by separating public power from the populace and locating it in the council chamber, parliament and law courts, whereby responsibility for political and economic decisions is transferred from supposedly equal citizens to elected or appointed representatives.

NEOLIBERALISM, however, has been accused of undermining the democratic legitimacy of the state by reducing its role to one of facilitating an expansion and intensification of market relations, through the ceding of powers to trade blocs like the NORTH AMERICAN FREE TRADE AGREEMENT and the European Union and to bodies like the WORLD BANK, the WORLD TRADE ORGANIZATION and the INTERNATIONAL MONETARY FUND. These bodies and the principles they practise are considered to prevent the state from acting as an agent of development, as a protector of community and from pursuing poverty-reducing, equitable and sustainable alternatives that advance the interests of poor and marginalized people.

From an anti-capitalist perspective, ANARCHISM and revolutionary syndicalism reject the need for the creation of a worker's state to replace its capitalist counterpart. The latter advocates the creation of revolutionary trade unions as the basis on which a future society can be organized. For

COMMUNISM, as outlined by Karl Marx (1818–1883) and Friedrich Engels (1820–1895) in the *Communist Manifesto* (1848), a truly democratic state would devolve the functions of coercion, consent and decision-making to the practice of everyday life. The Bolshevik model of the workers' state, however, was supposed to represent workers' interests, but in practice workers had no control or power over the state, which, due to the principles of peaceful coexistence and socialism in one country, remained with the party as a vanguard. In contrast to the majority of previous anti-capitalist activists and organizations, with the odd exception like AUTONOMIA, today's movement – as epitomized by the SOCIAL FORUM – mobilizes without aiming to capture or take over the state apparatus but seeks change at national and international levels through the practice of daily life. For a discussion of which, see John Holloway, *Change the World without Taking Power* (2002).

FURTHER INFORMATION

Lenin's *The State and Revolution*: www.marxists.org/archive/lenin/works/1917/
staterev
Weber's *Politics as a Vocation*: www2.pfeiffer.edu/~lridener/DSS/Weber/polvoc.
html

STRUCTURAL ADJUSTMENT PROGRAMMES (SAPs) are the

conditions imposed by the INTERNATIONAL MONETARY FUND (IMF) and the WORLD BANK in return for the credits, debt relief and loans they make to national governments – especially in developing countries. In return for financial assistance, governments are required to adopt what is essentially a neoliberal programme of reform. More often than not, this means one or more of the following prescriptions: currency devaluation, decontrol of exchange rates, DEREGULATION of the financial sector of the economy and of labour markets, increased interest rates, liberalization of trade, privatization, reductions in public services due to budget cuts and wage cuts. These measures are invariably accompanied by higher prices for food and other essentials of daily life, increased POVERTY, rising unemployment and reductions in education, health and social welfare programmes. For examples see the SAPRIN report *Structural Adjustment* (2004).

In contrast, CORPORATIONS are able to exploit cheap labour, devalued currency, favourable exchange rates and the absence of environmental protection controls to produce commodities that are not only too expensive for local people, but are sold at exorbitant prices in the developed world. While the prices and profits do not reflect the financial costs of production, they no doubt provide an inverse reflection of the human costs. The costs associated with SAPs are borne by the local population and not the people who negotiate the loans or who created the need for financial assistance – which is often needed to pay interest on debt owed to foreign banks. Furthermore, the fact that international institutions like the IMF and the World Bank can dictate domestic policy to governments raises questions of ACCOUNTABILITY and DEMOCRACY.

During the 1990s, for example, the Campaign Against Neoliberalism in South Africa (CANSA) noted that the IMF – which had supported the apartheid regime – required the African National Congress (ANC) to retain the National Party finance minister and Reserve Bank governor. Later in the decade it was also instrumental in persuading the ANC government to abandon policies of social justice and redistribution contained in its Reconstruction and Development Programme and replace them with neoliberal principles and programmes. By using SAPs in this way, the IMF and the World Bank prevent governments from implementing policies designed to reduce poverty through equitable and sustainable economic and social development. They are also open to accusations of ignoring – even encouraging – human rights abuses that result from the imposition of SAPs, and of subverting popular participation in government by overriding democratic mandates.

FURTHER INFORMATION

The African experience: www.africaaction.org/action/sap0204.htm
CANSA statement: www.twnside.org.sg/title/afri-cn.htm
SAP and Poverty: www.globalissues.org/TradeRelated/SAP.asp

STUDENT MOVEMENTS, activists, organizations and protests have formed an integral part of a variety of progressive struggles waged since World War II. These include but are not restricted to gay, national and women's liberation movements and campaigns for greater accountability, democratic practice and free speech. Examples include student protests in countries of the former Soviet bloc, like Poland in 1956, and in 1968 when students in the erstwhile Czechoslovakia participated in the 'Prague Spring', and protests took place in what was then Yugoslavia. In China, Tiananmen Square has been a favourite site of student protests, like those that followed the death of Zhou Enlai (1898–1976). Protests by students and intellectuals also took place in 1987, and again as part of the movement that was crushed by the military in 1989, which had support from urban workers and involved strikes at colleges in Beijing and other cities. Pro-democracy student movements and organizations have also targeted military regimes around the world, such as the Free Burma Coalition founded by a group of Burmese and American graduate students at the University of Wisconsin in 1995.

In the USA students from the South and the North took part in the civil rights movement. The Student Nonviolent Coordinating Committee, for example, developed and coordinated sit-in campaigns and organized freedom rides on public buses, voter registration drives and other activities. Student-organized sit-ins took place in all Southern and border states, spread to Nevada, Illinois and Ohio, and focused on public spaces where racial segregation was practised: beaches, buses, libraries, lunch counters, museums, parks and theatres. Students were also involved in the activities of 'Freedom Summer' of 1964, which was intended to publicize the disenfranchisement of Southern blacks; the autumn of the same year also witnessed unrest at the University of California, Berkeley. Organizations like Students for a Democratic Society (SDS), the Southern Student Organizing Committee and the Free Speech Movement opposed the imposition of restrictions on campus political activity with demonstrations, sit-ins and student strikes. The SDS also achieved a national profile in leading campus opposition to the Vietnam War, against which students protested in London, Paris, Berlin and Rome, and in Australia and New Zealand.

Perhaps above all others, the year 1968 is associated with student protest. In addition to the examples already cited, months of conflict raged between the authorities at the University of Paris at Nanterre and students led by activists like Daniel Cohn-Bendit, ENRAGÉS and the Situationists. Closure of the university on 2 May and threats of expulsions were met with opposition by students and staff at the Sorbonne, including Jean-Paul Sartre (1905–1980). The Sorbonne was subsequently closed by university administrators, a decision that met with protests on 6 and 10 May, which ended in street battles with the police, who had occupied both institutions. A general strike was called for school and college students and the Confédération Générale du Travail and Force Ouvrière trade unions called a one-day general strike and demonstration for 13 May. The following day the Sorbonne was reopened by the authorities, occupied by students and declared an autonomous 'people's university'. Workers staged a sit-in at the Sud Aviation plant near Nantes on 14 May, strikes spread to the Renault parts plant near Rouen and manufacturing complexes at Flins in the Seine

233

Valley and the Paris suburb of Boulogne-Billancourt. By 16 May workers had occupied up to fifty factories and by the following week 10 million, or roughly two-thirds of the French workforce, had joined the strike. The protests only ended after the trade unions negotiated a 35 per cent increase in the minimum wage, a 7 per cent wage rise in general and half normal pay for the time on strike, and a general election was agreed.

Student protests and months of political unrest also occurred in Mexico as dissatisfaction with government policy and corruption grew into demonstrations in the run-up to the 1968 Olympic Games to be held in Mexico City. In September, President Gustavo Díaz Ordaz ordered the army to occupy the campus of the National Autonomous University of Mexico, the largest university in Latin America. After student strikes lasting nine weeks, a demonstration of students from various universities marched against the army's occupation of the university campus on 2 October. The march culminated in the Plaza de las Tres Culturas in Tlatelolco, Mexico City, where workers joined in, until the movement was put down in much the same manner as the Tiananmen Square protests in China two decades later. In apartheid South Africa, students were also at the forefront of the liberation movement, including Steve Biko (1946–1977), who helped found the South African Students' Organization at black universities, again in 1968, and became its first president. The African Students' Movement changed its name to the South African Students Movement, in January 1972, as part of the attempt to build a national movement of high-school students. This body organized protests over the practice of only allowing lessons to be taught in Afrikaans, including children at Orlando West Junior School in Soweto, who went on strike over this and other grievances on 30 April 1976. Their rebellion spread to other schools in Soweto until a student-organized rally on 16 June was ended by police action that left anywhere between the official estimate of 23 and unofficial estimates of 200 dead.

Today, students are also active participants at campus, local, regional and international levels, the range of which is indicated by the now dated Philip Altbach study, *Student Political Activism* (1989), and analysed in an American context by Robert Rhoads, *Freedom's Web* (1998). Opposition to NEOLIBERALISM, for example, takes the form of individual and organized action and is represented in myriad student-based groups and causes. In Britain, the People & Planet network was formed as Third World First, in 1969, and is now represented at over 70 per cent of UK universities and colleges and at more than 150 sixth-form and further education colleges. In the USA, the Student Alliance To Reform Corporations is an organization of activists in high schools, colleges, communities and cities that works with existing campus groups, faculty, staff and neighbourhood associations, trade unions, businesses and others who share their goals. On an international scale, the United Students Against Sweatshops represents a movement of campus groups and individuals fighting for sweatshop-free labour conditions and WORKERS' RIGHTS in universities, in the businesses they deal with and in CORPORATIONS in general.

The motivations of these groups provide a fair summary of anti-capitalist issues in general, and matters relating to world poverty, SUSTAINABLE DEVELOPMENT and economic, environmental and social justice. Other causes cover INTERNATIONAL DEBT and the importance of the multilateral treaties on trade and investment administered by the WORLD TRADE ORGANIZATION. The principles of human rights expressed as dignity, EQUALITY and FREEDOM also form an integral aspect of these concerns and involve respect for INDIGENOUS PEOPLE and their cultures, workers' right to self-determination, and opposition to discrimination and oppression within capitalist society based on race, sex, sexuality or CLASS. Organizations like the Freechild Project also advocate radical democracy, and others see grassroots democratic decision-making as a necessary component of the fair distribution of goods and services and equal access to resources, opportunities and information.

Monitoring the actions of governments and corporations through right-to-know initiatives and shareholder activism has produced changes in PepsiCo's cooperation with Burma's military dictatorship, and has also persuaded a lecturers' pension fund, the third biggest in Britain, to adopt a socially responsible investment policy. The adoption by universities and corporations of ethical codes of conduct, full public disclosure of company information and independent verification systems are also advocated as means of protecting workers' rights. The ultimate aim is a global society where workers, consumers and producers are all directly involved in decision-making processes, rather than them taking place behind the closed doors of the INTERNATIONAL MONETARY FUND, WORLD BANK and WORLD ECONOMIC FORUM.

FURTHER INFORMATION

People & Planet: www.peopleandplanet.org
Student Alliance to Reform Corporations: www.starcalliance.org
United Students Against Sweatshops: www.studentsagainstsweatshops.org
Canadian Federation of Students: www.cfs-fcee.ca
School student activism: soundout.org

SUSTAINABLE DEVELOPMENT and sustainability are often used interchangeably as general terms that indicate the kind of human socio-economic activity and organization that will enable the indefinite satisfaction of fundamental human needs and the realization of individual potential in harmony with the preservation of BIODIVERSITY and ecosystems. Perhaps it is more appropriate to consider 'sustainable development' to be part of a process – along with sustainable agriculture, sustainable economy and sustainable industries – through which sustainability in general can be achieved. Understood thus, sustainability can be defined as ensuring that people and the environment enjoy the highest possible standards of welfare – now and in the future – so that future generations will be able to live in a safe environment while improving standards of living. There is a general recognition, however, that, to be effective, solutions must embrace economic, social and ecological aspects of everyday living, conflict prevention and TRADE, while addressing every level of organization from local communities to global society. Among other issues, for example, P.K. Rao, *Sustainable Development* (1998), discusses the need to deal with problems such as debt and poverty in the developing world.

The World Commission on Environment and Development – also known as the Brundtland Commission – is credited with introducing the concept of sustainable development in its 1987 report *Our Common Future*. In 1992, a United Nations Conference for Environment and Development – the Earth Summit – was held as a consequence of concerns raised by the report, and invited proposals on how to promote sustainable development. Since then the issues have become part of international environmental law, and a series of UN conferences have been held to consider environmental and development issues, including the World Summit on Sustainable Development (Rio + 10) in Johannesburg, September 2002.

Although the Brundtland report was influential in bringing concerns about sustainability to a broader audience, similar issues had been the cause of disquiet among environmentalists since the 1960s. In 1968, for example, Paul Ehrlich published *The Population Bomb*, and several European economists and scientists formed the Club of Rome, which later published *Limits to Growth* (1972) with Donella Meadows. The 1970s also witnessed the birth and growth of a number of organizations that, among other things, accepted the general premiss that the world is growing too quickly and using up its resources. These include various political parties calling themselves GREEN, Friends of the Earth, Greenpeace and the Worldwatch Institute.

Central to the sustainability thesis is the idea that humanity is using up the earth's resources in an attempt to feed and accommodate an ever-growing population by expanding agricultural production and urbanization. This process is exacerbated by corporate and governmental desires, especially in the industrialized world, for infinite economic growth to fuel and feed insatiable demands for consumption, and leads inevitably to the degradation of ecosystems and life supporting systems on which humanity depends. As evidence, campaigners point to the interconnectivity of the destruction of tropical rainforests, air pollution and acid rain, increased traffic levels, depletion of the ozone layer, fossil fuel power stations and GLOBAL WARMING. Proposals to address the problems range from abandoning economic development altogether, through slowing economic development, to establishing environmental standards and enforcing them. A focus on population growth, control and reduction, however, raises concerns about human rights such as involuntary or induced sterilization and infanticide – said to have resulted from the Chinese government's one-child policy.

In contrast to strategies that require the imposition of restraint or retrogression, sustainable development is presented as a constructive and progressive agenda that incorporates demands for environmental, economic and social justice. The preservation of natural resources through sustainable use, for example, is not only essential for the survival and well-being of the natural world but also forms part of a symbiotic relationship that gives people the opportunity to enjoy healthy, fulfilling and economically secure ways of living, working and being. Some advocates therefore equate projects to develop life-enhancing technologies with the redistribution of PRIVATE PROPERTY and wealth under various forms of democratic control and the common ownership and organization of socially useful production and distribution.

Integral to this approach is the creation of democratic urban communities and regions; ideas which are explored by Diane Warburton, *Community and Sustainable Development* (1998). Ultimately such initiatives are aimed at the use of existing resources and organizations to develop an urban ecology based on health, safety and environmental protection, including the use of clean, safe and sustainable energy sources, ecologically benign lifestyles and sustainable food production. Understood in this context, sustainable development involves much more than the orthodox economic category of sustainable growth that focuses on increases in income and output without regard to environmental impact. For economic activity to be sustainable

237

it must meet people's present needs, improve their quality of life while enhancing environmental conditions, and not endanger the welfare of future generations and of the planet itself.

Examples of sustainable economic activities include projects that are designed to provide work for local people. *Taking the High Road to Forest Restoration* (2001), by Chris Van Daalen, for example, describes exercises in the USA that provide well-trained, well-paid jobs in forest and stream restoration. Other initiatives include efforts to redress the impact of global warming through the development of cleaner, renewable energy programmes, enhancing energy efficiency, reducing waste and greenhouse gas emissions from fossil fuel power plants, while at the same time protecting jobs and creating new employment. From the perspective of creating jobs and protecting the environment, ecologically sustainable projects include natural heritage protection, involving the protection of endangered species, and water resource management to meet peoples needs for water, prevent flooding and clean up pollution and degradation.

Sustainable industries such as the production of ecological paper alternatives – like the use of kenaf, wheat straw and corn advocated by the Earth Island Institute – offer a solution to deforestation and logging. Similarly, the Alliance for Sustainable Jobs and the Environment argues that short-sighted corporate policies place profitability above the welfare of working people, communities and the natural world. They therefore advocate the development and promotion of business models, public policies and global trade agreements that include enforceable labour and environmental standards that plan for sustainability over the long term, protect and conserve the environment and provide stable, fair waged employment.

Similar criteria are advocated for the sustainable management and use of agricultural biodiversity based on people's control over genetic resources and local knowledge. Organic agriculture is therefore promoted as a sustainable alternative to intensive farming methods. The loss of biological diversity either through industrial farming techniques or GENETIC ENGINEERING is considered by Kok Peng Khor, *Intellectual property, Biodiversity and Sustainable Development* (2002), and regarded by activists as undermining sustainable agriculture by destroying choices for the future and depriving people of a key resource base for survival. Michael Stowell, *The Remarkable Mother of Invention* (2001), notes that Cuba, with its unique status and circumstances, has become a pioneer in the search for alternative technologies and policies that promote sustainable, ecological agriculture. This involves a combination

238

of support for small organic farms to provide affordable food to the population and the recycling of waste for energy production.

FURTHER INFORMATION

Centre for Neighbourhood Technology: www.cnt.org

Cuba and Sustainability: www.globalexchange.org/countries/cuba/sustainable/index.html

UN Earth Summit: www.earthsummit2002.org

SWEATSHOP conditions include one or more of the following: CHILD LABOUR, intimidation of workers, long working hours, forced overtime, low wages, suppression of independent workforce organization, sexual harassment, coercive birth control, unsafe working conditions, poor ventilation and restricted toilet breaks. In short, they represent some of the worst characteristics of CAPITALISM and the process of EXPLOITATION. Usually a consequence of 'sweating' – a process whereby work is subcontracted to the lowest bidder – sweatshop conditions are frequently associated with the manufacture of clothing, due to the labour-intensive sewing and finishing processes, but are also common in the electronics industry and in agriculture.

Modern-day multinational corporations, including Gap, Kappa, Nike and Disney, have been accused of moving or subcontracting production to developing countries to take advantage of poor wages, the absence of legislation requiring minimum working standards, and authoritarian governments that outlaw economic and political dissent. See Andrew Ross, *No Sweat* (1997), for a comprehensive list of examples. In Latin America, the term *Maquila* is a synonym for sweatshop, and EXPORT-PROCESSING ZONES throughout the developing world, but particularly in Asia, are notorious harbingers. Anti-sweatshop motivation combines promotion of human rights and a concern that lower-cost production threatens jobs and employment standards elsewhere. Illegal sweatshops can still be found in developed countries, for example, especially among the employment of new and illegal immigrants who are either devoid or ignorant of statutory rights and often the victims of HUMAN TRAFFICKING.

FURTHER INFORMATION

www.nosweat.org.uk

www.labourbehindthelabel.org

United Students Against Sweatshops: www.usasnet.org

239

T

TAXATION is that aspect of fiscal policy (from the Latin *fiscus*, purse) concerned with raising money to cover government expenditure at local and national levels. This includes administration costs, overseas aid, subsidies to agriculture and industry, as well as the provision of infrastructure, like the arts, education, health, housing, judiciary, military, policing, social security, transport and welfare. According to Adam Smith (1723–1790), *The Wealth of Nations* (1776), taxation should be proportional to the taxpayer's income, be known in advance, easily collected and raise more than it costs to collect. Subsequent theorists have also suggested that all taxpayers should be treated the same and that taxation should not be a disincentive for work.

There are three main ways in which taxes can be levied so that the payer is treated impartially and those with the same circumstances therefore pay the same tax. These are a per capita or poll tax where everyone pays the same amount, a proportional tax where everyone pays the same proportion of their income, and a progressive tax where the amount paid increases with the level of income. Neoclassical and neoliberal economists believe that all taxation is detrimental to the smooth operation of the MARKET and prefer the second option. In contrast, direct taxation based on ability to pay is the norm, because it effects a redistribution of wealth, from rich to poor, by spreading the tax burden whilst financing social and welfare provision and enhancing the proportion of disposable income available to the lower paid.

There are two main forms of taxation: direct taxes that fall on individuals and CORPORATIONS and indirect taxes that are levied on the sale, purchase and use of specific commodities. Examples of direct taxes are income tax, corporation tax, inheritance tax, surtax, capital gains tax – levied when the increase in value of an asset like art, property or shares is realized – and windfall tax targeted at unusually high profits. Indirect taxes include purchase tax, sales tax and taxes on commodities like alcohol, tobacco, petrol, motor vehicles and pastimes like gambling. They also include stamp duty (intended to discourage speculation through the now moribund practice of charging for a contract to be stamped as valid), tariffs that are levied on imports, and excise charged on things produced domestically.

These and other forms of tax are levied at a particular rate against a given base. In other words, a percentage or proportion of income or wealth is liable for taxation once it has reached and exceeded a predetermined level. Where the base is represented by a monetary value, the tax is categorized as *ad valorem*. If the tax rate is set as a specific sum, regardless of price, the tax is fixed according to the quantity sold. In general terms, *ad valorem* taxes on purchases and sales are regressive because they account for a greater proportion of a low-paid person's disposable income than that of a wealthier person. They also fall entirely on the final consumer. Imposition of the tax on essential items like household electricity and gas supply also has a disproportionate impact on poorer individuals and families who spend a greater proportion of their income on such costs.

In the European Union, for example, a value-added tax is applied at each stage of the production of commodities and services that are considered to add VALUE. According to economists, the addition of tax at each stage of the process minimizes market distortion and tax avoidance, but discriminates against manufacturing activity. As indirect taxes can be avoided, at least in theory, they are often levied to discourage a form of activity or consumption, such as car use, drinking, gambling or smoking, by increasing the price. Likewise, levying tariffs on imports can discourage trade in certain commodities, while exemptions from excise afford advantages to domestic products when traded overseas. Where demand is inelastic and does not drop as the price increases, however, the result is not less activity or consumption, but increased revenue.

Nevertheless, groups like Friends of the Earth that are concerned about the impact of industrial development on BIODIVERSITY, ecosystems and GLOBAL WARMING propose that the consumption of carbon, gas and oil-based non-renewable fuels be taxed to reduce the release of carbon into the atmosphere. Others like the Association for the Taxation of Financial Transactions for the Aid of Citizens and War on Want advocate the introduction of an international TOBIN TAX to deter currency speculation and the damage wreaked by CAPITAL FLOWS. Some supporters call for revenue raised to be hypothecated – that is, spent on redressing the problems caused by fuel consumption or capital flows, for example, and supporting programmes of SUSTAINABLE DEVELOPMENT.

At the macroeconomic level, taxation is used as an instrument to regulate economic activity; a method particularly associated with the KEYNESIAN approach. According to such prescriptions, taxation is reduced in order to increase the amount of money circulating in the economy, thereby boosting demand and employment levels and preventing economic recession. Conversely, taxation is increased in an attempt to reduce the money supply and therefore combat inflation. After World War II, social-democratic parties employed Keynesian demand-management techniques in Europe and elsewhere as a way of maintaining levels of employment and welfare provision.

James O'Connor, *The Fiscal Crisis of the State* (1973), and Samuel Brittan, *The Economic Consequences of Democracy* (1977), have argued, from different perspectives, that developments made it impossible for governments to cover costs through taxation without reducing the profitability of corporations and therefore deterring investment. Paradoxically, the nostrums of MONETARISM and NEOLIBERALISM were accepted and practised in Britain, New Zealand and the USA during the 1980s, as solutions to the perceived social-democratic crisis rather than attempting to find ways of transcending the profit motive. Consequently, income was redistributed, from poor to wealthy, as corporation tax and top rates of income tax were reduced in an attempt to encourage investment. At the same time, the emphasis was switched from direct to indirect taxation, which compounded the effects of high unemployment and reduced social security payments by pricing 'luxuries' out of the reach of the many.

Such effects have been exacerbated by the fact that the vast majority of people who work for a living have no means of avoiding income tax, as employers collect it directly from their wages and the STATE takes it from social security. Danny Burns, *Poll Tax Rebellion* (1992), for example, describes what happens when other forms of direct taxation and collection are attempted. In contrast, those individuals and corporations able to employ a NETWORK of accountants, banks and lawyers can reduce financial transparency in order to evade paying tax. Methods include flags of convenience in shipping, holding assets offshore as in the case of tax havens, and the competition between countries – developing and industrialized – to encourage investment by offering tax breaks. At the same time, governments are increasingly adopting the mantra that social security and old-age pensions are no longer affordable.

As well as focusing the tax burden onto ordinary citizens, at the same time that social security payments are falling, such processes also reduce the democratic control of taxation and enhance the power of corporations to dictate tax policy in their own interests. Among other things, this is facilitated by an absence of TRANSPARENCY between countries about tax laws and treaties negotiated with financial service corporations, businesses and trusts, concerning their turnover and tax paid. Groups like Tax Justice Network campaign for accountants, auditors, lawyers and their financial and corporate clients to publish all details relevant to the possible shifting of profits to low-tax jurisdictions and for the same residency principles to be applied to corporate taxation in each national jurisdiction.

FURTHER INFORMATION

Ecological tax: www.progress.org/banneker/shift.html
Tax Justice: www.taxjustice.net

TERRORISM is defined by Section 2331 of title 18, Part I, Chapter 113B of the United States Code as: 'activities that (A) involve acts dangerous to human life that are a violation of the criminal laws of the United States or of any State…; (B) appear to be intended (i) to intimidate or coerce a civilian population; (ii) to influence the policy of a government by intimidation or coercion; or (iii) to affect the conduct of a government by mass destruction, assassination, or kidnapping…'. As Noam Chomsky, 9–11 (2001), argues, however, governments do not abide by their official definitions of the term. In other words, all governments accept the concept and practice of violence – and therefore terror – as a tactic to achieve particular ends, such as maintaining public order, while the term 'terrorism' is used to imply an illegitimate use of violence. In capitalist society, the legitimate use of violence is presented as the sole preserve of the STATE – exercised through the police and military apparatus – and anyone else who uses violence to further their aims is categorized as a terrorist.

The meaning of the term has changed with time, however, as has the importance attached to it; see Jonathan Barker, *Guide to Terrorism* (2003), for a broader discussion. The Online Etymology Dictionary, for example, attributes the first appearance of the word in English to a 1795 description of attempts by the Committee of Public Safety, under Maximilien de Robespierre (1758–1794), to eradicate threats to the French Revolution, both external and internal, between September 1793 and July 1794. Meanwhile, those who took part in the American Revolution of 1775–76 or in the revolutions that swept Europe in 1848 considered their use of violence to be legitimate and were not considered 'terrorists' at the time. The same applies to advocates of insurrection – like Gracchus Babeuf (1760–1797) and Louis-Auguste Blanqui (1805–1881) in France – and to Chartists in England

243

and Wales who advocated the use of 'physical force' to obtain reform of the electoral system.

The term 'terrorist' was used in the nineteenth century to describe the actions of the People's Will (Narodnaia Volia) in Russia and the 'propaganda of the deed'. The latter was articulated by Errico Malatesta (1853–1932) as a tactic of employing insurrectionary acts to inspire mass revolt and taken to include assassination by certain exponents of ANARCHISM. In the twentieth century, 'terrorist' and 'terrorism' were used to describe the activities of the Lohamei Herut Israel (Lehi) and Irgun Tsevai Leummi (Etsel) Zionist groups in the British Mandate of Palestine. The terms were also applied to anti-capitalist groups like the Red Brigades (Brigate Rosse) in Italy, the Red Army Fraction (Rote Armee Fraktion) in West Germany, and November 17 in Greece in the 1970s and beyond. Such groups organized in secret, consisted of small numbers and represented no real constituency. Their tactics of assassination, bombing and kidnapping were intended to facilitate societal change by encouraging state repression, which would in turn result in popular disillusionment with the status quo and lead to demands for change.

Also in the twentieth century, national liberation movements adopted armed struggle as a means of defeating and expelling colonial regimes, but could be viewed either as freedom fighters or as terrorists, depending on the allegiances of the observer. Similarly, those who fought racist regimes in Rhodesia and South Africa were only considered to be terrorists by supporters of the regimes, and who is regarded as a terrorist in the province of Northern Ireland ('the North' to Republicans) depends on what side you are on. After World War II, such struggles became part of the cold war, but were generally referred to as guerrilla warfare, as armed combatants such as the Viet Cong and other liberation movements adopted overt organizational forms. Similar problems of identification still apply today where groups – like the FARC in Columbia and Maoists in India, Nepal and the Philippines – control large swathes, but are labelled by government as terrorists.

Governments, in general, have a long history of double standards when it comes to condemning any kind of violence carried out by opponents – even self-defence in the face of police aggression as in the case of the BLACK BLOC – while authorizing the use of violence to repress dissent. As part of the cold war, armed groups fighting colonial occupation and capitalist exploitation were condemned by governments who were financing armed opposition to non-capitalist governments in Africa and Latin America. Government officials in the USA, for example, allowed cocaine trafficking to finance and arm the Contra group in Nicaragua and, as John Cooley, *Unholy Wars* (2002), documents, the government also recruited and trained Islamic extremists to fight the Afghan regime backed by the Soviet Union. The Military Western Hemisphere Institute for Security Co-operation and its predecessor have also been used to train allies in 'counter-terrorism' measures.

Frederick Gareau, *State Terrorism and the USA* (2004), examines the practices of regimes in Latin America and elsewhere that sanctioned the torture and extrajudicial killing of dissidents – be they academics, clergy, human rights activists, indigenous campaigners, journalists or trade-union leaders. These and other forms of repression have been carried out covertly by the military, police and secret services and by militia and paramilitaries to give the illusion that such violence is connected to criminal activity. The military government of Indonesia was also accused of similar tactics in Acheh, East Timor and Irian Jaya. Parallels can also be drawn between such activities and Israel's extrajudicial killing of Palestinians, allegations of collusion between Loyalists and the British state in Ireland and clandestine attacks on members of the Basque separatist group Fatherland and Liberty (Euzkadi Ta Askatasuna, ETA). Once again, however, there is no consensus about which of these actions constitute terrorism or which groups are terrorists.

Since the September 2001 atrocities in the USA, terrorism and terrorists have replaced the cold war communist enemy and existing conflicts have been reinterpreted so that opponents who were referred to as guerrillas or revolutionaries are designated terrorists in Chechnya, Colombia, Iraq, Israel and elsewhere. This definition now includes anyone who is alleged to have damaged property on a demonstration or resisted police aggression. In Britain, for example, peace protestors have been arrested and detained under prevention-of-terrorism legislation; this is considered by civil and human rights campaigners to use the abstract threat of terrorism as a pretext for governments to remove restrictions on state activity and reduce the RIGHTS of individuals. Witness, for example, the 2002 decision by US President George W. Bush to allow the Central Intelligence Agency to carry out extrajudicial killings of anyone alleged to be working for or with al-Qaeda.

These and other examples beg the question of whether a government can legitimately use terror tactics to combat terrorism and whether such activity is counterproductive. Likewise, the doctrine of 'shock and awe' espoused by Harlan Ullman and James Wade in *Rapid Dominance* (1998) is intended to weaken the will of an adversary through the intensive bombardment of military and strategic targets, as in Serbia in 1999 and Iraq in 2003. Apart from in the realm of semantics, however, there is little qualitative difference between the use of 'shock and awe' tactics and terror; just as it is also improbable that bombing military targets only affects military personnel and does not instil terror into the civilian population. Using a Manichaean dichotomy to portray governments as good and dissidents and opponents as evil, antipatriotic terrorists leaves no room for the consideration of inconsistencies in thought and practice. Periodic atrocities are also given greater media attention and afforded more importance by governments than the daily suffering of people who live and die in POVERTY because they lack the basic living requirements of food, safe water, shelter and health care. Perhaps such people feel that the only way to air their grievances is to commit outrages.

FURTHER INFORMATION

Why Marxists oppose individual terrorism: www.marxists.org/archive/trotsky/works/1909/tia09.htm
United Nations and terrorism: www.unodc.org/unodc/terrorism.html
USA and terrorism: www.cooperativeresearch.org/timeline.jsp?timeline=us_terror
USA government view: www.state.gov/coalition; www.state.gov/s/ct

TOBIN TAX is named after James Tobin (1918–2002), who in 1972 proposed the idea of an international tax on foreign exchange transactions as a form of monetary system regulation that would discourage speculative currency trading by making it more costly and thereby reduce exchange rate volatility. By taxing all transactions involving the conversion of one currency into another, in both domestic security and foreign exchange markets, the tax is intended to target short-term CAPITAL FLOWS that are often speculative. Even a slight increase in the cost of trading in currencies is expected to make short-term money movements unprofitable – due to the volumes required to make speculation on very small differences between currencies worthwhile – and thereby deter destructive attacks on a country's currency. He reiterated his ideas on many occasions, including in *A Proposal for International Monetary Reform* (1978) and *International Currency Regimes* (1991), and argued that a tax paid on entry and exit would penalize tax havens, fiscal fraud and money laundering. As is evident from the contributions to Mahbub ul Haq, Inge Kaul and Isabelle Grunberg, *The Tobin Tax* (1996), however, opinion is divided over the extent to which the proposal could work and whether it is in fact desirable.

Advocates like the Association for the Taxation of Financial Transactions for the Aid of Citizens, the Halifax Initiative and War on Want argue that action is required to prevent recurrence of the financial and socio-economic crises that affected Brazil, Mexico, Russia, Thailand and others in the 1990s. Rather than react to an emergency once it has happened, the Tobin Tax is intended to prevent crises occurring, enhance international cooperation and coordination to address short-term speculation, and rectify underlying structural problems. By allowing traders to react to economic and policy changes, the tax is preferred to alternative devices like capital controls that prevent capital being moved out of a country. Less responsive measures also include taxing foreign assets to encourage investment in domestic corporations, an interest rate equalization tax of all capital outflows or inflows and a national withholding tax that would increase tax levels for short-term capital gains. Exponents of NEOLIBERALISM, on the other hand, abhor attempts to restrict the movement of capital and press the case – through the INTERNATIONAL MONETARY FUND (IMF), ORGANIZATION FOR ECONOMIC COOPERATION AND DEVELOPMENT (OECD) and WORLD TRADE ORGANIZATION (WTO) – for deregulated financial markets that others see as the source instability.

Although the tax is intended to be universal in its application, 84 per cent of all foreign exchange transactions take place in nine countries that host the main markets and the large banks and financial institutions that are the key players. The same countries are home to the strongest currencies – the US dollar, the euro, sterling and the yen. Their participation is therefore seen as a prerequisite for the tax's effectiveness and could even form the basis of a workable regime to be expanded to other economies. On a day-to-day basis, the tax could be collected at the national level, by central banks or financial regulatory bodies, as all transactions are tracked through a centralized system of settlements. Problems arise, however, when a national–international dichotomy is introduced into the equation. On the one hand, the tax could be used to engender international coordination of macroeconomic policies to develop a stable global financial and monetary system and as a tool to enhance international cooperation over competition and between the industrialized and developing countries. Tobin, however, proposed the World Bank and the IMF as agencies that could set and enforce the tax parameters. There is little support for the tax from within those organizations at present, and advocates of the tax view the bodies with deep suspicion. The issue of how to administer and distribute revenues raised by the tax faces almost identical obstacles.

The size of foreign exchange markets – spot, forward and derivative contracts – means that the proceeds of the tax could be enormous. Conservative estimates that do not take into account behavioural reactions to the tax even exceed what the United Nations Program for Development specify as necessary to meet the essential needs of the world's poorest populations. Expectations of what the tax could fund are equally vast and range from the global provision of basic education and health care, food security, water and sanitation, to environmental protection and the eradication of world poverty. War on Want and Emily Willmott, *The Robin Hood Tax* (2002), for example, propose a new accountable, democratic and transparent authority under the auspices of the United Nations General Assembly to deal with the administration of the tax, to distribute its collateral and to initiate programmes of SUSTAINABLE DEVELOPMENT. For such a scheme to work, however, developing countries would have to participate within its decision-making process and an audit for eligibility be instituted to prevent allocations to corrupt governments and those that seek to use proceeds from the tax to redress budget deficits or cut existing welfare programmes.

Although the tax would give national or community governments – in the case of the European Union – more control over currency markets, assigning proceeds from the tax to an international institution responsible for implementing it is considered to be preferable to returning revenue to national governments. Redistribution to the countries from where tax is levied, for example, would afford disproportionate benefit to developed nations with important financial centres and institutions. Similarly, redistributing proceeds according to voting shares in an international organization like the IMF or the WTO would also have inequitable outcomes, while determining the regional incidence of proceeds would be difficult.

Supporters like Heikki Patomaki, *Democratizing Globalization* (2001), also argue that as a system of REGULATION and redistribution – using revenue raised to tackle world poverty – the tax will help prioritize development over speculation and therefore produce stability. In contrast, unregulated financial markets and institutions are accused of favouring fiscal policies that cause financial crises and remedial social policies that have a disproportionate impact on the poorest members of society. The tax is therefore considered to form a central aspect of any programme designed to develop a world economy in which international finance is subservient to the goals of sustainable economic growth, redistribution of wealth and social justice. There are, however, several practical problems that could impair the tax's effectiveness.

The first involves administrative difficulties posed by the numbers of people and organizations that would have to be covered by the tax in order to minimize financial market distortions. In other words, everyone who makes a financial market transaction – financial institutions, governments and international organizations, producers of goods and services, commercial enterprises and private households – would have to be included, unless Treasury activity and other positive transactions were exempted in developing nations. The next question is at what level the tax should be set, if it is to be uniform and deter speculation on the sale and repurchase of foreign currencies. Speculators who expect a short-term devaluation of 3 per cent are unlikely to be deterred by a tax rate less than that level, but that could impose a disproportionate penalty on private households and public bodies. At the other end of the spectrum a lower tax on currency transactions would not be expected to hold back productive business transactions for trade and investment, stop all speculation or prevent all crises, but would at least make them less likely and more manageable. A balance would therefore have to be struck between the tax base, tax rate and range of exempt trading needed to raise enough revenue to meet political objectives, while deterring speculation and crises, but not disrupting normal trading.

In recognizing and discussing such difficulties, Paul Bernd Spahn, *The Tobin Tax and Exchange Rate Stability* (1996), suggests a two-tier structure. A minimal-rate transaction tax would run on a continual basis and raise revenue without impairing normal trading activity. In addition, an exchange surcharge would be administered with the transaction tax to act as an anti-speculation device and a 'circuit-breaker' that would be activated during periods of exchange rate turmoil and impending crisis. To deter attempts at tax evasion, such as swapping speculative activity between forms of trading, the transaction tax could also be varied according to the activity. Different rates would be levied for foreign exchange and derivative transactions, for example, and thereby avoid the problem – associated with the Tobin tax – of disrupting normal trade.

This scheme is similar to the European Monetary System's mechanism for achieving exchange rate stability through a target rate and an acceptable range of differences among member states, but would need universal application – like the Tobin tax – to prevent speculation between the US dollar, the euro, sterling and the yen. Both the exchange surcharge and the Tobin tax are designed to avoid the social deprivation that follows an increase in interest rates to combat speculative attacks. Likewise they would also eliminate the use of currency reserves to deter speculation and to bail out failing financial institutions. Although they would help restore a degree of autonomy and sovereignty to national governments, they would be unlikely to prevent speculative trading triggered by sudden fears of payment defaults or political crises.

FURTHER INFORMATION

Halifax Initiative: www.halifaxinitiative.org
Initiative in the United States of America: www.tobintax.org
War on Want site: www.tobintax.org.uk

TRADE involves the exchange of commodities like currency, manufactured items and natural resources, as well as the provision of services such as banking, telecommunications, transportation and utilities like heating, lighting and water. As part of the exchange process, commodities and services are bought and sold for a price, which is expressed as an amount of money, and the form of trade can be bilateral, multilateral, retail or wholesale and occur locally, regionally or internationally. According to economic theory, trade takes place for a number of reasons and these include the geographic distribution of resources, the effect of climate and terrain on fauna, flora and human activity, and the capacity for domestic production to meet domestic demand.

The classical economist David Ricardo (1772–1823) developed the law of comparative advantage to explain the propensity for trade in terms of the differing costs of production. Variables involved in this process include the level of demand for a particular commodity, together with the availability and costs involved in acquiring buildings, energy, equipment, EXCHANGE RATE, labour-power, natural resources, skills and transport. Trade therefore occurs because it is more profitable for people in a certain area to concentrate on manufacturing steel, for example, so that they can then sell their product in order to purchase something it would be difficult or expensive for them to produce. According to this way of thinking, all parties benefit and the notion that traders exploit others is not entertained. In areas like the ARMS TRADE, however, it is difficult to see who, other than the traders themselves, are the main beneficiaries.

At the international level, trade can be between two parties (bilateral) or involve several participants (multilateral) in the export and import of commodities and services. Trade between nations and their CORPORATIONS has a tradition of being regulated in order to minimize risks to traders, such as default, expropriation, insolvency, licensing or rejection. Originally, this operated in the form of bilateral treaties like the imperial preference exercised under the British Commonwealth and German customs union (*Zollverein*), in which members applied a common tariff to imports from non-members. More recently free-trade areas like those in Europe and North America have been established to remove barriers between signatories. Unlike customs unions, relations with non-members are decided unilaterally, and imports from outside the trade bloc are governed by a 'rule of origin' to govern their movement among and between member countries.

Since the end of World War II, international trade has been regulated under the auspices of the GENERAL AGREEMENT ON TARIFFS AND TRADE (GATT) and more recently through the resultant WORLD TRADE ORGANIZATION (WTO). The stated aim of both is the expansion of free trade – that is, the negotiated removal of administration systems, duties, import controls, licensing, public procurement, quotas, regulations, subsidies and tariffs in order to afford equal rights to domestic and foreign producers. Competition engendered by open international trade is expected to maximize global economic product and consequently raise living standards for all. Economies with a balance-of-payments surplus, because they export more than they import, for example, are expected to give higher rewards to employees and thereby stimulate demand for imports.

Free trade was also a popular economic doctrine in the nineteenth century and a central element of British policy until 1932. The theory was challenged by Friedrich List (1789–1846), *The National System of Political Economy* (*Das Nationale System der olitischen Okonomie*) (1841), and abandoned by some countries during the economic recession of the 1870s and 1880s. A central reason for doing so was the conviction that free trade gives a disproportionate advantage to established industries and economies, because of existing specialization and large-scale production. There is therefore nothing new about the idea that terms of trade favour rich and highly capitalized countries at the expense of underdeveloped countries and that those who advocate free trade are generally already in a strong, competitive position and likely to profit from an expansion of trade. Hence the Netherlands and Britain were vociferous advocates of free trade in the past, while the USA is the main advocate today.

Free trade is supposed to improve economic efficiency by encouraging competition, forcing unprofitable concerns to change or fold, and creating new jobs due to foreign investment. Efficiency in this context is purely financial, however, and makes no allowance for the socio-economic costs of unemployment and **POVERTY** that arise as a consequence. John Madeley, *Hungry for Trade* (2000), Oxfam, *Rigged Rules and Double Standards* (2002), and Yilmaz Akyuz, *Developing Countries and World Trade* (2003), provide other examples of disingenuous argument and practice, not least of which is the fact that today's main advocates of free trade still practise protectionism. Japan and the USA both protect domestic agricultural, clothing and textile industries through subsidy and tariff and the European Union Common Agricultural Policy is equally designed to protect domestic production from imports. Developing countries are unable to retaliate by subsidizing domestic production to make it competitive and they therefore lose any theoretical comparative advantage. These circumstances are a remnant of the GATT, which favoured developed countries by guaranteeing a limited form of free trade in manufactured commodities, while excluding agriculture from this arrangement.

Local producers are unable to compete with **MULTINATIONAL CORPORATIONS** (MNCs), and much of the trade that takes place in the world today comprises the exchange or transfer of components within MNCs and between corporate subsidiaries at managed rather than market mechanisms and prices. The theory of comparative advantage therefore becomes one that is utilized by corporations that can move investment and production to take advantage of local circumstances and is exploited to minimize employment, environmental, health and safety and social protection; these processes are explored by Graham Dunkley, *Free Trade* (2004). There is also a conflict of interest between the ideas of free trade and intellectual property, with the latter acting to prevent developing countries from producing cheaper, generic medicine, for example. There is therefore a paradox in the fact that membership of the WTO is conditional on acceptance of **TRADE-RELATED INTELLECTUAL PROPERTY RIGHTS**. Perhaps an accurate description of the current state of affairs is organized rather than free trade, as even trade blocs exhibit varying degrees of free trade.

The concept and practice of **FAIR TRADE** is advocated by organizations like Equal Exchange, Greenpeace, Max Havelaar, Oxfam, Rainforest Alliance and Transfair as an antidote to the iniquities of normal capitalist trade. As such it has its roots in the alternative trading groups like Ten Thousand Villages and SERRV and the Oxfam world shop initiative and therefore accepts the basic principles of capitalist trade, while espousing the same ultimate goal as free-trade advocates, namely increased prosperity. Since 1988, fair-trade producers and sellers of bananas, chocolate, honey, fruit juice, sugar and tea have used a certification system that includes the Fairtrade, Fair Trade Certified, Max Havelaar and Transfair labels, the standards and accreditation of which are coordinated by the Fairtrade Labelling Organizations International. See David Ransom, *The No-nonsense Guide to Fair Trade* (2001), for an overview of the issues and developments.

FURTHER INFORMATION

Fair Trade advocate: www.fairtrade.net
Free Trade advocate: www.freetrade.org
Sceptical view: www.tradeobservatory.org

TRADE MARK is a category of INTELLECTUAL PROPERTY whereby corporations register a sign – made up of colours, a logo, slogans or three-dimensional shapes or words – as a marketing tool to distinguish their commodities and services from those of another trader. See also BRAND.

TRADE-RELATED INTELLECTUAL PROPERTY RIGHTS (TRIPS) came into being as a multilateral agreement in 1994, following negotiations that took place as part of the process to establish the WORLD TRADE ORGANIZATION (WTO). Under its auspices, all WTO members and therefore national governments and their citizens are required to guarantee stringent levels of protection for INTELLECTUAL PROPERTY, including COPYRIGHT, patents and TRADE MARKS. Failure to do so can result in the implementation of sanctions through TRIPS' prevention and settlement of disputes procedures. Although TRIPS is ostensibly a modernization of the 1883 Paris Convention for the Protection of Industrial Property and the 1886 Berne Convention for the Protection of Literary and Artistic Works, Peter Drahos and John Braithwaite, *Information Feudalism* (2002), catalogue the agreement's negative aspects. Likewise, 3D – a NON-GOVERNMENTAL ORGANIZATION based in Switzerland that campaigns for trade rules that promote an equitable economy – published a series of briefing papers in 2004 that analysed the impact of regional trade agreements and domestic implementation of TRIPS on access to medicine in developing countries.

Curiosities in the agreement include the classification of computer programs as works of literature, so that they qualify for copyright protection.

253

Furthermore, Article 27 decrees that patents have to be granted in all fields of technology regardless of whether it is in the public interest to do so. Due to the nature of patent laws in the USA, however, this has led to allegations of BIOPIRACY, where traditional knowledge has been registered as new to the USA. These and other controversies – especially those relating to the need for generic AIDS drugs in sub-Saharan Africa – contributed to the Doha Declaration of 2001, which implied that TRIPS should not be used to create obstacles to the solution of public health crises. Nevertheless, the WORLD INTELLECTUAL PROPERTY ORGANIZATION and the European Union have sought to develop stricter rules on enforcing intellectual property rights and preventing their circumvention, while others have sought to minimize the possibility of patent holders being forced to grant licences in certain circumstances.

FURTHER INFORMATION

3D Briefing papers: www.3dthree.org/en/page.php?IDpage=23&IDcat=5
Health issues: www.cptech.org/ip/health
Provisions of the agreement: www.wto.org/english/docs_e/legal_e/27-trips_01_
e.htm

TRADE-RELATED INVESTMENT MEASURES (TRIMs) is a multi-lateral trade agreement negotiated and implemented as part of the 1994 Uruguay Round of talks that established the WORLD TRADE ORGANIZATION (WTO). The terms of the accord are designed to prevent restrictions and distortions of the trade in goods, especially discrimination against foreign investors or products. A precise definition is not included in the text of the agreement, but Annex One provides a list of things that are prohibited. These include requirements for a corporation to use or purchase domestic commodities; limits placed on the level of imports in an attempt to balance the levels of exports and imports; and linking the value of a corporation's exports and imports in an attempt to produce a foreign exchange surplus.

A gradual timetable was devised for implementation of these measures and gave developed countries two years, developing countries five years and least developed countries seven years. A Committee on TRIMs was also established to oversee the execution of the provisions of the agreement. Nevertheless, attempts to extend the DEREGULATION of international investment are ongoing within the WTO and external initiatives include the abortive negotiation of the MULTILATERAL AGREEMENT ON INVESTMENT, which, among other things, would have allowed investors to challenge national laws and seek monetary compensation from governments for restricting TRADE.

Opponents contend that TRIMs is anti-democratic, because it undermines the ability of national governments and thereby citizens to manage or regulate their economy. In 2000, for example, a broad coalition of non-governmental organizations and activist groups launched the 'Shrink or Sink' campaign and petition. Aimed at the WTO in general, the coalition calls for the elimination of TRIMs and for the right for developing countries to adopt policies that enhance their own productive sectors, in recognition of their weak position in the international trading system and their overriding need to benefit from world trade.

FURTHER INFORMATION

Shrink it or sink it: uuhome.de/global/english/WTO010b.html
Treaty text: www.wto.org/english/docs_e/legal_e/19-adp.pdf

TRADE UNION or labour union is a collective organization comprising people who work in the same occupation, have the same employer or work in the same branch of industry. Its main purpose is collective bargaining so that the comparative economic weakness of workers as unorganized individuals is counteracted. Negotiations with an employer or employers usually concern the maintenance and improvement of members' living standards in general and wages, hours and other terms and conditions of employment in particular. The development of trade unionism accompanied the growth of factory industry and wage labour, initially in Britain in the early nineteenth century; it remained illegal in France until 1884 and in Germany until 1890.

Penalties for attempting to organize workers included execution and transportation in Britain, where the Tolpuddle Martyrs were sent to Australia for breaching the Combination Acts of 1799 and 1800. As John Orth, *Combination and Conspiracy* (1991), records, the repeal of the Acts in 1824 allowed secret local associations of craftspeople to form national amalgamated trade unions – the first of which was the Amalgamated Society of Engineers in 1850 – while the Trade Union Act of 1871 provided legal status. These 'new model unions' only represented skilled workers, but differed from guilds, which were groups of self-employed skilled craftsmen who had ownership and control over the materials and tools they needed to produce their goods. Towards the end of the nineteenth century, general unions were introduced among agricultural labourers, dockers, municipal workers and seamen, who were usually low-paid and unskilled. The growth of this 'new unionism' saw a change in approach from the skilled unions' reliance on control over apprenticeships and participation in joint negotiating boards, to the general unions' use of the strike weapon.

The organization and functions of trade unions are permitted by law, but are also restricted so as to codify the relationship between employers and those who belong to unions. For the main part, trade unions are considered to be economic bodies, a division that was reinforced by the provisions of the 1927 Trades Disputes Act that followed the 1926 General Strike in Britain, and by the 1947 Taft–Hartley Act in the USA. Prior to such acts, trade unions formed long-term relationships with socialist or social-democratic parties, like the Labour Party in Britain, but in some European countries like France and Italy trade unions and party allegiances split along Christian, socialist and communist party lines. In the USA, by contrast, unions are historically aligned with the Democratic Party, but there are no formal ties of affiliation.

Although trade unions are a force for democratizing the workplace, national and international trade-union bodies accept capitalist production relations as the framework for trade-union aims and methods. Most trade unions in Britain belong to the Trades Union Congress, while in the USA there is the American Federation of Labour–Congress of Industrial Organizations (AFL–CIO). The largest global organization of trade-union members is the Brussels-based International Confederation of Free Trade Unions; formed in 1849, it has 231 affiliated organizations in 150 countries and territories, with a combined membership of 158 million. The ORGANIZATION FOR ECONOMIC COOPERATION AND DEVELOPMENT (OECD) has a Trade Union Advisory Committee (TUAC) and there is also a European Trades Union Confederation.

In anti-capitalist terms, Vladimir (Ulyanov) Lenin (1870–1924), *On Trade Unions* (1970), took a dim view of the trade unions' potential for change, though revolutionary syndicalism or anarcho-syndicalism was derived from the French 'syndicats' or associations of workers that unite members of the same trade or industry. Between 1895 and 1920 the idea that capitalist society could be overthrown by means of DIRECT ACTION or a general strike and an alternative society practising industrial democracy organized through trade unions gained varying degrees of credence in Europe and the continents of America. In Britain, the movement was associated with Tom Mann (1856–1941), *The Industrial Syndicalist* (1910), and bears comparison to the 'guild socialism' of G.D.H. Cole (1889–1959). Following the merger of the Labour Exchanges (Bourses du Travail) and General Confederation of Labour (Confédération Générale du Travail) (CGT) in 1902 the ideas were influential in France until the formation of the Communist Party of France (Parti Communiste Français) in 1920 and its subsequent takeover of the CGT.

The movement was also represented in Argentina by the Federación Obrera Regional, in Germany by the Freie Arbeiter Union, in Italy by the Unione Sindicale Italiana, and in Portugal by the Confederação Geral dos Trabahaladores Portugueses. In the USA, the industrial unionism advocated by the Industrial Workers of the World (Wobblies), formed in 1905, did not use the term 'syndicalist', but analogies can be drawn between the policies and tactics of each. The other notable example of syndicalist influence was in Spain where Solidaridad Obrera was formed in Barcelona in 1907 and the Conferación Nacional del Trabajo operated from its inception in Seville in 1910 until the victory of Franco in 1939.

Today, individual unions together with their national and international organizations campaign on issues that reflect the concerns of the current anti-capitalist movement. These include economic, environmental and social justice, SUSTAINABLE DEVELOPMENT and the impact of multinational corporations, international financial institutions and multilateral trade agreements on WORKERS' RIGHTS and the lives of working people in general; the reality of which is captured by Henk Thomas, *Globalisation and Third World Trade Unions* (1995). More specifically, such concerns translate into campaigns about corporate accountability over executive pay, pension plans and the use of sweatshops. The AFL–CIO produces a shoppers' guide to products and services produced by unionized workers and to companies that abuse workers and the environment, for example, while in Britain the network Labour Behind the Label undertake similar initiatives. The TUAC also produces reports and lobbies the G8 summits and OECD on related matters.

FURTHER INFORMATION

Current issues: www.labourstart.org
Industrial Workers of the World: www.iww.org; www.iww.org.uk
International trade-union campaigns: www.global-unions.org

TRANSNATIONAL CORPORATIONS (TNCs) literally operate
– have investments, production facilities and markets – in more than one

country. They are not restricted by national boundaries and their interests and involvement are evident within and across nations. Although the term is often used instead of 'multinational corporations', in practice there is no qualitative difference between the two. See also **CORPORATIONS**.

TRANSPARENCY implies an openness of decision-making processes in the realms of business practice, law enforcement, corporate management and **POLITICS**. This means public participation in and scrutiny of decisions from start to finish and is considered to be an essential element of **DEMOCRACY**. This is sometimes referred to as open government, whereby all arguments for and against proposals, the manner in which decisions are made and all outcomes are in the public domain. All related documents, draft or otherwise, should also be made available throughout and archived afterwards. Varying degrees of openness exist in legislative processes that allow public observation of debates – either in person or on television – as in Britain and the USA, and full records of discussions are recorded and published together with the texts of proposed laws and final laws.

The advent of the Internet has made published material more widely available, including evidence submitted to public inquiries. In practice, however, such bodies make decisions in private and are therefore more akin to the principle of **ACCOUNTABILITY**. The same applies to day-to-day policymaking in and by commissions and political parties. Meanwhile, the legalistic linguistic conventions adopted while drafting legislation also act as a barrier to public participation. Along similar lines, groups like Tax Justice Network argue that accountants, banks and lawyers create complex and secret financial structures in a deliberate attempt to reduce transparency, and in doing so contribute to catastrophes like the collapse of Barings Bank in the 1990s and of Enron early in the twenty-first century.

The Halifax Initiative also argues for a fundamental reform of the way the international financial system and its institutions operate through the introduction of democratic governance that consists of full and open public participation. They also campaign for transparency in **EXPORT CREDIT** decisions, whereas the DATA group focus on international institutions like the **INTERNATIONAL MONETARY FUND**, **WORLD BANK** and **WORLD TRADE ORGANIZATION** and Transparency International target political corruption, including multinational corporations' dealings with national governments. For others, the Internet has facilitated the development of open source ideals and their application to decision-making, governmental and other organizational processes. Networks like the GNU/Linux community and Indymedia, for example, advocate using the Internet to allow the involvement of interested groups and individuals in policy formulation. Such processes are considered to be more legitimate and more efficient through the correction and improvement of proposals before they are accepted and implemented.

FURTHER INFORMATION

Indymedia process: docs.indymedia.org
Campaign groups: www.datadata.org; www.halifaxinitiative.org; www.transparency.org

TROTSKYISM is a radical theory of COMMUNISM and form of MARXISM that is derived from or claimed to relate to the work of Leon Trotsky (1879–1940) – original name Lev Davidovitch Bronstein – one of the leading figures of the Bolshevik Revolution in 1917. As a member of the Left Opposition that disagreed with developments within the Soviet Union under Joseph (Dzhugashvili) Stalin (1879–1953), Trotsky attracted support from those who were critical of and opposed to the Bolshevik Revolution in general. Following his expulsion from the Communist Party of the Soviet Union Union (CPSU, Kommunistischeskaya Partiya Sovetskogo Soyuza) and his forced deportation in 1929, he helped found the Fourth International or World Party of Socialist Revolution in 1938, as an alternative to the Third International.

INTERNATIONALISM, the need for a revolutionary strategy that breaks with the existing order and for REVOLUTION to take place on a global scale as a way of ensuring the success of communism represent the cornerstones of Trotskyism. This approach is outlined by Trotsky as part of his transitional programme, *The Death Agony of Capitalism* (1938), and sits in direct contrast to the idea of 'socialism in one country', which is equated with bureaucratization, forced industrialization and a predicted reintroduction of PRIVATE PROPERTY. The popularity of this critique, which included advocacy of a pluralistic form of socialism that involved workers' control and competition between parties that accepted socialist organization of production and distribution, receded after Trotsky's death, but re-emerged during the 1960s.

A defining feature of groups that associate themselves with the legacy of Trotsky has been their propensity towards extreme fragmentation – evidence of which is provided by the list of International Trotskyist Tendencies from 1928 by the Encyclopaedia of Trotskyism online. Disagreements include whether the Soviet Union was state capitalist or a form of 'degenerated workers' state' in line with Trotsky's analysis in *The Revolution Betrayed* (1937). Organizational differences range from broad and loosely organized groups, through centralized democratic forms, to democratic centralism; the justification for which is attributed to different stages of Trotsky's thought. Similarly, the concept of permanent revolution as a series of interconnected and interdependent social, political and economic upheavals that proceed on a variety of levels and in diverse social structures has been (mis)understood in a number of ways.

FURTHER INFORMATION

Encyclopedia of Trotskyism Online: www.marxists.org/history/etol
Trotsky's works online: www.marxists.org/archive/trotsky/index.htm

U

UNITED NATIONS (UN) is a voluntary association open to all countries that accept its charter. The charter was ratified in 1945 following negotiations between France, the then Republic of China, Britain, the USA and the USSR at Dumbarton Oaks in 1944 and the United Nations Conference on International Organization in 1945 in San Francisco. The preamble to the Charter (1945) summarizes its aims as avoiding the scourge of war and promoting fundamental human rights, social progress, better standards of life as well as EQUALITY between men and women and between countries. Ultimately, the aims of maintaining international peace and security together with economic and social cooperation are based on the general principle of INTERNATIONALISM. From an original membership of 51, by 2004 the number had risen to 191, the majority of which are developing countries. The 24th of October is also recognized as United Nations Day.

The UN comprises six main bodies. The General Assembly is the main arena for deliberation, consists of all member states and was first convened in London in 1946. The Assembly votes on resolutions, which are recommendations and therefore not binding. This and other UN bodies are serviced by a Secretariat of almost 9,000 people, based primarily at the organization's headquarters in New York, officially opened in 1951, and at offices in Addis Ababa, Bangkok, Beirut, Geneva, The Hague, Nairobi, Santiago and Vienna. The Secretariat is headed by a Secretary-General, whom it assists in administering peacekeeping operations, gathering information on economic and social trends and problems, human rights and SUSTAINABLE DEVELOPMENT, implementing Security Council decisions, mediating international disputes, consulting members and organizing international conferences. Seven men have been Secretary-General: Norwegian Trygve Halvdan Lie (1896–1968) between 1945 and 1953; Swede Dag Hammarskjöld (1905–1961) until 1961; Burmese U Thant (1909–1974) until 1971; Austrian Kurt Waldheim until 1981; Peruvian Javier Pérez de Cuéllar until 1991; Egyptian Boutros Boutros-Ghali until 1996; and Ghanaian Kofi Annan.

The Security Council has responsibility for maintaining international peace and security and has the power to make binding decisions. The first session was held in London in 1946, when the Council consisted of five permanent members and six elected. The nations that took part in the Dumbarton Oaks conference form the permanent members, though the People's Republic of China replaced Taiwan in 1971 and Russia replaced the USSR in 1991. In 1965, the number of elected members was also increased to fifteen, each of which is selected by a regional group and confirmed by the General Assembly, and serves for two years; five new members are chosen each year. Security Council Resolutions require the approval of nine votes, though each of the permanent members has a right to veto.

The original permanent members reflected the major victorious powers from World War II and are now considered to be anomalous. The defeated powers of Germany and Japan, for example, were not afforded permanent status, though rank among the world's largest economies, constitute the third and second largest contributors to UN funding respectively, while only the USA contributes more troops to UN-mandated missions than Germany. Although the five permanent members were the original nuclear powers, the reality of this situation has also changed with India, Israel and Pakistan acquiring such weapons. The preponderance of developing countries in the General Assembly also means that they can influence its agenda, debates and decisions, but they have less influence in the Security Council.

Proposed solutions to these irregularities include making permanent members of Brazil, Germany, India, Japan and an unspecified African country. This does not address the predominance of industrialized countries, however, though the suggestion from Italy and the Netherlands to combine European representation under a European Union (EU) representative might help address this imbalance, though the EU is not a country. Other alternatives include removing the right of veto, thereby affording equal weight to the votes of Security Council members, or weighting votes according to population size. These and other issues are considered by Vicenc Fisas, *Blue Geopolitics* (1995), and by South Centre, *For a Strong and Democratic United Nations* (1997).

The Economic and Social Council (ECOSOC) promotes international economic and social cooperation and development, has fifty-four members, eighteen of whom are elected each year by the General Assembly for a three-year term. ECOSOC oversees and sets policy for UN operational development and other activities that, in turn, involve the UN's five Regional Commissions and nine Functional Commissions, which include those on Social Development, Human Rights, Sustainable Development and the Status of Women. ECOSOC also coordinates the activities of the UN and fifteen autonomous specialized agencies, such as the International Labour Organization, World Health Organization, WORLD BANK, INTERNATIONAL MONETARY FUND and the WORLD INTELLECTUAL PROPERTY ORGANIZATION.

The final organ of the UN system is the International Court of Justice, which was set up as the judicial arm of the UN in 1945 and saw its inaugural sitting take place the following year. The Court hears disputes submitted by consenting countries and makes decisions according to international law. It also gives advisory opinions on legal questions referred to it by General Assembly, Security Council or UN agencies. Located at The Hague, in the Netherlands, the court comprises fifteen judges elected by the General Assembly and Security Council and makes decisions by a majority vote of judges. Each judge is elected for a nine-year term and five positions are elected every three years. Individuals can be re-elected, but the Court must be made up of representatives from fifteen different countries.

Where countries agree to submit a case before the Court, decisions are supposed to be binding, but the USA ignored a 1984 Court order that it should pay reparations to Nicaragua for breaching international law by using force against it. In theory, the Security Council could have punished the USA for not complying, but, as a permanent member, the USA could veto any such action. The Court also issues advisory opinions on questions of international law submitted by UN institutions. Although advisory opinions are not usually binding, where they involve specific instruments or regulations they can be binding on agencies or countries. One of the most recent advisory opinions of the International Court of Justice, for example, involved the construction of a concrete wall around the West Bank Palestinian territories occupied by Israel.

The UN and its institutions are often at the forefront of debates about issues that concern present-day anti-capitalists. A non-exhaustive list of examples is provided by the UN's Millennium Development goals. These include: eradicating extreme poverty and hunger; achieving universal primary education; promoting gender equality and empowering women; reducing child mortality; improving maternal health, combating HIV/AIDS, malaria and other diseases; ensuring environmental sustainability; and developing a global partnership for development. These and other matters are addressed by agencies, commissions and programmes such as the Children's Fund, the Commission on the Status of Women, the Development Fund for Women, the Development Programme, the Educational, Scientific and Cultural

Organization, the Environment Programme, the High Commissioner for Refugees, the Programme on HIV/AIDS, the World Bank, the World Food Programme and the World Health Organization.

Taking these commitments at face value, there appears to be a conflict of interest between the stated aims of the UN, its agencies and the policies that are implemented in its name. In particular, the goals of eradicating POVERTY, promoting DEMOCRACY and sustainable development, protecting the environment and recognizing workers' rights appear to be at odds with the implications of DEREGULATION, STRUCTURAL ADJUSTMENT PROGRAMMES and trade liberalization. So, too, concern about the impact of INTERNATIONAL DEBT on each DEVELOPING COUNTRY and the role of the World Bank in such processes. Despite adopting the UNIVERSAL DECLARATION OF HUMAN RIGHTS in 1948, for example, cases of arbitrary detention, disappearance and torture continued to occur; often with the complicity of permanent members of the Security Council. Allegations of BIOPIRACY contrast with efforts to protect INTELLECTUAL PROPERTY, and there appears to be an inherent conflict of interest between attempts to guarantee food safety and market deregulation.

While the UN extols its virtues in helping countries in transition to democracy by providing technical assistance for the holding of free and fair elections, groups like Global Policy Forum campaign to make the UN administration more transparent, more accountable and therefore more democratic. Based on the present one-state, one-vote principle, countries are supposed to cast votes at the UN in accordance with the wishes of their electors. With advances in technology, however, it should soon be possible for global citizens to participate directly in the election of UN officials and representatives. Alternatively, national governments could consult electorates through referenda, before casting votes and ratifying appointments.

Making the UN more democratic and therefore responsive to the will of the global populace would have the effect of changing the role of the UN from one of a debating forum to more of a world government. Such moves are supported by the Committee for a Democratic UN, part of the World Federalist Movement and advocates of the creation of a United Nations Parliamentary Assembly. Criticism of the UN includes its apparent reluctance or inability to influence certain aspects of national policy and practice due, in part, to the fact that decisions taken by the General Assembly and judgments of the International Court of Justice are not binding. The UN would therefore be able to impose sanctions on members who are in breach of agreed decisions and treaties; in much the same way as the World Trade

Organization does now, but with a global democratic mandate. Coupled to such demands are the ideas that the UN should play a greater role in world affairs. The Association for the Taxation of Financial Transactions for the Aid of Citizens and War on Want, for example, call for a UN feasibility study on the TOBIN TAX and for it to be involved in its administration. Likewise, Tax Justice Network's advocacy of a democratic global forum to improve cooperation and to increase the democratic control of taxation could conceivably fall under the auspices of a reformed UN.

FURTHER INFORMATION

Global Policy Forum: www.globalpolicy.org
Official UN site: www.un.org
World Federalist Movement: www.wfm.org

UNIVERSAL DECLARATION OF HUMAN RIGHTS contains articles relating to areas, especially regarding education, health, social security and work, that do not always appear to be high on the agenda of certain countries that present themselves as champions of human rights. These areas do, however, motivate many anti-capitalist activists, groups and organizations. The full text is as follows:

PREAMBLE: Whereas recognition of the inherent dignity and of the equal and inalienable rights of all members of the human family is the foundation of freedom, justice and peace in the world,

Whereas disregard and contempt for human rights have resulted in barbarous acts which have outraged the conscience of mankind, and the advent of a world in which human beings shall enjoy freedom of speech and belief and freedom from fear and want has been proclaimed as the highest aspiration of the common people,

Whereas it is essential, if man is not to be compelled to have recourse, as a last resort, to rebellion against tyranny and oppression, that human rights should be protected by the rule of law,

Whereas it is essential to promote the development of friendly relations between nations,

Whereas the peoples of the United Nations have in the Charter reaffirmed their faith in fundamental human rights, in the dignity and worth of the human person and in the equal rights of men and women and have determined to promote social progress and better standards of life in larger freedom,

Whereas Member States have pledged themselves to achieve, in cooperation with the United Nations, the promotion of universal respect for and observance of human rights and fundamental freedoms,

Whereas a common understanding of these rights and freedoms is of the greatest importance for the full realization of this pledge,

Now, therefore the general assembly proclaims this universal declaration of human rights as a common standard of achievement for all peoples and all nations, to the end that every individual and every organ of society, keeping this Declaration constantly in mind, shall strive by teaching and education to promote respect for these rights and freedoms and by progressive measures, national and international, to secure their universal and effective recognition and observance, both among the peoples of Member States themselves and among the peoples of territories under their jurisdiction.

ARTICLE 1. All human beings are born free and equal in dignity and rights. They are endowed with reason and conscience and should act towards one another in a spirit of brotherhood.

ARTICLE 2. Everyone is entitled to all the rights and freedoms set forth in this Declaration, without distinction of any kind, such as race, colour, sex, language, religion, political or other opinion, national or social origin, property, birth or other status. Furthermore, no distinction shall be made on the basis of the political, jurisdictional or international status of the country or territory to which a person belongs, whether it be independent, trust, non-self-governing or under any other limitation of sovereignty.

ARTICLE 3. Everyone has the right to life, liberty and security of person.

ARTICLE 4. No one shall be held in slavery or servitude; slavery and the slave trade shall be prohibited in all their forms.

ARTICLE 5. No one shall be subjected to torture or to cruel, inhuman or degrading treatment or punishment.

ARTICLE 6. Everyone has the right to recognition everywhere as a person before the law.

ARTICLE 7. All are equal before the law and are entitled without any discrimination to equal protection of the law. All are entitled to equal protection against any discrimination in violation of this Declaration and against any incitement to such discrimination.

ARTICLE 8. Everyone has the right to an effective remedy by the competent national tribunals for acts violating the fundamental rights granted him by the constitution or by law.

ARTICLE 9. No one shall be subjected to arbitrary arrest, detention or exile.

ARTICLE 10. Everyone is entitled in full equality to a fair and public hearing by an independent and impartial tribunal, in the determination of his rights and obligations and of any criminal charge against him.

ARTICLE 11.

(1) Everyone charged with a penal offence has the right to be presumed innocent until proved guilty according to law in a public trial at which he has had all the guarantees necessary for his defence.

(2) No one shall be held guilty of any penal offence on account of any act or omission which did not constitute a penal offence, under national or international law, at the time when it was committed. Nor shall a heavier penalty be imposed than the one that was applicable at the time the penal offence was committed.

ARTICLE 12. No one shall be subjected to arbitrary interference with his privacy, family, home or correspondence, nor to attacks upon his honour and reputation. Everyone has the right to the protection of the law against such interference or attacks.

ARTICLE 13.

(1) Everyone has the right to freedom of movement and residence within the borders of each state.

(2) Everyone has the right to leave any country, including his own, and to return to his country.

ARTICLE 14.

(1) Everyone has the right to seek and to enjoy in other countries asylum from persecution.

(2) This right may not be invoked in the case of prosecutions genuinely arising from non-political crimes or from acts contrary to the purposes and principles of the United Nations.

ARTICLE 15.

(1) Everyone has the right to a nationality.

(2) No one shall be arbitrarily deprived of his nationality nor denied the right to change his nationality.

ARTICLE 16.

(1) Men and women of full age, without any limitation due to race, nationality or religion, have the right to marry and to found a family. They are entitled to equal rights as to marriage, during marriage and at its dissolution.

(2) Marriage shall be entered into only with the free and full consent of the intending spouses.

(3) The family is the natural and fundamental group unit of society and is entitled to protection by society and the State.

ARTICLE 17.

(1) Everyone has the right to own property alone as well as in association with others.

(2) No one shall be arbitrarily deprived of his property.

ARTICLE 18. Everyone has the right to freedom of thought, conscience and religion; this right includes freedom to change his religion or belief, and freedom, either alone or in community with others and in public or private, to manifest his religion or belief in teaching, practice, worship and observance.

ARTICLE 19. Everyone has the right to freedom of opinion and expression; this right includes freedom to hold opinions without interference and to seek, receive and impart information and ideas through any media and regardless of frontiers.

ARTICLE 20.

(1) Everyone has the right to freedom of peaceful assembly and association.

(2) No one may be compelled to belong to an association.

ARTICLE 21.

(1) Everyone has the right to take part in the government of his country, directly or through freely chosen representatives.

(2) Everyone has the right of equal access to public service in his country.

(3) The will of the people shall be the basis of the authority of government; this will shall be expressed in periodic and genuine elections which shall be by universal and equal suffrage and shall be held by secret vote or by equivalent free voting procedures.

ARTICLE 22. Everyone, as a member of society, has the right to social security and is entitled to realization, through national effort and international cooperation and in accordance with the organization and resources of each State, of the economic, social and cultural rights indispensable for his dignity and the free development of his personality.

ARTICLE 23.

(1) Everyone has the right to work, to free choice of employment, to just and favourable conditions of work and to protection against unemployment.

(2) Everyone, without any discrimination, has the right to equal pay for equal work.

(3) Everyone who works has the right to just and favourable remuneration ensuring for himself and his family an existence worthy of human dignity, and supplemented, if necessary, by other means of social protection.

(4) Everyone has the right to form and to join trade unions for the protection of his interests.

ARTICLE 24. Everyone has the right to rest and leisure, including reasonable limitation of working hours and periodic holidays with pay.

ARTICLE 25.

(1) Everyone has the right to a standard of living adequate for the health and well-being of himself and of his family, including food, clothing, housing and medical care and necessary social services, and the right to security in the event of unemployment, sickness, disability, widowhood, old age or other lack of livelihood in circumstances beyond his control.

(2) Motherhood and childhood are entitled to special care and assistance. All children, whether born in or out of wedlock, shall enjoy the same social protection.

ARTICLE 26.

(1) Everyone has the right to education. Education shall be free, at least in the elementary and fundamental stages. Elementary education shall be compulsory. Technical and professional education shall be made generally available and higher education shall be equally accessible to all on the basis of merit.

(2) Education shall be directed to the full development of the human personality and to the strengthening of respect for human rights and fundamental

freedoms. It shall promote understanding, tolerance and friendship among all nations, racial or religious groups, and shall further the activities of the United Nations for the maintenance of peace.

(3) Parents have a prior right to choose the kind of education that shall be given to their children.

ARTICLE 27.

(1) Everyone has the right freely to participate in the cultural life of the community, to enjoy the arts and to share in scientific advancement and its benefits.

(2) Everyone has the right to the protection of the moral and material interests resulting from any scientific, literary or artistic production of which he is the author.

ARTICLE 28. Everyone is entitled to a social and international order in which the rights and freedoms set forth in this Declaration can be fully realized.

ARTICLE 29.

(1) Everyone has duties to the community in which alone the free and full development of his personality is possible.

(2) In the exercise of his rights and freedoms, everyone shall be subject only to such limitations as are determined by law solely for the purpose of securing due recognition and respect for the rights and freedoms of others and of meeting the just requirements of morality, public order and the general welfare in a democratic society.

(3) These rights and freedoms may in no case be exercised contrary to the purposes and principles of the United Nations.

ARTICLE 30. Nothing in this Declaration may be interpreted as implying for any State, group or person any right to engage in any activity or to perform any act aimed at the destruction of any of the rights and freedoms set forth herein.

See also RIGHTS.

Source: www.un.org/Overview/rights.html

UTOPIA is generally used to refer to notions about an ideal form of society in which there exists complete human fulfilment, EQUALITY, FREEDOM, JUSTICE and other preferred standards. In this respect, the term and the concept derive from the eponymous publication of 1516 by Thomas More (1478–1535), the title of which is taken to be a derivation from the Greek (*outopia*, no place; *eutopia*, good place). The genre also includes *The City of the Sun* by Tommaso Campanella (1568–1639) – written in 1602, though not published in printed form until 1623 – and *The New Atlantis*, written by Francis Bacon (1561–1626) in 1626 and published posthumously in 1627.

Both works have the distinction of being the earliest expositions of societies transformed by the application of knowledge and economic-technological development. John Bellers (1654–1725) published his *Proposals for Raising a College of Industry for All Useful Trades and Husbandry* in 1695 as a means of alleviating poverty without inconveniencing the wealthy. Étienne Cabet (1788–1856) later sought to popularize communism of production based on machine industry in *Travels in Icaria* (*Voyages en Icarie*) (1839) and later founded colonies in the USA based on his ideas.

Writing before the convergence of socialist and class interests in 1830s' Britain and France, a variety of theorists advocated class reconciliation as opposed to class struggle, amelioration of social conditions, reorganization of the labour process, communal ownership and free distribution of essential goods and services according to need. These include Claude-Henri de Rouvroy, Comte de Saint Simon (1760–1825), who advocated a rationally planned and collectively controlled mode of production based on modern industry in *Letters from an Inhabitant of Geneva* (*Lettres d'un habitant de Genève à ses contemporains*) (1803). Similar views were expressed by Robert Owen (1771–1858) in *A New View of Society* (1813) and by François-Charles Fourier (1772–1837) in *Theory of the Four Movements* (*La Theorie de Quatrres Mouvements*) (1808).

The term 'utopian' was co-opted as a pejorative description of such theories by Friedrich Engels (1820–1895) and Karl Marx (1818–1883) in the *Manifesto of the Communist Party* (1848); a concept elaborated by Engels, *Socialism: Utopian and Scientific* (1892). Stated briefly, they defined utopianism as a failure to recognize the revolutionary role of the PROLETARIAT as the agent of human and therefore self-emancipation. Interestingly, the word is still used to categorize and demonize concepts that are antithetical to capitalism as idealistic or impractical, and has even been adapted by Ernest Callenbach, *Ecotopia* (1978). There is, however, a conspicuous reluctance to recognize the utopian nature of neoliberal proposals for free trade and LAISSEZ-FAIRE, especially as existing inequalities of wealth and power between CORPORATIONS, individuals and nations in the form of monopolies, subsidies and tariffs make such schemes unrealistic.

FURTHER INFORMATION

Engels, *Socialism: Utopian and Scientific* online: www.marxists.org/archive/marx/
   works/1880/soc-utop
Literary and other genres: www.utoronto.ca/utopia

V

VALUE is understood by economists to be an expression of worth that exists in two forms: as use-value and as exchange-value. The use-value of a COMMODITY indicates its utility to someone and is the reason why it becomes available for exchange in the first place. Without a use-value the commodity would be worthless, as no one would want it. Exchange-value, on the other hand, is deemed to be the quantitative aspect of value, expressed as the worth of one commodity in relation to another. Under CAPITALISM, one particular commodity – that of money – is set apart to represent the value of all commodities; and, as the medium of exchange, the money form of value appears to be a common characteristic of all commodities. As a consequence, money is believed to constitute the universal equivalent of value.

Adam Smith (1723–1790), *Wealth of Nations* (1776), and David Ricardo (1722–1823), *On the Principles of Political Economy* (1817), considered the innate worth of a commodity to be based on the amount of LABOUR needed to produce it. Subsequent economists sought to explain value as something that is external to the nature of a commodity and therefore to divorce the substance of value from the relations of production. They chose to interpret exchange-value as price expressed as a quantity of money and therefore a form of value that is not based on and therefore separate from the inherent, concrete qualities of the commodity itself. In other words, a price expresses the money form of value and money represents the standard by which commodities are priced. The tendency of this ratio of exchange to vary according to circumstance, place and time is explained in terms of supply and demand. Originators of this approach include William Jevons (1835–1882) *The Theory of Political Economy* (1871), Carl Menger (1840–1921), *Principles of Economics* (1871), and Marie-Esprit-Léon Walras (1834–1910), *Elements of Pure Economics* (1954).

Contingent on this form of analysis is the conclusion that the only common, consistent elements that apply to all commodities are the human motivations that fuel supply and demand. As a consequence of focusing on the abstract notions of human experience, value is considered to be the product of commodity exchange and not an inherent, concrete property of the commodity itself. Taking this view at face value, therefore, value can be enhanced by manipulating demand through ADVERTISING and encouraging CONSUMERISM. A further corollary of this approach is the assumption that the total value circulating in the economy must be constant, as this justifies the maxim that a fair exchange is no robbery.

In contrast, Karl Marx (1818–1883) in *Capital* (1867) argued that value has both an abstract and a material existence in the social relations of production and exchange; especially as all economic categories reflect some form of human activity. A materialist analysis therefore recognizes that the only common, consistent element of commodities is that people produce them. They are the products of human labour and their value is measured in units of time necessary for them to be made – socially necessary labour-time – and therefore the expenditure of labour-power as part of the process of creation. This labour-power has, in turn, a use-value that is specific to capitalist commodity relations and an exchange-value as a commodity that is bought from workers by employers. The fact that the labour-power has a greater value than the wage paid for it forms the basis of capitalist EXPLOITATION.

As the appearance form of value, exchange-value is expressed independently of the reality of the productive process, is obscured by the operations of markets, competition, supply and demand, and therefore serves to mask the underlying SOCIAL RELATIONS involved in production. The process of exchange also reduces the different kinds of LABOUR embodied in different commodities to an abstract category of labour in general. The connections between independent commodity producers therefore appear as relations between things – commodities of goods, money and services – and are symptomatic of the processes of ALIENATION and REIFICATION.

An alternative yet related understanding of the term 'value' is evident in society as a whole and as part of academic social science in particular. In this instance, beliefs, ideas or opinions are equated with aesthetic, ethical and ideological assessments of worth and described as value judgements or truth claims. The positivist school that originated with Auguste Marie François Xavier Comte (1798–1857) is particularly influential in the conception and practice of orthodox economics. Also associated with the logical positivism of Karl Popper (1902–1994), it seeks to exclude value judgements through the concentration on observable facts and relationships. In other words, researchers are expected to act impartially and not allow individual preferences to bias research, data collection or conclusions.

There are, however, a number of factors that can influence research and the selection of topics studied, such as the preferred theory of the researcher or their employer and the interests of the funding organization. The value system(s) of the researcher, the dominant value system(s) of society, and interactions between the two also exert an influence on research and on the presentation of findings. According to David Held, *Introduction to Critical Theory* (1980), for example, Max Horkheimer (1895–1973) argued that there is no objective reality upon which social theorists can reflect, because social theorists are part of the societal process analysed. In order to overcome such obstacles, an account and explanation of research undertaken can include details of the author's epistemological and methodological understanding, of her/his approach to the question of research, and of her/his value system(s) and truth claims. Perhaps the ultimate paradox is the fact that the idea that social science should be free of value judgements is itself a value judgement.

FURTHER INFORMATION

Essays on Marx's theory of value: www.marxists.org/subject/economy/rubin/ch12.htm

International Working Group on Value Theory: www.gre.ac.uk/~fa03/iwgvt

Capital Volume I: www.marxists.org/archive/marx/works/1867-c1/ch01.htm#S3

W

WORKERS' RIGHTS and employment or labour rights are the economic equivalent to the concept of RIGHTS in the civil sphere of society. They are also enshrined in the UNIVERSAL DECLARATION OF HUMAN RIGHTS in Articles 4, 20, 23 and 24. The first two involve protection from slavery and servitude and guarantee freedom of association. Articles 23 and 24 guarantee the right to work, to choose employment, to enjoy just and favourable conditions, equal pay for equal work, an absence of discrimination, a fair wage, the right to form and join a TRADE UNION and to limited working hours and paid holidays. Accredited as a specialized agency of the UNITED NATIONS (UN) in 1946, the Independent Labour Organization (ILO) is charged with ensuring that governments and employers provide working conditions that are compatible with these standards.

This function involves the drafting, agreement and ratification of conventions among member states. Of the 185 conventions agreed since its inception as part of the 1919 Treaty of Versailles, eight are considered to be fundamental. These cover Forced or Compulsory Labour; Freedom of Association and Protection of the Right to Organize; the Right to Organize and Collective Bargaining; Equal Remuneration for Work of Equal Value; Abolition of Forced Labour; Discrimination in Employment and Occupation; Minimum Age for Employment; and Worst Forms of Child Labour. Government, employer and worker representatives at the International Labour Conference of 1998 also adopted the Declaration on Fundamental Principles and Rights at Work. The ILO describes the Declaration as a global consensus on minimum social and labour standards that commits all ILO members to respect the principles, irrespective of whether fundamental conventions have been ratified. These minima are identified as freedom of association and the effective recognition of the right to collective bargaining, together with the eradication of forced or compulsory labour, of child labour and of discrimination in respect of employment and occupation.

The creation of a consensus on such matters began with the social clause debate during negotiations to establish the WORLD TRADE ORGANIZATION (WTO) in 1994 and includes the identification of four fundamental categories of principles and rights at work by the 1995 UN World Summit for Social Development in Copenhagen. Trade ministers that attended the WTO Ministerial Conference in Singapore also accepted the standards recognized as part of these deliberations the following year. The same criteria are also included in the ILO Tripartite Declaration of Principles Concerning Multinational Enterprises (1977), accepted by the ORGANIZATION FOR ECONOMIC COOPERATION AND DEVELOPMENT and form part of the UN Global Compact.

The ILO Declaration on Fundamental Principles is designed to encourage member governments that have not ratified the equivalent convention to adopt and abide by prescribed standards. This involves a requirement for all governments to produce an annual report that outlines the rights afforded to working people in that country. If one or more conventions have not been ratified, the report must also include an explanation why ratification cannot be completed and can include requests for assistance in achieving compliance in the form of technical cooperation projects. Employer and worker organizations are also invited to comment on their national situations and all reports are published in the form of an *Annual Review*. In addition, a report of global and regional trends is published as a means of highlighting areas of the Declaration that are of most concern. The reporting process started in 2000 with a global report on freedom of association and collective bargaining and began an annual reporting cycle that thereafter focuses on one of the areas of principles and rights in turn.

The rights identified in the various conventions and declarations remain the very minimum acceptable; the extent of which can be illustrated by considering some of the provisions of the European Union Labour Law. This covers the working environment and health and safety, working conditions, information and consultation, EQUALITY between men and women, representation, and the right of association and to strike. Such provisions are aimed at achieving career and employment security, contributing to the development of skills and helping to achieve a work–life balance. In addition, the Works Council directive requires consultation to take place before workplace changes, and the Parental Leave directive stipulates that parents should be allowed up to three months' unpaid leave following the birth of a child. The Working Time directive, which limits the consensual working week to 48 hours, was also adopted under the health and safety clause of the Single European Act.

By way of contrast, workers in developing countries and those with authoritarian governments, experience the daily abuses of CHILD LABOUR,

275

SWEATSHOP conditions in EXPORT-PROCESSING ZONES and the suppression of economic and political dissent. While international bodies proclaim their commitment to increasing employment, reducing POVERTY and promoting social integration and SUSTAINABLE DEVELOPMENT, there appear to be inconsistencies in the prescribed approaches. Advocates of neoliberalism and free trade, for example, seek DEREGULATION of the labour market, and the ILO Declaration on Fundamental Principles includes the caveat that 'labour standards should not be used for protectionist trade purposes'. Furthermore, the International Confederation of Free Trade Unions, *Annual Survey of Violations of Trade Union Rights* (2004), reveals that intimidation of workers, long working hours, forced overtime, low wages, suppression of independent workforce organization and unsafe working conditions are all too prevalent in the industrialized world. This is yet further evidence that declarations and legislation count for little unless they are enforced.

FURTHER INFORMATION

Annual Survey of Violations of Trade Union Rights: www.icftu.org/survey
ILO: www.ilo.org/public/english/standards/index.htm
European labour Law: http://europa.eu.int/comm/employment_social/labour_law/
    index_en.htm
Trade Union Advisory Committee (TUAC) to the OECD: www.tuac.org/state-
    men/clabourrights.htm

WORLD BANK is the collective name used to refer to the International Bank for Reconstruction and Development (IBRD), the International Development Association (IDA), the International Finance Corporation (IFC), the Multilateral Investment Guarantee Agency (MIGA) and the International Centre for Settlement of Investment Disputes (ICSID). The IBRD, also commonly referred to as the 'World Bank', was set up as a UNITED NATIONS special agency in 1945 with the ratification of the BRETTON WOODS SYSTEM, and its functions are therefore different to those of a clearing bank that people use every day. Like its sister organization, the INTERNATIONAL MONETARY FUND (IMF), the IBRD is based in Washington DC, the US capital, and consists of and is governed by 184 member countries. Unlike the IMF, however, most of its finances come from the sale of US$ bonds on the world's financial markets – $23 billion in 2002. In the same year around $9 billion was donated to the IDA by forty member countries, as part of a four-year cycle and $6.6 billion was paid from the Bank's resources.

Under the guise of providing member countries with finance for development and **POVERTY** reduction, the World Bank has mainly focused on increasing living standards in developing countries through the provision of financial support for development projects, thereby transferring resources from the industrialized world to stimulate economic growth. The manner in which this is achieved has changed over time, however, though the central function has always been deciding which countries receive assistance and which do not. Since 1956, for example, the IFC has also helped promote private-sector investment for high-risk sectors and countries. Similarly, the IDA was set up in 1960 to provide interest-free credit and grant financing, the ICSID in 1966 to help settle investment disputes between foreign investors and host countries, and the MIGA in 1988 to provide political risk insurance (guarantees) to investors in and lenders to developing countries.

There has also been a change in the kind of projects that the Bank has supported since its first and, in real terms, its largest ever loan of $250 million was awarded to France in 1947 for post-war reconstruction. Many of the early development programmes it sponsored in developing countries involved large, prestigious and sophisticated industrial and infrastructure projects that, once completed, required skilled workers that the existing education system of the host countries was unlikely to provide. Similarly, because finished projects were not labour-intensive, there was little likelihood that many people would have the chance to acquire the necessary skills or that there would be much benefit to the local economy in terms of employment. The need for a change in approach was recognized and from the 1970s onward emphasis was placed on addressing basic needs through training programmes and, rather controversially, population control schemes. Moreover, because developing countries in general were net importers of agricultural products, attention was given to improving production through the provision of basic equipment, fertilizer and the development of new strains of rice and wheat. From the 1980s, the World Bank also began to make lending conditional on the acceptance of sectoral and **STRUCTURAL ADJUSTMENT PROGRAMMES** (SAPs) and, following criticism from Walden Bello, Shea Cunningham and Bill Rau, *Dark Victory* (1994), and others, sought to emphasize its role in poverty reduction and environmental protection.

The IBRD provided loans totalling $11.5 billion in support of 96 projects in 40 countries during 2002. Recipients include countries that are unable to borrow from commercial sources and those that can but would have to pay high rates of interest. Both have more time to repay than if they borrowed from a commercial bank, with the former being given 35–40 years to repay, including a 10-year period before repayment starts, while the latter are given 15–20 years to repay after a 3–5 year non-payment period. About one-quarter of the World Bank's financial assistance comes in the form of concessional assistance from the IDA – interest-free credit and grants amounting to $8.1 billion for 133 projects in 62 countries in 2002. Although assistance is described as contributing to poverty reduction – building schools and health centres, providing water and electricity, delivering social services, protecting the environment and producing economic growth that will improve living standards – the aims of projects are not always compatible. There might, for example, be a conflict of interest between dam and bridge construction to provide jobs, create energy and stimulate economic growth and environmental protection. Similarly, the effects of economic reform programmes and technical expertise often seem to be at odds with the provision of social services and poverty reduction.

Nevertheless, there are also tangible achievements, such as the projected debt relief saving of $40 billion for 26 nations under the Heavily Indebted Poor Countries (HIPC) Initiative. In 2002, approval was given for an increased use of up to 21 per cent of IDA grants for special difficulties, such as the HIV/AIDS problem, while the World Bank has commitments that exceed $1.3 billion, 50 per cent of which goes to sub-Saharan Africa. As a special agency of the United Nations it is subject to the Millennium Development Goals, agreed in 2000 – that set specific targets for sustainable poverty reduction – in terms of school enrolments, child mortality, maternal health, disease and access to water to be met by 2015. The development of mechanisms to assist corruption and fraud prevention in over 1,800 bank-financed projects has also been given a prominent role since the Department of Institutional Integrity was set up.

In contrast to the appearance described above, critics like Catherine Caufield, *Masters of Illusion* (1998), argue that the reality of the policies and practices of the World Bank has a somewhat different outcome. Campaign groups like 50 Years is Enough and World Bank Bonds Boycott call for an end to SAPs and related policies; as well as to environmentally destructive projects, especially drilling for oil and gas, mining and building dams; and, 100 per cent debt cancellation. SAPs and other macroeconomic 'reform' require economic austerity measures and PRIVATIZATION, for example, as conditions for the granting of loans, credits or debt relief. Critics therefore call for the suspension of conditions in existing programmes and the HIPC

Initiative to be abandoned because it conditions debt relief on socio-economic policy compliance.

Demands also include the payment of reparations to people relocated due to projects funded by the World Bank, to those harmed by SAPs, and for compensation to be paid to governments where loan repayments have been made on projects that have failed on economic, social, cultural and environmental grounds. Examples of such projects and policies include support for the proposed Bujagali dam hydroelectric project in Uganda, which is opposed by the International Rivers Network. Probe International also works to highlight the environmental impact of loans for oil exploration in the Amazon rainforest in Ecuador and for land-use planning in Brazil. Similarly, the Ghana National Coalition Against Water Privatization campaigns against the Bank's requirement for the privatization of water in order to gain access to external assistance and soft loans.

The Bank is also considered to exert undue leverage as a creditor, coupled with the ability to influence prospective foreign investors, to direct national economic policies in a neoliberal direction and thereby undermine national sovereignty under the euphemism 'economic liberalization'. Existing debt relief is therefore considered to be insufficient and to allow the World Bank and the wealthiest nations represented in the G8 to impose policies consistent with their interests and those of the international financial institutions and **CORPORATIONS** as opposed to the interests of local people. In this way, governments of indebted countries are not accountable to the will of their electorates, but to the agents and beneficiaries of free-market economic experimentation, which reduces the ability to pursue equitable, sustainable development alternatives aimed at reducing poverty and thereby advancing the interests of the poor and marginalized.

A lack of democratic practice is also a concern in the decision-making process of the World Bank, which is considered to give power to the wealthiest nations. Remedies reviewed by Richard Peet, *Unholy Trinity* (2003), range from outright abolition, through stopping government allocations, to a radical transformation into agencies that serve the interests of poor people and workers. Contributors to Jonathan Pincus and Jeffery Winters, *Reinventing the World Bank* (2002), meanwhile, call for enhanced **ACCOUNTABILITY** and **TRANSPARENCY**. This would include making all board meetings public and all project and programme agreements, board meeting minutes, evaluations of programme failures and successes available to the public in local languages. Likewise, measures adopted by the World Bank, in the form of the

Department of Institutional Integrity, to address corruption and fraud are deemed to be inadequate. They do not suspend or write off loans being repaid by the population as a whole but used to enrich public and private officials, politicians, dictators or military juntas. Neither is the recovery/return of stolen money sought, nor the provision of compensation for unrecoverable stolen resources considered.

FURTHER INFORMATION

World Bank: www.worldbank.org
World Bank Bonds Boycott: www.econjustice.net/wbbb
Social Justice Committee: www.worldbunk.org

WORLD INTELLECTUAL PROPERTY ORGANIZATION (WIPO)

was established in 1967 and since 1974 has been a specialized agency of the UNITED NATIONS with responsibility for administering and promoting international unions and treaties concerned with the protection – that is, REGULATION – of intellectual property rights. Through its International Bureau, for example, the WIPO maintains registration services for geographical indications of source, industrial designs, patents and trademarks among its 177 members. Prior to creation of the WIPO, the 1883 Paris Convention for the Protection of Industrial Property and the 1886 Berne Convention for the Protection of Literary and Artistic Works served to regulate INTELLECTUAL PROPERTY. The United International Bureaux for the Protection of Intellectual Property (Bureaux Internationaux Réunis pour la Protection de la Propriété Intellectuelle) administered the provisions of each convention.

Since 1 January 1996, the WIPO and WORLD TRADE ORGANIZATION have worked together to implement the WTO's TRADE-RELATED INTELLECTUAL PROPERTY RIGHTS (TRIPS) agreement – introduced in January 1995. This cooperation covers the notification of relevant national laws and regulations, technical cooperation, and ensuring that developing countries abide by the requirements of the agreement. Significantly, TRIPS was not negotiated under WIPO regulations, because each member has one vote, and developing countries therefore have a better chance of blocking unfavourable provisions.

FURTHER INFORMATION

Official site: www.wipo.int
Movement for patent-free software: www.ffii.org
Consumer perspective: www.cptech.org/ip

WORLD SOCIAL FORUM is an annual convention that has been held in Porto Alegre, Brazil, since 2001 to coincide with the WORLD ECONOMIC FORUM. See SOCIAL FORUM.

WORLD TRADE ORGANIZATION (WTO) came into existence on 1 January 1995 as the secretariat that administers the GENERAL AGREEMENT ON TARIFFS AND TRADE (GATT). Constituted by the Marrakesh Agreement, it represents the culmination of the Uruguay Round of negotiations that lasted from 1986 to 1994; a process examined by Graham Dunkley, *The Free Trade Adventure* (2000). The WTO supervises TRADE between countries according to the provisions of the GATT, but also promotes the principles of free trade when hosting negotiations, assessing national policies and providing assistance and training. By October 2004, the WTO had 148 members and up to 30 countries attempting to join, although the USA has effectively vetoed Iran's application, which was first submitted in 1996.

Based in Geneva, Switzerland, the Secretariat has a Director-General and a General Council consists of ambassadors, heads of delegations and officials. Council responsibilities include trade policy reviews and dispute settlement, while the body is also convened to consider other matters during the year. Subcommittees of the General Council include those dealing with matters related to trade in Goods, Services and Intellectual Property, while ad hoc committees, working groups and working parties are charged with administering agreements and issues concerning development, the environment and membership applications. The main decision-making body of the WTO is the Ministerial Conference, which is convened every two years, or more frequently if necessary.

As such the secretariat does not take decisions, but plays a role in supporting the councils, committees and ministerial conferences of the WTO, advising applicants, offering legal advice for dispute settlement, providing technical assistance, analysing world trade and undertaking public relations activities. WTO decisions concerning the adoption or amendment of agreements are the responsibility of the General Council and can be taken by consensus or majority voting. While the WTO brochures *Ten Common Misunderstandings about the WTO* and *The WTO in Brief* extol the virtues of consensus decision-making, little attention is paid to the disproportionate ability of industrialized countries to devote resources to analysis and negotiation, to veto proposals and suppress opposition to policy. WTO publicity also ignores the inherent difficulties of revising agreements by consensual agreement.

281

The GATT was originally concerned with reducing tariffs on manu-factured commodities, but the Uruguay Round of negotiations also intro-duced a number of new multilateral agreements such as the TRADE-RELATED INTELLECTUAL PROPERTY RIGHTS (TRIPS) and TRADE-RELATED INVESTMENT MEASURES (TRIMs). In all, there are sixty such agreements and schedules, including the 1997 agreements between 69 countries to deregulate telecom-munications services, 40 countries on information technology products and on financial services involving 70 members. These agreements are contractu-ally binding and are enforced by the Dispute Settlement Body, which has the power to impose sanctions against transgressors. The WTO estimates that there were 300 such disputes between 1995 and 2003, compared to the same number of complaints under the GATT between 1947 and 1994.

Negotiations on a GENERAL AGREEMENT ON TRADE IN SERVICES (GATS) covering agriculture and services such as banking, insurance, telecommuni-cations, tourism and transport began in 2000 and became known as the Doha Development Agenda following the fourth WTO Ministerial Conference held in Qatar, November 2001. See Bhagirath Lal Das, *WTO: The Doha Agenda* (2003), for a discussion of related issues. Although a deadline of 1 January 2005 was imposed on these negotiations, the fifth Ministerial Conference held in Cancún, Mexico, in September 2003 failed to reach agreement due to the concerns of twenty-two developing countries over a range of issues relat-ing to competition, investment, government procurement and agricultural subsidies. The meeting was also faced with massive demonstrations similar to those that greeted the third ministerial conference in Seattle, USA, in Novem-ber 1999. Nevertheless, individual WTO members are entering into bilateral agreements on such matters and similar provisions are being incorporated into draft regional trade agreements like the FREE TRADE AGREEMENT OF THE AMERICAS. Interestingly enough, the WTO estimates that service industries account for 70 per cent of economic activity in developed countries.

Although WTO publicity claims that developing countries are allowed flexibility in implementing agreements and commitments, the fact that twenty-two countries formed a coalition to protect their interests against the USA and the European Union suggests a conflict of interests. Once an agree-ment is in force, developing countries have recourse to the dispute settlement process, but more powerful trading partners can allocate greater resources to contest cases. Training and technical assistance are offered to developing and least-developed countries in the form of reference centres, regional seminars, technical cooperation missions, trade policy courses under the auspices of the committee on trade and development and a subcommittee that focuses on least-developed countries. Such activity is neither altruistic nor tolerant of heterodox policy, however, as it is designed to integrate countries into the global trading system based on WTO agreements and neoliberal doctrine; a role also performed by the Trade Policy Review Mechanism that scrutinizes and reports on each country's performance. Fatoumata Jawara, Aileen Kwa and Shefali Sharma, *Behind the Scenes at the WTO* (2003), provide an insight into these and other processes.

CORPORATIONS are also represented in WTO seminars and symposia by corporate lobby groups and seek to influence governmental input into the WTO through similar channels; as do campaigners and NON-GOVERNMENTAL ORGANIZATIONS like the International Centre for Trade and Sustainable Development. According to Aziz Choudry, *How Low Can You Go?* (2002), however, the International Chamber of Commerce CORPORATE LOBBY GROUP has permanent representation at the WTO and uses intergovernmental organizations to influence processes. Such involvement, together with the level of resources allocated to promoting free trade in the name of economic growth, job creation and POVERTY reduction, leads to charges that the WTO pursues a primarily corporate-friendly agenda.

Groups like People & Planet, Peoples Global Action and War on Want, among others, see a conflict of interest between DEREGULATION and the optimal use of the world's resources, SUSTAINABLE DEVELOPMENT and environmental protection. Such goals are stipulated in the preamble to the Marrakesh Agreement and Article 20 of the GATT, which includes a general commitment to protect human, animal or plant life or health, conserve natural resources and protect the environment, but are subject to constraints designed to prevent protectionism. In fact, the WTO literature appears to make multiple use of the same examples: rulings on shrimp imports, the protection of sea turtles and the banning of asbestos products. For a study of the interaction between development, environment and trade, see P.K. Rao, *The World Trade Organization and the Environment* (2000).

Perhaps a more accurate picture of the WTO's outlook is provided by the assertion that it does not set international rules for environmental protection. Agencies and conventions, such as the Codex Alimentarius of the United Nations Food and Agriculture Organization and World Health Organization, are attributed that function, even though compliance cannot be compelled. These and other factors have resulted in calls by campaign groups like 50 Years is Enough, the Association for the Taxation of Financial Transactions for the Aid of Citizens and the World Development Movement for the abolition or reform of the INTERNATIONAL MONETARY FUND, the WORLD BANK and the WTO. The combination of INTERNATIONAL DEBT, trade and financial policies are considered to represent an agenda of NEOLIBERALISM that benefits international financiers and transnational corporations; as argued by Richard Peet, *Unholy Trinity* (2003).

FURTHER INFORMATION

Official site: www.wto.org
Caricature of the official site: www.gatt.org
Trade Observatory: www.wtowatch.org

XYZ

XENOPHOBIA is literally a fear of strangers or things foreign and un-known, but is more commonly used to imply contempt or hatred. As a social phenomenon, it is employed as a negative means of establishing identity for a group or community through the intolerance of immigrants and minorities. See RACISM.

XENOTRANSPLANTATION is the branch of GENETIC ENGINEERING that involves the transplantation of tissues or organs from one species of plant or animal into an individual of another species.

YA BASTA is a Spanish term meaning 'enough is enough', adopted as a slogan by the ZAPATISTA uprising in Chiapas, Mexico, to mark the intro-duction of the NORTH AMERICAN FREE TRADE AGREEMENT on 1 January 1994. The term has also been adopted by a number of groups and networks inspired by or established in support of the 1994 uprisings.

FURTHER INFORMATION
Ya Basta: free.freespeech.org/yabasta/faq.html
Italian language site: www.ecn.org/yabasta

ZAPATISTAS refers to the Zapatista Army of National Liberation (Ejér-cito Zapatista De Liberación Nacional, EZLN), which takes its name from the early-twentieth-century revolutionary and leader of rural peasantry in Mexico, Emiliano Zapata (1879–1919). On 1 January 1994 the organiza-tion seized five towns in Chiapas, Mexico, in protest at the treatment of INDIGENOUS PEOPLE and the implications for them of the expected po-larization of wealth in Mexico due to the NORTH AMERICAN FREE TRADE AGREEMENT (NAFTA), which also came into effect on that day. The origins of EZLN, which is based mainly in southern Chiapas, and its insurrection can be traced back to the 1980s, in the popular campaigns, movements and organizations that defended agrarian reforms and WORKERS' RIGHTS and resisted discrimination against indigenous communities. Although primarily a national movement campaigning to change the Mexican constitution, the EZLN also has a global outlook that identifies the neoliberal policies of the WORLD BANK, INTERNATIONAL MONETARY FUND and multilateral trade treaties as the source of social and economic travails that affect many developing countries. In this sense, the international struggle is motivated by a desire to preserve the distinct human identities of all peoples.

The EZLN differs from other guerrilla movements in ways that have captured the imagination of the disaffected, and has therefore helped influence the development of present-day anti-capitalism. From its inception, the uprising in Chiapas has attracted unprecedented media attention – both mainstream and alternative – that reflects and engenders new international strategies of resistance and the emergence of human rights organizations. In 1996, for example, the EZLN called a series of meetings that resulted in over 3,000 activists and intellectuals from 42 countries on 5 continents meeting in Chiapas at the end of July, to enhance the global struggle against neoliberalism. The Intercontinental Meeting for Humanity and Against Neoliberalism inspired the development of the Intercontinental Network of Alternative Communication (Red Intercontinental de Comunicación Alternativa, RICA) to accelerate the intercontinental struggle, share experiences and develop strategies for the fight against neoliberal capitalism, while developing and sharing ideas about alternative social organization. Through such initiatives and the use of various forms of communication – Internet, radio, television, music and film – the EZLN is able to reach out to, involve and influence other sectors and develop networks of support and solidarity that help guard against the potential isolation of the EZLN's struggle. Juana Ponce de Leon also edited a selection of written communications: *Our Word is our Weapon* (2001). The enduring international interest and presence in Chiapas include MEDIA, human rights organizations, the International Red Cross, as well as donors of foodstuffs and clothing.

The democratic and political practices of the EZLN also help distinguish them from other guerrilla insurgencies and connect with current anti-capitalist sentiment. This is particularly so in the way they combine the experiences and communal culture of indigenous peoples with western socialist ideas. They therefore employ a collective and horizontal decision-making process that gathers the views of the people living in Chiapas and those who support their cause. Setting out to be a form of civil resistance with a new political focus, rather than a traditional political party, the

286

EZLN emulates and co-opts the traditional authority structure of the indigenous people – akin to what others have called primitive communism. There is, for example, a supreme Zapatista authority – the Clandestine Indigenous Revolutionary Committee (CIRC) – which is organized along communal lines and whose decision-making process starts with public discussion where everyone's opinion is respected and accorded equal weight. Issues are negotiated until a consensus is reached, so that the will of the majority is not imposed on a minority, or vice versa – a principle and practice that bears comparison to the SOCIAL FORUM. The General Command represents the armed wing of the EZLN, is headed by Subcomandante Insurgente Marcos, and has to obey the community as represented by the CIRC. The title 'subcommandante' is an indication that the office holder and the movement are subservient to the will and the consent of the community.

The EZLN has been adept at advocating and practising indigenous values, which include collective ownership of land, collective labour, loyalty to tradition and to the community as a whole – including the poor. Likewise civil authorities are rotated annually, while political, religious and domestic values of sharing goods, feeding the community and guests of the community also form important connections. By integrating the military, political and community organizations with the culture of the people, the movement has become indivisible from the populace. A series of family networks provide information, food, safe passage, clothing, arms and medicines for those they consider to be their fighters, and form a bulwark against external pressures to become subservient to the neoliberal prescriptions of NAFTA and the WORLD TRADE ORGANIZATION.

FURTHER INFORMATION

Chiapas Watch: www.zmag.org/chiapas1/index.htm
Discussion Group: www.zapatistas.org
Indymedia site: chiapas.mediosindependientes.org
Irish Mexico Group: flag.blackened.net/revolt/mexico.html
Resource page, largely in Spanish: www.ezln.org

Timeline

PERSON	BORN	INDICATIVE WORK	MOVEMENT
Gerrard Winstanley (c. 1609–1660)	English	*The True Levellers' Standard Advanced* (1649)	True Levellers/ Diggers
François-Noel 'Gracchus' Babeuf (1760–1797)	French	*Manifesto of the Equals* (1796)	Conspiracy of Equals
Charles-Henri Saint-Simon (1760–1825)	French	*Social Organisation* (1825)	Utopian socialism
William Godwin (1756–1836)	English	*Enquiry Concerning Political Justice* (1793)	Anarchism
Charles Fourier (1772–1837)	French	*Theory of the Four Movements* (1808)	Utopian socialism
Étienne Cabet (1788–1856)	French	*Travels in Icaria* (1839)	Utopian socialism
Robert Owen (1771–1858)	Welsh	*A New View of Society* (1813)	Utopian socialism
Pierre-Joseph Proudhon (1809–1865)	French	*What is Property?* (1840)	Mutualism/ anarchism
Frederick Denison Maurice (1805–1872)	English	*The Kingdom of Christ* (1838)	Christian socialism
Mikhail Bakunin (1814–1876)	Russian	*Statism and Anarchy* (1872)	Anarchism/ collectivism
Louis Blanc (1811–1882)	French	*The Organisation of Labour* (1839)	Socialism
Karl Marx (1818–1883)	German	*Capital: A Critique of Political Economy* (1865, 1885, 1894)	Communism
Albert Parsons (1848–1887)	American	*Anarchism* (1889)	Anarchism
Friedrich Engels (1820–1895)	German	*Socialism: Utopian and Scientific* (1892)	Communism
William Morris (1834–1896)	English	*News from Nowhere* (1890)	Socialism
Henry George (1839–1897)	American	*Progress and Poverty* (1879)	Socialism
Laurence Gronlund (1846–1899)	Danish/ American	*Co-operative Commonwealth* (1886)	Socialism
Lafargue, Paul (1841–1911)	Cuban	*The Right To Be Lazy* (1907)	Socialism
Daniel De Leon (1852–1914)	Curaçaon/ American	*Revolutionary Socialism in US Congress* (1931)	Industrial unionism
Georgii Plekhanov (1856–1918)	Russian	*In Defence of Materialism* (1895)	Marxism
Rosa Luxemburg (1871–1919)	Polish	*Social Reform or Revolution* (1899)	Communism
Piotr Kropotkin (1842–1921)	Russian	*Mutual Aid* (1897)	Anarcho-communism

PERSON	BORN	INDICATIVE WORK	MOVEMENT
Georges Sorel (1847–1922)	French	*Reflections on Violence* (1906)	Anarcho-syndicalism
Ricardo Flores Magon (1873–1922)	Mexican	*Land and Liberty* (1913)	Anarchist communism
Vladimir (Ulyanov) Lenin (1870–1924)	Russian	*What Is To Be Done?* (1902)	Bolshevism/communism
Eugene Victor Debs (1855–1926)	American	*Industrial Unionism* (1905)	Industrial unionism
Mary 'Mother' Jones (1830–1930)	Irish/American	*Mother Jones Speaks* (1983)	Industrial unionism
Jose Carlos Mariátegui (1894–1930)	Peruvian	*Seven Interpretative Essays on Peruvian Reality* (1928)	Socialism
Eduard Bernstein (1850–1932)	German	*Evolutionary Socialism* (1899)	Socialism
Florence Kelley (1859–1932)	American	*Modern Industry in Relation to the Family, Health, Education, Morality* (1914)	Feminism
Alexander Berkman (1870–1936)	Russian/American	*ABC of Anarchism* (1929)	Anarchism
Antonio Gramsci (1891–1937)	Italian	*Prison Notebooks* (1929–35)	Communism
Nikolai Bukharin (1888–1938)	Russian	*Historical Materialism* (1921)	Bolshevism/communism
Karl Kautsky (1854–1938)	German	*The Road to Power* (1909)	Marxism
Leon (Lev Bronstein) Trotsky (1879–1940)	Russian	*The Death Agony of Capitalism* (1938)	Bolshevism/communism
Emma Goldman (1869–1940)	Lithuanian/American	*Anarchism and Other Essays* (1910)	Anarchism
Tom Mann (1856–1941)	English	*The Industrial Syndicalist* (1910)	Syndicalism
Chen Duxiu (1879–1942)	Chinese	*Chen Duxiu's Last Articles and Letters* (1998)	Communism
James Shaver Woodsworth (1874–1942)	Canadian	*My Neighbor* (1911)	Socialism
Joseph (Dzhugashvili) Stalin (1879–1953)	Russian	*The Foundations of Leninism* (1924)	Bolshevism/communism
Manabendra Nath Roy (1887–1954)	Indian	*India in Transition* (1922)	Communism
Albert Einstein (1879–1955)	German/American	*Why Socialism* (1949)	Socialism
Diego Rivera (1886–1957)	Mexican	*Manifesto for a Free Revolutionary Art* (1938)	Trotskyism
G.D.H. Cole (1889–1959)	English	*Self-Government in Industry* (1917)	Guild socialism
William Zebulon Foster (1881–1961)	American	*The Twilight of World Capitalism* (1949)	Industrial unionism
Rachel Carson (1907–1964)	American	*Silent Spring* (1962)	Green
Elizabeth Gurley Flynn (1890–1964)	American	*Sabotage* (1916)	Communism

PERSON	BORN	INDICATIVE WORK	MOVEMENT
Georg Lukács (1885–1971)	Hungarian	*History and Class Consciousness* (1923)	Communism
Dipa Nusantara Aidit (1923–1965)	Indonesian	*The Indonesian Revolution* (1964)	Communism
Mary Heaton Vorse (1907–1966)	American	*Labor's New Millions* (1938)	Communism
Fabricio Ojeda (1929–1966)	Venezuelan	*The True Revolution* (1967)	Communism
Camilo Torres (1929–1966)	Colombian	*Liberation or Death* (1967)	Liberation theology
Michael Gold (1894–1967)	American	*Change the World!* (1937)	Socialism
Upton Beall Sinclair (1878–1968)	American	*The Industrial Republic* (1907)	Socialism
Norman Mattoon Thomas (1884–1968)	American	*As I See It* (1932)	Communism
Ho Chi Minh (1890–1969)	Vietnamese	*On Revolution* (1984)	Communism
Liu Shaoqi (1898–1969)	Chinese	*Three Essays on Party-Building* (1980)	Communism
Max Shachtman (1904–1972)	American	*Race and Revolution* (2003)	Trotskyism
Salvador Allende (Gossens) (1908–1973)	Chilean	*Political Thought* (1972)	Socialism
Amílcar Lopes Cabral (1924–1973)	Guinea Cape Verdean	*Revolution in Guinea* (1969)	African Socialism
James Patrick Cannon (1890–1974)	American	*America's Road to Socialism* (1975)	Trotskyism
Paul Robeson (1898–1976)	African American	*Paul Robeson Speaks* (1978)	Communism
Carlos Fonseca Amador (1936–1976)	Nicaraguan	*Viva Sandino* (1982)	Sandinista
Steve Biko (1946–1977)	South African	*I Write What I Like* (1979)	Black Power/ student
Evelyn Reed (1905–1979)	American	*Problems of Women's Liberation* (1971)	Women's liberation
Peng Shu-Tse (1895–1983)	Chinese	*Behind China's 'Great Cultural Revolution'* (1967)	Trotskyism
Farrell Dobbs (1907–1983)	American	*Teamster Politics* (1975)	Trotskyism
Samora Moisés Machel (1933–1986)	Mozambican	*Establishing People's Power* (1977)	Socialism
Michel Aflaq (1910–1989)	Syrian	*Choice of Texts* (1977)	Pan Arab socialism
Cyril Lionel Robert James (1901–1989)	Trinidadean	*Marxism for Our Times* (1999)	Communism
Mao Zedong (1893–1976)	Chinese	*A Critique of Soviet Economics* (1977)	Communism
Paulo Freire (1921–1977)	Brazilian	*The Pedagogy of the Oppressed* (1970)	Liberation theology
Louis Althusser (1918–1990)	French	*For Marx* (1969)	Communism

PERSON	BORN	INDICATIVE WORK	MOVEMENT
Edward Thompson (1924–1993)	English	*The Making of the English Working Class* (1963)	New Left
Guy Debord (1931–1994)	French	*Society of the Spectacle* (1967)	Situationist
Stokely Carmichael/ Kwame Ture (1941–1998)	American	*Black Power* (1967)	Black liberation
Tony Cliff (1917–2000)	Palestinian	*State Capitalism in Russia* (1974)	Trotskyism
Liborio Justo (1902–2003)	Argentinian	*Bolivia: The Defeated Revolution* (1967)	Trotskyism
Betty Friedan (1921–2006)	American	*The Feminine Mystique* (1963)	Feminism
Jean Bertrand Aristide	Haitian	*Eyes of the Heart* (2000)	Liberation theology
Baburam Bhattarai	Nepalese	*The Nature of Underdevelopment and Regional Structure of Nepal* (2003)	Maoism
Bob Black	American	*The Abolition of Work and Other Essays* (1985)	Anarchism
Hugo Blanco	Peruvian	*Land or Death* (1972)	Trotskyism
Hugo Rafael Chávez Frías	Venezuelan	*The Fascist Blow against Venezuela* (2003)	Socialism
Noam Chomsky	American	*Profit Over People* (1999)	Libertarian socialism
Teresa Ebert	American	*(Untimely) Critiques for a Red Feminism* (1995)	Women's liberation
Duane Elgin	American	*Voluntary Simplicity* (1998)	Green
Shulamith Firestone	American	*Dialectic of Sex* (1970)	Women's liberation
Vo Nguyen Giap	Vietnamese	*People's War People's Army* (1961)	Communism
Gustavo Gutierrez	Peruvian	*A Theology of Liberation* (1971)	Liberation theology
Abimael Reynoso Guzmán Gonzalo	Peruvian	*Popular War in Peru* (1989)	Maoism
Naomi Klein	Canadian	*No Logo* (2000)	Anti-capitalism
James Lovelock	English	*Gaia* (1979)	Green
Subcomandante Marcos	Mexican	*Our Word is Our Weapon* (2001)	Zapatista
David Miller	English	*Market, State and Community* (1990)	Market socialism
Kate Millett	American	*Sexual Politics* (1969)	Women's liberation
Arne Naess	Norwegian	*Ecology, Community and Lifestyle* (1989)	Deep ecology
Antonio Negri	Italian	*Marx Beyond Marx* (1991)	Communism
Humberto Ortega Saavedra	Nicaraguan	*50 Years of Sandinista Struggle* (1978)	Sandinista
René Viénet	French	*Enragés and Situationists* (1992)	Situationism
Robert Wolff	American	*In Defense of Anarchism* (1970)	Anarchism

Postscript

Whether you are already acquainted with the ideas discussed in this book or new to the subject I hope that it has proved enjoyable and useful. It isn't enough to write and read anti-capitalist literature, however; it needs to be shared with others – especially future generations.

If you found any of the texts included here to be of interest or particularly stimulating, please ask your local libraries – in your school, college or university, and those open to the public – to stock them. Similarly, ask bookshops to include them for sale. That way, we can preserve these works for new generations and hopefully continue the spread of alternative ideas.

In recognition of the contradiction of making money from a book about anti-capitalism, 10 per cent of the proceeds made by the author from its sale will be donated to relevant groups and organizations. You can find details of this at www.atozofanti-capitalism.info. The site also offers an opportunity for you to provide constructive feedback on the book and its contents and to make suggestions for additional entries or amendments to existing ones.

Bibliography

Adams, D.W. (1995) *Education for Extinction: American Indians and the Boarding School Experience, 1875–1928*, Lawrence: University Press of Kansas.

Adorno, T.W. (1981) *Prisms*, Cambridge: MIT Press.

——— (1991) *The Culture Industry: Selected Essays on Mass Culture*, London: Routledge.

Adorno, T.W., and M. Horkheimer (1979) *Dialectic of Enlightenment*, London: Verso.

Aflaq, M. (1977) *Choice of Texts from the Ba'ath Party Founder's Thought*, Baghdad: Arab Ba'ath Socialist Party.

Agamben, G. (1993) *The Coming Community*, Minneapolis: University of Minnesota Press.

Agathangelou, A.M. (2004) *The Global Political Economy of Sex: Desire, Violence, and Insecurity in Mediterranean Nation States*, London: Palgrave Macmillan.

Aeschylus (1976) 'Seven Against Thebes', *The Complete Plays of Aeschylus*, trans. G. Murray, London: Allen & Unwin.

Aglietta, M. (1979) *A Theory of Capitalist Regulation: The US Experience*, London: New Left Books.

Agnoli, J. (2000) 'Die Transformation der Linken', *Die Zeit*, 17 February 2002, www.glasnost. de/autoren/athan/agnoli2000.html.

Aidit, D.N. (1964) *The Indonesian Revolution and the Immediate Tasks of the Communist Party of Indonesia*, Peking: Foreign Language Press

Akyuz, Y. (2003) *Developing Countries and World Trade: Performance and Prospects*, London: Zed Books.

Allende, S. (1972) *Salvador Allende: su pensamiento*, Santiago de Chile: Empresa Editora Nacional Quimantu.

Altbach, P.G. (ed.) (1989) *Student Political Activism: An International Reference Handbook*, London: Greenwood Press.

Althusser, L. (1969) *For Marx*, London: Allen Lane.

——— (1971) *Lenin and Philosophy, and Other Essays*, London: New Left Books.

——— and É. Balibar (1979) *Reading 'Capital'*, London: Verso.

Altman, D. (1987) *AIDS and the New Puritanism*, London: Pluto.

Amador, C.F. (1982) *Viva Sandino*, Managua: Nueva Nicaragua.

Amnesty International (2004) *Undermining Global Security: The European Unions Arms Exports*, London: Amnesty International.

Anderson, B. (2000) *Doing the Dirty Work?: The Global Politics of Domestic Labour*, London: Zed Books.

Anker, C. Van Den (2004) *The Political Economy of New Slavery*, London: Macmillan.

Aristide, J.B. (2000) *Eyes of the Heart: Seeking a Path for the Poor in the Age of Globalization*, Monroe ME: Common Courage Press.

Aristotle (1984) 'Politics', in *The Complete Works of Aristotle: The Revised Oxford Translation*, Princeton NJ: Princeton University Press.

Bacon, D. (2004) *The Children of NAFTA: Labor Wars on the U.S./Mexico Border*, Berkley: University of California Press.

Bacon, F. (1989 [1627]) *The New Atlantis and The Great Instauration*, Arlington Heights IL: Harlan Davidson.

Bakan, J. (2004) *The Corporation: The Pathological Pursuit of Profit and Power*, New York: Free Press.

Bakunin, M.A. (1871) *The Paris Commune and the Idea of the State*, Marseilles: Centre International de Recherches sur l'Anarchisme.

——— (1990 [1872]) *Statism and Anarchy*, Cambridge: Cambridge University Press.

Balakrishnan, G. (2003) *Debating Empire*, London: Verso.

Balibar, É. (1991) 'Is there a Neo-racism?', in É. Balibar and I. Wallerstein, *Race, Nation, Class: Ambiguous Identities*, London: Verso.

Baran, P. (1957) *The Political Economy of Growth*, London: Calder.

Barbrook, R. (1995) *Media Freedom: The Contradictions of Communication in the Age of Modernity*, London: Pluto.

Barker, J. (2003) *The No-nonsense Guide to Terrorism*, London: Verso.

Barratt Brown, M. (1974) *The Economics of Imperialism*, Harmondsworth: Penguin.

Baudrillard, J. (1983) *Simulations*, New York: Semiotext(e).

Baumert, K. (ed.) (2002) *Building on the Kyoto Protocol: Options for Protecting the Climate*, Washington DC: World Resources Institute.

Beck, U. (2000) *What is Globalisation?*, Cambridge: Polity Press.

Bellers, J. (1916 [1695]) *Proposals for Raising a College of Industry etc.*, London: Headley Bros.

Bello, W., S. Cunningham and B. Rau (1994) *Dark Victory: The United States, Structural Adjustment and Global Poverty*, London: Pluto.

Bello, W., N. Bullard and K. Malhotra (eds) (2000) *Global Finance: New Thinking on Regulating Speculative Capital Markets*, London: Zed Books.

Berkman, A. (1984 [1929]) *A.B.C. of Anarchism*, London: Freedom Press.

Berlin, I. (1969) *Four Essays on Liberty*, London: Oxford University Press.

Bernays, E.L. (1928) *Propaganda*, New York: Horace Liveright

Bernstein, E. (1967 [1899]) *Evolutionary Socialism: A Criticism and Affirmation*, New York: Schocken Books.

Bhattarai, B. (2003) *The Nature of Underdevelopment and Regional Structure of Nepal: A Marxist Analysis*, Delhi: Adroit Publishers.

Biko, S. (1979) *I Write What I Like: A Selection of His Writings*, London: Heinemann.

Black, B. (1996) *The Abolition of Work and Other Essays*, http://inspiracy.com/black/abolition/part1.html.

Blanc, L. (1848 [1839]) *The Organisation of Labour*, London: H.G. Clarke.

Blanco. H. (1972) *Land or Death: The Peasant Struggle in Peru*, New York: Pathfinder Press.

Blaser, M., H.A. Feit and G. Mcrae (2004) *In the Way of Development: Indigenous Peoples, Life Projects and Globalization*, London: Zed Books.

Blauner, R. (1972) *Racial Oppression in America*, New York: Harper & Row.

Bonefield, W., R. Gunn and K. Psychopedis (eds) (1991, 1992, 1995) *Open Marxism*, London: Pluto.

Boron, A.A. (2005) *Empire and Imperialism: A Critical Reading of Michael Hardt and Antonio Negri*, London: Zed Books.

Bottomore, T. (ed.) (1991) *A Dictionary of Marxist Thought*, Oxford: Blackwell.

Bourdieu, P.F., and J.C. Passeron (1977) *Reproduction in Education, Society and Culture*, London: Sage Publications.

Braverman, H. (1974) *Labour and Monopoly Capital: The Degradation of Work in the Twentieth Century*, New York: Monthly Review Press.

Brittan, S. (1977) *The Economic Consequences of Democracy*, London: Temple Smith.

Brunner, K. (1968) *The Role of Money and Monetary Policy*, http://research.stlouisfed.org/publications/review/68/07/Money_July1968.pdf.

Bukharin, N. (1978 [1921]) *Historical Materialism: A System of Sociology*, New York: University of Michigan Press.

Burdon, R.H. (2003) *The Suffering Gene: Environmental Threats to Our Health*, London: McGill-Queen's University Press.

Burke, E. (1774) *Speech to the Electors of Bristol*, www.econlib.org/library/LFBooks/Burke/brkSWv4c1.html.

Burns, D. (1992) *Poll Tax Rebellion*, London: A.K. Press.

Burton, B., and S. Rampton (1998) 'The PR Plot to Overheat the Earth', www.earthisland.org/eijournal/spring98/sp98a_fe.htm.

Cabet, E. (2003 [1839]) *Travels in Icaria*, Syracuse: Syracuse University Press.

Cabral, A.L. (1969) *Revolution in Guinea: An African People's Struggle*. London: Stage 1.

Caffentzis, G. (2000) 'Notes on the Antiglobalization Movement 1985-2000: Where do we come from? Who are we now? Where do we go to?', www.endpage.com/Archives/Subversive_Texts/Midnight_Notes_Collective/Caffentzis_Antiglobalisation_Movement.xhtml.

Callenbach, E. (1978) *Ecotopia: A Novel about Ecology, People and Politics in 1999*, London: Pluto Press.

Cannon, J.P. (1975) *America's Road to Socialism*, New York: Pathfinder Press.

Campanella, T. (1981 [1602]) *The City of the Sun*, London: Journeyman.

Carson, R. (1962) *Silent Spring*, Boston MA: Riverside Press.

Castells, M. (1977) *The Urban Question: A Marxist Approach*, London: Edward Arnold.

—— (1978) *City, Class and Power*, London: Macmillan.

Caufield, C. (1998) *Masters of Illusion: The World Bank and the Poverty of Nations*, London: Pan.

Chamberlain, H.S. (1968) *The Foundations of the Nineteenth Century*, New York: H. Fertig.

Chattopadhyaya, D. (1980) *Indian Atheism: A Marxist Analysis*, New Delhi: People's Publishing House.

Chávez Frías, H.R. (2003) *El Golpe Fascista Contra Venezuela: 'Aquí está en juego la vida de la patria': Discursos e Intervenciones, Diciembre de 2002–Enero de 2003*, Havana: Ediciones Plaza.

Chomsky, N. (1993) *Mandate for Change or Business as Usual*, www.chomsky.info/articles/199302-.htm.

—— (1999) *Profit Over People: Neo-liberalism and Global Order*, New York: Seven Stories Press.

—— (2001) *9–11*, New York: Seven Stories Press.

Chossudovsky, M. (1997) *The Globalisation of Poverty: Impacts of IMF and World Bank Reforms*, London: Zed Books.

Choudry, A. (2002) *How Low Can You Go: The Corruption of Corporate Imperialism*, www.zmag.org/content/showarticle.cfm?SectionID=10&ItemID=2196.

Cliff, T. (1974) *State Capitalism in Russia*, London: Pluto.

Coase, R.H. (1991) 'The Nature of the Firm', in O.E. Williamson and S.G. Winter, *The Nature of the Firm: Origins, Evolution, and Development*, New York: Oxford University Press.

Coates, K. (2004) *A Global History of Indigenous Peoples: Struggle and Survival*, London: Palgrave Macmillan.

Cobb, C., and J. Cobb (1994) *The Green National Product: A Proposed Index of Sustainable Economic Welfare*, London: University Press of America.

Cobb, C., T. Halstead and J. Rowe (1995) *The Genuine Progress Indicator: A Summary of Data and Methodology*, San Francisco: Redefining Progress.

Cohen, D., R. de la Vega and G. Watson (2001) *Advocacy for Social Justice: A Global Action and Reflection Guide*, Oxford: Oxfam.

Cohen, L. (2003) *A Consumer's Republic: The Politics of Consumption in Postwar America*, New York: Knopf.

Cole, G.D.H. (1973 [1913]) *The World of Labour: Discussion of the Present and Future of Trade Unionism*, Brighton: Harvester Press.

—— (1917) *Self-Government in Industry*, London: Bell.

Cooley, J.K. (2002) *Unholy Wars: Afghanistan, America and International Terrorism*, London: Pluto.

Correa, C.M. (1993) *Intellectual Property Rights and Foreign Direct Investment*, New York:United Nations.

Coyote, P. (1998) *Sleeping Where I Fall: A Chronicle*, Washington DC: Counterpoint.

Crick, B. (2000) *In Defence of Politics*, London: Continuum.

Daalen Van, C. (2001) *Taking the High Road to Forest Restoration: A Quality Jobs Approach*, www.biodiversitynorthwest.org/Restoration/qualityjobs.htm.

D'Adesky, C. (2004) *Moving Mountains: Dispatches from the Frontlines of Global AIDS*, London: Verso.

Dakar Conference (2000) *The Dakar Declaration for the Total and Unconditional Cancellation of African and Third World Debt*, www.nycsocialforum.org/articles/dakar.html.

Daly, H.E., and J.B. Cobb (1989) *For the Common Good: Redirecting the Economy toward Community, the Environment, and a Sustainable Future*, Boston MA: Beacon Press.

Darwin, C. (2003) *On the Origin of Species*, London: Routledge.

Das, B.L. (2003) *WTO: The Doha Agenda: The New Negotiations on World Trade*, London: Zed Books.

Dean, J., and P. Passavant (eds) (2003) *The Empire's New Clothes: Reading Hardt and Negri*, New York: Routledge.

Debord, G. (1994 [1967]) *Society of the Spectacle*, New York: Zone Books.

Debs, E.V. (1905) *Industrial Unionism: An Address Delivered at Grant Central Palace, New York, Sunday, December 10 1905*, New York: Labor News.

De Leon, D. (1931) *Revolutionary Socialism in US Congress: Parliamentary Idiocy vs. Marxian Socialism*, New York: New York Labor News.

Department of Justice Canada (1985) *An Act Respecting Indians*, http://laws.justice.gc.ca/en/I-5.

Derrida, J. (1983) *Letter to a Japanese Friend*, http://lucy.ukc.ac.uk/Simulate/Derrida_deconstruction.html.

De Tocqueville, A. (2003) *Democracy in America and Two Essays on America*, London: Penguin.

Dobbs, F. (1975) *Teamster Politics*, New York: Monad Press.

Dommen, C. (2002) *Trading Rights? Human Rights and the WTO*, London: Zed Books.

Dooley, B. (1998) *Black and Green: Civil Rights Struggles in Northern Ireland and Black America*, London: Pluto.

Drahos, P., and J. Braithwaite (2002) *Information Feudalism: Who Owns the Knowledge Economy?*, London: Earthscan.

Dros, J.M. (2004) *Managing the Soy Boom: Two Scenarios of Soy Production Expansion in South America*, www.panda.org/downloads/forests/managingthesoyboomenglish.pdf.

Dunkley, G. (2000) *The Free Trade Adventure: The WTO, the Uruguay Round and Globalism. A Critique*, London: Zed Books.

———(2004) *Free Trade: Myth Reality and Alternatives*, London: Zed Books.

Durkheim, E. (1897) *Le Suicide: Étude de Sociologie*, Paris: Alcan.

Duxiu, C. (1998) *Chen Duxiu's Last Articles and Letters, 1937–1942*, Richmond: Curzon.

Dyer-Witherford, N. (1999) *Cyber Marx: Cycles and Circuits of Struggle in High-technology Capitalism*, Urbana: University of Illinois Press.

Ebert, T. (1995) *(Untimely) Critiques for a Red Feminism*, www.marxists.org/reference/subject/philosophy/works/us/ebert.htm.

Ehrlich, P.R. (1971 [1968]) *The Population Bomb*, London: Ballantine.

Einstein, A. (1949) 'Why Socialism', *Monthly Review*, May, www.monthlyreview.org/598einst.htm.

Electronic Disturbance Theatre (2003) *Hacktivism: Network Art Activism*, New York: Autonomedia.

Elgin, D. (1981) *Voluntary Simplicity: Toward a Way of Life that is Outwardly Simple, Inwardly Rich*, New York: Morrow.

Engels, F. (1947 [1878]) *Anti-Dühring*, Moscow: Progress Publishers.

———(1890) Letter to C. Schmidt, 5 August, www.marxists.org/archive/marx/works/1890/letters/90_08_05.htm.

——— 1892 (1960) *Socialism: Utopian and Scientific*, The Essential Left.

Engler, A. (1995) *Apostles of Greed: Capitalism and the Myth of the Individual in the Market*, London: Pluto.

Ewen, S. (1996) *PR! A Social History of Spin*, New York: Basic Books

Fári, M.G., R. Bud and P.U. Kralovánszky (2001) *History of the Term Biotechnology: K. Ereky & His Contribution*, www.redbio.org/portal/encuentros/enc_2001/index.htm.

Felix, D. (1998) 'IMF Bailouts and Global Financial Flows', *Foreign Policy in Focus*, vol. 3, no. 5, April, www.fpif.org/briefs/vol3/v3n5imf.html.

Filmer, R. (1991) *Patriarcha and Other Writings*, Cambridge: Cambridge University Press.

Firestone, S. (1979 [1970]) *Dialectic of Sex: The Case for Feminist Revolution*, London: Women's Press.

Fisas, A.V. (1995) *Blue Geopolitics: The United Nations Reform and the Future of the Blue Helmets*, London: Pluto.

Fisher, I. (1931) *The Purchasing Power of Money: Its Determination and Relation to Credit, Interest and Crises*, New York: Macmillan.

Fisher, W.F., and T. Ponniah (eds) (2003) *Another World Is Possible: Popular Alternatives to Globalization at the World Social Forum*, London: Zed Books.

Foner, P. S. (1969) *The Autobiographies of the Haymarket Martyrs*, New York: Humanities Press.

Foster, W.Z. (1949) *The Twilight of World Capitalism*, New York: International Publishers.

Foucault, M. (1995 [1977]) *Discipline and Punish: The Birth of the Prison*, New York: Vintage Books.

——(1982) 'The Subject and Power', in H.L. Dreyfus and P. Rabinow (eds), *Michel Foucault: Beyond Structuralism and Hermeneutics*, Chicago: University of Chicago Press.

Fourier, C. (1996 [1808]) *The Theory of the Four Movements*, Cambridge: Cambridge University Press.

Frank, A.G. (1991) *The Underdevelopment of Development*, Stockholm: Bethany Books.

Fraser, R. (1999) *Shadow Child: A Memoir of the Stolen Generation*, Alexandria NSW: Hale & Iremonger.

French National Assembly (1789) *Declaration of the Rights of Man and of the Citizen*, www.magnacartaplus.org/french-rights/1789.htm.

Freire, P. (1985) *The Pedagogy of the Oppressed*, Harmondsworth: Penguin.

Friedan, B. (1997 [1963]) *The Feminine Mystique*, New York: W.W. Norton.

Friedman, M. (1962) *Capitalism and Freedom*, Chicago: University of Chicago Press.

——(1980) *Free to Choose: A Personal Statement*, Harmondsworth: Penguin.

Friends of the Earth (2000) The Politics of Climate change, www.foe.co.uk/resource/briefings/politics_climate_change.pdf.

Furedi, F. (1994) *New Ideology of Imperialism: Renewing the Moral Imperative*, London: Pluto.

GAATW (1999) *Human Rights Standards for the Treatment of Trafficked Persons*, www.gaatw.org/downloads/human_rights_standards_1999.pdf.

Gareau, F.H. (2004) *State Terrorism and the United States: From Counterinsurgency to the War on Terrorism*, London: Zed Books.

Gellner, E. (1981) *Muslim Society*, Cambridge: Cambridge University Press.

George, S. (1992) *The Debt Boomerang: How Third World Debt Harms Us All*, London: Pluto.

Giap, V.N. (1961) *People's War People's Army*, Hanoi: Foreign Languages Publishing House.

Ginsborg, P. (2004) *Silvio Berlusconi: Television, Power and Patrimony*, London: Verso.

Gobineau, A. J. (1998) *The Inequality of Human Races*, New York: H. Fertig.

Godrej, D. (2001) *The No-nonsense Guide to Climate Change*, London: Verso.

Godwin. W. (1976 [1793]) *Enquiry Concerning Political Justice, and Its Influence on Modern Morals and Happiness*, Harmondsworth: Penguin.

Gold, M. (1937) *Change the World!*, London: Lawrence & Wishart.

Goldman, E. (1910) *Anarchism and Other Essays*, New York: Mother Earth.

Goldman, M. (1998) *Privatizing Nature: Political Struggles for the Global Commons*, London: Pluto.

Gordon, D., C. Pantazis, P. Townsend, S. Nandy and S. Pemberton (2003) *Child Poverty in the Developing World*, Bristol: Policy Press.

Gott, R. (1973) *Rural Guerrillas in Latin America*, Harmondsworth: Penguin.

Gramsci, A. (1991 [1929–35]) *Prison Notebooks*, New York: Columbia University Press.

Grogan, E. (1972) *Ringolevio: A Life Played for Keeps*, London: Heinemann.

Gronlund, L. (1886) *Co-operative Commonwealth: An Exposition of Modern Socialism*, London: Swan Sonnenschein Le Bas & Lowrey.

Gumbel, A. (2004) 'How the War Machine is Driving the US Economy', *Independent*, 9 January 2004.

Gupta, J. (2001) *Our Simmering Planet: What to Do about Global Warming*, London: Zed Books.

Gurley Flynn, E. (1916) *Sabotage: The Conscious Withdrawal of the Workers' Efficiency*, Cleveland OH: Industrial Workers of the World.

Gutiérrez, G. (2001) *A Theology of Liberation: History, Politics, and Salvation*, London: SCM.

Guzmán, A.R. (1989) *Guerra popular en el Peru: el pensamiento Gonzalo*, Lima: L. Arce Borja.

Habermas, J. (1988) *Legitimation Crisis*, Cambridge: Polity Press.

Haeckel, E. (1866) *Generelle Morphologie der Organismen*, Berlin: Georg Reimer.

Hagopian, E.C. (ed.) (2004) *Civil Rights in Peril: The Targeting of Arabs and Muslims*, London: Pluto.

ul-Haq, M., I. Kaul and I. Grunberg (1996) *The Tobin Tax: Coping with Financial Volatility*, Oxford: Oxford University Press.

Harding, J. (2000) *The Uninvited: Refugees at the Rich Man's Gate*, London: Profile.

Hardt, M., and T. Negri (2000) *Empire*, London: Harvard University Press.

——— (2004) *Multitude: War and Democracy in the Age of Empire*, New York: Penguin.

Hawken, P. (1993) *The Ecology of Commerce: A Declaration of Sustainability*, New York: Harper-Collins.

Hayek, F.A. (1986) *The Road to Serfdom*, London: Ark.

Heaton Vorse, M. (1938) *Labor's New Millions*, New York: Modern Age Books.

Hechter, M. (1978) *Internal Colonialism: The Celtic Fringe in British National Development 1536–1966*, London: Routledge & Kegan Paul.

Held, D. (1980) *Introduction to Critical Theory: Horkheimer to Habermas*, London: Hutchinson.

Herman, E.S., and N. Chomsky (2002) *Manufacturing Consent: The Political Economy of the Mass Media*, New York: Pantheon Books.

Hill, C.E. (1972) *The World Turned Upside Down: Radical Ideas during the English Revolution*, London: Maurice Temple Smith.

Hirst, P., and G. Thompson (1996) *Globalization in Question: The International Economy and the Possibilities of Governance*, Cambridge: Polity Press.

Hobbes, T. (1968) *Leviathan*, Harmondsworth: Penguin.

Hobsbawm, E.J. (1972) *Primitive Rebels: Studies in Archaic Forms of Social Movement in the 19th and 20th Centuries*, Manchester: Manchester University Press.

Hobson, J.A. (1938) *Imperialism: A Study*, London: Unwin Hyman.

Ho Chi Minh (1984) *On Revolution*, Boulder CO: Westview.

Hoggart, R. (2004) *Mass Media in a Mass Society*, New York: Continuum.

Holloway, J. (2002) *Change the World without Taking Power*, London: Pluto.

Hume, D. (1748) *Of the Original Contract*, www.constitution.org/dh/origcont.htm.

Independent Commission on International Development Issues (1980) *North–South, a Programme for Survival: Report of the Commission on International Development Issues*, Cambridge MA: MIT Press.

International Confederation of Free Trade Unions (2004) *Annual Survey of Violations of Trade Union Rights*, www.icftu.org/survey.

International Labour Organization (1977) *Tripartite Declaration of Principles Concerning Multinational Enterprises and Social Policy*, www.ilo.org/public/english/employment/multi/index.htm.

——— (1989) *Convention Concerning Indigenous and Tribal Peoples in Independent Countries*, www.ilo.org/public/english/employment/skills/recomm/instr/c_169.htm.

——— (1998) *Declaration of Fundamental Principles of Rights at Work*, www.ilo.org/dyn/declaris/declarationweb.indexpage.

——— (2004) *Organising for Social Justice*, www.ilo.org/dyn/declaris/declarationweb.global reportslist?var_language=EN.

IPCC (2001) *Third Assessment Report – Climate Change 2001*, www.ipcc.ch/index.htm.

IWMA (1871) *General Rules*, www.marxists.org/archive/marx/works/1864/10/27b.htm.

Jackson, T., and N. Marks (1994) *Measuring Sustainable Economic Welfare: A Pilot Index 1950–1990*, Stockholm: Stockholm Environment Institute.

James, C.L.R. (1999) *Marxism for Our Times: C.L.R. James on Revolutionary Organization*, Jackson MS: University Press of Mississippi.

Jawara, F., A. Kwa, S. Sharma and D. Woodward (2003) *Behind the Scenes at the WTO*, London: Zed Books.

Jetin, B. (2000) *Utility of the Tobin Tax and of the Control of Capital Flows for Building a New Architecture for the International Financial System*, www.attac.org/fra/list/doc/jetinen.htm.

Jevons, W.S. (2001 [1871]) *The Theory of Political Economy*, London: Palgrave Macmillan.

Jha, P.S. (2002) *The Perilous Road to the Market: The Political Economy of Reform in Russia, India and China*, London: Pluto.

Jomo K.S. (1998) *Tigers in Trouble: Financial Governance, Liberalisation and Crises in East Asia*, Hong Kong: Hong Kong University Press.

Jones, M. (1983) *Mother Jones Speaks: Collected Writings and Speeches*, New York: Monad Press.

Jones, N. (1999) *Sultans of Spin*, London: Gollancz.

Jordan, T., and P. Taylor (2004) *Hacktivism and Cyberwars: Rebels with a Cause?*, London: Routledge.

Juma, C., and J.B. Ojwang (eds) (1996) *In Land We Trust: Environment, Private Property and Constitutional Change*, Nairobi: ACTS Press.

Justo, L. (1967) *Bolivia: la Revolución Derrotada*, Cochabamba.

Kahler, M. (ed.) (1998) *Capital Flows and Financial Crises*, Manchester: MUP.

Kautsky, K. (1996 [1909]) *The Road to Power: Political Reflections on Growing into the Revolution*, Atlantic Highlands NJ: Humanities Press.

——— (1981 [1918]) *The Dictatorship of the Proletariat*, Westport CT: Greenwood Press.

Kelley, F. (1914) *Modern Industry in Relation to the Family, Health, Education, Morality*, New York: Longmans.

Kenny, M. (1995) *The First New Left: British Intellectuals after Stalin*, London: Lawrence & Wishart.

Keynes, J.M. (1936) *General Theory of Employment, Interest and Money*, London: Macmillan.

Khor, K.P. (2002) *Intellectual Property, Biodiversity and Sustainable Development: Resolving the Difficult Issues*, London: Zed Books.

Kirkup, T. (1976) *A History of Socialism*, Geneva: Minkoff Reprint.

Klein, M. (2000) *No Logo*, London: Flamingo.

——— (2002) 'Introduction', in M. Prokosch and L. Raymond (eds), *The Global Activist's Manual: Local Ways to Change the World*, New York: Thunder's Mouth Press.

Knox, R. (1850) *The Races of Men: A Fragment*, London: Henry Renshaw.

Korsch, K. (1972) *Marxism and Philosophy*, London: New Left Books.

Kropotkin, P.A. (1985) *The Conquest of Bread*, London: Elephant.

——— (1985) *Fields, Factories and Workshops Tomorrow*, London: Freedom.

——— (1987) *Mutual Aid: A Factor of Evolution*, London: Freedom.

Lafargue, P. (1907) *The Right To Be Lazy and Other Studies*, Chicago: Charles H. Kerr.

Lange, O.R. (1948) *On the Economic Theory of Socialism*, Minneapolis: University of Minnesota Press.

Larrain, J. (1979) *The Concept of Ideology*, London: Hutchinson.

Lasn, K. (1999) *Culture Jam: The Uncooling of America*, New York: Eagle Brook.

Lenin, V.I. (1978 [1902]) *What Is To Be Done? Burning Questions of Our Movement*, Moscow: Progress Publishers.

——— (2000 [1916]) *Imperialism the Highest Stage of Capitalism: A Popular Outline*, New Delhi: Leftword.

——— (1992 [1917]) *The State and Revolution*, London: Penguin.

——— (1929 [1918]) *The Proletarian Revolution and Kautsky the Renegade*, London: Modern Books.

——— (1970 [1920]) *Left-Wing Communism, an Infantile Disorder*, Moscow: Progress.

——— (1920) *Theses on Fundamental Tasks of The Second Congress of the Communist International*, http://marx.galizalivre.org/archive/lenin/works/1920/jul/04.htm.

——— (1978 [1970]) *On Trade Unions*, Moscow: Progress Publishers.

Lentin, A. (2004) *Racism and Anti-racism in Europe*, London: Pluto.

Leon, J.P. de (2001) *Our Word is Our Weapon: Selected Writings*, London: Serpent's Tail.

Lessig, L. (2004) *Free Culture: How Big Media Uses Technology and the Law to Lock Down Culture and Control Creativity*, New York: Penguin Press.

Leys, C. (2001) *Market Driven Politics: Neo-liberal Democracy and the Public Interest*, London: Verso.

Liberty (ed.) (1999) *Liberating Cyberspace: Civil Liberties, Human Rights, and the Internet*, London: Pluto.

Lipsey, R.G., and K.A. Chrystal (1999) *Principles of Economics*, Oxford: Oxford University Press.

List, F. (1909 [1841]) *The National System of Political Economy*, London: Longmans, Green.

Locke, J. (1988) *Two Treatises of Government*, Cambridge: Cambridge University Press.

Lovejoy, T.E. (1980) 'Foreword', in M. Soulé and B. Wilcox, *Conservation Biology: An Evolutionary–Ecological Perspective*, Sunderland: Sinauer Associates.

Lovelock, J. (1979) *Gaia: A New Look at Life on Earth*, Oxford: Oxford University Press.

Lukács, G. (1971 [1923]) *History and Class Consciousness: Studies in Marxist Dialectics*, London: Merlin Press.

Luxemburg, R. (1973 [1899]) *Social Reform or Revolution*, Colombo: Sydney Wanasinghe.

——— (1964 [1906]) *The Mass Strike, the Political Party and the Trade Unions*, Colombo: Sydney Wanasinghe.

——— (1963 [1913]) *The Accumulation of Capital*, London: Routledge.

Machel, S.M. (1977) *Establishing People's Power to Serve the Masses*, Dar es Salaam: Tanzania Publishing House.

Machiavelli, N. (1999 [1532]) *The Prince*, London: Penguin.

Madeley, J. (2000) *Hungry for Trade: How the Poor Pay for Free Trade*, London: Zed Books.

Madison, J. (1774) *The Federalist*, www.law.emory.edu/FEDERAL/federalist.

Magon, R.F. (1913) *Land and Liberty: Mexico's Battle for Economic Freedom and its Relation to Labor's World-Wide Struggle*, Los Angeles CA: Mexican Liberal Party.

Malthus, T. (1798) *An Essay on the Principle of Population, as it Affects the Future Improvement of Society with Remarks on the Speculations of Mr. Godwin, M. Condorcet, and Other Writers*, www. ac.wwu.edu/~stephan/malthus/malthus.o.html.

Manes, C. (1990) *Green Rage: Radical Environmentalism and the Unmaking of Civilization*, Boston MA: Little, Brown.

Mann, T. (1974 [1910]) *The Industrial Syndicalist*, Nottingham: Bertrand Russell Peace Foundation.

Mao Zedong (1977) *A Critique of Soviet Economics*, London: Monthly Review Press.

Marcuse, H. (1987 [1955]) *Eros and Civilisation: A Philosophical Enquiry into Freud*, London: Ark.

——— (1971 [1958]) *Soviet Marxism: A Critical Analysis*, Harmondsworth: Penguin.

——— (1972 [1964]) *One-Dimensional Man: Studies in the Ideology of Advanced Industrial Society*, London: Abacus.

Mariategui, J.C. (1971 [1928]) *Seven Interpretative Essays on Peruvian Reality*, Austin: University of Texas Press.

Martinez Cobo, J.R. (1987) *Study of the Problem of Discrimination Against Indigenous Populations*, New York: United Nations.

Maurice, J.F.D. (1958 [1838]) *The Kingdom of Christ; or, Hints on the principles, ordinances, and constitution of the Catholic Church. In letters to a member of the Society of Friends. By a Clergyman of the Church of England*, London: SCM Press.

Marx, K. (1975 [1844]) 'Excerpts from James Mill's Elements of Political Economy', in *Early Writings*, Harmondsworth: Penguin.

——— (1975 [1844]) 'Economic and Philosophical Manuscripts', in *Early Writings*, Harmondsworth: Penguin.

——— and F. Engels (1983 [1848]) *Manifesto of the Communist Party*, London: Lawrence & Wishart.

——— (1956–59 [1867]) *Capital*, Volume I: *A Critique of Political Economy*, London: Lawrence & Wishart.

——— (1964) *Theories of Surplus Value: Volume Four of Capital*, Moscow: Foreign Languages Publishing House.

——— (1992 [1871]) 'The Civil War in France', in *The First International and After*, London: Penguin.

——— (1992 [1875]) 'Critique of the Gotha Programme', in *The First International and After*, London: Penguin.

McChesney, R.W. (1999) *Rich Media, Poor Democracy: Communication Politics in Dubious Times*, Urbana: University of Illinois Press.

McLean, I. (ed.) (1996) *Oxford Concise Dictionary of Politics*, Oxford: Oxford University Press.

McMillan, J., and P. Buhle (eds) (2003) *The New Left Revisited*, Philidelphia: Temple University Press.

McNally, D. (1993) *Against the Market: Political Economy, Market Socialism and the Marxist Critique*, London: Verso.

Meadows, D.H. (1972) *The Limits to Growth: A Report for the Club of Rome's Project on the Predicament of Mankind*, New York: Potomac Associates.

Mellor, W. (1920) *Direct Action*, London: Leonard Parsons.

Menger, C. (1981 [1871]) *Principles of Economics*, New York: New York University Press.

Michels, R. (1915) *Political Parties: A Sociological Study of the Oligarchical Tendencies of Modern Democracy*, London: Jarrold.

Miliband, R. (1973) *The State in Capitalist Society*, London: Quartet Books.

Mill, J.S. (1992) *On Liberty and Utilitarianism*, London: D. Campbell.

——— (1998) *Utilitarianism*, Oxford: Oxford University Press.

Miller, D. (1989) *Market, State and Community: Theoretical Foundations of Market Socialism*, Oxford: Clarendon Press.

Miller, D. (ed.) (2004) *Tell Me Lies: Propaganda and Media Distortion in the Attack on Iraq*, London: Pluto.

Millet, D., E. Toussaint and V. Briault Manus (2004) *Who Owes Who? 50 Questions about World Debt*, London: Zed Books.

Millett, K. (2000) *Sexual Politics*, Urbana: University of Illinois Press.

Molloy, I. (2001) *Rolling Back Revolution: The Emergence of Low Intensity Conflict*, London: Pluto.

More, T. (2003 [1516]) *Utopia*, London: Penguin.

Morgan, L.H. (1985) *Ancient Society*, Tucson: University of Arizona Press.

Morris, W. (1995 [1890]) *News from Nowhere: or an Epoch of Rest: Being Some Chapters from a Utopian Romance*, Cambridge: Cambridge University Press.

Myers, C. (2002) *The Biblical Vision of Sabbath Economics*, Washington DC: Tell the Word Press.

Nace, T. (2003) *Gangs of America: The Rise of Corporate Power and the Disabling of Democracy*, London: McGraw-Hill.

Naess, A. (1989) *Ecology, Community and Lifestyle: Outline of an Ecosophy*, Cambridge: Cambridge University Press.

Negri, T. (1991) *Marx Beyond Marx: Lessons on the Grundrisse*, London: Pluto.

New Shorter Oxford English Dictionary, Volume 1 (1993), Oxford: Clarendon Press.

Nion, A. (1846) *Droits Civils des Auteurs, Artistes et Inventeurs*, Paris.

Nkrumah, K (1965) *Neo-colonialism: The Last Stage of Imperialism*, London: Nelson.

Notes from Nowhere (2003) *We Are Everywhere: The Irresistible Rise of Global Anti-capitalism*, London: Verso.

Nottingham, S. (2002) *Genescapes: The Ecology of Genetic Engineering*, London: Palgrave.

O'Connor, J. (1973) *The Fiscal Crisis of the State*, New York: St Martin's Press.

Ojeda, F. (1967) 'La Revolución Verdadera, la Violencia y el Fatalismo Geo-Político', *Pensamiento Crítico*, February, pp. 54–73; www.filosofia.org/hem/dep/pch/n01p054.htm.

Orford, M. (2004) *Climate Change and the Kyoto Protocol's Clean Development Mechanism: Stories from the Developing World*, Rugby: ITDG Publishing.

Ortega Saavedra, H. (1978) *50 Años de Lucha Sandinista*, Caracas.

Orth, J.V. (1991) *Combination and Conspiracy: A Legal History of Trade Unionism 1721–1906*, Oxford: Clarendon Press.

Owen, R. (1970 [1813]) *A New View of Society; and Report to the County of Lanark*, Harmondsworth: Penguin.

Oxfam (2002) *Rigged Rules and Double Standards: Trade, Globalisation, and the Fight Against Poverty*, www.maketradefair.com/assets/english/report_english.pdf.

Paine, T. (1995 [1792]) *The Rights of Man: Common Sense and other Writings*, Oxford: Oxford University Press.

Pakulski, J., and M. Waters (1996) *The Death of Class*, London: Sage

Palast, G. (2002) *The Best Democracy Money can Buy: An Investigative Reporter Exposes the Truth about Globalization, Corporate Cons and High Finance Fraudsters*, London: Pluto.

Panitch, L. (1976) *Social Democracy and Industrial Militancy: The Labour Party, Trade Unions and Incomes Policy 1945–1974*, Cambridge: Cambridge University Press.

Pareto, V. (1935) *The Mind and Society*, London: Jonathan Cape.

Parsons, A. (1889) *Anarchism: Its Philosophy and Scientific Basis as Defined by Some of its Apostles*, Chicago: Parsons.

Patomaki, H. (2001) *Democratizing Globalization: The Leverage of the Tobin Tax*, London: Zed Books.

Peet, R. (2003) *Unholy Trinity: The IMF, World Bank and WTO*, London: Zed Books.

Perelman, M. (2002) *Steal this Idea: Intellectual Property Rights and the Corporate Confiscation of Creativity*, New York: Palgrave.

Pincus, J.R., and J.A. Winters (eds) (2002) *Reinventing the World Bank*, London: Cornell University Press.

Plato (1997) 'Republic', in *Complete Works*, ed. D.S. Hutchinson and J.M. Cooper, Cambridge: Hackett Publishing.

Plekhanov, G.V. (1947 [1895]) *In Defence of Materialism: The Development of the Monist View of History*, London: Lawrence & Wishart.

Poulantzas, N. (1978) *State, Power, Socialism*, London: New Left Books.

Pratkanis, A., and E. Aronson (2001) *Age of Propaganda: The Everyday Use and Abuse of Persuasion*, New York: W.H. Freeman.

Prokosch, M., and L. Raymond (eds) (2002) *The Global Activist's Manual: Local Ways to Change the World*, New York: Thunder's Mouth Press.

Proudhon, P.J. (1994 [1840]) *What is Property?*, Cambridge: Cambridge University Press.

Ransom, D. (2001) *The No-nonsense Guide to Fair Trade*, Oxford: New Internationalist Publications.

Rao, P.K. (1998) *Sustainable Development: Economics and Policy*, Oxford: Blackwell.

———— (2000) *World Trade Organization and the Environment*, London: Macmillan.

Rawls, J. (1972) *A Theory of Justice*, Oxford: Clarendon Press.

Reed, E. (1971) *Problems of Women's Liberation: A Marxist Approach*, New York: Pathfinder Press.

Rhoads, R.A. (1998) *Freedom's Web: Student Activism in an Age of Cultural Diversity*, London: Johns Hopkins University Press.

Ricardo, D. (1971 [1817]) *On The Principles of Political Economy, and Taxation*, Harmondsworth: Penguin.

Richards, D.A.J. (1998) *Women, Gays and the Constitution: The Grounds for Feminism and Gay Rights in Culture and Law*, Chicago: University of Chicago Press.

Rivera, D., and Breton, A. (1938) *Manifesto for a Free Revolutionary Art*, www.marxists.org/subject/art/lit_crit/works/rivera/manifesto.htm.

Robeson, P. (1978) *Paul Robeson Speaks: Writings, Speeches, Interviews, 1918–1974*, London: Quartet Books.

Rose, R.B. (1966) *The Enragés: Socialists of the French Revolution*, Carlton: Melbourne University Press.

Rosmini-Serbati, A. (1848) *La Costitutione Civile Secondo la Giustizia Sociale*, Naples.

Ross, A. (ed.) (1997) *No Sweat: Fashion, Free Trade, and the Rights of Garment Workers*, London: Verso.

Rousseau, J.-J. (1993) *The Social Contract: And, Discourses*, London: Dent.

Rowland, C. (1988) *Radical Christianity: A Reading of Recovery*, London: Polity.

Roy, M.N. (1922) *India in Transition*, Geneva: J.B. Target

Saad-Filho, A. (ed.) (2003) *Anti-capitalism: A Marxist Introduction*, London: Pluto.

Saint-Simon, C.H. (1976 [1803]) 'Letters from an Inhabitant of Geneva to His Contemporaries', in *Political Thought of Saint-Simon*, London: Oxford University Press.

———— (1964 [1825]) *Social Organisation, the Science of Man and Other Writings*, New York: Harper & Row.

SAPRIN (2004) *Structural Adjustment: The Policy Roots of Economic Crisis, Poverty and Inequality*, London: Zed Books.

Sassoon, D. (1997) *One Hundred Years of Socialism: The West European Left in the Twentieth century*, London: Fontana.

Sauvy, A. (1952) 'Trois Mondes, Une Planète', *L'Observateur*, 14 August.

Schumpeter, J.A. (1976) *Capitalism, Socialism and Democracy*, London: Allen & Unwin.

Seabrook, J. (1996) *Travels in the Skin Trade: Tourism and the Sex Industry*, London: Pluto.

———— (2001) *Children of Other Worlds: Exploitation in the Global Market*, London: Pluto.

Sen, J., and A. Anand (eds) (2004) *World Social Forum: Challenging Empires*, New Delhi: Viveka Foundation.

Shachtman, M. (2003) *Race and Revolution*, London: Verso.

Shaoqi, L. (1980) *Three Essays on Party-Building*, Beijing: Foreign Languages Press.

Shaw, E. (1988) *Discipline and Discord in the Labour Party: The Politics of Managerial Control in the Labour Party 1951–87*, Manchester: Manchester University Press.

Shaw, R. (1996) *The Activist's Handbook: A Primer for the 1990s and Beyond*, Berkley: University of California Press.

Shiva, V. (1997) *Biopiracy: The Plunder of Nature and Knowledge*, Boston MA: South End Press.

Shu-Tse, P. (1967) *Behind China's 'Great Cultural Revolution'*, New York: Merit.

Sinclair, U.B. (1907) *The Industrial Republic: A Study of the America of Ten Years Hence*, London: William Heinemann.

Singer, P. (2002) *Animal Liberation*, New York: Ecco.

Smith, A. (1976 [1776]) *An Enquiry into the Nature and Causes of the Wealth of Nations*, Chicago: University of Chicago Press.

Smith, J.W. (1994) *The World's Wasted Wealth: Save our Wealth, Save Our Environment*, Cambria CA: Institute for Economic Democracy.

Soederberg, S. (2005) *The Politics of the New International Financial Architecture: Reimposing Neoliberal Domination in the Global South*, London: Zed Books.

Soon, W. (2000) *Solar Variability and Climate Change*, www.marshall.org/article.php?id=91.

Sorel, G. (1999) *Reflections on Violence*, Cambridge: Cambridge University Press.

South Centre (1997) *For a Strong and Democratic United Nations: A South Perspective on UN Reform*, London: Zed Books.

Spahn, P.B. (1996) *The Tobin Tax and Exchange Rate Stability*, www.worldbank.org/fandd/english/0696/articles/0130696.htm.

Spender, D. (1998) *Man Made Language*, London: Pandora.

Stalin, J. (1994 [1924]) *The Foundations of Leninism*, Quilon: Massline.

Stallman, R. (2001) *Biopiracy or Bioprivateering?*, www.stallman.org/articles/biopiracy.html.

Stauber, J.C., and S. Rampton (1995) *Toxic Sludge Is Good For You: Lies, Damn Lies, and the Public Relations Industry*, Monroe ME: Common Courage Press.

Stott, P., S. Tett, G. Jones, M. Allen, J. Mitchell and G. Jenkins (2000) *External Control of 20th Century Temperature by Natural and Anthropogenic Forcings*, http://funnel.sfsu.edu/courses/gm310/articles/GlblWrming20thCenturyCauses.pdf.

Stowell, M.W. (2001) *The Remarkable Mother of Invention*, www.swans.com/library/art7/mws005.html.

Stuart, J. (1996) *The True Law of Free Monarchies; and, Basilikon Doron*, Toronto: Centre for Reformation and Renaissance Studies. Also at www.jesus-is-lord.com/basilico.htm.

Students for a Democratic Society (1962) *Port Huron Statement of the Students for a Democratic Society*, http://coursesa.matrix.msu.edu/~hst306/documents/huron.html.

Tansley, A.G. (1935) 'The Use and Abuse of Vegetational Concepts and Terms', *Ecology*, vol. 16, no. 3, July, pp. 284–307.

Tawney, R.H. (1938) *Religion and the Rise of Capitalism*, Harmondsworth: Penguin.

Taylor, F.W. (1986) *The Principles of Scientific Management*, Easton: Hive Publishing.

Thomas, H. (ed.) (1995) *Globalisation and Third World Trade Unions: The Challenge of Rapid Economic Change*, London: Zed Books.

Thomas, N.M. (1932) *As I See It*, New York: Macmillan.

Thompson, E.P. (1980 [1963]) *The Making of the English Working Class*, London: Gollancz.

Thompson, W. (1997) *The Left in History: Revolution and Reform in Twentieth century Politics*, London: Pluto.

Thoreau, H.D. (1849) *On the Duty of Civil Disobedience*, www.cs.indiana.edu/statecraft/civ.dis.html.

Tobin, J. (1978) 'A Proposal for International Monetary Reform', *Eastern Economic Journal*, www.globalpolicy.org/socecon/glotax/currtax/original.htm.

——— (1991) 'International Currency Regimes, Capital Mobility, and Macroeconomic Policy', *Cowles Foundation Discussion Paper No. 993*, http://netec.mcc.ac.uk/WoPEc/data/Papers/cwl-cwldpp993.html.

Tokar, B. (2001) *Redesigning Life: The Worldwide Challenge to Genetic Engineering*, London: Zed Books.

Torres, C. (1967) *Liberación o Muerte*, Havana: Instituto del Libro.

303

Trotsky, L. (1999 [1937]) *The Revolution Betrayed: What is the Soviet Union and Where is it Going?*, London: Union Books.

———— (1942 [1938]) *The Death Agony of Capitalism and the Tasks of the Working Class*, London: Periodical Publications.

———— (1971) *The Permanent Revolution: Results and Prospects*, London: New Park Publications.

Tuitt, P. (1996) *False Images: Law's Construction of the Refugee*, London: Pluto.

Ture, K., and C. Hamilton (1992) *Black Power: The Politics of Liberation in America*, New York: Vintage Books.

Turton, H. (2004) Greenhouse Gas Emissions in Industrialized Countries: Where does Australia Stand? www.tai.org.au/Publications_Files/DP_Files/Dp66sum.pdf.

Ullman, H., and J. Wade (1998) *Rapid Dominance: A Force for All Seasons; Technologies and Systems for Achieving Shock and Awe – A Real Revolution in Miliatry Affairs*, Royal United Services Institute for Defence Studies.

United Nations (1945) *Charter*, www.un.org/aboutun/charter.

———— (1949) *Convention for the Suppression of the Traffic in Persons and of the Exploitation of Prostitutes and of Others*, www.ohchr.org/english/law/trafficpersons.htm.

———— (1949–51) *Statement on Race: Part One*, www.unesco.org/general/eng/infoserv/archives/files_online/32312A102_I.pdf.

———— (1951) *Statement on Race: Part Two*, www.unesco.org/general/eng/infoserv/archives/files_online/32312A102_II.pdf.

———— (1951) *Convention Relating to the Status of Refugees*, www.unhchr.ch/html/menu3/b/o_c_ref.htm.

———— (1973) *Convention on International Trade in Endangered Species of Wild Fauna and Flora*, www.cites.org/eng/disc/text.shtml.

———— (1982) *Convention on the Law of the Sea*, www.un.org/Depts/los/convention_agreements/convention_overview_convention.htm.

———— (1989) *Convention on the Rights of the Child*, www.unhchr.ch/html/menu3/b/k2crc.htm.

———— (1989) *Convention on the Control of Transboundary Movements of Hazardous Wastes and Their Disposal*, www.basel.int/text/con-e.htm.

———— (1992) *Convention on Biological Diversity*, www.biodiv.org/convention/articles.asp.

———— (1992) *Framework Convention on Climate Change*, http://unfccc.int/essential_background/convention/background/items/2853.php.

———— (1998) *Human Development Report*, http://hdr.undp.org/reports/global/1998/en.

———— (2000) *Protocol to Prevent, Suppress and Punish Trafficking in Persons*, www.unodc.org/unodc/en/trafficking_protocol.html.

———— (2000) *Protocol against the Smuggling of Migrants by Land, Sea and Air*, http://untreaty.un.org/English/notpubl/18–12-b.E.htm.

United States Code (2004) *Section 2331 of title 18, Part I, Chapter 113B*, www.law.cornell.edu/uscode/html/uscode18/usc_sec_18_00002331----000-.html.

United States of America (1776) *The Declaration of Independence*, www.ushistory.org/declaration/document.

———— (1868) Fourteenth Amendment to the Constitution of the United States, www.usconstitution.net/const.html#Am14.

Usdin, S. (2003) *The No Nonsense Guide to HIV/AIDS*, London: Verso.

Vadez, J. (1993) *Internationalism and the Ideology of Soviet Influence in Eastern Europe*, Cambridge: Cambridge University Press.

Vandemoortele, J. (2002) *Are We Really Reducing Global Poverty*, www.undp.org/mainundp/propoor/docs/arewereally-reducing-gobal-poverty.pdf.

Veblen, T. (1994) *The Theory of the Leisure Class*, London: Penguin.

Vernadsky, V.I. (1926) *The Biosphere*, New York: Copernicus.

Viénet, R. (1992) *Enragés and Situationists in the Occupation Movement, France, May, '68*, London: Rebel Press.

Vogt, R. (1999) *Whose Property? The Deepening Conflict between Private Property and Democracy in Canada*, London: University of Toronto Press.

Waldron, J. (1988) *The Right to Private Property*, Oxford: Clarendon Press.

Wallerstein, I.M. (2004) *World-systems Analysis: An Introduction*, London: Duke University Press.

———— (1991) *Geopolitics and Geoculture: Essays on the Changing World-System*, Cambridge: Cambridge University Press.

Walras, L. (1954) *Elements of Pure Economics*, London: George Allen & Unwin.

Warburton, D. (ed.) (1998) *Community and Sustainable Development: Participation in the Future*, London: Earthscan.

Warren, B. (1980) *Imperialism: Pioneer of Capitalism*, London: Verso.

Webb, S., and B. Webb (1920) *Industrial Democracy*, London: Longmans Green.

Weber, M. (1919) *Politics as a Vocation*, www2.pfeiffer.edu/~lridener/DSS/Weber/polvoc.html.

———— (1923) *General Economic History*, London: Allen & Unwin.

———— (1979) 'Class, Status and Party', in *Economy and Society*, Berkeley: University of California Press.

———— (2001) *The Protestant Ethic and the Spirit of Capitalism*, Chicago: Fitzroy Dearborn.

Weitling, W. (1854) *Garantien der Harmonie und Freiheit*, Vivis.

Whitelegg, J. (1997) *Critical Mass: Transport Environment and Equity in the Twenty-First Century*, London: Pluto.

Wilde, O. (2001) *The Soul of Man under Socialism and Selected Critical Prose*, London: Penguin.

Willmott, E. (2002) *The Robin Hood Tax: Concrete Proposals for Fighting Global Poverty and promoting Sustainable Development by Harnessing the Proceeds from a Currency Transaction Tax*, London: War on Want.

Wilson, E.O., and F.M. Peter (eds) (1988) *Biodiversity*, Washington DC: National Academy Press.

Wilson, J., and B. Drozdek (2004) *Broken Spirits: The Treatment of Traumatized Asylum Seekers, Refugees, War and Torture Victims*, New York: Brenner-Routledge.

Winstanley, G. (1941 [1649]) 'The True Levellers' Standard Advanced', in *The Works of Gerrard Winstanley: with an Appendix of Documents Relating to the Digger Movement*, ed. G.H. Sabine, Ithaca: Cornell University Press.

———— (1941 [1652]) 'The Law of Freedom in a Platform', in *The Works of Gerrard Winstanley: with an Appendix of Documents Relating to the Digger Movement*, ed. G.H. Sabine, Ithaca: Cornell University Press.

Wolff, R.P. (1998) *In Defense of Anarchism*, Berkeley: University of California Press.

Wollstonecraft, M. (1992 [1792]) *A Vindication of the Rights of Woman*, London: Everyman's Library.

Wolvekamp, P., A.D. Usher, V. Paranjpye and M. Ramnath (eds) (1999) *Forests for the Future: Local Strategies for Forest Protection, Economic Welfare and Social Justice*, London: Zed Books.

Woodcock, G. (1986) *Anarchism: A History of Libertarian Ideas and Movements*, Harmondsworth: Penguin.

Woodsworth, J.S. (1911) *My Neighbor: A Study of City Conditions*, Toronto: Missionary Society of the Methodist Church.

World Commission on Environment and Development (1987) *Our Common Future*, Oxford: Oxford University Press.

World Social Forum (2001) *Charter of Principles*, www.forumsocialmundial.org.br/main.php?id_menu=4&cd_language=2.

World Trade Organization, *Ten Common Misunderstandings about the WTO*, www.wto.org/english/thewto_e/whatis_e/10mis_e/10m00_e.htm.

———— *The WTO in Brief*, www.wto.org/english/thewto_e/whatis_e/inbrief_e/inbr00_e.htm.

Wright, S. (2002) *Storming Heaven: Class Composition and Struggle in Italian Autonomist Marxism*, London: Pluto.

Wright Mills, C. (1959) *The Power Elite*, New York.

———— (1960) 'Letter to the New Left', in *New Left Review* 5, September–October.

Zimmerman, J.F. (1999) *The Initiative: Citizen Law-making*, London: Praeger.

Index

309